The Python Workshop

Write Python code to solve challenging real-world problems

Corey Wade

Mario Corchero Jiménez

Andrew Bird

Dr. Lau Cher Han

Graham Lee

BIRMINGHAM—MUMBAI

The Python Workshop

Group Product Manager: Gebin George

Publishing Product Manager: Kunal Sawant

Senior Editor: Rohit Singh

Technical Editor: Pradeep Sahu

Copy Editor: Safis Editing

Project Coordinator: Deeksha Thakkar

Proofreader: Safis Editing

Indexer: Subalakshmi Govindhan

Production Designer: Vijay Kamble

Business Development Executive: Debadrita Chatterjee

Marketing Coordinator: Sonakshi Bubbar

First published: November 2019

Second edition: October 2022

Production reference: 1271022

Published by Packt Publishing Ltd.

Livery Place

35 Livery Street

Birmingham

B3 2PB, UK.

ISBN 978-1-80461-061-9

www.packt.com

Contributors

About the authors

Corey Wade, MS Mathematics, MFA Writing & Consciousness, is the director and founder of Berkeley Coding Academy where he teaches Python and data science to teenagers from around the world. A regular contributor to Towards Data Science, Corey has also authored *Hands-On Gradient Boosting with XGBoost and scikit-learn*. Corey has taught math and programming for 18 years at the Independent Study program of Berkeley High School. When not teaching or building machine learning models in Python, Corey reads poetry and studies the stars. You can visit his website at `berkeleycodingacademy.com`.

Mario Corchero Jiménez is a senior software developer at Bloomberg. He leads the Python infrastructure team, enabling the company to work effectively with Python and building company-wide libraries and tools. His professional experience is mainly in C++ and Python and he has contributed patches to multiple Python open source projects. He is a PSF fellow, having received the PSF Q3 2018 Community Award, and the vice president of Python España (Spain's Python association). He has also served as the chairperson of PyLondinium, PyConES17, and PyCon Charlas at PyCon 2018. Mario is passionate about the Python community, open source and inner source.

Andrew Bird is the data and analytics manager at Vesparum Capital. He leads the software and data science teams at Vesparum, overseeing full-stack web development in Django and React. He is an Australian actuary (FIAA, CERA) who has previously worked with Deloitte Consulting in financial services. Andrew also currently works as a full-stack developer for Draftable Pvt. Ltd. He voluntarily manages the ongoing development of the donation portal for the Effective Altruism Australia website.

Dr. Lau Cher Han is a chief data scientist and is currently the CEO of LEAD, an institution that provides programs on data science, full-stack web development, and digital marketing. Well-versed in programming languages such as JavaScript, Python, C#, and so on, he is experienced in MEAN Stack, ASP.NET, and Python Django web frameworks. He is multilingual and speaks English, Chinese, and Bahasa fluently. His knowledge of Chinese even includes its dialects of Hokkien, Teochew, and Cantonese.

Graham Lee is an experienced programmer and writer. He has written several books, including *Professional Cocoa Application Security*, *Test-Driven iOS Development*, *APPropriate Behaviour*, and *APPosite Concerns*. He is a developer who's been programming for long enough to want to start telling other people about the mistakes he's made in the hope that they'll avoid repeating them. In his case, this means having worked for about 12 years as a professional. His first programming experience can hardly be called professional at all, as it was in BASIC on a Dragon 32 microcomputer.

About the reviewer

Jeyapriya Udayanakumar is currently an associate professor at Stella Maris College, Chennai, India, and she has been pursuing her passion for teaching for more than 20 years. She has an interest in computer programming and believes that programming should be taught to students as an art. She has guided many student projects and been a part of some of them in real time. She has headed the department of computer science for 7 years and has been the dean of academic affairs for 3 years. She is known for her teaching skills and competency, has a penchant for clarity in terms of gauging goals and learning outcomes, and can connect with learners and assess their needs with ease. She has completed a master's degree in computer applications.

Table of Contents

2

Python Data Structures   57

3

Executing Python – Programs, Algorithms, and Functions   89

4

Extending Python, Files, Errors, and Graphs   137

5

Constructing Python – Classes and Methods   171

6

The Standard Library   215

7

Becoming Pythonic   277

8

Software Development   303

9

Practical Python – Advanced Topics   339

10

Data Analytics with pandas and NumPy   381

11

Machine Learning   439

12

Deep Learning with Python   483

13

The Evolution of Python – Discovering New Python Features   527

Preface

Welcome to the second edition of Python Workshop! This book is for anyone new to the Python programming language. Our objective is to teach you Python 3.11 so that you can solve real-world problems as a Python developer and data scientist.

This book will combine theory, examples, exercises, questions, and activities for all core concepts so that you can learn to use Python best practices to solve real-world problems. The exercises and activities have been chosen specifically to help you review the concepts covered and extend your learning. The best way to learn Python is to solve problems on your own.

The material (in this book) is targeted at beginners but will be equally as beneficial to experienced developers who are not yet familiar with Python. We are not teaching computer science per se but rather Python, the most beautiful and powerful coding language in the world. If you have never studied computer science, you will learn the most important concepts here, and if you have studied computer science, you will discover tools and tricks for Python that you have never seen before.

Python has become the most popular programming language in the world due to its simple syntax, extensive range, and dominance in the field of machine learning. In this book, you will become fluent in Python syntax, and you will take significant steps toward producing Pythonic code. You will gain experience in Python development, data science, and machine learning. In this new second edition, you will learn all important updates since Python 3.7, and you will gain experience in deep learning by building neural networks.

Many introductory Python books provide full introductions to computer science. Learning computer science with Python is an excellent way to start, but it is not the method of this book. Units on software development and data science are rarely covered in such books. They may be touched upon elsewhere, but here, software development and data science represent 50% of our book.

By contrast, many books on software development and data science are not designed for beginners. If they are, the Python fundamentals that they teach are usually summarized in one brief unit. This book devotes considerable space to Python fundamentals and essentials. Beginners are not only welcome; they are guided every step of the way.

In addition to the unique focus on Python fundamentals and essentials, the fact that the content is written by seasoned educators, data scientists, and developers makes this Python book more than just a text or reference. It's a comprehensive Python book designed to empower learners at all levels.

Python is not the language of tomorrow; Python is the language of today. By learning Python, you will become empowered as a developer and data scientist, and you will gain a significant edge over the competition. The journey will be fun, compelling, challenging, and ultimately rewarding.

Who this book is for

This book is for professionals, students, and hobbyists who want to learn Python and apply it to solve challenging real-world problems. Although this is a beginner's course, it's helpful to know standard programming topics such as variables, if-else statements, and functions. Experience with another object-oriented programming language, though not essential, is beneficial. If Python is your first attempt at computer programming, we will cover the basics with adequate detail for a motivated student.

What this book covers

Chapter 1, Python Fundamentals – Math, Strings, Conditionals, and Loops, explains how to code basic Python concepts, and outlines the fundamentals of the Python language.

Chapter 2, Python Data Structures, covers the essential elements that are used to store and retrieve data using general Python.

Chapter 3, Executing Python – Programs, Algorithms, and Functions, explains how to write more powerful and concise code through an increased appreciation of well-written algorithms, and an understanding of functions.

Chapter 4, Extending Python, Files, Errors, and Graphs, covers the basic I/O (input/output) operations for Python and covers using the matplotlib and seaborn libraries to create visualizations.

Chapter 5, Constructing Python – Classes and Methods, introduces one of the most central concepts in object-oriented programming classes, and it will help you write code using classes, which will make your life easier.

Chapter 6, The Standard Library, explains the importance of the Python standard library. It explains how to navigate in the standard Python libraries and overviews some of the most commonly used modules.

Chapter 7, Becoming Pythonic, covers the Python programming language, with which you will enjoy writing succinct, meaningful code. It also demonstrates some techniques for expressing yourself in ways that are familiar to other Python programmers.

Chapter 8, Software Development, shows how to debug and troubleshoot our applications, how to write tests to validate our code, and the documentation for other developers and users.

Chapter 9, Practical Python – Advanced Topics, explains how to take advantage of parallel programming, how to parse command-line arguments, how to encode and decode Unicode, and how to profile Python to discover and fix performance problems.

Chapter 10, Data Analytics with pandas and NumPy, introduces data science, which is a core application of Python. Loading, graphing, analyzing, and manipulating big data are all covered.

Chapter 11, Machine Learning, explains the concept of machine learning along with the necessary steps in building, scoring, and making predictions from a wide range of machine learning algorithms.

Chapter 12, Deep Learning with Python, explains the fundamental ideas and code behind neural networks, using Keras. Regularization techniques, including Dropout, and a full section on convolutional neural networks are included.

Chapter 13, New Features in Python, focuses on explaining the new features available in Python versions, from 3.7 to 3.11. It lists the enhancements in each version, with code samples on how to use them and why they are beneficial to the user, helping you to keep up to date with the evolution of the language.

To get the most out of this book

It's not assumed that you know any Python or computer science to get started. All you need is basic problem-solving skills at the level of high school algebra. All Python, computer science, software development, and data science will be taught assuming little to no knowledge.

Software/hardware covered in the book	Operating system requirements
Python 3.11	Windows, macOS, or Linux
Jupyter notebooks	Windows, macOS, or Linux

Each great journey begins with a humble step. Our upcoming adventure in the land of Python is no exception. Before you can begin, you need to be prepared with the most productive environment. In this section, you will see how to do that. We will be using Python 3.11 (from `https://python.org`). Future versions of Python 3 will be compatible.

Installing Jupyter on your system

We will be using Jupyter Notebooks to run Python for most of this book. To install Jupyter Notebook on Windows, macOS, or Linux, it's recommended that you download Anaconda, which includes Python and nearly all data science libraries that we will use in this text. To download Anaconda, follow these steps:

1. Head to `https://www.anaconda.com/distribution/` to install the Anaconda Navigator, which is an interface through which you can access your local Jupyter Notebook.

2. Now, based on your operating system (Windows, macOS, or Linux), you need to download the Anaconda installer.

3. Have a look at the following figure, which shows where we can download the Anaconda files for Windows, with other options presented:

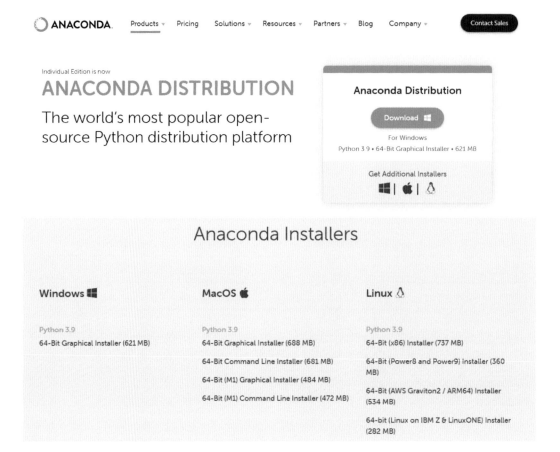

Figure 0.1 – The Anaconda home page

Launching the Jupyter Notebook

To launch the Jupyter Notebook from Anaconda Navigator, you need to follow these steps:

1. Once you launch Anaconda Navigator, you will see the following screen:

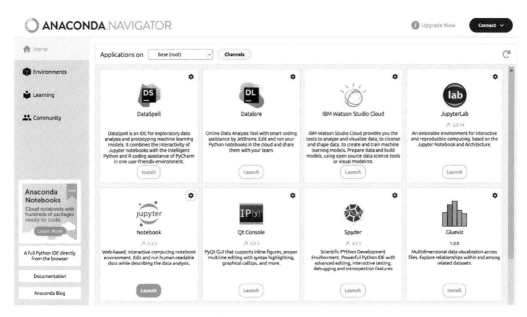

Figure 0.2 – The Anaconda installation screen

2. Now, click on **Launch** under the Jupyter Notebook option and launch the notebook on your local system. When that happens, you should see a Jupyter Notebook open in a web browser window similar to the following screenshot:

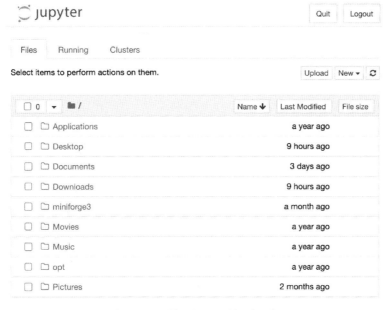

Figure 0.3 – The Jupyter Notebook

Congratulations! You have successfully installed a Jupyter Notebook on your system.

To install the Python terminal on your system

Jupyter Notebook comes with Python pre-installed; however, we will show you how to install Python directly to the terminal on your system using the following steps:

1. Open the following link, which is the Python community website URL: `https://www.python.org/downloads/`.

2. Select the operating system (Windows, macOS, or Linux):

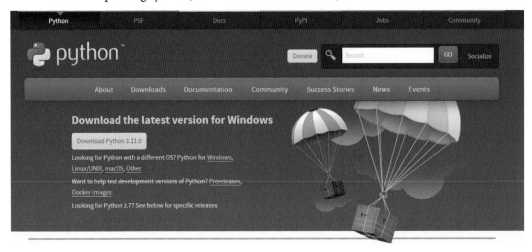

Figure 0.4 – The Python home page

3. Once you have downloaded the software, you need to install it.

4. Have a look at the following screenshot in which we have installed the Python terminal on a Windows system. We load it through the **Start** menu, search for `Python`, and click on the software.

    The Python terminal will look like this:

```
Python 3.11 (tags/v3.10.4:9d38120, Mar 23 2022, 23:13:41) [MSC v.1929 64 bit (AMD64)] on win32
Type "help", "copyright", "credits" or "license" for more information.
>>>
```

Figure 0.5 – The Python terminal interface

Congratulations! You have successfully installed the Python terminal on your system.

A few important packages

Some of the exercises in this book require the following packages:

- Matplotlib
- Seaborn
- NumPy
- Pandas
- Scikit-learn
- Keras

All these packages are automatically included with Jupyter Notebook, with the exception of Keras, which will be used in *Chapter 12*, *Deep Learning with Python*, where you are encouraged to use Google Colab notebooks online, which include Keras automatically.

If you ever need to download any package or library explicitly, you can do so as follows:

- Direct terminal installation of NumPy:

```
pip install numpy
```

- Direct terminal installation using Anaconda:

```
conda install numpy
```

Note that most packages and libraries may be installed in a similar fashion.

To install Docker

1. Head to `https://docs.docker.com/docker-for-windows/install/` to install Docker for Windows.

2. Head to `https://docs.docker.com/docker-for-mac/install/` to install Docker for macOS.

3. Head to `https://docs.docker.com/v17.12/install/linux/docker-ce/ubuntu/` to install Docker on Linux.

If you are using the digital version of this book, we advise you to type the code yourself or access the code from the book's GitHub repository (a link is available in the next section). Doing so will help you avoid any potential errors related to the copying and pasting of code.

Download the example code files

You can download the example code files for this book from GitHub at https://github.com/ PacktPublishing/The-Python-Workshop-Second-Edition. If there's an update to the code, it will be updated in the GitHub repository. Solutions to the chapter activities are provided on GitHub in the Appendix folder.

We also have other code bundles from our rich catalog of books and videos available at https:// github.com/PacktPublishing/. Check them out!

Download the color images

We also provide a PDF file that has color images of the screenshots and diagrams used in this book. You can download it here: https://packt.link/KB0O0.

Conventions used

There are a number of text conventions used throughout this book.

Code in text: Indicates code words in text, database table names, folder names, filenames, file extensions, pathnames, dummy URLs, user input, and Twitter handles. Here is an example: "Mount the downloaded WebStorm-10*.dmg disk image file as another disk in your system."

A block of code is set as follows:

```
s1 = set([1,2,3,4,5,6])
print(s1)
s2 = {1,2,2,3,4,4,5,6,6}
print(s2)
s3 = {3,4,5,6,6,6,1,1,2}
print(s3)
```

The output of a code block is highlighted in bold:

```
{1, 2, 3, 4, 5, 6}
```

When we wish to draw your attention to a particular part of a code block, the relevant lines or items are set in bold:

```
[default]
import math
def factorial_sum(numbers):
    total = 0
```

```
    for n in numbers:
        total += math.factorial(n)
    return total
```

Any command-line input or output is written as follows:

```
$ mkdir css
$ cd css
```

Bold: Indicates a new term, an important word, or words that you see on screen. For instance, words in menus or dialog boxes appear in **bold**. Here is an example: "Select **System info** from the **Administration** panel."

> **Tips or Important Notes**
> Appear like this.

Get in touch

Feedback from our readers is always welcome.

General feedback: If you have questions about any aspect of this book, email us at customercare@packtpub.com and mention the book title in the subject of your message.

Errata: Although we have taken every care to ensure the accuracy of our content, mistakes do happen. If you have found a mistake in this book, we would be grateful if you would report this to us. Please visit www.packtpub.com/support/errata and fill in the form.

Piracy: If you come across any illegal copies of our works in any form on the internet, we would be grateful if you would provide us with the location address or website name. Please contact us at copyright@packt.com with a link to the material.

If you are interested in becoming an author: If there is a topic that you have expertise in and you are interested in either writing or contributing to a book, please visit authors.packtpub.com.

Share Your Thoughts

Once you've read *The Python Workshop, Second Edition*, we'd love to hear your thoughts! Scan the QR code below to go straight to the Amazon review page for this book and share your feedback.

https://packt.link/r/1-804-61061-5

Your review is important to us and the tech community and will help us make sure we're delivering excellent quality content.

Download a free PDF copy of this book

Thanks for purchasing this book!

Do you like to read on the go but are unable to carry your print books everywhere?

Is your eBook purchase not compatible with the device of your choice?

Don't worry, now with every Packt book you get a DRM-free PDF version of that book at no cost.

Read anywhere, any place, on any device. Search, copy, and paste code from your favorite technical books directly into your application.

The perks don't stop there, you can get exclusive access to discounts, newsletters, and great free content in your inbox daily

Follow these simple steps to get the benefits:

1.   Scan the QR code or visit the link below

https://packt.link/free-ebook/9781804610619

2.   Submit your proof of purchase
3.   That's it! We'll send your free PDF and other benefits to your email directly

1

Python Fundamentals – Math, Strings, Conditionals, and Loops

Overview

By the end of this chapter, you will be able to simplify mathematical expressions with the order of operations using integers and floats; assign variables and change Python types to display and retrieve user information; apply global functions including `len()`, `print()`, and `input()`; manipulate strings using indexing, slicing, string concatenation, and string methods; apply Booleans and nested conditionals to solve problems with multiple pathways; utilize `for` loops and `while` loops to iterate over strings and repeat mathematical operations, and create new programs by combining math, strings, conditionals, and loops.

> **Note**
> This chapter covers the fundamentals of the Python language.

Introduction

In this chapter, we will present vital Python concepts; that is, the core elements that everyone needs to know when starting to code. We will cover a breadth of topics while focusing on math, strings, conditionals, and loops. By the end of this chapter, you will have a strong foundation in Python, and you will be able to write significant Python programs as you continue with the rest of this book.

You will start with a very famous developer example, *Python as a calculator*. In addition to the standard operations of addition, subtraction, multiplication, division, and exponentiation, you will learn integer division and the modulus operator. By using only basic Python, you can outperform most calculators on the market.

Next, you'll learn about **variables**. Python is dynamically typed, meaning that variable types are unknown before the code runs. Python variables do not require special initialization. The first variables we will look at will be `integers`, `floats`, and `strings`. Here, you will identify and convert between types.

Next, to work with strings, you will utilize string methods, in addition to **indexing**, **slicing**, and string **concatenation**. You'll also use built-in functions such as `print()` and `input()` to communicate with the user.

Moving ahead, you'll encounter Booleans, `true` or `false` Python types, which precede conditionals, statements with `if` clauses, which lead to branching. Booleans and conditionals allow us to write more complex programs by taking a greater number of possibilities into account.

Finally, we will close this chapter with loops, which allow us to repeat operations. In particular, we will apply `while` loops and `for` loops by utilizing `break` and `continue`.

For true beginners, this introductory chapter will get you up to speed with basic programming concepts. If you are new to Python, you will see why the Python language is so clear, powerful, and invaluable. By the end of this chapter, you will be comfortable running Python basics on your own, and you will be prepared to tackle more of the advanced concepts ahead.

We will be looking at the following topics in this chapter:

- Python as a calculator
- Strings – concatenation, methods, and input()
- String interpolation
- String indexing and slicing
- Slicing
- Booleans and conditionals
- Loops

Let's start coding in Python 3.11

Technical requirements

The code files for this chapter are available on GitHub at `https://github.com/PacktPublishing/The-Python-Workshop-Second-Edition/tree/main/Chapter01`.

In the *Preface*, we learned how to install Anaconda, which comes with the most updated version of Python and Jupyter Notebook. We are using Jupyter Notebook as the default **integrated development environment (IDE)** for this book because it is sufficient for your entire *Python Workshop* journey, including the later chapters on data science.

It's time to open a Jupyter Notebook and begin our Pythonic journey.

> **Note**
>
> The Python code in most of the chapters of this book will work on almost any IDE that supports Python. Feel free to use Colab notebooks, terminals, Sublime Text, PyCharm, or any other IDE that suits your purposes.

Opening a Jupyter Notebook

To get started with this book, you need to make sure that you have a Jupyter Notebook open. Here are the steps:

1. Locate and open Anaconda Navigator.

2. Search for `Jupyter Notebook` in Anaconda Navigator and click on it.

    A new window should open in the web browser of your choice:

Figure 1.1 – The Jupyter Notebook interface

> **Note**
>
> If you are having trouble accessing a Jupyter Notebook, it may mean that your Jupyter Notebook is not set up properly. Go back to the *Preface* or see `https://jupyter-notebook.readthedocs.io/en/stable/troubleshooting.html` for a troubleshooting guide.

> **Option**
>
> Depending on how you set up your Jupyter Notebook, you may also open Jupyter Notebook by typing `jupyter notebook` in your terminal.

Python as a calculator

Python is an incredibly powerful calculator. By leveraging the `math` library, `numpy`, and `scipy`, Python typically outperforms pre-programmed calculators. In later chapters, you will learn how to use the `numpy` and `scipy` libraries. For now, we'll introduce the calculator tools that most people use daily.

Addition, subtraction, multiplication, division, and **exponentiation** are core operations. In computer science, the modulus operator and **integer division** are essential as well, so we'll cover them here.

The `modulus` operator is the remainder in mathematical division. **Modular arithmetic** is also called **clock arithmetic**. For instance, in mod5, which is a modulus of 5, we count 0,1,2,3,4,0,1,2,3,4,0,1... This goes in a circle, like the hands on a clock, which uses mod12.

The difference between division and integer division depends on the language. When dividing the integer 9 by the integer 4, some languages return 2; others return 2.25. In your case, Python will return 2.25.

There are many advantages to using Python as your calculator of choice. The first is that you are not limited to using programs that others have written. You can write a program to determine the greatest common divisor or the Euclidean distance between two points.

Other advantages include reliability, precision, and speed. Python generally prints out more decimal places than most standard calculators, and it always does what you command it to do.

We'll cover a small sample of what Python can calculate. Complex numbers are previewed as a Python type. Great `math` libraries such as `Turtle`, which creates polygons and circles with ease, may be explored in your own time and are referenced in *Chapter 6, The Standard Library*. The depth of math required for data analysis and machine learning starts with the foundations laid here.

> **Note**
>
> In this book, copy everything in highlighted coding cells in your Jupyter Notebook; be sure to exclude >>> when you see it later. To run code in Jupyter, make sure the cell is highlighted, then press *Shift + Enter*. You may also press the **Run** button at the top of the Notebook, but this takes more time. Start thinking like a developer and use keystrokes instead.

Standard math operations

Let's have a look at the standard math operations and their symbols since we will be using these while coding. The following table covers these:

Operation	Symbol
Addition	+
Subtraction	-
Multiplication	*
Division	/
Integer Division	//
Exponentiation	**
Modulo/Remainder	%

Figure 1.2 – Standard math operations

> **Note**
>
> The ** symbol is not universal for exponentiation, but it should be. By definition, exponentiation is repeated multiplication. Using the * symbol twice is representative of repeated multiplication. It's terse, fast, and efficient. Other programming languages require functions to exponentiate.

Python provides an optional method from the math library, math.pow(), but ** is cleaner and easier to use.

Basic math operations

We can perform all standard math operations on the numbers 5 and 2. Python uses the same math symbols as most calculators:

1. Add 5 and 2 using the + addition operator by entering the following code:

   ```
   5 + 2
   ```

   After running the code, by pressing *Shift + Enter* in a Jupyter Notebook, you will get the following output:

   ```
   7
   ```

2. Subtract 2 from 5 using the – subtraction operator, as follows:

   ```
   5 - 2
   ```

   The output is as follows:

   ```
   3
   ```

3. Use the * multiplication operator to multiply 5 by 2:

```
5 * 2
```

The output is as follows:

```
10
```

4. Now, use the / division operator to divide 5 by 2:

```
5 / 2
```

The output is as follows:

```
2.5
```

When dividing two numbers, Python always returns a decimal, which is different than other languages. Python is math-positive, so it gives the correct mathematical answer.

5. Integer division can be done using the // integer division operator:

```
5 // 2
```

6. Observe the change in the output:

```
2
```

The result of the integer division is the integer before the decimal point. It is not rounded.

7. Now, use the ** exponential operator to take 5 to the 2nd power:

```
5 ** 2
```

The output is as follows:

```
25
```

8. Finally, use the % modulus operator to find 5 mod 2:

```
5 % 2
```

The output is as follows:

```
1
```

The modulus operator returns the remainder when the first number is divided by the second.

In the aforementioned examples, you used the different math operators and performed operations with them in a Jupyter Notebook. Next, let's move on to the order of operations in Python.

Order of operations

Parentheses are meaningful in Python. When it comes to computation, Python always computes what is in parentheses first.

The Python language follows the same order of operations as in the math world. You may remember the acronym PEMDAS: parentheses first, exponentiation second, multiplication/division third, and addition/subtraction fourth.

Consider the following expression: 5 + 2 * -3.

The first thing to note is that the negative sign and subtraction sign are the same in Python. Let's have a look at the following example:

1. Without parentheses, Python will first multiply 2 and -3, and then add 5:

    ```
    5 + 2 * -3
    ```

    The output is as follows:

    ```
    -1
    ```

2. If parentheses are placed around 5 and 2, we obtain a different result since 5 and 2 will be added before multiplying by -3:

    ```
    (5 + 2) * -3
    ```

    Here is the output:

    ```
    -21
    ```

If you're ever in doubt, use parentheses. Parentheses are very helpful for complex expressions, and extra parentheses do not affect code.

In the first exercise, we are going to dive into Python code and work with math operations.

Exercise 1 – getting to know the order of operations

The goal of this exercise is to work with the primary math operations in Python and understand their order of execution. This exercise can be performed on the Python terminal, your Jupyter Notebook, or any other IDE:

1. Subtract 5 to the 3rd power from 100 and divide the result by 5:

    ```
    (100 - 5 ** 3) / 5
    ```

    The output is as follows:

    ```
    -5.0
    ```

2.   Add 6 to the remainder of 15 divided by 4:

```
6 + 15 % 4
```

The output is as follows:

```
9
```

3.   Add 2 to the 2nd power, which is 4, to the integer division of 24 and 4:

```
2 ** 2 + 24 // 4
```

The output is as follows:

```
10
```

In this quick exercise, you used Python to perform basic math using the order of operations. As you can see, Python is an excellent calculator. You will use Python often as a calculator in your career as a developer.

Python concept – spacing

You may have wondered about the spaces between numbers and symbols. In Python, spaces after a number or symbol do not carry any meaning. So, 5**3 and 5   **   3 both result in 125.

Spaces are meant to enhance readability. Although there is no correct way to space code, spaces are generally encouraged between operands and operators. Thus, 5   **   3 is slightly preferable.

Trying to follow certain conventions is it's acceptable. If you develop good habits early on, it will make reading and debugging code easier later. Whatever conventions you choose, try to be consistent.

Number types – integers and floats

Now, you will address the difference between an integer and a float. Consider 8 and 8.0. You know that 8 and 8.0 are equivalent mathematically. They both represent the same number, but they are different types in Python. 8 is an integer, while 8.0 is a decimal, technically referred to in Python as a float.

An integer in Python is classified as being of the int type, short for integer. Integers include all positive and negative whole numbers, including 0. Examples of integers include 3, -2, 47, and 10000.

Floats, by contrast, are Python types represented as decimals. All rational numbers expressed as fractions can be represented as floats. Examples of floats include 3.0, -2.0, 47.45, and 200.001.

> **Note**
> We are only covering text and numeric types in this chapter. Other types will be discussed in subsequent chapters.

Python types can be obtained explicitly using the `type()` keyword, as you will see in the following exercise.

Exercise 2 – integer and float types

The goal of this exercise is to determine types and then change those types in our Python code. This can be performed in your Jupyter Notebook:

1. Begin by explicitly determining the type of 6 using the following code:

    ```
    type(6)
    ```

    The output is as follows:

    ```
    int
    ```

2. Now, enter `type(6.0)` in the next cell of your notebook:

    ```
    type(6.0)
    ```

    The output is as follows:

    ```
    float
    ```

3. Now, add 5 to 3.14. Infer the type of their sum:

    ```
    5 + 3.14
    ```

    The output is as follows:

    ```
    8.14
    ```

    It's clear from the output that combining an `int` and a `float` gives us a `float`. This makes sense. If Python returned 8, you would lose information. When possible, Python converts types to preserve information.

    You can, however, change types by using the `type` keyword.

4. Now, convert 7.999999999 into an `int`:

    ```
    int(7.999999999)
    ```

    The output is as follows:

    ```
    7
    ```

5. Convert 6 into a `float`:

    ```
    float(6)
    ```

The output is as follows:

```
6.0
```

In this exercise, you determined types using the `type()` keyword, and you changed types between integers and floats. As a developer, you will need to use your knowledge of variable types more often than you might expect. It's standard to be unsure of a type when dealing with hundreds of variables simultaneously, or when editing other people's code.

> **Note**
>
> Changing types, referred to as **casting**, will be revisited later in this chapter in the *Casting – changing types* section.

Complex number types

Python includes complex numbers as an official type. This is not common in other languages and it gives us a hint of the mathematical depth that Python contains.

Complex numbers arise when taking the square roots of negative numbers. There is no real number whose square is -9, so we say that the square root of -9 equals 3i. Another example of a complex number is 2i + 3. Python uses `j` instead of `i`.

You can take a look at the following code snippet to learn how to work with complex number types.

Divide `2 + 3j` by `1 - 5j`, enclosing both operations within parentheses:

```
(2 + 3j) / (1 - 5j)
```

The output will be as follows:

```
-0.5+0.5j
```

> **Note**
>
> For more information on complex numbers, check out `https://docs.python.org/3.7/library/cmath.html`.

Errors in Python

In programming, errors are not to be feared; errors are to be welcomed. Errors are common not only for beginners but for all developers.

Different IDEs show different outputs when errors arise. At this point in your journey, if you get an error, check your code carefully and try again.

When you're getting started with a new language, many errors are referred to as "syntax errors." A syntax error means that Python cannot compile the code that you wrote because it's grammatically incorrect. For instance, you cannot write the letter i after a number, or any other letter besides j, which gives the complex numbers listed previously.

You will learn about important skills for handling errors in *Chapter 4, Extending Python, Files, Errors, and Graphs*.

And don't worry! Python errors in Jupyter Notebooks won't crash your computer or cause any serious problems beyond the inability to run Python code at that moment.

Variable assignment

In Python, variables are memory slots that can store elements of any type. The name variable is meant to be suggestiveas the values assigned to variables may change throughout a program Python variables are introduced the same way as in math: by using the equals sign. In most programming languages, however, order matters; that is, x = 3.14 means that the value 3.14 gets assigned to the x variable. However, 3.14 = x will produce an error because it's impossible to assign a variable to a number. In other words, variable assignment must have the variable on the left of the equals sign, and the value on the right. In the following exercise, we will implement this concept in code.

Exercise 3 – assigning variables

The goal of this exercise is to assign values to variables. This exercise can be performed in a Jupyter Notebook:

1. Set x equal to the number 2, then add 1 to the x variable:

```
x = 2
x + 1
```

The output is as follows:

```
3
```

Once we add 1 to x, we get the output of 3, because the x variable has had 1 added to it.

2. Check the value of x by entering x in a coding cell and running the code:

```
x
```

The output is as follows:

```
2
```

Note that the value of x has not changed.

3.   Change x to 3.0, set x equal to x+1, and check the value of x:

```
x = 3.0
x = x + 1
x
```

The output is as follows:

```
4.0
```

In this step, we changed the value of x by setting x equal to x+1. This is permissible in Python because of the right to left order in variable assignment. On the right-hand side, x+1 has a value of 4.0; this value may be assigned to any variable, including x.

By the end of this exercise, you may have noticed that, in programming, you can assign a variable in terms of its previous value. This is a powerful tool, and many developers use it quite often. Furthermore, the type of x changed. x started as an int, but later became a float. This is allowed in Python because Python is dynamically typed.

> **Pythonic note**
>
> Incrementing a variable by 1 is so common in computer programming that there's a shortcut for it. Instead of writing x=x+1, you can write x+=1 in Python, a Pythonic shortcut that you will apply later.

Casting – changing types

In some languages, a variable can't change types. This means that if the y variable is an integer, then y must always be an integer. Python, however, is dynamically typed, as we saw in *Exercise 3 – assigning variables*, and as illustrated in the following example:

1.   y starts as an integer:

```
y = 10
```

2.   y becomes a float:

```
y = y - 10.0
```

3.   Check the type of y:

```
type(y)
```

The output is as follows:

```
float
```

In the first activity, you will practice math operations with variable assignment.

Activity 1 – assigning values to variables

In this activity, you will assign a number to the x variable, increment the number, and perform additional operations.

By completing this activity, you will learn how to perform multiple mathematical operations using Python. This activity can be performed in your Jupyter Notebook.

The steps are as follows:

1. First, set 14 to the x variable.

2. Now, add 1 to x.

3. Finally, divide x by 5 and square the result.

    The output is as follows:

    ```
    9.0
    ```

> **Note**
> The solution for this activity can be found in *Appendix* on GitHub.

Variable names

To avoid confusion, it's recommended to use variable names that make sense to readers. Instead of using x, the variable may be income or age. Although x is shorter, someone else reading the code might not understand what x is referring to. Try to use variable names that are indicative of the meaning.

There are some restrictions when naming variables. For instance, variable names can only contain alphanumeric characters and the underscore symbol (_). Variable names can only start with an alphabetic character or an underscore, not with a digit.

According to Python conventions, it's best to use lowercase letters when defining variables.

Python keywords are reserved in the language, and also may not be used for variable names. Python keywords have special meanings. We will go over most of these keywords later.

Running the following two lines of code always shows a current list of Python keywords:

```
import keyword
print(keyword.kwlist)
```

The output is as follows:

```
['False', 'None', 'True', 'and', 'as', 'assert', 'async', 'await', 'break', 'class', 'continue',
'def', 'del', 'elif', 'else', 'except', 'finally', 'for', 'from', 'global', 'if', 'import', 'i
n', 'is', 'lambda', 'nonlocal', 'not', 'or', 'pass', 'raise', 'return', 'try', 'while', 'with',
'yield']
```

Figure 1.3 – Output showing the Python keywords

> **Note**
>
> If you use any of the preceding keywords as variable names, Python will throw an error.

Exercise 4 – naming variables

The goal of this exercise is to learn standard ways to name variables by considering good and bad practices. This exercise can be performed in a Jupyter Notebook:

1. Create a variable called `1st_number` and assign it a value of `1`:

    ```
    1st_number = 1
    ```

    Let's see the output:

    ```
    File "<ipython-input-2-ac9b8cc41192>", line 1
        1st_number=1
                 ^
    SyntaxError: invalid syntax
    ```

    Figure 1.4 – Output throwing a syntax error

    You'll get the error mentioned in the preceding screenshot because you cannot begin a variable with a number.

2. Now, let's try using letters to begin a variable:

    ```
    first_number = 1
    ```

3. Now, use special characters in a variable name, as in the following code:

    ```
    my_$ = 1000.00
    ```

    The output is as follows:

    ```
    File "<ipython-input-3-e3c03546ed83>", line 1
        my_$ = 1000.00
             ^
    SyntaxError: invalid syntax
    ```

    Figure 1.5 – Output throwing a syntax error

You will get the error mentioned in *Figure 1.5* because you cannot include a variable with a special character.

4. Now, use letters again instead of special characters for the variable name:

```
my_money = 1000.00
```

In this exercise, you learned how to use underscores to separate words when naming variables, and not to start variables' names with numbers or include any symbols. In Python, you will quickly get used to these conventions.

Multiple variables

Most programs contain multiple variables. The same rules when working with single variables apply here. You will practice working with multiple variables in the following exercise.

Exercise 5 – assigning multiple variables

In this exercise, you will perform mathematical operations using more than one variable. This exercise can be performed in your Jupyter Notebook:

1. Assign 5 to x and 2 to y:

```
x = 5
y = 2
```

2. Add x to x and subtract y to the second power:

```
x + x - y ** 2
```

This will give you the following output:

```
6
```

Python has a lot of cool shortcuts, and multiple variable assignment is one of them. Let's look at the Pythonic way of declaring two variables.

> **Note**
> Pythonic is a term used to describe code written in the optimum readable format. This will be covered in *Chapter 7, Becoming Pythonic*.

3. Assign 8 to x and 5 to y in one line:

```
x, y = 8, 5
```

4. Find the integer division of x and y:

```
x // y
```

This will give you the following output:

```
1
```

In this exercise, you practiced working with multiple variables, and you even learned the Pythonic way to assign values to multiple variables in one line. It's rare to only work with one variable in practice.

Comments

Comments are extra blocks of code that do not run. They are meant to clarify code for readers. In Python, any text following the # symbol on a single line is a comment. Comments followed by the # symbol may be inline or above the statement.

> **Note**
>
> Consistent use of comments will make reviewing and debugging code much easier. It's strongly advisable to practice this from here on out.

Exercise 6 – comments in Python

In this exercise, you will learn two different ways to display comments in Python. This exercise can be performed in a Jupyter Notebook:

1. Write a comment that states This is a comment:

```
# This is a comment
```

When you execute this cell, nothing should happen.

2. Set the pi variable equal to 3.14. Add a comment above the line stating what you did:

```
# Set the variable pi equal to 3.14
pi = 3.14
```

Adding this comment clarifies what follows.

3. Now, try setting the pi variable equal to 3.14 again, but add the comment stating what you did on the same line:

```
pi = 3.14  # Set the variable pi equal to 3.14
```

Although it's less common to provide comments on the same line of code, it's acceptable and often appropriate.

The output from the Jupyter notebook is shown here:

```
In [1]:  # This is a comment

In [2]:  # Set the variable pi equal to 3.14
         pi = 3.14

In [3]:  pi = 3.14    # Set the variable pi equal to 3.14
```

Figure 1.6 – Output from the Jupyter Notebook using comments

In this exercise, you learned how to write comments in Python. As a developer, writing comments is essential to making your code legible to others.

Docstrings

Docstrings, short for document strings, state what a given document, such as a program, a function, or a class, actually does. The primary difference in syntax between a docstring and a comment is that docstrings are intended to be written over multiple lines, which can be accomplished with triple quotes, `"""`. They also introduce a given document, so they are placed at the top.

Here is an example of a docstring:

```
"""
This document will explore why comments are particularly
    useful when writing and reading code.
"""
```

Docstrings, like comments, are designed as information for developers reading and writing code. Unlike comments, docstrings may be accessed later using _doc_.

Activity 2 – finding the area of a triangle

In this activity, you will determine the area of a triangle using variables, comments, type conversion, and docstrings.

You need to assign numbers to the base and height variables, then multiply the base and height by ½ to find the area. You will also include a docstring and comments to clarify the code.

The steps are as follows:

1. Write a docstring that describes what the code is going to do.
2. Set base and height equal to 2 and 4, respectively.

3. Determine the area of a triangle using `base` and `height`.

4. Convert the area of the triangle into an integer.

5. Display the final output.

6. Include comments to clarify each line of code.

    The following is the output:

    4

> **Note**
>
> The solution for this activity can be found in *Appendix* on GitHub.

So far, in this chapter, you have used Python as a basic calculator, along with the order of operations. You examined the difference between the `int` and `float` values and learned how to convert between them, a process known as type casting. Now, you can implement variable assignment and reassign variables to make programs run more smoothly. You also utilized comments to make code more readable and learned how to identify syntax errors. In addition, you learned a couple of cool Python shortcuts, including assigning multiple variables to one line. As a bonus, you explored Python's complex number types.

Next, you'll explore Python's other main type: strings.

Strings – concatenation, methods, and input()

So far, you have learned how to express numbers, operations, and variables. But what about words? In Python, anything that goes between single (`'`) or double (`"`) quotes is considered a string. Strings are commonly used to express words, but they have many other uses, including displaying information to the user and retrieving information from a user.

Examples include `'hello'`, `"hello"`, `'HELLoo00'`, `'12345'`, and `'fun_characters: !@ #$%^&*('`.

In this section, you will gain proficiency with strings by examining string methods, string concatenation, and useful built-in functions, including `print()` and `len()`, by covering a wide range of examples.

String syntax

Although strings may use single or double quotes, a given string must be internally consistent. That is, if a string starts with a single quote, it must end with a single quote. The same is true of double quotes.

We'll look at valid and invalid strings in the next exercise.

Exercise 7 – string error syntax

The goal of this exercise is to learn appropriate string syntax:

1. Open a Jupyter Notebook.

2. Enter a valid string:

    ```
    bookstore = 'City Lights'
    ```

3. Now, enter an invalid string:

    ```
    bookstore = 'City Lights"
    ```

    The output is as follows:

    ```
    File "<ipython-input-2-9c3a3fab8dfa>", line 1
        bookstore = 'City Lights"
                                 ^
    SyntaxError: EOL while scanning string literal
    ```

    Figure 1.7 – Output with invalid string format

    If you start with a single quote, you must end with a single quote. Since the string has not been completed, you receive a syntax error.

4. Now, you need to enter a valid string format again, as shown in the following code snippet:

    ```
    bookstore = "Moe's"
    ```

    This is okay. The string starts and ends with double quotes. Anything can be inside the quotation marks, except for more of the same quotation marks.

5. Now, add an invalid string again:

    ```
    bookstore = 'Moe's'
    ```

    Let's look at the output:

    ```
    File "<ipython-input-4-0ef68cccb92b>", line 1
        bookstore = 'Moe's'
                         ^
    SyntaxError: invalid syntax
    ```

    Figure 1.8 – Output with the invalid string

This is a problem. You started and ended with single quotes, and then you added another single quote and an `s`.

A couple of questions arise. The first is whether single or double quotes should be used. The answer is that it depends on developer preference. Double quotes are more traditional, and they can be used to avoid potentially problematic situations such as the aforementioned `Moe's` example. Single quotes save space and require one less keystroke.

In this exercise, you learned the correct and incorrect ways of assigning strings to variables with single and double quotes.

Escape characters

Python uses the backslash character, \, called an **escape** sequence in strings, so that you can insert any type of quote inside strings. The character that follows the backslash in an escape sequence may be interpreted as mentioned in Python's official documentation, shown in the following table. Of particular note is \n, which is used to create a new line:

Escape Sequence	Meaning
\newline	Ignored
\\	Backslash (\)
\'	Single quote (')
\"	Double quote (")
\a	ASCII Bell (BEL)
\b	ASCII Backspace (BS)
\f	ASCII Formfeed (FF)
\n	ASCII Linefeed (LF)
\r	ASCII Carriage Return (CR)
\t	ASCII Horizontal Tab (TAB)
\v	ASCII Vertical Tab (VT)
\ooo	ASCII character with octal value ooo
\xhh...	ASCII character with hex value hh...

Figure 1.9 – Escape sequences and their meaning

> **Note**
>
> For more general information on strings, you can refer to https://docs.python.org/2.0/ref/strings.html.

Escape sequences with quotes

Here is how an escape sequence works with quotes. The backslash overrides the single quote as an end quote and allows it to be interpreted as a string character:

```
bookstore = 'Moe\'s'
```

Multiline strings

Short strings often display nicely, but what about multiline strings? It can be cumbersome to define a paragraph variable that includes a string over multiple lines. In some IDEs, the string may run off the screen, and it may be difficult to read. In addition, it might be advantageous to have line breaks at specific points for the user.

> **Note**
> Line breaks will not work inside single or double quotes if you press the *Return* key.

When strings need to span multiple lines, Python provides an escape option, \n, and triple quotes.

Here is an example of triple quotes (''') being used to write a multiline string:

```
vacation_note = '''
During our vacation to San Francisco, we waited in a long
    line by Powell St. Station to take the cable car. Tap
        dancers performed on wooden boards. By the time our
            cable car arrived, we started looking online for a
                good place to eat. We're heading to North Beach.
'''
```

> **Note**
> Multiline strings take on the same syntax as a docstring. The difference is that a docstring appears at the beginning of a document, and a multiline string is defined within the program.

The print() function

The print() function is used to display information to the user or the developer. It's one of Python's most widely used built-in functions.

Exercise 8 – displaying strings

In this exercise, you will learn about different ways to display strings:

1. Open a new Jupyter Notebook.
2. Define a greeting variable with a value of 'Hello'. Display the greeting using the print() function:

```
greeting = 'Hello'
print(greeting)
```

The output is as follows:

```
Hello
```

`Hello`, as shown in the display, does not include single quotes. This is because the `print()` function is generally intended for the user to print the output.

> **Note**
> The quotes are for developer syntax, not user syntax.

3. Display the value of `greeting` without using the `print()` function in a Jupyter Notebook:

```
greeting
```

The output is as follows:

```
'Hello'
```

When we input `greeting` without the `print()` function, we are obtaining the encoded value, hence the quotes.

4. Consider the following sequence of code in a single cell in a Jupyter Notebook:

```
spanish_greeting = 'Hola.'
spanish_greeting
arabic_greeting = 'Ahlan wa sahlan.'
```

When the preceding cell is run, the output does not display `spanish_greeting`. If the code were run as three separate cells, it would display `Hola.`, the string assigned to `spanish_greeting`. For consistency, it's useful to use `print()` any time information should be displayed.

5. Now, display the Arabic greeting message defined in *Step 4* using the global `print()` function:

```
print(arabic_greeting)
```

We will see the following output:

```
Ahlan wa sahlan.
```

In this exercise, you learned different ways to display strings, including using the `print()` function. You will use the `print()` function very frequently as a developer.

String operations and concatenation

The multiplication and addition operators work with strings as well. In particular, the + operator combines two strings into one and is referred to as **string concatenation**. The * operator, for multiplication, repeats a string multiple times. In the following exercise, you will look at string concatenation in our string samples.

Exercise 9 – string concatenation

In this exercise, you will learn how to combine strings using string concatenation:

1. Open a new Jupyter Notebook.

2. Combine `spanish_greeting`, which we used in *Exercise 8 – displaying strings*, with `'Senor.'` using the + operator and display the results:

    ```
    spanish_greeting = 'Hola'
    print(spanish_greeting + 'Senor.')
    ```

    The output is as follows:

    ```
    HolaSenor.
    ```

    Notice that there are no spaces between the greeting and the name. If we want spaces between strings, we need to explicitly add them.

3. Now, combine `spanish_greeting` with `'Senor.'` using the + operator, but this time, include a **space**:

    ```
    spanish_greeting = 'Hola '
    print(spanish_greeting + ' Senor.')
    ```

    The output is as follows:

    ```
    Hola Senor.
    ```

4. Display the `greeting` variable five times using the * multiplication operator:

    ```
    greeting = 'Hello'
    print(greeting * 5)
    ```

    The output is as follows:

    ```
    HelloHelloHelloHelloHello
    ```

By completing this exercise successfully, you have concatenated strings using the + and * operators.

String interpolation

When writing strings, you may want to include variables in the output. String interpolation includes the variable names as placeholders within the string. There are two standard methods for achieving string interpolation: **comma separators** and **format**.

Comma separators

Variables may be interpolated into strings using commas to separate clauses. It's similar to the + operator, except it adds spacing for you.

Look at the following example, where we add Ciao within a print statement:

```python
italian_greeting = 'Ciao'
print('Should we greet people with', italian_greeting,
    'in North Beach?')
```

The output is as follows:

```
Should we greet people with Ciao in North Beach?
```

f-strings

Perhaps the most effective way to combine variables with strings is with f-strings. Introduced in Python 3.6, f-strings are activated whenever the f character is followed by quotations. The advantage is that any variable inside curly brackets will automatically be converted into a string.

Here is an example:

```python
poet = 'Amanda Gorman'
age = 22
f'At age {age}, {poet} became the youngest inaugural poet
    in US history.'
```

The output is as follows:

```
'At age 22, Amanda Gorman became the youngest inaugural
    poet in US history.'
```

The spacing works out well, and you can use as many variables as desired.

> **Note**
>
> For more information on f-strings, along with the string literals that they replaced, check out the official documentation at `https://docs.python.org/3/tutorial/inputoutput.html`.

In the next section, you will look at some built-in string functions available to Python developers.

The len() function

Many built-in functions are useful for strings. One such global function is `len()`, which is short for length. The `len()` global function returns the length of any object. For a string, the `len()` function returns the number of characters in a string.

Note that the `len()` function will also count any blank spaces in a given string.

Let's determine the length of the `arabic_greeting` variable that we used in *Exercise 8 – displaying strings*:

```
len(arabic_greeting)
```

The output is as follows:

```
16
```

> **Note**
>
> When entering variables in Jupyter notebooks, you can use **tab completion**. After you type in a letter or two, you can press the *Tab* key. Python then displays all valid continuations that will complete your expression. If done correctly, you will see your variable listed after entering the first few characters. Then, you can highlight the variable and press *Enter*. Using tab completion will limit errors.

String methods

All Python types, including strings, have their own methods. These methods generally provide shortcuts for implementing useful tasks. Methods in Python, as in many other languages, are accessed via dot notation.

You can use a new variable, `name`, to access a variety of methods. You can see all methods by pressing the *Tab* button after the variable name and a dot (.).

Exercise 10 – implementing string methods

In this exercise, you will learn how to implement string methods:

1. Set a new variable, called name, to any name that you like:

    ```
    name = 'Josephine'
    ```

> **Note**
>
> In Jupyter Notebooks, you can access string methods by pressing the *Tab* button after the variable name and dot (.), as demonstrated in the following screenshot:

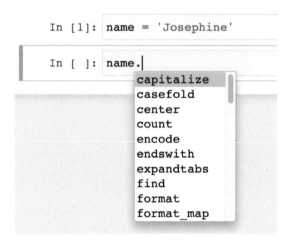

Figure 1.10 – Setting a variable name via the drop-down menu

You can scroll down the list to obtain all available string methods.

2. Now, convert the name variable into lowercase letters using the lower() method:

    ```
    name.lower()
    ```

    The output is as follows:

    ```
    'josephine'
    ```

3. Now, capitalize the name variable using the capitalize() method:

    ```
    name.capitalize()
    ```

    The output is as follows:

    ```
    'Josephine'
    ```

4. Convert the `name` variable into uppercase letters using `upper()`:

    ```
    name.upper()
    ```

    The output is as follows:

    ```
    'JOSEPHINE'
    ```

5. Finally, count the number of e instances in the `name` variable:

    ```
    name.count('e')
    ```

    The output is as follows for `name=Josephine`:

    ```
    2
    ```

In this exercise, you learned about a variety of string methods, including `lower()`, `capitalize()`, `upper()`, and `count()`.

Methods may only be applied to their representative types. For instance, the `lower()` method only works on strings, not integers or floats. By contrast, global functions such as `len()` and `print()` can be applied to a variety of types.

> **Note**
>
> Methods do not change the original variable unless we explicitly reassign the variable. So, the name has not been changed, despite the methods that we have applied. An example of changing a variable would be `name = name.lower()`.

Casting

It's common for numbers to be expressed as strings when dealing with input and output. Note that `'5'` and `5` are different types. We can easily convert between numbers and strings using the appropriate types and keywords. In the following exercise, we are going to be using types and casting to understand the concepts much better.

Exercise 11 – types and casting

In this exercise, you will learn how types and casting work together:

1. Open a new Jupyter Notebook.

2. Determine the type of `'5'`:

    ```
    type('5')
    ```

The output is as follows:

```
str
```

3. Now, add `'5'` and `'7'`:

```
'5' + '7'
```

The output is as follows:

```
'57'
```

The answer is not 12 because, here, 5 and 7 are of the string type, not of the int type. Recall that the + operator concatenates strings. If we want to add 5 and 7, we must convert them first.

4. Convert the `'5'` string into an int using the following line of code:

```
int('5')
```

The output is as follows:

```
5
```

Now that 5 is a number, it can be combined with other numbers via standard mathematical operations.

5. Add `'5'` and `'7'` by converting them into the int type first:

```
int('5') + int('7')
```

The output is as follows:

```
12
```

In this exercise, you learned how strings may be cast as ints, and how ints may be cast as strings via a general procedure that will work for all transferable types.

The input() function

The input() function is a built-in Python function that allows user input. Note that the input given by the user will be taken as a string in Python, irrespective of the type of input the user gives. It's a little different than what we have seen so far. Let's see how it works in action.

Exercise 12 – using the input() function

In this exercise, you will utilize the input () function to obtain information from the user. Note that in computer programming, the user generally refers to the person or entity using the program that you are writing:

1. Open a new Jupyter Notebook.

2. Ask a user for their name using the input () function, as follows:

```
name = input('What is your name?')
```

The output is as follows:

```
name = input('What is your name?')

What is your name?[            ]
```

Figure 1.11 – The user is prompted to answer a question

The text following input is displayed, and the computer is waiting for the user's response. Enter a response and then press *Enter*:

```
[1] name = input('What is your name?')

    What is your name?Alenna
```

Figure 1.12 – The user may type anything into the provided space

Now that a name has been provided to the input () function, it has been stored as the name variable and may be referenced later.

Access the provided name using the global input () function, as follows:

```
print(f'Hello, {name}.')
```

The output will be as follows:

```
Hello, Alenna.
```

> **Note**
>
> `input()` can be finicky in Jupyter Notebooks. If an error arises when you're entering the code, try restarting the kernel using the **Runtime: Restart Runtime** tab. Restarting the kernel will erase the current memory and start each cell afresh. This is advisable if the notebook stalls.

In this exercise, you learned how the `input()` function may be used to access and retrieve information from the user.

Activity 3 – using the input() function to rate your day

In this activity, you will create an input type where you ask the user to rate their day on a scale of 1 to 10.

Using the `input()` function, you will prompt a user for input and respond with a comment that includes the input. In this activity, you will print a message to the user asking for a number. Then, you will assign the number to a variable and use that variable in a second message that you display to the user.

The steps are as follows:

1. Open a new Jupyter Notebook.

2. Display a question prompting the user to rate their day on a number scale of 1 to 10.

3. Save the user's input as a variable.

4. Display a statement to the user that includes the number.

> **Note**
> The solution for this activity can be found in *Appendix* on GitHub.

String indexing and slicing

Indexing and **slicing** are crucial parts of programming. Indexing and slicing are regularly used in lists, a topic that we will cover in *Chapter 2, Python Data Structures*. In data analysis, indexing and slicing DataFrames is essential to keep track of rows and columns, something you will practice in *Chapter 10, Data Analytics with pandas and NumPy*.

Indexing

The characters in strings exist in specific locations. In other words, their order counts. The index is a numerical representation of where each character is located. The first character is at index 0, the second character is at index 1, the third character is at index 2, and so on.

> **Note**
>
> We always start at 0 when indexing in computer programming!

Consider the following string:

```
destination = 'San Francisco'
```

`'S'` is in the 0th index, `'a'` is in the 1st index, `'n'` is in the 2nd index, and so on, as shown in the following table:

String	S	a	n		F	r	a	n	c	i	s	c	o
Index	0	1	2	3	4	5	6	7	8	9	10	11	12

Figure 1.13 – Diagrammatic representation of the character values
and the corresponding positive index values

The characters of each index are accessed using bracket notation, as follows:

```
destination[0]
```

The output is as follows:

```
'S'
```

To access the data from the first index, enter the following:

```
destination[1]
```

The output is as follows:

```
'a'
```

Now, try adding `-1` as the index value to access the last character of the string:

```
destination[-1]
```

The output is as follows:

```
'o'
```

> **Note**
>
> Negative numbers start at the end of the string. (It makes sense to start with -1 since -0 is the same as 0.)

To access the data from the end of any string, always use the negative sign:

```
destination[-2]
```

The output is as follows:

```
'c'
```

The following figure shows the negative indexing of the sco characters from the word Francisco:

Character value	s	c	o
Index Count	-3	-2	-1

Figure 1.14 – Negative index values at the end of San Francisco

Here is one more example:

```
bridge = 'Golden Gate'
bridge[6]
```

The output is as follows:

```
' '
```

You may be wondering whether you did something wrong because no letter is displayed. On the contrary, it's perfectly fine to have an empty string. An empty string is one of the most common strings in programming.

Slicing

A **slice** is a subset of a string or other element. A slice could be the whole element or one character, but it's more commonly a group of adjoining characters.

Let's say you want to access the fifth through eleventh letters of a string. So, you start at index 4 and end at index 10, as was explained in the *Indexing* section. When slicing, the colon symbol (:) is inserted between indices, like so: [4:10].

There is one caveat: the lower bound of a slice is always included, but the upper bound is not. So, in the preceding example, if you want to include the 10th index, you must use [4:11].

Now, let's have a look at the following example for slicing.

Retrieve the fifth through eleventh letters of the destination variable, which you used in the *Indexing* section:

```
destination[4:11]
```

The output is as follows:

```
'Francis'
```

Retrieve the first three letters of `destination`:

```
destination[0:3]
```

The output is as follows:

```
'San'
```

There is a shortcut for getting the first n letters of a string. If the first numerical character is omitted, Python will start at the 0th index.

Now, to retrieve the first eight letters of `destination` using the shortcut, use the following code:

```
destination[:8]
```

The output is as follows:

```
'San Fran'
```

Finally, to retrieve the last nine letters of `destination`, use the following code:

```
destination[-9:]
```

The output is as follows:

```
'Francisco'
```

The negative sign, `-`, means that we start at the end. So, the `-9` parameter means start at the ninth-to-last letter, and the colon means we end at the last letter.

Strings and their methods

We started with string syntax before moving on to a variety of ways to concatenate strings. We also looked at useful global functions, including `len()`, and examined a sample of string methods. Next, we cast numbers as strings and vice versa.

The `input()` function is used to access user input. This extends what you can do. Responding to user feedback is a core element of programming that you will continue to develop. Finally, we closed by looking at two powerful tools that developers frequently use: indexing and slicing.

There is a great deal more to learn about strings. You will encounter additional problems and methods throughout this book. This introductory chapter is meant to equip you with the basic skills needed to handle strings going forward.

Next, you will learn how to branch programs using Booleans and conditionals.

Booleans and conditionals

Booleans, named after George Boole, take the values of **True** or **False**. Although the idea behind Booleans is rather simple, they make programming much more powerful.

When writing programs, it's useful to consider multiple cases. If you prompt the user for information, you may want to respond differently, depending on the user's answer.

For instance, if the user gives a rating of 0 or 1, you may give a different response than a rating of 9 or 10. The keyword here is `if`.

Programming based on multiple cases is often referred to as branching. Each branch is represented by a different conditional. Conditionals often start with an `if` clause, followed by `else` clauses. The choice of a branch is determined by Booleans, depending on whether the given conditions are `True` or `False`.

Booleans

In Python, a Boolean class object is represented by the `bool` keyword and has a value of `True` or `False`.

> **Note**
> Boolean values must be capitalized in Python.

Exercise 13 – Boolean variables

In this short exercise, you will use, assign, and check the types of Boolean variables:

1. Open a new Jupyter Notebook.
2. Now, use a Boolean to classify someone as being over 18 using the following code snippet:

```
over_18 = True
type(over_18)
```

The output is as follows:

```
bool
```

The given output is `bool`, which is short for Boolean.

In this short, quick exercise, you learned about `bool`, one of Python's most important types.

Logical operators

Booleans may be combined with the **and**, **or**, and **not** logical operators, as indicated in the following table:

Logical Operators

	not	and	or
A = True	not A = False	A and A = True	A or A = True
B = False	not B = True	A and B = False	A or B = True
		B and B = False	B or B = False

Figure 1.15 – Table of logical operators

As you can see, the **not** operator changes the value of the Boolean, the **and** operator returns **True** if both Booleans are true, and the **or** operator returns **True** if only one Boolean is true.

Now, let's use them in the following practice example:

1. First, assign `True` and `False` to `over_18` and `over_21`, respectively:

    ```
    over_18, over_21 = True, False
    ```

2. Next, check if the individual is `over_18` and `over_21`:

    ```
    over_18 and over_21
    ```

    The output is as follows:

    ```
    False
    ```

3. Now, check if the individual is `over_18` or `over_21`:

    ```
    over_18 or over_21
    ```

The output is as follows:

```
True
```

4. Now, check if the individual is not `over_18`:

```
not over_18
```

The output is as follows:

```
False
```

5. Now, check if the individual is not `over_21` or (`over_21 or over_18`):

```
not over_21 or (over_21 or over_18)
```

The output is as follows:

```
True
```

In the next section, you will learn about the comparison operators that go along with Booleans.

Comparison operators

Python objects may be compared using a variety of symbols that evaluate to Booleans.

Figure 1.16 shows the comparison table with their corresponding operators:

Symbol	Meaning
<	Greater than
<=	Greater than or equal to
>	Less than
>=	Less than or equal to
==	Equivalant to
!=	Not equivalent to

Figure 1.16 – Comparison table and the corresponding symbols

> **Note**
> The = and == symbols are often confused. The = symbol is an assignment symbol. So, x = 3 assigns the 3 integer to the x variable. The == symbol makes a comparison. Thus, x == 3 checks to see whether x is equivalent to 3. The result of x == 3 will be True or False.

Exercise 14 – comparison operators

In this exercise, you will practice using comparison operators. You will start with some basic mathematical examples:

1. Open a new Jupyter Notebook.

2. Now, set `income` equal to `80000` and include a comparison operator to check whether `income` is less than `75000`:

    ```
    income = 80000
    income < 75000
    ```

    The output is as follows:

    ```
    False
    ```

3. Using the following code snippet, you can check whether `income` is greater than or equal to `80000` and less than or equal to `100000`:

    ```
    income >= 80000 and income <= 100000
    ```

    The output is as follows:

    ```
    True
    ```

4. Now, check whether `income` is not equivalent to `10000`:

    ```
    income != 100000
    ```

    The output is as follows:

    ```
    True
    ```

5. Now, check whether `income` is equivalent to `90000`:

    ```
    income == 90000
    ```

    The output is as follows:

    ```
    False
    ```

The double equals sign, or the equivalent operator, `==`, is very important in Python. It allows us to determine whether two objects are equal. You can now address the question of whether 6 and 6.0 are the same in Python.

6. Is 6 equivalent to 6.0 in Python? Let's find out:

    ```
    6 == 6.0
    ```

    The output is as follows:

    ```
    True
    ```

    This may come as a bit of a surprise. 6 and 6.0 are different types, but they are equivalent. Why would that be?

    Since 6 and 6.0 are equivalent mathematically, it makes sense that they would be equivalent in Python, even though the types are different. Consider whether 6 should be equivalent to 42/7. The mathematical answer is yes. Python often conforms to mathematical truths, even with integer division. From this, you can conclude that different types can have equivalent objects.

7. Now, find out whether 6 is equivalent to the '6' string:

    ```
    6 == '6'
    ```

    This will result in the following output:

    ```
    False
    ```

    Different types usually do not have equivalent objects. In general, it's a good idea to cast objects as the same type before testing for equivalence.

8. Next, let's find out whether someone who is 29 is in their 20s or 30s:

    ```
    age=29
    (20 <= age < 30) or (30 <= age < 40)
    ```

    Now, the output will be as follows:

    ```
    True
    ```

    Although the parentheses in the preceding code line are not strictly required, they make the code more readable. A good rule of thumb is to use parentheses for clarity. When using more than two conditions, parentheses are generally a good idea.

By completing this exercise, you have practiced using different comparison operators.

Comparing strings

Does `'a' < 'c'` make sense? What about `'New York' > 'San Francisco'`?

Python uses the convention of alphabetical order to make sense of these comparisons. Think of a dictionary: when comparing two words, the word that comes later in the dictionary is considered greater than the word that comes before.

Exercise 15 – practicing comparing strings

In this exercise, you will be comparing strings using Python:

1. Open a new Jupyter Notebook.

2. Let's compare single letters:

    ```
    'a' < 'c'
    ```

    Let's see the output:

    ```
    True
    ```

3. Now, let's compare `'New York'` and `'San Francisco'`:

    ```
    'New York' > 'San Francisco'
    ```

    Now, the output changes:

    ```
    False
    ```

    This is `False` because `'New York' < 'San Francisco'`. `'New York'` does not come later in the dictionary than `'San Francisco'`.

In this exercise, you learned how to compare strings using comparison operators.

Conditionals

Conditionals are used when we want to express code based on a set of circumstances or values. Conditionals evaluate Boolean values or Boolean expressions, and they are usually preceded by `'if'`.

Let's say we are writing a voting program, and we only want to print something if the user is under 18.

The if syntax

Consider the following example:

```
if age < 18:
    print('You aren\'t old enough to vote.')
```

There are several key components to a condition. Let's break them down.

The first is the `if` keyword. Conditionals start with an `if` clause. Everything between `if` and the colon is the condition that we are checking.

The next important piece is the colon, `:`. The colon indicates that the `if` clause has been completed. At this point, the compiler decides whether the preceding condition is `True` or `False`.

All statement(s) to be executed when the condition evaluates to `True` need to be indented.

Indentation can be advantageous when dealing with nested conditionals because it avoids cumbersome notation. Python indentation is expected to be **four spaces** and may usually be achieved by pressing *Tab* on your keyboard.

Indented lines will only run if the condition evaluates to `True`. If the condition evaluates to `False`, the indented lines will be skipped over entirely.

Indentation

Indentation is one of Python's singular features. Indentation is used everywhere in Python. One advantage is the number of keystrokes. It takes one keystroke to tab, and two keystrokes to insert brackets. Another advantage is readability. It's clearer and easier to read code when it all shares the same indentation, meaning the block of code belongs to the same branch.

One potential drawback is that dozens of tabs may draw text offscreen, but this is rare in practice, and can usually be avoided with elegant code. Other concerns, such as indenting or unindenting multiple lines, may be handled via shortcuts. Select all of the text and press *Tab* to indent. Select all of the text and press *Shift + Tab* to unindent.

> **Note**
> Indentation is unique to Python. This may result in strong opinions on both sides. In practice, indentation is very effective, and developers used to other languages will appreciate its advantages in time.

Exercise 16 – using the if syntax

In this exercise, you will be using conditionals using the `if` clause:

1. Open a new Jupyter Notebook.
2. Now, run multiple lines of code where you set the `age` variable to `20` and add an `if` clause, as mentioned in the following code snippet:

```
age = 20
if age >= 18 and age < 21:
```

```
print('At least you can vote.')
print('US Poker will have to wait.')
```

The output is as follows:

```
At least you can vote.

US Poker will have to wait.
```

There is no limit to the number of indented statements. Each statement will run in order, provided that the preceding condition is `True`.

3. Now, use nested conditionals:

```
if age >= 18:
  print('You can vote.')
  if age >= 21:
    print('You can play poker in the US.')
```

The output is now as follows:

```
You can vote.
```

In this case, it's true that `age >= 18`, so the first statement prints `You can vote`. The second condition, `age>= 21`, however, is false, so the second statement does not get printed.

In this exercise, you learned how to use conditionals using the `if` clause. Conditionals will always start with `if`.

if else

`if` conditionals are commonly joined with `else` clauses. The idea is as follows. Say you want to print something to all users unless the user is under 18. You can address this with an `if-else` conditional. If the user is under 18, you print one statement. Otherwise, you print another. The otherwise clause is preceded with `else`.

Exercise 17 – using the if-else syntax

In this exercise, you will learn how to use conditionals that have two options – one following `if`, and one following `else`:

1. Open a new Jupyter Notebook.

2. Introduce a voting program only to users over 18 by using the following code snippet:

```
age = 20
if age < 18:
  print('You aren\'t old enough to vote.')
```

```
else:
    print('Welcome to our voting program.')
```

The output will be as follows:

Welcome to our voting program.

> **Note**
> Everything after else is indented, just like everything after the if loop.

In this exercise, you learned how to use if-else in conjunction with loops.

The elif statement

elif is short for **else if**. elif does not have meaning in isolation. elif appears in between an if and else clause. Have a look at the following code snippet and copy it into your Jupyter notebook. The explanation is mentioned after the output:

```
if age <= 10:
    print('Listen, learn, and have fun.')
elif age<= 19:
    print('Go fearlessly forward.')
elif age <= 29:
    print('Seize the day.')
elif age <= 39:
    print('Go for what you want.')
elif age <= 59:
    print('Stay physically fit and healthy.')
else:
    print('Each day is magical.')
```

The output is as follows:

Seize the day.

Now, let's break down the code for a better explanation:

1. The first line checks if age is less than or equal to 10. Since this condition is false, the next branch is checked.

2. The next branch is elif age <= 19. This line checks if the specified age is less than or equal to 19. This is also not true, so we move to the next branch.

3. The next branch is `elif age <= 29`. This is true since `age = 20`. The indented statement that follows will be executed.

4. Once any branch has been executed, the entire sequence is aborted, and none of the subsequent `elif` or `else` branches are checked.

5. If none of the `if` or `elif` branches were true, the final `else` branch will automatically be executed.

In the next topic, you will learn about loops.

Loops

"Write the first 100 numbers."

There are several assumptions implicit in this seemingly simple command. The first is that the student knows where to start, namely at number 1. The second assumption is that the student knows where to end, at number 100. And the third is that the student understands that they should count by 1.

In programming, this set of instructions may be executed with a loop.

There are three key components to most loops:

1. The start of the loop
2. The end of the loop
3. The increment between numbers in the loop

Python distinguishes between two fundamental kinds of loops: `while` loops and `for` loops.

while loops

In a `while` loop, a designated segment of code repeats, provided that a particular condition is true. When the condition evaluates to false, the `while` loop stops running. A `while` loop may print out the first 10 numbers.

You could print the first 10 numbers by implementing the `print` function 10 times, but using a `while` loop is more efficient, and it scales easily. In general, it's not a good idea to copy and paste while coding. If you find yourself copying and pasting, there's probably a more efficient way. Let's have a look at the following example:

```
i = 1
while i <= 10:
    print(i)
    i += 1
```

Let's see the output:

```
1
2
3
4
5
6
7
8
9
10
```

You can break down the preceding code block and find out what's happening in concrete steps:

- **Initialize the variable**: Loops need to be initialized with a variable. The variable is going to change throughout the loop. The naming of the variable is up to you. `i` is often chosen because it stands for incrementor. In this example, `i = 1`.

- **Set up the while loop**: The `while` loop starts with the `while` keyword. Following `while` is the chosen variable. After the variable comes the condition that must be met for the loop to run. In general, the condition should have some way of being broken. When counting, the condition usually includes an upper limit, but it could also be broken in other ways, such as `i != 10`. This line of code is the most critical piece of the loop. It sets up how many times the loop is expected to run. In this example, we are using `while i <= 10:`.

- **Instructions**: The instructions include all indented lines after the colon. Anything could be printed, any function could be called, and any number of lines may be executed. It all depends on the program. So long as the code is syntactically correct, generally speaking, anything goes. This part of the loop is going to run over and over, so long as the aforementioned condition is true. In the example, we are using `print(i)`.

- **Increment**: The incrementor is a crucial part of this example. Without it, the preceding code will never stop running. It will print 1s endlessly because 1 is always less than 10. Here, you increment by 1, but you could also increment by 2, or any other number. An example is `i += 1`.

Now that you understand the separate pieces, let's look at how it works together:

1. The variable is initialized as `1`. The `while` loop checks the condition. `1` is less than or equal to `10`. `1` is printed. `1` is added to `i`. We increment to `i = 2`.

2. After all the indented code after the colon has run, the loop is executed again by returning to the `while` keyword.

3. The `while` loop checks the condition again. 2 is less than or equal to 10. 2 is printed to the console. 1 is added to i. We now increment to i = 3.

4. The `while` loop checks the condition again. 3 is less than or equal to 10. 3 is printed to the console. 1 is added to i. We increment to i = 4.

5. The `while` loop continues to increment and print out numbers until it reaches 10.

6. The `while` loop checks the condition. 10 is less than or equal to 10. 10 is printed to the console. 1 is added to i. We increment to i = 11.

7. The `while` loop checks the condition. 11 is not less than or equal to 10. We break out of the loop by moving beyond the indentation.

> **Note**
> You will get stuck in infinite loops. It happens to everyone. At some point, you will forget to add the increment, and you will be stuck in an infinite loop. In Jupyter Notebooks, just `restart` the kernel.

The break keyword

break is a special keyword in Python that is specifically designed for loops. If placed inside a loop, commonly in a conditional, `break` will immediately terminate the loop. It doesn't matter what comes before or after the loop. The break is placed on its own line, and it *breaks out of the loop*.

To practice, let's print the first number greater than 100 that is divisible by 17.

The idea is that you are going to start at 101 and keep counting until you find a number divisible by 17. Assume you don't know what number to stop at. This is where `break` comes into play. `break` will terminate the loop. You can set your upper bound at some number that you know you will never reach and break out of the loop when you print the first number divisible by 17:

```
# Find first number greater than 100 and divisible by 17.
x = 100
while x >= 100:
  x += 1
  if x % 17 == 0:
    print('', x, 'is the first number greater than 100
      that is divisible by 17.')
    break
```

The x += 1 iterator is placed at the beginning of the loop. This allows us to start with 101. The iterator may be placed anywhere in the loop.

Since 101 is not divisible by `17`, the loop repeats, and $x = 102$. Since `102` is divisible by `17`, the `print` statement executes and we break out of the loop.

This is the first time you have used **double indentation**. Since the `if` conditional is inside a `while` loop, it must be indented as well.

Activity 4 – finding the least common multiple (LCM)

In this activity, you will find the LCM of two divisors. The LCM of two divisors is the first number that both divisors can divide.

For instance, the LCM of 4 and 6 is 12, because 12 is the first number that both 4 and 6 can divide. You will find the LCM of two numbers. You will set the variables, then initialize a `while` loop with an iterator and a Boolean that is `True` by default. After that, you will set up a conditional that will break if the iterator divides both numbers. Finally, you will increase the iterator and print the results after the loop completes.

In this activity, using the following steps, you need to find the LCM of `24` and `36`.

The steps are as follows:

1. Set a pair of variables equal to `24` and `36`.
2. Initialize the `while` loop, based on a Boolean that is `True` by default, with an iterator.
3. Set up a conditional to check whether the iterator divides both numbers.
4. Break the while loop when the LCM is found.
5. Increment the iterator at the end of the loop.
6. Print the results using an f-string.

    The output is as follows:

    ```
    The Least Common Multiple of 24 and 36 is 72.
    ```

> **Note**
> The solution for this activity can be found in *Appendix* on GitHub.

Programs

You have been writing programs throughout this chapter. Every chunk of executable code that can be saved and run on demand is a computer program. You have written programs that greeted users, and you just wrote a program to compute the LCM of a given number in *Activity 4 – finding the least common multiple (LCM)*. In *Chapter 3, Executing Python – Programs, Algorithms, and Functions*, you will learn specific techniques for writing, saving, and executing Python programs.

Now that you have a lot of tools under your belt, you can combine them to write some interesting programs. You know how to generate input from a user, you know how to convert the input into desired types, and you know how to use conditionals and loops to iterate through cases and print various results, depending on the outcome.

Later in this book, you will get into the details of saving and testing programs. In the next exercise, you will write a program to identify perfect squares.

Exercise 18 – calculating perfect squares

The goal of this exercise is to prompt the user to enter a given number and find out whether it is a perfect square without using square roots.

The following steps will help you with this:

1. Open a new Jupyter Notebook.

2. Prompt the user to enter a number to see if it's a perfect square:

    ```
    print('Enter a number to see if it\'s a perfect
        square.')
    ```

3. Set a variable equal to input(). In this case, let's enter 64:

    ```
    number = input()
    ```

4. Ensure the user input is a positive integer:

    ```
    number = abs(int(number))
    ```

5. Choose an iterator variable:

    ```
    i = -1
    ```

6. Initialize a Boolean to check for a perfect square:

    ```
    square = False
    ```

7. Initialize a while loop from -1 to the square root of the number:

    ```
    while i <= number:
    ```

8. Increment i by 1:

    ```
    i += 1
    ```

9. Check the square root of `number`:

```
if i*i == number:
```

10. Indicate that we have a perfect `square`:

```
square = True
```

11. `break` out of the loop:

```
break
```

12. If the number is `square`, `print` out the result:

```
if square:
    print('The square root of', number, 'is', i, '.')
```

13. If the number is not a square, `print` out this result:

```
else:
    print('', number, 'is not a perfect square.')
```

The output is as follows:

The square root of 64 is 8.

In this exercise, you wrote a program to check whether the user's number is a perfect square.

In the next exercise, you are going to write a program based on making a real estate offer.

Exercise 19 – real estate offer

The goal of this exercise is to prompt the user to bid on a house and let them know if and when the bid has been accepted.

The following steps will help you with this:

1. Open a new Jupyter Notebook.

2. Begin by stating a market price:

```
print('A one bedroom in the Bay Area is listed at
    $599,000.')
```

3. Prompt the user to make an offer on the house using `input()` and convert it into an integer:

```
offer = int(input('Enter your first offer on the
    house.'))
```

4. Prompt the user to enter their highest offer for the house:

```
highest = int(input('Enter your highest offer on the
    house.'))
```

5. Prompt the user to choose increments:

```
increment = int(input('How much more do you want to
    offer each time if each time your offer is
        rejected ?'))
```

6. Set offer_accepted equal to False:

```
offer_accepted = False
```

7. Initialize the for loop from offer to best:

```
while offer <= best:
```

8. If offer is greater than 650000, they get the house:

```
if offer >= 650000:
    offer_accepted = True
    print('Your offer of', offer, 'has been
        accepted!')
    break
```

9. If offer does not exceed 650000, they don't get the house:

```
print(f'We\'re sorry, your offer of {offer} has
    not been accepted.' )
```

10. Add increment to offer:

```
offer += increment
```

The output is as follows:

```
A one bedroom in the Bay Area is listed at $599,000
Enter your first offer on the house.
600000
Enter your best offer on the house.
690000
How much more do you want to offer each time?
10000
We're sorry, you're offer of 600000 has not been accepted.
We're sorry, you're offer of 610000 has not been accepted.
We're sorry, you're offer of 620000 has not been accepted.
We're sorry, you're offer of 630000 has not been accepted.
We're sorry, you're offer of 640000 has not been accepted.
Your offer of 650000 has been accepted!
```

Figure 1.17 – Output showing the conditions mentioned in the code using loops

In this exercise, you prompted the user to bid for a house and let them know when and if the bid was accepted.

for loops

for loops are similar to while loops, but they have additional advantages, such as being able to iterate over strings and other objects.

Exercise 20 – using for loops

In this exercise, you will utilize for loops to print the characters in a string, in addition to a range of numbers:

1. Open a new Jupyter Notebook.

2. Print out the characters of 'Amazing':

```
for i in 'Amazing':
  print(i)
```

The output is as follows:

```
A
m
a
z
i
n
g
```

The `for` keyword often goes with the `in` keyword. The `i` variable is known as a dummy variable. The `for i in` phrase means that Python is going to check what comes next and look at its components. Strings are composed of characters, so Python will do something with each of the individual characters. In this particular case, Python will print out the individual characters, as per the `print (i)` command.

What if we want to do something with a range of numbers? Can `for` loops be used for that? Absolutely. Python provides another keyword, `range`, to access a range of numbers. `range` is often defined by two numbers – the first number and the last number – and it includes all numbers in between. Interestingly, the output of `range` includes the first number, but not the last number.

In the next step, you will use `range` to display the first 9 numbers:

1. Use a lower bound of `1` and an upper bound of `10` with `range` to print 1 to 9, as follows:

    ```
    for i in range(1,10):
        print(i)
    ```

    The output is as follows:

    ```
    1
    2
    3
    4
    5
    6
    7
    8
    9
    ```

    `range` does not print the number `10`.

2. Now, use `range` with one bound only, the number `10`, to print the first 10 numbers:

    ```
    for i in range(10):
        print(i)
    ```

    The output is as follows:

    ```
    0
    1
    2
    3
    4
    5
    ```

6

7

8

9

So, `range(10)` will print out the first 10 numbers, starting at 0, and ending with 9. By default, `range` will start with 0, and it will include the number of values provided in parenthesis.

Now, let's say that you want to count by increments of 2. You can add a third bound, a step increment, to count up or down by any number desired.

3. Use a step increment to count the odd numbers through 10:

```
for i in range(1, 11, 2):
    print(i)
```

The output is as follows:

1

3

5

7

9

Similarly, you can count down using negative numbers, which is shown in the next step.

4. Use a negative step increment to count down from 3 to 1:

```
for i in range(3, 0, -1):
    print(i)
```

The output is as follows:

3

2

1

And, of course, you can use nested loops, which are shown in the next step.

5. Now, `print` each letter of your name three times:

```
name = 'Alenna'
for i in range(3):
    for i in name:
        print(i+'!')
```

The output is as follows:

```
A
l
e
n
n
a
!
A
l
e
n
n
a
!
A
l
e
n
n
a
!
```

In this exercise, you utilized loops to print any given number of integers and characters in a string.

The continue keyword

continue is another Python keyword designed for loops. When Python reaches the continue keyword, it stops the code and goes back to the beginning of the loop. continue is similar to break because they both interrupt the loop process, but break terminates the loop, whereas continue continues the loop from the beginning.

Let's look at an example of continue in practice. The following code prints out every two-digit prime number:

```python
for num in range(10,100):
  if num % 2 == 0:
    continue
  if num % 3 == 0:
    continue
```

```
    if num % 5 == 0:
        continue
    if num % 7 == 0:
        continue
    print(num)
```

The output is as follows:

```
11
13
17
19
23
29
31
37
41
43
47
53
59
61
67
71
73
79
83
89
97
```

Let's go through the beginning of the code. The first number to check is 10. The first line checks if 10 can be divided by 2. Since 2 does divide 10, we go inside the conditional and reach the continue keyword. Executing continue returns us to the start of the loop.

The next number that is checked is 11. Since 2, 3, 5, and 7 do not divide 11, you reach the final line and print the number 11.

The code continues in this fashion for all two-digit numbers, only printing numbers that do not meet the criteria for any of the `continue` options.

Activity 5 – building conversational bots using Python

You are working as a Python developer and you are building two conversational bots for your clients. You create a list of steps beforehand to help you out. These steps will help you build two bots that take input from the user and produce a coded response.

This activity aims to make you use nested conditionals to build two conversational bots. The first bot will ask the user two questions and include the user's answer in each of its follow-up responses. The second bot will ask a question that requires a numerical answer. Different responses will be given to a different number of scales. This process will be repeated for a second question.

Let's look at the steps.

For the first bot, the steps are as follows:

1. Ask the user at least two questions.
2. Respond to each answer as the chatbot. Include the answer in the response.

For the second bot, the steps are as follows:

1. Ask a question that can be answered with a number scale, such as `On a scale of 1-10`....
2. Respond differently depending on the answer given.
3. State a different question following each answer that can be answered with a number scale.
4. Respond differently, depending on the answer given.

> **Note**
> The second bot should be written with nested conditionals.

> **Hint**
> Casting may be important.

One possible output for bot 1 is as follows:

```
We're kindred spirits, Corey. Talk later.
```

One possible output for bot 2 is as follows:

```
How intelligent are you? 0 is no intelligence. And 10 is a genius
8
Are you human by chance? Wait. Don't answer that.
How human are you? 0 is not at all and 10 is human all the way.
8
I think this courtship is over.
```

Figure 1.18 – Possible outcome from one of the possible values entered by the user

> **Note**
> The solution for this activity can be found in *Appendix* on GitHub.

Summary

You have gone over a lot of material in this introductory chapter. You have covered math operations, string concatenation and methods, general Python types, variables, conditionals, and loops. Combining these elements allows us to write programs of real value.

Additionally, you have been learning Python syntax. You now understand some of the most common errors, and you're becoming accustomed to the importance that indentation plays. You're also learning how to leverage important keywords such as range, in, if, and True and False.

Going forward, you now have the key fundamental skills to tackle more advanced introductory concepts. Although there is much to learn, you have a vital foundation in place to build upon the types and techniques discussed here.

In the next chapter, you will learn about some of the most important Python types, including lists, dictionaries, tuples, and sets.

2

Python Data Structures

Overview

By the end of this chapter, you will be able to encode and modify the different types of Python data structures, including lists, dictionaries, tuples, and sets, and describe the differences between them; create matrices and manipulate both a matrix as a whole and its individual cells; call the `zip()` function to create different Python structures; find what methods are available for lists, dictionaries, and sets; write a program using the most popular methods for lists, dictionaries, and sets, and convert between different Python data structures.

Introduction

In the previous chapter, you learned the basics of the Python programming language and essential elements such as `string` and `int`, as well as how to use conditionals and loops to control the flow of a Python program. By utilizing these elements, you should now be familiar with writing basic programs in Python.

In this chapter, you are going to learn how to use data structures to store more complex types of data that help model actual data and represent it in the real world.

In programming languages, data structures refer to objects that can hold some data together, which means they are used to store a collection of related data.

For instance, you can use a list to store our to-do items for the day. The following is an example that shows how lists are coded:

```
todo = ["pick up laundry", "buy Groceries", "pay electric
  bills"]
```

We can also use a dictionary object to store more complex information such as subscribers' details from our mailing list. Here is an example code snippet, but don't worry, we will cover this later in this chapter:

```
User = {
    "first_name": "Jack",
    "last_name":"White",
    "age": 41,
    "email": "jack.white@gmail.com"
}
```

Here is a tuple of a point in the *x-y* plane, another data type that will be covered later:

```
point = (1,2)
```

And here is a set of points, whose details will come at the end of this chapter:

```
my_set = {3, 5, 11, 17, 31}
```

There are four types of data structures in Python: `list`, `tuple`, `dictionary`, and `set`:

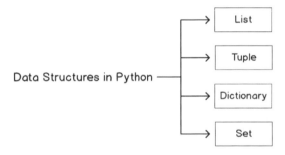

Figure 2.1 – The different data structures in Python

These data structures define the relationship between data and the operations that can be performed on data. They are a way of organizing and storing data that can be accessed efficiently under different circumstances.

In this chapter, we will cover the following topics:

- The power of lists
- List methods
- Matrix operations

- Dictionary keys and values
- Dictionary methods
- Tuples
- A survey of sets
- Choosing types

Let's start!

Technical requirements

The code files for this chapter are available on GitHub at `https://github.com/PacktPublishing/The-Python-Workshop-Second-Edition/tree/main/Chapter02`.

The power of lists

You will now look at the first type of data structure in Python: lists.

A list is a type of container in Python that is used to store multiple datasets at the same time. Python lists are often compared to arrays in other programming languages, but they do a lot more.

The following figure shows a list of fruits, along with their respective indices:

Figure 2.2 – A Python list with a positive index

A list in Python is written within square brackets, [ ]. Each element in the list has its own distinct **index**. The elements in a list have a finite sequence. Like other programming languages, the index of the first item of a list is 0, the second item has an index of 1, and so on. This has to do with how lists are implemented at a lower programming level, so do take note of this when you are writing index-based operations for lists and other iterable objects.

You will now look at the different ways that lists can be useful.

Exercise 21 – working with Python lists

In this exercise, you will learn how to work with a Python list by coding and creating a list and adding items to it. For example, this could prove useful if you have to use a list to store the items that are in a shopping cart:

1. Open a new Jupyter Notebook.

2. Now, enter the following code snippet:

```
shopping = ["bread","milk", "eggs"]
print(shopping)
```

The output is as follows:

```
['bread', 'milk', 'eggs']
```

Here, you created a list called `shopping` with `bread`, `milk`, and `eggs` inside it.

Since a list is a type of iterable in Python, you can use a `for` loop to iterate over all of the elements inside a list.

3. Now, enter and execute the code for a `for` loop and observe the output:

```
for item in shopping:
    print(item)
```

The output is as follows:

```
bread
milk
egg
```

> **Note**
> Python lists are different from arrays used in other languages, such as Java and C#. Python allows mixed types in a list – that is, `int` and `string`.

4. Now, use a `mixed` type of data within the list's content and enter the following code in a new cell:

```
mixed = [365, "days", True]
print(mixed)
```

The output is as follows:

```
[365, 'days', True]
```

But you might be wondering, in that case, shouldn't we be allowed to store a list of lists inside a list? We will take an in-depth look at **nested lists**, which can be used to represent complex data structures, after the next section.

In this exercise, you were introduced to the basics of Python lists.

Now, let's see what list methods are available in Python.

List methods

Since a list is a type of sequence, it supports all sequence operations and methods.

Lists are one of the best data structures to use. Python provides a set of list methods that makes it easy for us to store and retrieve values to maintain, update, and extract data. These common operations are what Python programmers perform, including **slicing**, **sorting**, **appending**, **searching**, **inserting**, and **removing** data.

You will learn about these handy list methods in the following exercises.

Exercise 22 – basic list operations

In this exercise, you are going to use the basic functions of lists to check the size of a list, combine lists, and duplicate lists:

1. Open a new Jupyter notebook.

2. Type the following code:

    ```
    shopping = ["bread","milk", "eggs"]
    ```

3. The length of a list can be found using the global `len()` function:

    ```
    print(len(shopping))
    ```

> **Note**
>
> The `len()` function returns the number of items in an object. When the object is a string, it returns the number of characters in the string.

The output is as follows:

```
3
```

4. Now, concatenate two lists using the + operator:

    ```
    list1 = [1,2,3]
    list2 = [4,5,6]
    ```

```
final_list = list1 + list2
print(final_list)
```

You will get the following output:

```
[1, 2, 3, 4, 5, 6]
```

As you can see, lists also support many string operations, one of which is concatenation, which involves joining two or more lists together.

5. Now, use the * operator, which can be used for repetition in a list, to duplicate elements:

```
list3 = ['oi']
print(list3*3)
```

It will repeat `'oi'` three times, giving us the following output:

```
['oi', 'oi', 'oi']
```

You are now familiar with some common operations that Python programmers use to interact with lists.

Accessing an item from a list

Just like other programming languages, in Python, you can use the index method to access elements in a list. You should complete the following exercise while continuing with the previous notebook.

Exercise 23 – accessing an item from shopping list data

In this exercise, you will work with lists and gain an understanding of how you can access items from a list. The following steps will enable you to complete this exercise:

1. Open a new Jupyter Notebook.
2. Enter the following code in a new cell:

```
shopping = ["bread","milk", "eggs"]
print(shopping[1])
```

The output is as follows:

```
milk
```

As you can see, the milk value from the shopping list has an index of 1 since the list begins from 0.

3. Now, access the first index and replace it with banana:

```
shopping[1] = "banana"
print(shopping)
```

The output is as follows:

```
['bread', 'banana', 'eggs']
```

4. Type the following code in a new cell and observe the output:

```
print(shopping[-1])
```

The output is as follows:

```
eggs
```

The output will print eggs – the last item.

Just like with strings, Python lists support **slicing** with the : notation in the format of list[i:j], where i is the starting element and j is the last element (non-inclusive).

5. Enter the following code to try out a different type of slicing:

```
print(shopping[0:2])
```

This prints the first and second elements, producing the following output:

```
['bread', 'banana']
```

6. Now, to print from the beginning of the list to the third element, run the following:

```
print(shopping[:3])
```

The output is as follows:

```
['bread', 'banana', 'eggs']
```

7. Similarly, to print from the second element of the list until the end, you can use the following:

```
print(shopping[1:])
```

The output is as follows:

```
['banana', 'eggs']
```

Having completed this exercise, you are now able to access items from a list in different ways.

Adding an item to a list

In the previous section and *Exercise 23 – accessing an item from shopping list data*, you learned how to access items from a list. Lists are very powerful and are used in many circumstances. However, you often won't know the data your users want to store beforehand. Here, you are going to look at various methods for adding items to and inserting items into a list.

Exercise 24 – adding items to our shopping list

The `append` method is the easiest way to add a new element to the end of a list. You will use this method in this exercise to add items to our `shopping` list:

1. In a new cell, type the following code to add a new element, `apple`, to the end of the list using the `append` method:

    ```python
    shopping = ["bread","milk", "eggs"]
    shopping.append("apple")
    print(shopping)
    ```

    Let's see the output:

    ```
    ['bread', 'milk', 'eggs', 'apple']
    ```

    The `append` method is commonly used when you are building a list without knowing what the total number of elements will be. You will start with an empty list and continue to add items to build the list.

2. Now, create an empty list, `shopping`, and keep adding items one by one to this empty list:

    ```python
    shopping = []
    shopping.append('bread')
    shopping.append('milk')
    shopping.append('eggs')
    shopping.append('apple')
    print(shopping)
    ```

    Here's the output:

    ```
    ['bread', 'milk', 'eggs', 'apple']
    ```

    This way, you start by initializing an empty list, and you extend the list dynamically. The result is the same as the list from the previous code. This is different from some programming languages, which require the array size to be fixed at the declaration stage.

3. Now, use the `insert` method to add elements to the `shopping` list:

    ```python
    shopping.insert(2, 'ham')
    print(shopping)
    ```

    The output is as follows:

    ```
    ['bread', 'milk', 'ham', 'eggs', 'apple']
    ```

As you coded in *Step 3*, you came across another way to add an element to a list: using the `insert` method. The `insert` method requires a positional index to indicate where the new element should be placed. A positional index is a zero-based number that indicates the position in a list. You can use `ham` to insert an item in the third position.

In the preceding code, you can see that `ham` has been inserted in the third position and shifts every other item one position to the right.

Having concluded this exercise, you are now able to `add` elements to our `shopping` list. This proves to be very useful when you get data from a customer or client, allowing you to add items to your list.

Exercise 25 – looping through a list

It's common to generate new lists by looping through previous lists. In the following exercise, you will loop through a list of the first 5 primes to generate a list of the squares of the first 5 primes:

1. In a new cell, enter the first 5 primes in a list called `primes`.

    ```
    primes = [2, 3, 5, 7, 11]
    ```

2. Now create an empty list, `primes_squared`, then loop through the `primes` list and append the square of each prime, as follows:

    ```
    primes_squared = []
    for i in primes:
        primes_squared.append(i**2)
    print(primes_squared)
    ```

    The output is as follows:

    ```
    [4, 9, 25, 49, 121]
    ```

This is the standard way to loop through lists to generate new lists. In *Chapter 7, Becoming Pythonic*, you will learn about a new way of using list comprehensions.

Now, let's examine matrices as nested lists.

Matrices as nested lists

Most of the data we store in the real world is in the form of a tabular data table – that is, **rows** and **columns** – instead of a one-dimensional flat list. Such tables are called **matrices** or **two-dimensional arrays**. Python (and most other programming languages) does not provide a table structure out of the box. A table structure is simply a way to present data.

What you can do is present the table structure shown in *Figure 2.3* using a list of lists; for example, let's say you want to store the following fruit orders using a list:

Apple	Banana	Orange
5	8	9
7	6	2

Figure 2.3 – A representation of lists of lists as a matrix

Mathematically, you can present the information shown in *Figure 2.3* using a 2 x 3 (2 rows by 3 columns) matrix. This matrix would look like this:

$$\begin{bmatrix} 1 & 2 & 3 \\ 4 & 5 & 6 \end{bmatrix}$$

Figure 2.4 – A matrix representation of data

In the next exercise, you will learn how to store this matrix as a nested list.

Exercise 26 – using a nested list to store data from a matrix

In this exercise, you will look at working with a nested list, storing values in it, and accessing it using several methods:

1. Open a new Jupyter notebook.

2. Enter the following code in a new cell:

    ```
    m = [[1, 2, 3], [4, 5, 6]]
    ```

    We can store the matrix as a series of lists inside a list, which is called a nested list.

    We can now access the elements using the `[row] [column]` variable notation.

3. Print the element indexed as the first row and first column:

    ```
    print(m[1][1])
    ```

    The output is as follows:

    ```
    5
    ```

    It prints the value of row 2, column 2, which is 5 (remember, we are using a zero-based index offset).

4. Now, access each of the elements in the nested list matrix by retaining their reference index with two variables, i and j:

    ```
    for i in range(len(m)):
        for j in range(len(m[i])):
            print(m[i][j])
    ```

The preceding code uses a `for` loop to iterate twice. In the outer loop (`i`), we iterate every single row in the m matrix, and in the inner loop (`j`), we iterate every column in the row. Finally, we `print` the element in the corresponding position.

The output is as follows:

```
1
2
3
4
5
6
```

5. Use two `for..in` loops to print all the elements within the matrix:

```
for row in m:
    for col in row:
        print(col)
```

The `for` loop in the preceding code iterates both `row` and `col`. This type of notation does not require us to have prior knowledge of the matrix's dimensions.

The output is as follows:

```
1
2
3
4
5
6
```

You now know how a nested list stored as a matrix works, and how to access values from nested lists. In the next activity, you will implement these concepts to store employee data.

Activity 6 – using a nested list to store employee data

In this activity, you are going to store table data using a nested list. Imagine that you are currently working in an IT company and have been given a list of employees. You are asked by your manager to use Python to store this data for further company use.

This activity aims to help you use nested lists to store data and print them as you need them.

The data provided to you by your company is shown in *Figure 2.5*:

Name	Age	Department
John Mckee	38	Sales
Lisa Crawford	29	Marketing
Sujan Patel	33	HR

Figure 2.5 – Table consisting of employee data

Follow these steps to complete this activity:

1. Open a new Jupyter Notebook.

2. Create a list and assign it to `employees`.

3. Create three nested lists in `employees` to store the information of each employee, respectively.

4. Print the `employees` variable.

5. Print the details of all employees in a presentable format.

6. Print only the details of `Lisa Crawford`.

By printing the details in a presentable format, the output will be as follows:

```
['Lisa Crawford', 29, 'Marketing']
Name: Lisa Crawford
Age: 29
Department: Marketing
--------------------
```

Figure 2.6 – Printed details of an employee using lists

> **Note**
> The solution for this activity can be found in *Appendix* on GitHub.

In the next section, you will learn more about matrices and their operations.

Matrix operations

Let's learn how to use nested lists to perform basic matrix operations. Although many developers use NumPy to perform matrix operations, it's very useful to learn how to manipulate matrices using straight Python. First, you will add two matrices in Python. Matrix addition requires both matrices to have the same dimensions; the results will also be of the same dimensions.

In the next exercise, you will perform matrix operations.

Exercise 27 – implementing matrix operations (addition and subtraction)

In this exercise, you will use the matrices in the following figures:

$$X = \begin{bmatrix} 1 & 2 & 3 \\ 4 & 5 & 6 \\ 7 & 8 & 9 \end{bmatrix}$$

Figure 2.7 – Matrix data for the X matrix

$$Y = \begin{bmatrix} 10 & 11 & 12 \\ 13 & 14 & 15 \\ 16 & 17 & 18 \end{bmatrix}$$

Figure 2.8 – Matrix data for the Y matrix

Now, let's add and subtract the X and Y matrices using Python.

The following steps will enable you to complete this exercise:

1. Open a new Jupyter Notebook.

2. Create two nested lists, X and Y, to store the values:

```
X = [[1,2,3],[4,5,6],[7,8,9]]
Y = [[10,11,12],[13,14,15],[16,17,18]]
```

3. Initialize a 3 x 3 zero matrix called `result` as a placeholder:

```
# Initialize a result placeholder
result = [[0,0,0],
     [0,0,0],
     [0,0,0]]
```

4. Now, implement the algorithm by iterating through the cells and columns of the matrix:

```
# iterate through rows
for i in range(len(X)):
# iterate through columns
   for j in range(len(X[0])):
      result[i][j] = X[i][j] + Y[i][j]
print(result)
```

As you learned in the previous section, first, you iterate the rows in the X matrix, then iterate the columns. You do not have to iterate the Y matrix again because both matrices are of the same dimensions. The result of a particular row (denoted by i) and a particular column (denoted by j) equals the sum of the respective row and column in the X and Y matrices.

The output will be as follows:

```
[[11, 13, 15], [17, 19, 21], [23, 25, 27]]
```

5. You can also perform subtraction using two matrices using the same algorithm with a different operator. The idea behind this is the same as in *Step 3*, except you are doing subtraction. You can implement the following code to try out matrix subtraction:

```
X = [[10,11,12],[13,14,15],[16,17,18]]
Y = [[1,2,3],[4,5,6],[7,8,9]]
# Initialize a result placeholder
result = [[0,0,0],
      [0,0,0],
      [0,0,0]]
# iterate through rows
for i in range(len(X)):
# iterate through columns
   for j in range(len(X[0])):
      result[i][j] = X[i][j] - Y[i][j]
print(result)
```

Here is the output:

```
[[9, 9, 9], [9, 9, 9], [9, 9, 9]]
```

In this exercise, you were able to perform basic addition and subtraction using two matrices. In the next section, you will perform multiplication on matrices.

Matrix multiplication operations

Let's use nested lists to perform matrix multiplication for the two matrices shown in *Figures 2.9* and *2.10*:

$$X = \begin{bmatrix} 1 & 2 \\ 4 & 5 \\ 7 & 8 \end{bmatrix}$$

Figure 2.9 – The data of the X matrix

$$Y = \begin{bmatrix} 11 & 12 & 13 & 14 \\ 15 & 16 & 17 & 18 \end{bmatrix}$$

Figure 2.10 – The data of the Y matrix

For matrix multiplication, the number of columns in the first matrix (X) must equal the number of rows in the second matrix (Y). The result will have the same number of rows as the first matrix and the same number of columns as the second matrix. In this case, the resulting matrix will be a 3 x 4 matrix.

Exercise 28 – implementing matrix operations (multiplication)

In this exercise, your end goal will be to multiply two matrices, X and Y, and get an output value. The following steps will enable you to complete this exercise:

1. Open a new Jupyter notebook.

2. Create two nested lists, X and Y, to store the value of the X and Y matrices:

    ```
    X = [[1, 2], [4, 5], [3, 6]]
    Y = [[1,2,3,4],[5,6,7,8]]
    ```

3. Create a zero-matrix placeholder to store the result:

    ```
    result = [[0, 0, 0, 0], [0, 0, 0, 0], [0, 0, 0, 0]]
    ```

4. Implement the matrix multiplication algorithm to compute the result:

    ```
    # iterating by row of X
    for i in range(len(X)):
      # iterating by column by Y
      for j in range(len(Y[0])):
        # iterating by rows of Y
        for k in range(len(Y)):
          result[i][j] += X[i][k] * Y[k][j]
    ```

    You may have noticed that this algorithm is slightly different from the one you used in *Step 3* of *Exercise 27 – implementing matrix operations (addition and subtraction)*. This is because you need to iterate the rows of the second matrix, Y, as the matrices have different shapes, which is what is mentioned in the preceding code snippet.

5. Now, print the final result:

    ```
    for r in result:
      print(r)
    ```

Let's look at the output:

```
[11, 14, 17, 20]
[29, 38, 47, 56]
[33, 42, 51, 60]
```

Figure 2.11 – Output of multiplying the X and Y matrices

> **Note**
>
> To review the packages that data scientists use to perform matrix calculations, such as NumPy, check out `https://docs.scipy.org/doc/numpy/`.

In the next section, you will work with and learn about a new data structure: Python dictionaries.

Dictionary keys and values

A Python dictionary is an unordered collection that contains **keys** and **values**. Dictionaries are written with curly brackets, and the keys and values are separated by colons.

Have a look at the following example, where you store the details of an employee:

```
employee = {
   'name': "Jack Nelson",
   'age': 32,
   'department': "sales"
}
```

Python dictionaries contain key-value pairs. They simply map keys to associated values, as shown here:

Key	Value
name	Jack Nelson
age	32
department	sales

Figure 2.12 – Mapping keys and values in Python dictionaries

Dictionaries are like lists. They both share the following properties:

- Both can be used to store values

- Both can be changed in place and can grow and shrink on demand

- Both can be nested: a dictionary can contain another dictionary, a list can contain another list, and a list can contain a dictionary and vice versa

The main difference between lists and dictionaries is how elements are accessed. List elements are accessed by their position index, which is [0,1,2…], while dictionary elements are accessed via keys. Therefore, a dictionary is a better choice for representing collections, and mnemonic keys are more suitable when a collection's items are labeled, as in the database record shown in *Figure 2.13*. The database here is equivalent to a list, and the database list contains a record that can be represented using a dictionary. Within each record, there are fields to store respective values, and a dictionary can be used to store a record with unique keys mapped to values:

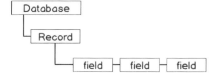

Figure 2.13 – A sample database record

There are, however, a few rules that you need to remember with Python dictionaries:

- Keys must be unique – no duplicate keys are allowed
- Keys must be immutable – they can be strings, numbers, or tuples

You will work with dictionaries and store a record in the next exercise.

Exercise 29 – using a dictionary to store a movie record

In this exercise, you will be working with a dictionary to store movie records, and you will also try and access the information in the dictionary using a key. The following steps will enable you to complete this exercise:

1. Open a Jupyter Notebook.

2. Enter the following code in a blank cell:

```
movie = {
    "title": "The Godfather",
    "director": "Francis Ford Coppola",
    "year": 1972,
    "rating": 9.2
}
```

Here, you have created a movie dictionary with a few details, such as `title`, `director`, `year`, and `rating`.

3. Access the information from the dictionary by using a key. For instance, you can use `'year'` to find out when the movie was first released using bracket notation:

    ```
    print(movie['year'])
    ```

    Here's the output:

    ```
    1972
    ```

4. Now, update the dictionary value:

    ```
    movie['rating'] = (movie['rating'] + 9.3)/2
    print(movie['rating'])
    ```

    The output is as follows:

    ```
    9.25
    ```

    As you can see, a dictionary's values can also be updated in place.

5. Construct a `movie` dictionary from scratch and extend it using key-value assignment:

    ```
    movie = {}
    movie['title'] = "The Godfather"
    movie['director'] = "Francis Ford Coppola"
    movie['year'] = 1972
    movie['rating'] = 9.2
    ```

    As you may have noticed, similar to a list, a dictionary is flexible in terms of size.

6. You can also store a list inside a dictionary and store a dictionary within that dictionary:

    ```
    movie['actors'] = ['Marlon Brando', 'Al Pacino',
        'James Caan']
    movie['other_details'] = {
        'runtime': 175,
        'language': 'English'
    }
    print(movie)
    ```

    The output is as follows:

```
{'title': 'The Godfather', 'director': 'Francis Ford Coppola', 'year': 1972, 'rating': 9.2,
'actors': ['Marlon Brando', 'Al Pacino', 'James Caan'], 'other_details': {'runtime': 175, 'la
nguage': 'English'}}
```

Figure 2.14 – Output while storing a dictionary within a dictionary

So far, you have learned how to implement nesting in both lists and dictionaries. By combining lists and dictionaries creatively, we can store complex real-world information and model structures directly and easily. This is one of the main benefits of scripting languages such as Python.

Activity 7 – storing company employee table data using a list and a dictionary

Remember the employee dataset, which you previously stored using a nested list? Now that you have learned about lists and dictionaries, you will learn how to store and access our data more effectively using dictionaries that contain lists.

The following table contains employee data:

Name	Age	Department
John Mckee	38	Sales
Lisa Crawford	29	Marketing
Sujan Patel	33	HR

Figure 2.15 – Employee data in a table

Follow these steps to complete this activity:

1. Open a Jupyter notebook (you can create a new one or use an existing one).
2. Create a list named `employees`.
3. Create three dictionary objects inside `employees` to store the information of each `employee`.
4. Print the `employees` variable.
5. Print the details of all employees in a presentable format.
6. Print only the details of `Sujan Patel`.

    The output is as follows:

```
Name: Sujan Patel
Age: 33
Department: HR
--------------------
```

Figure 2.16 – Output when we only print the employee details of Sujan Patel

> **Note**
> The solution for this activity can be found in *Appendix* on GitHub.

Dictionary methods

All Python types, including dictionaries, have their own methods. Since dictionaries include keys and values, it's common to access them using dictionary methods. In the following exercise, you will use dictionary methods to access and display dictionary elements.

Exercise 30 – accessing a dictionary using dictionary methods

In this exercise, you will learn how to access a dictionary using dictionary methods. The goal of this exercise is to print the order values against the item while accessing dictionary methods:

1. Open a new Jupyter Notebook.

2. Enter the following code in a new cell:

```
album_sales = {'barbara':150, 'aretha':75,
    'madonna':300, 'mariah':220}
print( album_sales.values())
print(list( album_sales.values()))
```

The output is as follows:

```
dict_values([150, 75, 300, 220])
 [150, 75, 300, 220]
```

The `values()` method in this code returns an iterable object. To use the values straight away, you can wrap them in a list directly.

3. Now, obtain a list of keys in a dictionary by using the `keys()` method:

```
print(list(album_sales.keys()))
```

The output is as follows:

```
['barbara', 'aretha', 'madonna', 'mariah']
```

4. Although you can't directly iterate a dictionary, you can loop through the dictionary by using the `items()` method, as in the following code snippet:

```
for item in  album_sales.items():
   print(item)
```

The output is as follows:

```
('barbara', 150)
aretha75('madonna', 300)
('mariah', 220)
```

In this exercise, you created a dictionary, accessed the keys and values of the dictionary, and looped through the dictionary.

The last step, showing the dictionary keys and values in parentheses, presents a new Python type, a tuple, as explained in the next section.

Tuples

A tuple object is similar to a list, but it cannot be changed. Tuples are immutable sequences, which means their values cannot be changed after initialization. You can use a tuple to represent fixed collections of items:

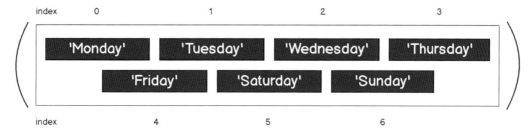

Figure 2.17 – A representation of a Python tuple with a positive index

For instance, you can define the weekdays using a list, as follows:

```
weekdays_list = ['Monday', 'Tuesday', 'Wednesday',
    'Thursday','Friday','Saturday', 'Sunday']
```

However, this does not guarantee that the values will remain unchanged throughout their life because a list is **mutable**. What you can do is define it using a tuple, as shown in the following code:

```
weekdays_tuple = ('Monday', 'Tuesday', 'Wednesday',
    'Thursday','Friday','Saturday', 'Sunday')
```

As tuples are immutable, you can be certain that the values are consistent throughout the entire program and will not be modified accidentally or unintentionally. In the next exercise, you will explore the different properties tuples provide a Python developer.

Exercise 31 – exploring tuple properties in a dance genre list

In this exercise, you will learn about the different properties of a tuple:

1. Open a Jupyter notebook.

2. Type the following code in a new cell to initialize a new tuple, t:

```
t = ('ballet', 'modern', 'hip-hop')
print(len(t))
```

The output is as follows:

```
3
```

> **Note**
>
> Remember, a tuple is immutable; therefore, you can't use the append method to add a new item to an existing tuple. You can't change the value of any existing tuple's elements since both of the following statements will raise an error.

3. Now, as mentioned in the note, enter the following lines of code and observe the error:

```
t[2] = 'jazz'
```

The output is as follows:

```
--------------------------------------------------------------------------
TypeError                                 Traceback (most recent call last)
<ipython-input-2-44651e94c673> in <module>
----> 1 t[2] = 'jazz'

TypeError: 'tuple' object does not support item assignment
```

Figure 2.18 – Errors occur when we try to modify the values of a tuple object

The only way to get around this is to create a new tuple by concatenating the existing tuple with other new items.

4. Now, use the following code to add two items, jazz and tap, to our tuple, t. This will give us a new tuple. Note that the existing t tuple remains unchanged:

```
print(t + ('jazz', 'tap'))
print(t)
```

The output is as follows:

```
('ballet', 'modern', 'hip-hop', 'jazz', 'tap')
('ballet', 'modern', 'hip-hop')
```

5. Enter the following statements in a new cell and observe the output:

```
t_mixed = 'jazz', True, 3
print(t_mixed)
t_dance = ('jazz',3), ('ballroom',2),
  ('contemporary',5)
print(t_dance)
```

Tuples also support mixed types and nesting, just like lists and dictionaries. You can also declare a tuple without using parentheses, as shown in the code you entered in this step.

The output is as follows:

```
('jazz', True, 3)
(('jazz', 3), ('ballroom', 2), ('contemporary', 5))
```

Zipping and unzipping dictionaries and lists using zip()

Sometimes, you obtain information from multiple lists. For instance, you might have a list to store the names of products and another list just to store the quantity of those products. You can aggregate these lists using the zip() method.

The zip() method maps a similar index of multiple containers so that they can be used as a single object. You will try this out in the following exercise.

Exercise 32 – using the zip() method to manipulate dictionaries

In this exercise, you will work on the concept of dictionaries by combining different types of data structures. You will use the zip() method to manipulate the dictionary with our shopping list. The following steps will help you understand the zip() method:

1. Open a new Jupyter Notebook.

2. Now, create a new cell and type in the following code:

```
items = ['apple', 'orange', 'banana']
quantity = [5,3,2]
```

Here, you have created a list of items and a list of quantity. Also, you have assigned values to these lists.

3. Now, use the zip() function to combine the two lists into a list of tuples:

```
orders = zip(items,quantity)
print(orders)
```

This gives us a `zip()` object with the following output:

```
<zip object at 0x0000000005BF1088>
```

4. Enter the following code to turn that `zip()` object into a `list`:

```
orders = zip(items,quantity)
print(list(orders))
```

The output is as follows:

```
[('apple', 5), ('orange', 3), ('banana', 2)]
```

5. You can also turn a `zip()` object into a `tuple`:

```
orders = zip(items,quantity)
print(tuple(orders))
```

Let's see the output:

```
(('apple', 5), ('orange', 3), ('banana', 2))
```

6. You can also turn a `zip()` object into a dictionary:

```
orders = zip(items,quantity)
print(dict(orders))
```

Let's see the output:

```
{'apple': 5, 'orange': 3, 'banana': 2}
```

Did you realize that you have to call `orders = zip(items,quantity)` every time? In this exercise, you will have noticed that a `zip()` object is an iterator, so once it has been converted into a list, tuple, or dictionary, it is considered a full iteration and it will not be able to generate any more values.

A survey of sets

So far, in this chapter, we have covered lists, dictionaries, and tuples. Now, let's look at sets, which are another type of Python data structure.

Sets are a relatively new addition to the Python collection type. They are unordered collections of unique and immutable objects that support operations mimicking mathematical set theory. Since sets do not allow multiple occurrences of the same element, they can be used to effectively prevent duplicate values.

A set is a collection of objects (called **members** or **elements**). For instance, you can define set A as containing even numbers between 1 to 10, and it will contain {2,4,6,8,10}; set B can contain odd numbers between 1 to 10, and it will contain {1,3,5,7,9}.

The following figure shows a visual of two sets without overlapping values:

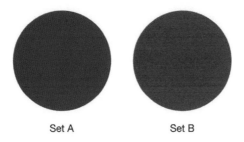

Set A   Set B

Figure 2.19 – Set A and Set B – each set contains a unique, distinct value

In the following exercise, you will work with sets in Python.

Exercise 33 – using sets in Python

In this exercise, you will practice working with sets in Python:

1. Open a Jupyter notebook.

2. Initialize a set using the following code. You can pass in a list to initialize a set or use curly brackets, as follows:

```
s1 = set([1,2,3,4,5,6])
print(s1)
s2 = {1,2,2,3,4,4,5,6,6}
print(s2)
s3 = {3,4,5,6,6,6,1,1,2}
print(s3)
```

The output is as follows:

```
{1, 2, 3, 4, 5, 6}
{1, 2, 3, 4, 5, 6}
{1, 2, 3, 4, 5, 6}
```

Here, you can see that the set is unique and unordered, so duplicate items and the original order are not preserved.

3. Enter the following code in a new cell:

```
s4 = {'martha graham, 'alivin ailey, 'isadora duncan'}
print(s4)
```

You can also initialize a set using curly brackets directly.

The output is as follows:

```
{'martha graham', 'alvin ailey', 'isadora duncan'}
```

4. Sets are mutable. Type the following code, which shows how to add a new item, `pineapple`, to an existing set, `s4`:

```
s4.add('katherine dunham')
print(s4)
```

The output is as follows:

```
{'martha graham', 'alvin ailey', 'isadora duncan'}
```

In this exercise, you were introduced to sets in Python. In the next section, you will dive in a bit deeper and understand the different set operations that Python offers.

Set operations

Sets support common operations such as unions and intersections. A `union` operation returns a single set that contains all the unique elements in both sets A and B; an `intersect` operation returns a single set that contains unique elements that belong to set A and also belong to set B at the same time. Let's look at the `union` operation in the following figure:

$A \cup B$

Figure 2.20 – Set A in union with Set B

The following figure represents the `intersect` operation:

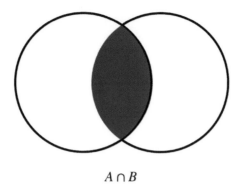

$$A \cap B$$

Figure 2.21 – Set A intersects with Set B

Now, let's implement these set operations in Python in the following exercise.

Exercise 34 – implementing set operations

In this exercise, we will be implementing and working with set operations:

1. Open a new Jupyter notebook.

2. In a new cell, type the following code to initialize two new sets:

    ```
    s5 = {1,2,3,4}
    s6 = {3,4,5,6}
    ```

3. Use the | operator or the `union` method for a union operation:

    ```
    print(s5 | s6)
    print(s5.union(s6))
    ```

    The output is as follows:

    ```
    {1, 2, 3, 4, 5, 6}
    {1, 2, 3, 4, 5, 6}
    ```

4. Now, use the & operator or the `intersection` method for an `intersection` operation:

    ```
    print(s5 & s6)
    print(s5.intersection(s6))
    ```

The output is as follows:

```
{3, 4}
{3, 4}
```

5. Use the – operator or the difference method to find the difference between two sets:

```
print(s5 - s6)
print(s5.difference(s6))
```

The output is as follows:

```
{1, 2}
{1, 2}
```

6. Now, enter the <= operator or the issubset method to check if one set is a subset of another:

```
print(s5 <= s6)
print(s5.issubset(s6))
s7 = {1,2,3}
s8 = {1,2,3,4,5}
print(s7 <= s8)
print(s7.issubset(s8))
```

The output is as follows:

```
False
False
True
True
```

The first two statements will return false because s5 is not a subset of s6. The last two statements will return True because s5 is a subset of s6. Note that the <= operator is a test for the subset. A proper subset is the same as a general subset, except that the sets cannot be identical. You can try it out in a new cell with the following code.

7. Check whether s7 is a formal subset of s8, and check whether a set can be a proper subset of itself by entering the following code:

```
print(s7 < s8)
s9 = {1,2,3}
s10 = {1,2,3}
print(s9 < s10)
print(s9 < s9)
```

The output is as follows:

```
True
False
False
```

Here, we can see that s7 is a proper subset of s8 because there are other elements in s8 apart from all the elements of s7. However, s9 is not a subset of s10 because they are identical. Therefore, a set is not a proper subset of itself.

8. Now, use the `>=` operator or the `issuperset` method to check whether one set is the superset of another. Try this using the following code in another cell:

```
print(s8 >= s7)
print(s8.issuperset(s7))
print(s8 > s7)
print(s8 > s8)
```

The output is as follows:

```
True
True
True
False
```

The first three statements will return `True` because s8 is the superset of s7 and is also a proper superset of s7. The last statement will return `false` because no set can be a proper superset of itself.

Having completed this exercise, you now know that Python sets are useful for efficiently preventing duplicate values and are suitable for common math operations such as unions and intersections.

> **Note**
>
> After all the topics covered so far, you may think that sets are similar to lists or dictionaries. However, sets are unordered and do not map keys to values, so they are neither a sequence nor a mapping type; they are a type by themselves.

Choosing types

So far, you have learned about most of the common data structures in Python. One of the challenges you might face is knowing when to use the various data types.

When choosing a collection type, it is useful to understand the unique properties of that type. For example, a list is used to store multiple objects and to retain a sequence, a dictionary is used to store unique key-value pair mappings, tuples are immutable, and sets only store unique elements. Choosing the right type for a particular dataset could mean an increase in efficiency or security.

Consider the following examples:

- Defining points on the *x-y* coordinate plane:

    A. List
    B. Dictionary
    C. **Tuple**
    D. Set

    Tuples are preferable for coordinate points that do not change, but some people prefer lists.

- Numbering students in order:

    E. **List**
    F. Dictionary
    G. Tuple
    H. Set

    A list is better than a dictionary here because order matters.

- Finding unique numbers from a bunch of numbers:

    I. List
    J. Dictionary
    K. Tuple
    L. **Set**

    Sets only include unique instances.

- Organizing a list of books and authors:

    M. List
    N. **Dictionary**
    O. Tuple
    P. Set

    Dictionaries are ideal for storing attributes regarding people or things.

Although there may be more than one reasonable choice for a data structure, choosing an incorrect type for your data may lead to data loss or low efficiency while running your code, or in the worst case, losing your data altogether.

Summary

To summarize, recall that Python data structures include lists, tuples, dictionaries, and sets. Python provides these structures to enable you to code better as a developer. In this chapter, we covered lists, which are one of the most important data types in Python since they can store multiple objects, as well as other data types, such as dictionaries, tuples, and sets. Each of these data types helps us store and retrieve data effectively.

Data structures are an essential part of all programming languages. Most programming languages only provide basic data types for storing different types of numbers, strings, and Booleans, as you learned in *Chapter 1*, *Python Fundamentals – Math, Strings, Conditionals, and Loops*. They are an essential part of any program. In this chapter, you learned that lists and dictionaries may be used to store complex data, including nested lists and mixed data types.

In the next chapter, you are going to learn how to use functions to write modular and understandable code that follows the **Don't Repeat Yourself** (**DRY**) principle.

Executing Python – Programs, Algorithms, and Functions

Overview

By the end of this chapter, you will be able to write and execute Python scripts from the command line; write and import Python modules; document your code with docstrings; implement basic algorithms in Python, including bubble sort and binary search; write functions utilizing iterative, recursive, and dynamic programming algorithms; modularize code to make it structured and readable; and use helper functions and lambda functions.

This chapter will leave you empowered to write more powerful and concise code through an increased appreciation of well-written algorithms and an understanding of functions.

Introduction

A computer is a machine with a huge volume of carefully organized logic. No one piece of this logic is necessarily complex or can capture what drives the result. Rather, the entire system is organized such that it comes together to provide the output you expect.

In previous chapters, you focused on basic Python idioms and data types. In this chapter, you will begin exploring more abstract concepts regarding how knowledge is formalized through logic in Python. You will explore a few fundamental algorithms that are used for solving typical problems in computer science, along with some simple logic.

For example, consider the problem of sorting a list of integers. Supermarkets use sorting techniques to sort through their customers to get an insight into the sales an individual customer provides. You may be surprised at the theoretical complexity behind writing such an algorithm in an efficient manner.

In this chapter, you will also learn about a few of the paradigms in Python for expressing code in a concise but readable way. You will learn the habits of a good programmer, and how to make sure you write code that is maintainable without repetition. In doing so, you will not need to rework your code unnecessarily, as requirements change constantly in the IT world.

This chapter begins by moving away from running code in Jupyter Notebooks and Python shells and toward Python scripts and modules. This will allow you more flexibility in writing clear, reusable, and powerful code.

We will be looking at the following topics:

- Python scripts and modules
- Python algorithms
- Basic functions
- Iterative functions
- Recursive functions
- Dynamic programming
- Helper functions
- Variable scope
- Lambda functions

Let's start!

Technical requirements

The code files for this chapter are available on GitHub at https://github.com/PacktPublishing/The-Python-Workshop-Second-Edition/tree/main/Chapter03.

Python scripts and modules

In previous chapters, you have been executing Python Jupyter Notebooks on an interactive Python console. However, most Python code lives in text files with a .py extension. These files are simply plain text that can be edited with any text editor. Programmers typically edit these files using either a text editor such as Notepad++, or **integrated development environments (IDEs)** such as Jupyter or PyCharm.

Typically, standalone .py files are either called **scripts** or **modules**. A script is a file that is designed to be executed usually from the command line. On the other hand, a module is usually imported into another part of the code or an interactive shell to be executed. Note that this is not a hard distinction; modules can be executed, and scripts can be imported into other scripts/modules.

Exercise 35 – writing and executing our first script

In this exercise, you will create a script called `my_script.py` and execute it on the command line to find the sum of the factorials of three numbers. The steps are as follows:

1. Using any text editor, create a new file called `my_script.py`. You can also use Jupyter (**New | Text File**).

2. Import the `math` library, as follows:

```
import math
```

3. Suppose that you have a list of numbers and you want to print the sum of the factorials of these numbers. Recall that a factorial is the product of all integers up to and equal to a given number.

   For instance, the factorial of 5 is calculated as 5! = 5 * 4 * 3 * 2 * 1 = 120.

   In the following code snippet, you are going to find the sum of factorials of 5, 7, and 11:

```
numbers = [5, 7, 11]
```

4. Using the `math.factorial` function, loop through the `numbers` list, add the factorials together, and print the total, like so:

```
total = 0
for n in numbers:
    total += math.factorial(n)
print(total)
```

5. Save the file as `my_script.py`.

6. Open a terminal or a Jupyter Notebook and ensure that your current directory is the same as the one with the `my_script.py` file. To check this, if you run `dir` in a Windows terminal or `ls` in a Mac terminal, you should see `my_script.py` in the list of files. If not, navigate to the correct directory using the `cd` command.

7. In the terminal, run `python my_script.py` to execute your script (in a Jupyter Notebook, run `!python my_script.py`).

   The output is as follows:

```
39921960
```

In this exercise, you successfully created and executed a file by navigating to the correct directory from the terminal or Jupyter Notebook.

In the next example, you will write your first module using a Python function. Although Python functions will be explored in depth later in this chapter, starting with the *Basic functions* section, here is a brief example to get you started.

Python function example

In Python, you always introduce a function with the def keyword, followed by a name of your choice, and the input of the function in parentheses before a colon. After the colon, you run indented code that typically manipulates the input. Finally, the output of the function comes after the return keyword.

Here is an example of a function that doubles a number:

```
def double(number):
    result = number * 2
    return result
```

Now, you call the function by stating the name, along with an appropriate value in parentheses:

```
double(16)
```

This will be the output:

```
32
```

When the function is called, Python finds the definition and follows the appropriate steps with the given input.

Now that you have an idea of how functions work, it's time to write your first module.

Exercise 36 – writing and importing our first module

In this exercise, as in *Exercise 35 – writing and executing our first script*, you will find the sum of the factorials of three numbers. However, this time, you will write the code inside of a function and save the function as a module called my_module.py. Here are the steps to write your first module:

1. Using any text editor, create a new file called my_module.py. You can also use Jupyter (**New | Text File**).

2. Add a function that returns the result of the computation in *Exercise 35 – writing and executing our first script*:

```
import math
def factorial_sum(numbers):
    total = 0
    for n in numbers:
        total += math.factorial(n)
    return total
```

3. Save the file as `my_module.py`.

4. Open a new Python shell or Jupyter Notebook and execute the following:

```python
python
>>>from my_module import factorial_sum
>>>factorial_sum([5, 7, 11])
```

The output is as follows:

```
39921960
```

> **Note**
>
> Writing this code as a module is useful if you want to reuse the function in another script or module. However, if you just want to execute the `print` statement once, and you don't want to have to import the function to a shell, a script is more convenient.

In this exercise, you created a module file called `my_module.py` and imported this module file to get the expected output on Jupyter or the Python shell.

Shebangs in Ubuntu

A shebang is a hashtag followed by an exclamation (`#!`) generally telling the interpreter where a script should run.

Using a shebang, the first line of a Python script will often look like this:

```
#!/usr/bin/env python3
```

This gives the script that follows permission to execute. Note that shebangs are rarely required, but they can provide additional clarity for developers.

As additional information, if you are using a Windows operating system, you can ignore this line. However, it is worth understanding its function. This path specifies the program that the computer should use to execute this file. In the previous example, you had to tell Command Prompt to use Python to execute our `my_script.py` script. However, on Unix systems (such as Ubuntu or Mac OS X), if your script has a shebang, you can execute it without specifying that the system should use Python. For example, using Ubuntu, you would simply write the following:

Figure 3.1 – Executing a script with a shebang statement in a Unix system

Docstrings

A docstring, which was mentioned in *Chapter 1, Python Fundamentals – Math, Strings, Conditionals, and Loops*, is a string appearing as the first statement in a script, function, or class. The docstring becomes a special attribute of the object, accessible with __doc__. Docstrings are used to store **descriptive information** to explain to the user what the code is for, and some high-level information on how they should use it.

Exercise 37 – adding a docstring to my_module.py

In this exercise, you extend your my_module.py module from *Exercise 36 – writing and importing our first module* by adding a docstring. Here are the steps:

1. Open my_module.py in Jupyter or a text editor.

2. Add a docstring to the script (as the first line before beginning with your code, as shown in the following code snippet):

```
""" This script computes the sum of the factorial of a
list of numbers"""
```

3. Open a Python console in the same directory as your my_module.py file.

4. Import the my_module module by running the following command:

```
import my_module
```

5. Call the help function on your my_module script to view the docstring. The help function can be used to obtain a summary of any available information regarding a module, function, or class in Python. You can also call it without an argument—that is, as help()—to start an interactive series of prompts:

```
help(my_module)
```

The output is as follows:

```
Help on module my_module:

NAME
    my_module - This script computes the sum of the factorial of a list of numbers

FUNCTIONS
    factorial_sum(numbers)

FILE
    /Users/coreyjwade/my_module.py
```

Figure 3.2 – The output of the help function

6. View the __doc__ property of my_module as a second way of viewing the docstring:

    ```
    my_module.__doc__
    ```

    The output is as follows:

    ```
    ' This script computes the sum of the factorial of a list of numbers'
    ```

Figure 3.3 – Viewing the docstring

Docstrings can span one line, such as in the preceding example, or multiple lines.

Importing libraries

After the optional shebang statement and docstring, Python files typically import classes, modules, and functions from other libraries. For example, if you wanted to compute the value of exp(2), which is the number *e* to the 2nd power, you could import the math module from the standard library (you will learn more about the standard library in *Chapter 6, The Standard Library*), like so:

```
import math
math.exp(2)
```

The output is as follows:

```
7.38905609893065
```

In the preceding example, you imported the math module and called an exp function that exists within the module. Alternatively, you could import the function itself from the math module, like so:

```
from math import exp
exp(2)
```

The output is as follows:

```
7.38905609893065
```

Note that there is a third way of importing, which should generally be avoided unless necessary:

```
from math import *
exp(2)
```

The output is as follows:

```
7.38905609893065
```

The `import *` syntax simply imports everything in the module. It is considered undesirable primarily because you end up with references to too many objects, and there's a risk that the names of these objects will clash. It's also harder to see where certain objects are imported from if there are multiple `import *` statements.

You can also rename modules or imported objects in the `import` statement itself:

```
from math import exp as exponential
exponential(2)
```

The output is as follows:

```
7.38905609893065
```

This is sometimes useful if you simply find the name of the object to be unwieldy, making your code less readable, or to follow Python standards to make certain names shorter. Or, it could be necessary if you want to use two modules that happen to have the same name.

In the following exercise, let's see how to use the `datetime` library.

Exercise 38 – finding the system date

In this exercise, you write a script that prints the current system date to the console by importing the `datetime` module. Let's look at the steps:

1. Create a new script called `today.py`.

2. Add a docstring to the script, as follows:

```
"""
This script prints the current system date.
"""
```

3. Import the `datetime` module by running the following command:

```
import datetime
```

4. Print out the current date using the `today()` property of `datetime.date`:

```
print(datetime.date.today())
```

5. Run the script from the command line, as shown:

```
(base) coreyjwade@Coreys-MacBook-Air-2 ~ % python today.py
2022-08-27
```

Figure 3.4 – The command-line output

In this exercise, you were able to write a script that prints the date and time using the `datetime` module.

The if __name__ == '__main__' statement

You will often see this cryptic statement in Python scripts. You won't cover this concept in depth, but it's worth understanding. It is used when you want to execute a script by itself, and to import objects from the script as though it were a regular module.

For example, suppose you want to sum the numbers from 1 to 10. If you execute the function from the command line, you may want the result printed to the console. However, you may also want to import the value to use it elsewhere in your code.

You may be tempted to write something like this:

```
result = 0
for n in range(1, 11):
# Recall that this loops through 1 to 10, not including 11
    result += n
print(result)
```

If you execute this program from the command line, it will print an output of 55, as expected. However, if you try importing the result in a Python console, as shown here, it will print the result again. When importing the result, however, you just want the variable; you don't expect it to print to the console:

```
from sum_to_10 import result
```

The output is as follows:

```
55
```

To fix this, you only call the `print` function in the case where __name__ == '__main__':

```
result = 0
for n in range(1, 11):
# Recall that this loops through 1 to 10, not including 11
    result += n
if __name__ == '__main__':
    print(result)
```

When executing from the command line, the Python interpreter sets the special __name__ variable equal to the '__main__' string, such that when you get to the end of your script, the result is printed, as shown here. However, when importing result, the print statement is never reached:

```
from sum_to_10 import result
result * 2
```

The output is as follows:

```
110
```

Activity 8 – what's the time?

You are asked to build a Python script that tells you the current time.

In this activity, you will use the datetime module to build a current_time.py script that outputs the current system time, and then you will import the current_time.py script into a Python console.

The steps to do this are as follows:

1. Create a new script called current_time.py in Jupyter or a text editor.
2. Add a docstring to the script to explain what it does.
3. Import the datetime module.
4. Get the current time using datetime.datetime.now().
5. Print the result, but only if the script is to be executed.
6. Execute the script from Command Prompt to check whether it prints the time.
7. Import the time into a Python console and check whether the console output prints the time.

You would get an output similar to the following:

```
14:24:30.321301
```

> **Note**
> The solution for this activity can be found in *Appendix* on GitHub.

Python algorithms

An algorithm is a series of instructions that can be executed to perform a certain task or computation. A recipe for a cake is an example of an algorithm—for example, preheat the oven, beat 125 g of sugar and 100 g of butter, and then add eggs and other ingredients. Similarly, simple computations in mathematics are algorithms. For example, when computing the perimeter of a circle, you multiply the radius by 2π. It's a short algorithm, but an algorithm nonetheless.

Algorithms are often initially defined in **pseudocode**, which is a way of writing down the steps a computer program will make without coding in any specific language. A reader should not need a technical background in order to read the logic expressed in pseudocode. For example, if you had a list of positive numbers and wanted to find the maximum number of positive numbers in that list, an algorithm expressed in pseudocode could be as follows:

1.   Set the `maximum` variable to `0`

2.   For each number in our list, check whether the number is bigger than the `maximum` variable

3.   If the number is greater than the `maximum` variable, set `maximum` equal to the number

4.   `maximum` is now equal to the largest number in the list

Pseudocode is useful because it allows us to show the logic of our code in a more universally accessible format than writing in a specific programming language. Programmers will often map out their thinking in pseudocode to explore the logic of their planned approach before writing the code itself.

In the next exercise, you will apply this pseudocode to find the maximum number from a list of numbers.

Exercise 39 – finding the maximum number

In this exercise, you will implement the pseudocode to find the maximum number from a list of positive numbers. The steps are as follows:

1.   Create a list of numbers, like so:

```
l = [4, 2, 7, 3]
```

2.   Set the `maximum` variable equal to `0`:

```
maximum = 0
```

3.   Look through each number, and compare it to `maximum`:

```
for number in l:
    if number > maximum:
        maximum = number
```

4.   Check the result by running the following command:

```
print(maximum)
```

The output is as follows:

7

In this exercise, you successfully implemented the pseudocode given and found the maximum number in a list of numbers.

Time complexity

So far in this book, we have become accustomed to our programs being executed at near-instantaneous speed. Computers are very fast, and the difference between performing 10 iterations in a loop and 1,000 iterations may seem immaterial to us. However, algorithms can quickly become inefficient as problems complexify. In measuring complexity, you are interested in knowing how the time it takes to execute the algorithm changes as the size of the problem changes. If the problem is 10 times as large, does the algorithm take 10 times as long to execute, 100 times as long, or 1,000 times as long? This relationship between the size of the problem and the steps taken is called the **time complexity** of an algorithm.

Of course, you could simply time the algorithm on problems of different sizes and observe the relationship on a graph. This technique is often useful when the algorithm is complex, and the theoretical relationship between size and time isn't computable. However, this isn't entirely satisfactory, as the actual time taken is also conditional on factors such as the memory that is available, the processor, the disk speed, and other process-consuming resources on the machine. It will only ever be an empirical approximation and may vary depending on the computer.

Instead, you simply count the number of operations required to execute the algorithm. The result of this counting is expressed with big-O notation. For example, $O(n)$ means that, for a problem of size n, the number of steps taken is proportional to n. This means that the actual number of steps required can be expressed as $\alpha * n + \beta$ where α and β are constants. Another way of thinking about this is that the steps required to execute the algorithm grow linearly with the problem size, as illustrated here:

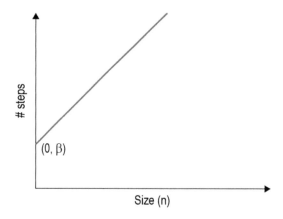

Figure 3.5 – Visual representation of linear time complexity

Any such problem where the complexity can be expressed as a linear function, $\alpha * n + \beta$, has a time complexity of $O(n)$.

Other common time complexities include the following:

- **O(1)—Constant time:** Here, the time taken is always the same, regardless of the problem size; for example, accessing an element of an array at a given index.

- **O(n^2)—Quadratic time:** Here, the time taken is proportional to the square of the problem size; for example, the bubble sort algorithm (this is covered in *Exercise 40 – using bubble sort in Python*)

- **O(log n)—Logarithmic time:** Here, the time taken is proportional to the natural logarithm of the problem size; for example, the binary search algorithm (this is covered in *Exercise 42 – binary search in Python*)

Time complexity for the maximum number algorithm

In the previous exercise, you computed the maximum of a list of positive numbers. Here, you express the complexity of the algorithm using the big-O notation. Follow these steps:

1. Our program starts by setting the `maximum = 0` variable. This is our first step: `total_ steps = 1`.

2. For a list of size n, you are going to loop through each number and perform the following operations:

    (a) Check whether it's greater than the maximum variable

    (b) If so, assign the maximum to the number

3. Sometimes, there will be one step executed for a number and, sometimes, there will be two steps (if that number happens to be the new maximum). You don't really care what this number is, so let's take its average, which you'll call α. That is, for each number, there will be an average of α steps executed, where α is a number between 1 and 2.

4. So, `total_steps` = $1 + \alpha * n$. This is a linear function, so the time complexity is `O(n)`.

Sorting algorithms

The most commonly discussed family of algorithms in computer science courses is sorting algorithms. Sorting algorithms come to your aid when, say, you have a list of values and you want to sort these into an ordered list. This problem is ever-present in our data-driven world; consider the following scenarios:

- You have a database of contacts and want to see them listed alphabetically

- You want to retrieve the five best test results from a classroom of students

- You have a list of insurance policies and want to see which ones have the most recent claims

The output of any sorting algorithm must satisfy two conditions:

- It must be in non-decreasing order. That is, each element must be equal to or greater than the element that came before it.

- It must be a permutation of the input. That is, the input elements must simply be rearranged and not altered.

Here is a simple example of what we want a sorting algorithm to accomplish:

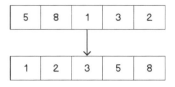

Figure 3.6 – A simple problem for a sorting algorithm to solve

One such algorithm for performing this operation is called **bubble sort**. It is explained as follows:

1. Start with the first two elements of this list. If the first is larger than the second, then switch the positions of the numbers. In this case, you leave them as is, as 5 < 8:

Figure 3.7 – Step 1 for the bubble sort algorithm

2. Move on to the next two elements. Here, you switch the positions of 8 and 1:

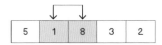

Figure 3.8 – Step 2 for the bubble sort algorithm

3. For the next pair, again, switch the positions, as 8 > 3:

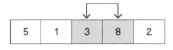

Figure 3.9 – Step 3 for the bubble sort algorithm

4. For the final pair, switch the positions again, as 8 > 2:

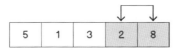

Figure 3.10 – Step 4 for the bubble sort algorithm

5. Go back to the start of the list and repeat the preceding process.

6. Continue looping through the list until no further swaps are required.

Exercise 40 – using bubble sort in Python

In this exercise, you will implement the bubble sort algorithm in Python with a list of numbers with the help of the following steps:

1. Start with a list of numbers, as shown here:

```
l = [5, 8, 1, 3, 2]
```

2. Create an indicator that will tell us when you can stop looping through the array:

```
still_swapping = True
```

3. Look through each number, and compare it to maximum by executing the following code:

```
while still_swapping:
    still_swapping = False
    for i in range(len(l) - 1):
        if l[i] > l[i+1]:
            l[i], l[i+1] = l[i+1], l[i]
            still_swapping = True
```

4. Check the result:

```
l
```

The output is as follows:

```
[1, 2, 3, 5, 8]
```

Bubble sort is a very simple but inefficient sorting algorithm. Its time complexity is $O(n^2)$, meaning that the number of steps required is proportional to the square of the size of the list.

Searching algorithms

Another important family of algorithms is searching algorithms. In a world where you are producing an exponentially increasing amount of data, these algorithms have a huge impact on our day-to-day lives. Simply considering the size of Google should give you an appreciation of the importance (and complexity) of these algorithms. Of course, you encounter the need for these algorithms just about every time you pick up a phone or open a laptop, as the following examples show:

- Searching your contacts list to send a message

- Searching your computer for a specific application

- Searching for an email containing a flight itinerary

With any of these examples, you can apply the simplest form of search—that is, a linear search. This will involve simply looping through all possible results and checking whether they match the search criteria. For example, if you were searching your contacts list, you would look through each contact one by one, and check whether that contact met the search criteria. If so, you would return the position of the result. This is a simple but inefficient algorithm, with time complexity of $O(n)$.

Exercise 41 – linear search in Python

In this exercise, you will implement the linear search algorithm in Python using a list of numbers. Proceed as follows:

1. Start with a list of numbers:

    ```
    l = [5, 8, 1, 3, 2]
    ```

2. Specify a value to search for:

    ```
    search_for = 8
    ```

3. Create a `result` variable that has a default value of `-1`. If the search is unsuccessful, this value will remain `-1` after the algorithm is executed:

    ```
    result = -1
    ```

4. Loop through the list. If the value equals the search value, set the `result` variable equal to the index of the value and exit the loop:

    ```
    for i in range(len(l)):
        if search_for == l[i]:
            result = i
            break
    ```

5. Check the result:

```
print(result)
```

The output is as follows:

```
1
```

> **Note**
>
> This means that the search found the required value at position 1 in the list (which is the second item in the list, as indices start from 0 in Python).

Another common sorting algorithm is called a **binary search**. The binary search algorithm takes a sorted array and finds the position of the target value. Suppose that you were trying to find the position of the number 11 in the following ordered list:

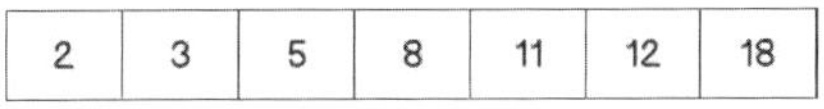

Figure 3.11 – A simple problem for a search algorithm to solve

The binary search algorithm is explained as follows:

1. Take the midpoint of the list. If this value is less than the target value, discard the left half of the list, and vice versa. In this case, our target value of 11 is greater than 8, so you know that you can restrict our search to the right side of the list (since you know the array is sorted):

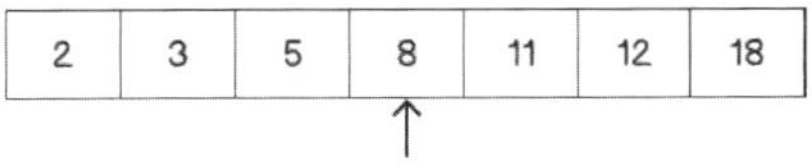

Figure 3.12 – Splitting the list at the midpoint, 8

> **Note**
>
> If there is an even number of items on the list, simply take one of the two middle numbers—it doesn't matter which.

2. You repeat this process with the right side of the list, picking the midpoint of the remaining values. Since the target value (11) is less than the midpoint (12), you discard the right side of our sublist:

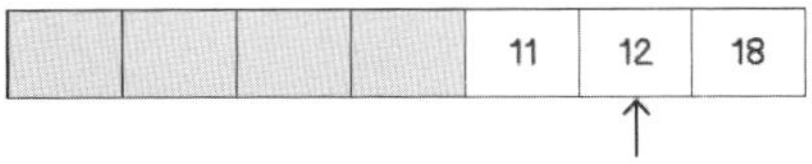

Figure 3.13 – Splitting the list at the midpoint of the remaining list

3.   This leaves you with the value that you were searching for:

Figure 3.14 – Reaching the final result

Exercise 42 – binary search in Python

In this exercise, you will implement the binary search algorithm in Python. Proceed as follows:

1.   Start with an ordered list of numbers:

```
l = [2, 3, 5, 8, 11, 12, 18]
```

2.   Specify a value to search for:

```
search_for = 11
```

3.   Create two variables that will represent the start and end locations of the sublist you are interested in. Initially, it will represent the start and end indices for the entire list:

```
slice_start = 0
slice_end = len(l) - 1
```

4.   Add a variable to indicate whether the search was successful:

```
found = False
```

5.   Find the midpoint of the list, and check whether the value is greater or less than the search term. Depending on the outcome of the comparison, either finish the search or update the locations for the start/end of the sublist:

```
while slice_start <= slice_end and not found:
    location = (slice_start + slice_end) // 2
    if l[location] == search_for:
        found = True
    else:
        if search_for < l[location]:
            slice_end = location - 1
        else:
            slice_start = location + 1
```

6. Check the results:

```
print(found)
print(location)
```

The output is as follows:

```
True
4
```

In this exercise, you successfully implemented the binary search algorithm on a list of numbers.

Basic functions

A function is a reusable piece of code that is only run when it is called. Functions can have inputs, and they usually return an output. For example, using a Python shell, you can define the following function that takes two inputs, `base` and `height`, and returns their product as the area:

```
def area(base, height):
    return base*height
area(2, 3)
```

The output is as follows:

```
6
```

Exercise 43 – defining and calling a function in the shell

In this exercise, you create a function that will return the second element of a list if it exists. Proceed as follows:

1. In a Python shell, enter the function definition. Note that the tab spacing needs to match the following output:

```
def get_second_element(mylist):
    if len(mylist) > 1:
        return mylist[1]
    else:
        return 'List was too small'
```

2. Try running the function on a small list of integers, like so:

```
get_second_element([1, 2, 3])
```

The output is as follows:

```
2
```

3. Try running the function on a list with only one element, like so:

```
get_second_element([1])
```

The output is as follows:

```
'List was too small'
```

Figure 3.15 – We are unable to get the second item with a list length of 1

Defining functions in a shell can be difficult, as the shell isn't optimized for editing multiple lines of code blocks. Instead, it's preferable for our functions to live inside a Python script.

Exercise 44 – defining and calling a function in a Python script

In this exercise, you will define and call a function in a `multiply.py` Python script and execute it from Command Prompt. The steps are set out here:

1. Create a new file using a text editor called `multiply.py`:

```python
def list_product(my_list):
    result = 1
    for number in my_list:
        result = result * number
    return result
print(list_product([2, 3]))
print(list_product([2, 10, 15]))
```

2. Using Command Prompt, execute this script, ensuring that your Command Prompt is in the same folder as the `multiply.py` file:

```
python multiply.py
```

You will see the output as this:

```
6
300
```

In this exercise, you worked on defining and calling a function within a Python script.

Exercise 45 – importing and calling the function from the shell

In this exercise, you will import and call the `list_product` function you defined in `multiply.py` with the following steps:

1. In a Python shell, import our `list_product` function:

    ```
    from multiply import list_product
    ```

    The output is as follows:

    ```
    6
    300
    ```

    One unintended consequence is that your `print` statements in `multiply.py` were also executed. Recall the `introduce __name__ == 'main'` code used before.

2. Call the function with a new list of numbers:

    ```
    list_product([-1, 2, 3])
    ```

    The output is as follows:

    ```
    -6
    ```

Now that you've completed this exercise, you have gained an understanding of how to import and call a function. You created the `multiply.py` file in the previous exercise and imported and used this function in this exercise.

Positional arguments

The preceding examples have all included positional arguments. In the following example, there are two positional arguments: x and y, respectively. When you call this function, the first value you pass in will be assigned to x, and the second value will be assigned to y:

```
def area(x, y):
    return x*y
```

You can also specify functions without any arguments, as shown here:

```
from datetime import datetime
def get_the_time():
    return datetime.datetime.now()
```

If you want to display the result of your function, call it inside of the global `print` function:

```
print(get_the_time())
```

The output is as follows:

```
2019-04-23 21:33:02.041909
```

Keyword arguments

Keyword arguments, also known as named arguments, are optional inputs to functions. These arguments sometimes include a default value that is taken when the function is called without the keyword argument specified.

Exercise 46 – defining a function with keyword arguments

In this exercise, you will use the Python shell to define an add_suffix function that takes an optional keyword argument. The steps for this exercise are as follows:

1. In a Python shell, define an add_suffix function:

    ```
    def add_suffix(suffix='.com'):
        return 'google' + suffix
    ```

2. Call the add_suffix function without specifying the suffix argument:

    ```
    add_suffix()
    ```

    The output is as follows:

    ```
    'google.com'
    ```

3. Call the function with a specific suffix argument:

    ```
    add_suffix('.co.uk')
    ```

    The output is as follows:

    ```
    'google.co.uk'
    ```

Exercise 47 – defining a function with positional and keyword arguments

In this exercise, you use the Python shell to define a convert_usd_to_aud function that takes a positional argument and an optional keyword argument, with the following steps:

1. In a Python shell, define a convert_usd_to_aud function:

    ```
    def convert_usd_to_aud(amount, rate=0.75):
        return amount / rate
    ```

2. Call the `convert_usd_to_aud` function without specifying the exchange rate argument:

    ```
    convert_usd_to_aud(100)
    ```

    You should get the following output:

    ```
    133.33333333333334
    ```

3. Call the `convert_usd_to_aud` function with a specific exchange rate argument:

    ```
    convert_usd_to_aud(100, rate=0.78)
    ```

    The output is as follows:

    ```
    128.2051282051282
    ```

The rule of thumb is to simply use positional arguments for required inputs that must be provided each time the function is called, and keyword arguments for optional inputs.

You will sometimes see functions that accept a mysterious-looking argument: `**kwargs`. This allows the function to accept any keyword arguments when it's called, and these can be accessed in a dictionary called `kwargs`. Typically, this is used when you want to pass arguments through to another function.

Exercise 48 – using **kwargs

In this exercise, you will write a Python script to pass named arguments through a `convert_usd_to_aud` function. Here are the steps:

1. Using a text editor, create a file called `conversion.py`.

2. Enter the `convert_usd_to_aud` function defined in the previous exercise:

    ```python
    def convert_usd_to_aud(amount, rate=0.75):
        return amount / rate
    ```

3. Create a new `convert_and_sum_list` function that will take a list of amounts, convert them to AUD, and return the sum:

    ```python
    def convert_and_sum_list(usd_list, rate=0.75):
        total = 0
        for amount in usd_list:
            total += convert_usd_to_aud(amount, rate=rate)
        return total
    print(convert_and_sum_list([1, 3]))
    ```

4. Execute this script from Command Prompt, as follows:

```
python conversion.py
```

The output is as follows:

```
5.3333333333333
```

> **Tip**
>
> Note that the `convert_and_sum_list` function didn't need the rate argument—it simply needed to pass it through to the `convert_usd_to_aud` function. Imagine that instead of one argument, you had 10 that needed to be passed through. There would be a lot of unnecessary code. Instead, you can use the `kwargs` dictionary.

5. Add the following function to `conversion.py`:

```
def convert_and_sum_list_kwargs(usd_list, **kwargs):
    total = 0
    for amount in usd_list:
        total += convert_usd_to_aud(amount, **kwargs)
    return total
print(convert_and_sum_list_kwargs([1, 3], rate=0.8))
```

6. Execute this script from Command Prompt:

```
python conversion.py
```

The output is as follows:

```
5.0
```

Activity 9 – formatting customer names

Suppose that you are building a **Customer Relationship Management (CRM)** system, and you want to display a user record in the following format: `John Smith (California)`. However, if you don't have a location in your system, you just want to see `John Smith`.

Create a `format_customer` function that takes two required positional arguments, `first_name` and `last_name`, and one optional keyword argument, `location`. It should return a string in the required format.

The steps are as follows:

1. Create a `customer.py` file.

2. Define a `format_customer` function.

3. Open a Python shell and import your `format_customer` function.

4. Try running a few examples, such as the following:

    ```
    from customer import format_customer
    format_customer('John', 'Smith', location='California')
    ```

    The output is as follows:

    ```
    'John Smith (California)'
    ```

    Run the following example:

    ```
    format_customer('Mareike', 'Schmidt')
    ```

    The output is as follows:

    ```
    'Mareike Schmidt'
    ```

> **Note**
> The solution for this activity can be found in *Appendix* on GitHub.

Iterative functions

In the *For loops* section of *Chapter 1, Python Fundamentals – Math, Strings, Conditionals, and Loops*, you were introduced to the syntax for looping over objects in Python. As a refresher, here is an example where you perform five iterations and print the `i` variable in each loop:

```
for i in range(5):
    print(i)
```

The output is as follows:

```
0
1
2
3
4
```

For loops can also be placed within functions.

Exercise 49 – a simple function with a for loop

In this exercise, you create a `sum_first_n` function that sums up the first n integers. For example, if you pass the n=3 function, it should return 1 + 2 + 3 = 6. Let's see the steps:

1. In a Python shell, enter the function definition. Note that the tab spacing needs to match the following output:

    ```python
    def sum_first_n(n):
        result = 0
        for i in range(n):
            result += i + 1
        return result
    ```

2. Test the `sum_first_n` function on an example:

    ```python
    sum_first_n(100)
    ```

    The output is as follows:

    ```
    5050
    ```

In this exercise, you successfully implemented a simple `sum_first_n` function with a `for` loop to find the total sum of n numbers.

Exiting early

You can exit the function at any point during the iterations. For instance, you might want the function to return a value once a certain condition is met.

Exercise 50 – exiting the function during the for loop

In this exercise, you will create a function that (inefficiently) checks whether a certain number x is a prime. The function does this by looping through all the numbers from 2 to x and checking whether x is divisible by it. If it finds a number that x is divisible by, the iteration will stop and return `False`, as it has ascertained that x is not prime. We will be performing the following steps:

1. In a Python shell, enter the following function definition. Note that the tab spacing needs to match the following output:

    ```python
    def is_prime(x):
        for i in range(2, x):
            if (x % i) == 0:
    ```

```
        return False
    return True
```

2. Test the function on a couple of examples:

```
is_prime(7)
```

The output is as follows:

```
True
```

3. Now, find out whether 1000 is a prime number or not.

```
is_prime(1000)
```

The output is as follows:

```
False
```

In this exercise, you successfully implemented code that checks whether the x variable is prime by looping through numbers. In the case that it is divisible, it will exit the loop and provide the output as False.

Activity 10 – the Fibonacci function with an iteration

You work in an IT firm, and your colleague has realized that being able to quickly compute elements of the Fibonacci sequence will reduce the time taken to execute the testing suite on one of your internal applications. You will use an iterative approach to create a fibonacci_iterative function that returns the nth value in the Fibonacci sequence. Recall that each term in the Fibonacci sequence is generated by summing the previous two terms. The Fibonacci sequence starts as follows: [0, 1, 1, 2, 3, 5, 8,...].

The steps are as follows:

1. Create a fibonacci.py file.

2. Define a fibonacci_iterative function that takes a single positional argument representing which number term in the sequence you want to return.

3. Run the following code:

```
from fibonacci import fibonacci_iterative
fibonacci_iterative(3)
```

The output is as follows:

```
2
```

Another example to test your code can be as shown in the following code snippet:

```
fibonacci_iterative(10)
```

The output is as follows:

```
55
```

> **Note**
>
> The solution for this activity can be found in *Appendix* on GitHub.

Recursive functions

When a function calls itself, this is known as a recursive function. This is similar to `for` loops; however, recursive functions allow you to write more elegant and terse functions than can be achieved with a loop.

You may imagine that a function that calls itself recursively might end up in an infinite loop; you can write a recursive function that will keep running indefinitely, as shown here:

```
def print_the_next_number(start):
        print(start + 1)
        return print_the_next_number(start + 1)
print_the_next_number(5)
```

The output starts as follows:

```
6
7
8
9
10
11
```

> **Note**
>
> This output is truncated.

If you run this code in a Python shell, it will continue printing integers until you interrupt the interpreter (*Ctrl + C*); in a Jupyter Notebook, you can interrupt or restart the kernel under the **Kernel** tab. Take a look at the preceding code and ensure you understand why it behaves in this manner. The function executes the following steps:

1. The function is called with $start = 5$.

2. It prints 6 to the console—that is, $(5 + 1 = 6)$.

3. It then calls itself, this time passing in the argument starting with 6.

4. The function starts again, this time printing 7—that is, $(6 + 1 = 7)$.

A terminating case

To avoid being stuck in an infinite loop, a recursive function will typically have a terminating case as a point where the chain of recursion is broken. In our previous example, you could make it stop once the start parameter is greater than or equal to 7, as illustrated here:

```
def print_the_next_number(start):
    print(start + 1)
    if start >= 7:
        return "I'm bored"
    return print_the_next_number(start + 1)
print_the_next_number(5)
```

The output is as follows:

```
6
7
8

"I'm bored"
```

Figure 3.16 – Terminating the loop

Exercise 51 – recursive countdown

In this exercise, you will create a `countdown` function that recursively counts down from integer n until we hit 0. Let's start:

1. In Jupyter Notebook, enter the function definition. Note that the tab spacing needs to match the output that follows:

```python
def countdown(n):
    if n == 0:
        print('liftoff!')
    else:
        print(n)
        return countdown(n - 1)
```

2. Test the function, like so:

```python
countdown(3)
```

The output is as follows:

```
3
2
1
liftoff!
```

Figure 3.17 – Counting down with recursion

In this exercise, you successfully implemented a termination statement after number 1, with the `liftoff` term. This shows us that the recursive countdown has ended.

Exercise 52 – factorials with iteration and recursion

In this exercise, you will create a `factorial_iterative` function that takes an integer and returns a factorial using both an iterative and a recursive approach. Recall that a factorial is the product of all integers up to and equal to the number.

Recall that the factorial of 5 is calculated as 5! = 5 * 4 * 3 * 2 * 1 = 120. The steps for this exercise are as follows:

1. In a Jupyter Notebook, enter the following function to compute factorials using iteration:

```python
def factorial_iterative(n):
    result = 1
    for i in range(n):
```

```
            result *= i + 1
        return result
```

2.   Test the function, like so:

```
factorial_iterative(5)
```

The output is as follows:

```
120
```

3.   Note that you can express *n! = n * (n – 1)!*; for instance, 5! = 5 * 4!. This means we can write the function with recursion, as follows:

```
def factorial_recursive(n):
        if n == 1:
                return 1
        else:
                return n * factorial_recursive(n - 1)
```

4.   Test the function, like so:

```
factorial_recursive(5)
```

The output is as follows:

```
120
```

In this exercise, you successfully implemented and used both iteration and recursion to find the factorial of n numbers.

Activity 11 – the Fibonacci function with recursion

Suppose that your colleague has told you that the iterative function you designed in *Activity 10 – the Fibonacci function with an iteration* is not elegant and should be written with fewer lines of code. Your colleague mentions that a recursive solution will be able to achieve this.

In this activity, you will use recursion to write a terse (but inefficient) function for computing the *n*th term of the Fibonacci sequence.

The steps are as follows:

1.   Open the `fibonacci.py` file created in *Activity 10 – the Fibonacci function with an iteration*.

2.   Define a `fibonacci_recursive` function that takes a single positional argument representing which number term in the sequence we want to return.

3. Try running a few examples in a Python shell, like so:

```
from fibonacci import fibonacci_recursive
```

To find the Fibonacci recursive for the value 3, use the following code:

```
fibonacci_recursive(3)
```

The output is as follows:

```
2
```

4. You can run the following code and find the Fibonacci recursive for the value 10:

```
fibonacci_recursive(10)
```

The output is as follows:

```
55
```

> **Note**
>
> The `fibonacci.py` file can be found on GitHub at `https://github.com/PacktPublishing/The-Python-Workshop-Second-Edition/tree/main/Chapter03/Activity11`.
>
> The solution for this activity can be found in *Appendix* on GitHub.

Dynamic programming

Our recursive algorithm for computing Fibonacci numbers may look elegant, but that doesn't mean it's efficient. For example, when computing the fourth term in the sequence, it calculates the value for both the second and third terms. Likewise, when calculating the value of the third term in the sequence, it calculates the value for the first and second terms. This isn't ideal, as the second term in the sequence was already being calculated in order to get the fourth term. Dynamic programming will help us to address this problem by ensuring you break down the problem into the appropriate subproblems, and never solve the same subproblem twice.

Exercise 53 – summing integers

In this exercise, you write a `sum_to_n` function to sum integers up to n. You store the results in a dictionary, and the function will use the stored results to return the answer in fewer iterations. For example, if you already know the sum of integers up to 5 is 15, you should be able to use this answer when computing the sum of integers up to 6. Let's see the steps:

1. Create a new `dynamic.py` Python file.

2. Write a `sum_to_n` function that starts with `result = 0`, and an empty dictionary for saving results:

```
stored_results = {}
def sum_to_n(n):
    result = 0
```

3. Add in a loop that computes the sum, returns the result, and stores the result in our dictionary:

```
stored_results = {}
def sum_to_n(n):
    result = 0
    for i in reversed(range(n)):
        result += i + 1
    stored_results[n] = result
    return result
```

4. Finally, extend the function further by checking in each loop whether you already have a result for this number; if so, use the stored result and exit the loop:

```
stored_results = {}
def sum_to_n(n):
    result = 0
    for i in reversed(range(n)):
        if i + 1 in stored_results:
            print('Stopping sum at %s because we have
previously computed it' % str(i + 1))
            result += stored_results[i + 1]
            break
        else:
            result += i + 1
    stored_results[n] = result
    return result
```

5. Test the function in a Python shell to find the sum of integers up to 5:

```
sum_to_n(5)
```

The output is as follows:

```
15
```

6.   Now, test the function once again to find the sum of integers up to 6:

```
sum_to_n(6)
```

The output is as follows:

```
Stopping sum at 5 because we have previously compu
ted it

21
```

Figure 3.18 – Stopping early with saved results

In this exercise, you were able to reduce the number of steps in our code using dynamic programming to find the sum of integers up to n. The results were stored in a dictionary, and the function used the stored result to output the answer in fewer iterations.

Timing your code

One measure of code efficiency is the actual time taken for your computer to execute it. In the examples given so far in this chapter, the code will execute too quickly to gauge any difference in the various algorithms. There are a few methods with which we can time programs in Python; you will focus on using the time module from the standard library.

Exercise 54 – calculating your code's timing

In this exercise, you will calculate the time taken to execute the function in the previous exercise using the following steps:

1.   Open the dynamic.py file created in the previous exercise and add the following import at the top of the file:

```
import time
```

2.   Modify the function to calculate the time at the start, and print out the time elapsed at the end:

```
stored_results = {}
def sum_to_n(n):
    start_time = time.perf_counter()
    result = 0
    for i in reversed(range(n)):
        if i + 1 in stored_results:
            print('Stopping sum at %s because we have
previously computed it' % str(i + 1))
```

```
                    result += stored_results[i + 1]
                    break
             else:
                    result += i + 1
      stored_results[n] = result
      print(time.perf_counter() - start_time, "seconds")
```

3.   Open a Python shell, import your new function, and try running an example with a large number:

```
sum_to_n(1000000)
```

The output is as follows:

```
0.17615495599999775 seconds

500000500000
```

Figure 3.19 – Timing our code

4.   Rerun the same code in the shell:

```
sum_to_n(1000000)
```

The output is as follows:

```
Stopping sum at 1000000 because we have previously
computed it
3.6922999981925386e-05 seconds

500000500000
```

Figure 3.20 – Speeding up the execution with dynamic programming

> **Note**
>
> In the preceding example, the function returned the value faster by simply looking up the stored value in the dictionary.

Activity 12 – the Fibonacci function with dynamic programming

Your colleague has tried to use the code written in *Activity 11 – the Fibonacci function with recursion*, and they notice that it is too slow when computing large Fibonacci numbers. They ask you to write a new function that can compute large Fibonacci numbers quickly.

In this activity, you will use dynamic programming to avoid the inefficient recursive loops that you implemented in *Activity 11 – the Fibonacci function with recursion*.

The steps to do this are as follows:

1. Open the `fibonacci.py` file created in *Activity 10 – the Fibonacci function with an iteration*.

2. Define a `fibonacci_dynamic` function that takes a single positional argument representing the number in the sequence that you want to return. Try starting with the `fibonacci_recursive` function from the previous activity and storing the results in a dictionary as the recursions are performed.

3. Try running a few examples in a Python shell, like so:

    ```
    from fibonacci import fibonacci_recursive
    fibonacci_dynamic(3)
    ```

    The output is as follows:

    ```
    2
    ```

> **Note**
> If you try to use our recursive or iterative functions to compute the 100th Fibonacci number, they will be too slow and will never finish executing (unless you're willing to wait a few years).

> **Note**
> The solution for this activity can be found in *Appendix* on GitHub.

Helper functions

A helper function performs part of the computation of another function. It allows you to reuse common code without repeating yourself. For instance, suppose you had a few lines of code that printed out the elapsed time at various points in a function, as follows:

```
import time
def do_things():
    start_time = time.perf_counter()
    for i in range(10):
        y = i ** 100
        print(time.perf_counter() - start_time, "seconds
elapsed")
    x = 10**2
```

```
        print(time.perf_counter() - start_time, "seconds elapsed")
        return x


do_things()
```

The output is as follows:

```
2.4620000012021137e-06 seconds elapsed
6.030800000189629e-05 seconds elapsed
8.65640000000667e-05 seconds elapsed
0.00010789800000310379 seconds elapsed
0.00012594900000095777 seconds elapsed
0.0002756930000025193 seconds elapsed
0.00030112900000034415 seconds elapsed
0.00032656500000172173 seconds elapsed
0.0003499490000002936 seconds elapsed
0.00037087300000138157 seconds elapsed
0.0003934370000031606 seconds elapsed

100
```

Figure 3.21 – Timing our helper functions

The print statement is repeated twice in the preceding code, and would be better expressed as a helper function, as follows:

```
import time
def print_time_elapsed(start_time):
    print(time.perf_counter() - start_time, "seconds elapsed")
def do_things():
    start_time = time.perf_counter()
    for i in range(10):
        y = i ** 100
        print_time_elapsed(start_time)
    x = 10**2
    print_time_elapsed(start_time)
    return x
```

Don't Repeat Yourself

The preceding example encapsulates the **Don't Repeat Yourself** (**DRY**) programming principle. In other words, "*Every piece of knowledge or logic must have a single, unambiguous representation within a system.*" If you want to do the same thing multiple times in your code, it should be expressed as a function, and called wherever it is needed.

Exercise 55 – helper currency conversion

In this exercise, you will take a function that computes the total USD for a transaction and use a `helper` function to apply the DRY principle. You will also add an optional margin into the currency conversion that should default to 0. Here are the steps:

1. Write a function that computes the total USD given aud or gdp values:

```
def compute_usd_total(amount_in_aud=0, amount_in_gbp=0):
    total = 0
    total += amount_in_aud * 0.78
    total += amount_in_gbp * 1.29
    return total
print(compute_usd_total(amount_in_gbp=10))
```

The output is as follows:

```
12.9
```

2. Create a currency conversion function with an optional `margin` variable:

```
def convert_currency(amount, rate, margin=0):
    return amount * rate * (1 + margin)
```

3. Modify the original function to use the `helper` function, like so:

```
def compute_usd_total(amount_in_aud=0, amount_in_gbp=0):
    total = 0
    total += convert_currency(amount_in_aud, 0.78)
    total += convert_currency(amount_in_gbp, 1.29)
    return total
```

4. Check the result:

```
print(compute_usd_total(amount_in_gbp=10))
```

The output is as follows:

```
12.9
```

5. Suppose that the business has decided to add a 1% margin for the conversion of the GBP component. Modify the function accordingly, like so:

```python
def compute_usd_total(amount_in_aud=0, amount_in_gbp=0):
    total = 0
    total += convert_currency(amount_in_aud, 0.78)
    total += convert_currency(amount_in_gbp, 1.29, 0.01)
    return total
```

6. Check the result:

```python
print(compute_usd_total(amount_in_gbp=10))
```

The output is as follows:

```
13.029
```

Note that it's possible to get ahead of yourself when applying the DRY principle in writing reusable code. In the currency example, if our application really did just require converting currency once, then it probably shouldn't be written as a separate function. It may be tempting to think that generalizing our code is always good because it insures us against the possibility of needing to repeat the same code later; however, this is not always optimal. You can end up spending a lot of time writing more abstract code than is necessary, and, often, this code can be less readable and may introduce unnecessary complexity to our code base. Typically, the time to apply the DRY principle is when you find yourself writing the code for the second time.

Variable scope

Variables are only available in the area where they are defined. This area is called the scope of the variable. Depending on how and where a variable is defined, it may or may not be accessible in certain parts of your code. Here, we will discuss what variables in Python represent, the difference in defining them inside or outside of a function, and how the `global` and `nonlocal` keywords can be used to override these default behaviors.

Variables

A variable is a mapping between a name and an object at a certain location in the computer's memory. For example, if you set $x = 5$, then x is the variable's name, and the value of 5 is stored in memory. Python keeps track of the mapping between the name x and the location of the value using namespaces. Namespaces can be thought of as dictionaries, with the names as the keys of the dictionary, and locations in memory as the values.

Note that when a variable is assigned to the value of another variable, as seen here, this just means they are pointing to the same value, not that their equality will be maintained when one of the variables is updated:

```
x = 2
y = x
x = 4
print("x = " + str(x))
```

The output is as follows:

```
x = 4
```

Now, check the value of y:

```
print("y = " + str(y))
```

The output is as follows:

```
y = 2
```

In this example, both x and y are initially set to point to the integer 2. Note that the line y = x here is equivalent to writing y = 2. When x is updated, it is updated to bind to a different location in memory, and y remains bound to the integer 2.

Defining inside versus outside a function

When you define a variable at the start of a script, it will be a global variable, accessible from anywhere in the script. It will even be available within the functions that you write. Consider the following example:

```
x = 5
def do_things():
    print(x)
do_things()
```

With this code, the output is as follows:

```
5
```

However, if you define a variable within a function, as seen here, it is only accessible within that function:

```
def my_func():
    y = 5
```

```
        return 2
print(my_func())
```

2

Now, enter the y value and observe the output:

```
y
```

The output is as follows:

```
-------------------------------------------------------------------
NameError                              Traceback (most recent call last)
<ipython-input-2-80d732a03aaf> in <module>
      4
      5 my_func()
----> 6 y

NameError: name 'y' is not defined
```

Figure 3.22 – We are unable to access the local y variable

Note that if you define a variable within a function that has already been defined globally, the value will change depending on where the variable is accessed. In the following example, x is defined globally as 3. However, it is defined within the function as 5, and when accessed within the function, you can see it takes the value of 5:

```
x = 3
def my_func():
    x = 5
    print(x)

my_func()
```

The output is as follows:

5

However, when it is accessed outside of the function, it takes the global value, 3.

This means you need to take care when updating global variables. For instance, can you see why the following fails to work? Take a look:

```
score = 0
def update_score(new_score):
```

```
        score = new_score
update_score(100)
print(score)
```

The output is as follows:

```
0
```

Within the function, the `score` variable is indeed updated to be equal to `100`. However, this variable is only local to the function, and outside the function, the global score variable is still equal to `0`. However, you can get around this with the `global` keyword.

The global keyword

The `global` keyword simply tells Python to use the existing globally defined variable, where the default behavior will be to define it locally. You can do this using the same example as before:

```
score = 0
def update_score(new_score):
    global score
    score = new_score
print(score)
```

The output is as follows:

```
0
```

Now, you update the score to 100, as shown in the following code snippet:

```
update_score(100)
```

Print the scores, like so:

```
print(score)
```

The output is as follows:

```
100
```

The nonlocal keyword

The `nonlocal` keyword behaves in a similar way to the `global` keyword, in that it does not define the variable locally, and instead picks up the existing variable definition. However, it doesn't go straight to the global definition. It first looks at the closest enclosing scope; that is, it will look "one level up" in the code.

For example, consider the following:

```
x = 4
def myfunc():
    x = 3
    def inner():
        nonlocal x
        print(x)
    inner()
myfunc()
```

The output is as follows:

```
3
```

In this example, the `inner` function takes the variable definition's x variable from `myfunc`, and not the `global` keyword's x variable. If you instead write `global x`, then the integer 4 will be printed.

Lambda functions

Lambda functions are small, anonymous functions that can be defined in a simple one-line syntax, like so:

```
lambda arguments : expression
```

For example, take the following function that returns the sum of two values:

```
def add_up(x, y):
    return x + y
print(add_up(2, 5))
```

```
7
```

This function can equivalently be written using the lambda function syntax, as follows:

```
add_up = lambda x, y: x + y
print(add_up(2, 5))
```

```
7
```

Note that the main restriction of a lambda function is that it can only contain a single expression—that is, you need to be able to write the expression to return the value in a single line of code. This makes lambda functions convenient only in situations where the function is sufficiently simple such that it can be expressed in a single statement.

Exercise 56 – the first item in a list

In this exercise, you will write a lambda function, `first_item`, to select the first item in a list containing cat, dog, and mouse items. The steps are as follows:

1. Create a `lambda` function, like so:

```
first_item = lambda my_list: my_list[0]
```

2. Test the function, as follows:

```
first_item(['cat', 'dog', 'mouse'])
```

```
'cat'
```

Lambda functions can be particularly useful in passing custom functions to a map, as you can quickly define a function on the fly without assigning it to a variable name. The next two sections look at contexts where this is particularly useful.

Mapping with lambda functions

map is a special function in Python that applies a given function to all items in a list. For instance, suppose that you had a list of names and you wanted to get the average number of characters:

```
names = ['Magda', 'Jose', 'Anne']
```

For each name in the list, you want to apply the `len` function, which returns the number of characters in a string. One option is to iterate manually over the names, and add the lengths to a list, like so:

```
lengths = []
for name in names:
    lengths.append(len(name))
```

An alternative is to use the map function:

```
lengths = list(map(len, names))
```

The first argument is the function to be applied, and the second argument is an iterable (in this case, a list) of names. Note that the map function returns a generator object, not a list, so you convert it back to a list.

Finally, you take the average length of the list, as follows:

```
sum(lengths) / len(lengths)
```

The output is as follows:

```
4.33333333333
```

Exercise 57 – mapping with a logistic transform

In this exercise, you use map with a lambda function to apply a logistic function to a list of values.

A logistic function is often used in predictive modeling when dealing with binary response variables. It is defined as follows:

$$f(x) = \frac{1}{1 + e^{-x}}$$

Figure 3.23 – Logistic function

The steps for this exercise are set out here:

1. Import the math module as needed for the exponential function:

    ```
    import math
    ```

2. Create a list of values:

    ```
    nums = [-3, -5, 1, 4]
    ```

3. Use a lambda function to map the list of values using a logistic transform:

    ```
    list(map(lambda x: 1 / (1 + math.exp(-x)), nums))
    ```

    You will get the following output:

    ```
    [0.04742587317756678,
     0.0066928509242848554,
     0.7310585786300049,
     0.9820137900379085]
    ```

Figure 3.24 – Applying the logistic function to a list

In this exercise, you used a lambda function to find the list of values by using map.

Filtering with lambda functions

`filter` is another special function that, like `map`, takes a function and an iterable (for example, a list) as inputs. It returns the elements for which the function returns `True`.

For example, suppose that you had a list of names and wanted to find those that were three letters long:

```
names = ['Josefina', 'Jim', 'Kim']
list(filter(lambda name: len(name) == 3, names))
['Jim', 'Kim']
```

You should get the following output:

```
['Jim', 'Kim']
```

Figure 3.25 – Filtering using a lambda function

Exercise 58 – using a filter lambda

Consider a list of all-natural numbers below 10 that are multiples of 3 or 7. The multiples will be 3, 6, 7, and 9, and the sum of these numbers is 25.

In this exercise, you will be calculating the sum of all multiples of 3 or 7 below 1,000. The steps are as follows:

1. Create a list of numbers from 0 to 999:

    ```
    nums = list(range(1000))
    ```

2. Use a lambda function to filter the values that are divisible by 3 or 7:

    ```
    filtered = filter(lambda x: x % 3 == 0 or x % 7 == 0,
    nums)
    ```

    Recall that the % (modulo) operator returns the remainder from the division of the first argument by the second. So, $x \% 3 == 0$ is checking that the remainder of x divided by 3 is 0.

3. Sum the list to get the result:

    ```
    sum(filtered)
    ```

    The output is as follows:

    ```
    214216
    ```

In this exercise, you successfully used filter lambdas that took a function as an input, and then returned the output as the sum of `filtered`.

Sorting with lambda functions

Another useful function that lambdas are often used with is `sorted`. This function takes an iterable, such as a list, and sorts it according to a function given by the `key` parameter.

For example, suppose that you had a list of names, and wanted them sorted by length:

```
names = ['Ming', 'Jennifer', 'Andrew', 'Boris']
sorted(names, key=lambda x : len(x))
```

You should get the following output:

```
['Ming', 'Boris', 'Andrew', 'Jennifer']
```

Figure 3.26 – Sorting using a lambda function

This is a great example of how utilizing Python functions can make writing Python code shorter and more efficient.

Summary

In this chapter, you were introduced to a few fundamental tools in Python for formalizing your knowledge. You learned how to write scripts and modules and save them appropriately. You were introduced to several different ways of writing functions, including iterative, recursive, and lambda functions. Additionally, common algorithms widely featured in basic computer science courses were presented, including bubble sort and binary search. You also learned why the DRY principle is important, and how general functions and helper functions help us to adhere to this principle to express the logical components of our code succinctly. Finally, you learned the importance of variable scope, timers, and dynamic programming.

In the next chapter, you will turn to Python applications that you will need in your Python toolkit, such as how to read and write files and how to plot visual graphs of data.

4

Extending Python, Files, Errors, and Graphs

Overview

By the end of this chapter, you will be able to use Python to read and write to files; use defensive programming techniques, such as assertions, to debug your code; use exceptions, assertions, and tests with a defensive mindset; and plot, draw, and create graphs as outputs.

You will also learn about the basic **input/output** (**I/O**) operations for Python and how to use the `matplotlib` and `seaborn` libraries to create visualizations.

Introduction

In *Chapter 3, Executing Python – Programs, Algorithms, and Functions*, you covered the basics of Python programs and learned how to write algorithms, functions, and programs. Now, you will learn how to make your programs more relevant and usable in the IT world.

In this chapter, you are going to look at file operations. File operations are essential for scripting as a Python developer, especially when you need to process and analyze a large number of files, such as in data science. In companies that deal with data science, you often do not have direct access to a database. Rather, they receive files in text format. These include CSV files for column data and TXT files for unstructured data (such as patient logs, news articles, user comments, and so on).

In this chapter, we will cover the following topics:

- Reading files
- Writing files
- Preparing for debugging (defensive code)

- Plotting techniques
- The don'ts of plotting graphs

Technical requirements

You can find the code files for this chapter on GitHub at `https://github.com/PacktPublishing/The-Python-Workshop-Second-Edition/tree/main/Chapter04`.

Reading files

While databases such as MySQL and Postgres are popular and widely used in many web applications, a large amount of data is still stored and exchanged using text file formats. Popular formats such as **comma-separated values (CSV)**, **JavaScript Object Notation (JSON)**, and **plain text** are used to store information such as weather data, traffic data, and sensor readings. In the following exercise, you will learn how to read text from a file using Python.

Exercise 59 – reading a text file using Python

In this exercise, you will be downloading a sample data file from the internet and reading data as the output. Follow these steps:

1. Open a new Jupyter notebook.

2. Now, copy the entire text from `https://packt.live/2MIHzhO`, save it to a local folder as `pg37431.txt`, and remember where it is located.

3. Upload the file to your Jupyter notebook by clicking on the **Upload** button in the top-right corner. Select the `pg37431.txt` file from your local folder, and then click on the **Upload** button again to store it in the same folder where your Jupyter notebook runs:

Figure 4.1 – The Upload button

4. Now, you should extract the content of the file using Python code. Open a new Jupyter notebook file and type the following code into a new cell. You will be using the open() function in this step. Don't worry too much about this; it will be explained in more detail later:

```
f = open('pg37431.txt')
text = f.read()
print(text)
```

You would get the following output:

```
_PRIDE AND PREJUDICE_

_A PLAY_

[Illustration: "_Mr. Darcy, I have never desired your good opinion, and
you have certainly bestowed it most unwillingly._"]




_PRIDE AND PREJUDICE_

_A PLAY_

_FOUNDED ON JANE AUSTEN'S
NOVEL_
```

Figure 4.2 – Output showing the extracted content from the file

Note that you can scroll within the cell and check the entire content.

5. Now, in a new cell, type text only, without the print command:

```
text
```

You will get the following output:

```
Out[6]: '\ufeffThe Project Gutenberg EBook of Pride and Prejudice, a play, by \nMary Keith Medbery Mackaye\n\nThis eBook is f
or the use of anyone anywhere at no cost and with\nalmost no restrictions whatsoever.  You may copy it, give it away
or\nre-use it under the terms of the Project Gutenberg License included\nwith this eBook or online at www.gutenberg.o
rg\n\n\nTitle: Pride and Prejudice, a play\n\nAuthor: Mary Keith Medbery Mackaye\n\nRelease Date: September 15, 2011
[EBook #37431]\n\nLanguage: English\n\n*** START OF THIS PROJECT GUTENBERG EBOOK PRIDE AND PREJUDICE, A PLAY ***\n
\n\n\nProduced by Chuck Greif and the Online Distributed\nProofreading Team at http://www.pgdp.net (This book was\n
produced from scanned images of public domain material\nfrom the Internet Archive.)\n\n\n\n\n\n\n\n_PRIDE AND PREJU
DICE_\n\n_A PLAY_\n\n[Illustration: "_Mr. Darcy, I have never desired your good opinion, and\nyou have certainly best
owed it most unwillingly._"]\n\n\n\n_PRIDE AND PREJUDICE_\n\n_A PLAY_\n\n_FOUNDED ON JANE AUSTEN\'S\nNOVEL_\n\n_BY_
\n\n_MRS. STEELE MACKAYE_\n\n[Illustration: colophon]\n\n_NEW YORK_\n_DUFFIELD AND COMPANY_\n_1906_\n\n\n
COPYRIGHT, 1906, BY DUFFIELD & COMPANY.\n\n                    Published September, 1906.\n\n
------\n\n                    SPECIAL COPYRIGHT NOTICE.\n\n        This play is fully protected by copyright, all r
equirements of the\n    law having been complied with. Performances may be given only with\n    the written permiss
ion of Duffield & Company, agents for Mrs.\n    Steele Mackaye, owner of the acting rights.\n\n        Extract from the
law relating to copyright:\n\n    "SEC. 4996. Any person publicly performing or representing any\n    dramatic or m
usical composition for which a copyright has been\n    obtained, without the consent of the proprietor of said drama
tic or\n    musical composition or his heirs or assigns, shall be liable for\n    damages therefor, such damages in
all cases to be assessed at such\n    sum not less than one hundred dollars for the first and fifty\n    dollars fo
r every subsequent performance as to the Court shall\n    appear just. If the unlawful performance and representatio
```

Figure 4.3 – Output after using only the text command

The difference in the output between this cell and the previous cell, as shown in *Figures 4.2* and *4.3*, is the presence of control characters. Using the `print` command helps us render the control characters while calling `text` shows the actual content and does not render as output.

In this exercise, you learned how to read the content of the entire data sample file.

Moving on, you will take a look at the `open()` function that you used in this exercise. It opens the file to let us access it. The `open()` function requires the name of the file you want to open as the argument. If you provide a filename without the full path, Python will look for the file in the same directory where it is currently running. In our case, it looks for the text file under the same folder where our `ipynb` file is, and where the Jupyter notebook started. The `open()` function returns an object, which you store as `f` (which represents **file**), and you use the `read()` function to extract its content.

You may also be wondering whether you need to close the file. The answer is that it depends. Usually, when you call a `read()` function, you can assume that Python will close the file automatically, either during garbage collection or when the program exits. However, your program may end prematurely, and the file may never close. Files that have not been closed properly can cause data to be lost or corrupted. However, calling `close()` too early in our program will also lead to more errors. It's not always easy to know exactly when you should close a file. Even though Python closes the file when the program is exited, it is always better to close the file explicitly as all the content in the buffer gets written to the file.

Text files can be exchanged and opened in all operating systems without requiring any special parser. Text files are also used to record ongoing information, such as server logs in the IT world.

But what if you are dealing with a large file or you only need to access parts of the content or read the file line by line? We will cover this in the next exercise.

Exercise 60 – reading partial content from a text file

In this exercise, you will be using the same sample data file from *Exercise 59 – reading a text file using Python*. Here, however, you will only be partially reading the content from the text file. Follow these steps:

1. Open a new Jupyter notebook.
2. Copy the `pg37431.txt` text file that you used in the previous exercise and save it in a separate folder that will be used to execute this exercise.
3. Write the following code in a new cell to read the first 5 characters:

```
with open("pg37431.txt", encoding="utf-8") as f:
    print(f.read(5))
```

The output is as follows:

```
The P
```

By doing this, you have included an argument in `read()` to tell Python to read the first 5 characters each time.

Notice that you use a `with` statement here. The `with` statement is a control flow structure in Python. It guarantees that the file object, `f`, will close automatically after the code block exits, no matter how the nested block exits.

If an exception occurs before the end of the block, it will still close the file before the exception is caught. Of course, it will close the file even if the nested block runs successfully.

4. Now, access the `text` file by reading it line by line using the `.readline` function. To do this, you need to enter the following code in a new cell on your notebook:

```
with open("pg37431.txt", encoding="utf-8") as f:
    print(f.readline())
```

You will get the following output as the very first line in the text file:

```
The Project Gutenberg EBook of Pride and Prejudice, a play, by
```

Figure 4.4 – Output after accessing the text line by line

By completing this exercise, you have learned how to use control structures in Python to close a code block automatically. By doing so, you were able to access the raw data text file and read it one line at a time.

Writing files

Now that you have learned how to read the content of a file, you are going to learn how to write content to a file. Writing content to a file is the easiest way for us to store content in our database storage, save our data by writing it to a particular file, and save data on our hard disk. This way, the output will still be available for us after we have closed the terminal or terminated the notebook that contains our program output. This will allow us to reuse the content later with the `read()` method, which we covered in the previous section, *Reading files*.

You will still be using the `open()` method to write to a file, except for when it requires an extra argument to indicate how you want to access and write to the file.

For instance, consider the following:

```
f = open("log.txt","w+", encoding="utf-8")
```

The preceding code snippet allows us to open a file in w+, a mode that supports both **reading** and **writing** – that is, to update the file. Other modes in Python include the following:

- r: The default mode. This opens a file for reading.
- w: Write mode. This opens a file for writing, creates a new file if the file does not exist, and overwrites the content if the file already exists.
- x: This creates a new file. This operation fails if the file exists.
- a: This opens a file in append mode and creates a new file if a file does not exist.
- b: This opens a file in binary mode.

In the following exercise, you will learn how to write content to a file.

Exercise 61 – creating and writing content to files to record the date and time in a text file

In this exercise, we will be writing content to a file. We are going to create a log file, which records the value of our counter every second. Follow these steps:

1. Open a new Jupyter notebook.
2. In a new cell, type the following code:

```
f = open('log.txt', 'w', encoding="utf-8")
```

The preceding code will open the log.txt file in write mode, which we will be using to write our values.

3. Now, in the next cell of your notebook, type the following code:

```
from datetime import datetime
import time
for i in range(0,10):
    print(datetime.now().strftime("%Y%m%d_%H:%M:%S-"),i)
    f.write(datetime.now().strftime("%Y%m%d_%H:%M:%S-")
    time.sleep(1)
    f.write(str(i))
    f.write""""\"")
f.close()
```

In this code block, we are importing the datetime and time modules that Python provides us with. We are also using a for loop to print the year, month, and day, as well as the hour, minutes, and seconds. Finally, we are using the write() function to add to the previous condition; that is, every time the loop exits, the write command prints a number in place of i.

You will get the following output:

```
20220523_03:32:09 - 0
20220523_03:32:10 - 1
20220523_03:32:11 - 2
20220523_03:32:12 - 3
20220523_03:32:13 - 4
20220523_03:32:14 - 5
20220523_03:32:15 - 6
20220523_03:32:16 - 7
20220523_03:32:17 - 8
20220523_03:32:18 - 9
```

Figure 4.5 – Output after using the write() function

4. Now, go back to the main page of your Jupyter notebook, or browse to your Jupyter notebook folder using **Windows Explorer** or **Finder** (if you are using a Mac). You will see the newly created log.txt file:

.ipynb_checkpoints	7/26/2019 9:00 AM	File folder	
Exercise03.ipynb	7/26/2019 9:01 AM	IPYNB File	1 KB
log	7/26/2019 9:03 AM	Text Document	1 KB

Figure 4.6 – The log file has been created

5. Open the file inside Jupyter notebook or your favorite text editor (for example, Visual Studio Code or Notepad); you will see content similar to the following:

```
1   20190420_23:47:08 - 0
2   20190420_23:47:09 - 1
3   20190420_23:47:10 - 2
4   20190420_23:47:11 - 3
5   20190420_23:47:12 - 4
6   20190420_23:47:13 - 5
7   20190420_23:47:14 - 6
8   20190420_23:47:15 - 7
9   20190420_23:47:16 - 8
10  20190420_23:47:17 - 9
11
```

Figure 4.7 – Content added to the log.txt file

With that, you have created your first text file. The example shown in this exercise is very common in most data science processing tasks; for instance, recording the readings of sensors and the progress of a long-running process.

The `close()` method at the very end makes sure that the file is closed properly and that all content in the buffer is written to the file.

Preparing for debugging (defensive code)

In the programming world, a bug refers to defects or problems that prevent code or programs from running normally or as expected. Debugging is the process of finding and resolving those defects. Debugging methods include interactive debugging, unit testing, integration testing, and other types of monitoring and profiling practices.

Defensive programming is a form of debugging approach that ensures the continuing function of a piece of a program under unforeseen circumstances. Defensive programming is particularly useful when we require our programs to have high reliability. In general, we practice defensive programming to improve the quality of software and source code, and to write code that is both readable and understandable.

We can use exceptions to handle unexpected inputs or user actions that can potentially reduce the risk of crashing our programs and make our software behave predictably.

Writing assertions

The first thing you need to learn about writing defensive code is how to write an assertion. Python provides a built-in `assert` statement for using the `assertion` condition in the program. The `assert` statement assumes the condition will always be true. It halts the program and raises an `AssertionError` message if it is false.

The simplest code to showcase `assert` is shown in the following code snippet:

```
x = 2
assert x < 1,"Invalid value"
```

Here, since 2 is not smaller than 1, and the statement is false, it raises an `AssertionError` message, as follows:

```
------------------------------------------------------------------
AssertionError                          Traceback (most recent call last)
<ipython-input-14-3a9a99a5e24a> in <module>
      1 x = 2
----> 2 assert x < 1, "Invalid value"

AssertionError: Invalid value
```

Figure 4.8 – Output showing AssertionError

> **Note**
> You can also write the `assert` function without the optional error message.

Next, you will learn how to use `assert` in a practical example.

Say that you want to calculate the average marks of a student in a semester. You need to write a function to calculate the average, and you want to make sure that the user who calls the function passes in the marks. You will learn how to implement this in the following exercise.

Exercise 62 – working with incorrect parameters to find the average using assert with functions

In this exercise, you will be using the assertion error with functions to check the error message when you enter incorrect parameters to calculate the average marks of students. Follow these steps:

1. Continue in the previous Jupyter notebook.

2. Type the following code into a new cell:

```
def avg(marks):
    assert len(marks) != 0
    return round(sum(marks)/len(marks), 2)
```

Here, you created an `avg` function that calculates the average from a given list, and you used the `assert` statement to check for any incorrect data that will throw the assertion error output.

3. In a new cell, type the following code:

```
sem1_marks = [62, 65, 75]
print("Average marks for semester 1:", avg(sem1_marks))
```

Here, you provided a list and calculated the average marks using the `avg` function.

The output is as follows:

```
Average marks for semester 1: 67.33
```

4. Next, test whether the `assert` statement is working by providing an empty list. In a new cell, type the following code:

```
ranks = []
print("Average of marks for semester 1:", avg(ranks))
```

You will get the following output:

```
-------------------------------------------------------------------------------
AssertionError                              Traceback (most recent call last)
<ipython-input-21-cec864bd4977> in <module>
      1 ranks = []
----> 2 print("Average of mark1:",avg(ranks))
      3

<ipython-input-18-5b6c83fe5ee4> in avg(marks)
      1 def avg(marks):
----> 2     assert len(marks) != 0
      3     return round(sum(marks)/len(marks), 2)

AssertionError:
```

Figure 4.9 – The assertion fails when we pass in an empty list

In the cell with the code where you provide three scores, the `len(marks) !=0` statement returns `true`, so no `AssertionError` will be raised. However, in the next cell, you did not provide any marks, so it raises an `AssertionError` message.

In this exercise, you used the `AssertionError` message to throw the output in case it is incorrect or if missing data is provided. This has proved to be useful in the real world when data is in an incorrect format; you can use this message to debug the incorrect data.

Note that although `assert` behaves like a check or data validation tool, it is not. Asserts in Python can be disabled globally to nullify all of the assert statements. Do not use `assert` to check whether a function argument contains an invalid or unexpected value, as this can quickly lead to bugs and security holes. The baseline is to treat Python's `assert` statement like a debugging tool and not to use it to handle runtime errors. The goal of using assertions is to let us detect a bug more quickly. An `AssertionError` message should never happen unless there's a bug in your program. In the next section, you will look at plotting techniques so that you get a visual output when using Python.

Plotting techniques

Unlike machines, humans are terrible at understanding data without graphics. Various visualization techniques have been invented to make humans understand different datasets. There are various types of graphs that you can plot, each with its strengths and weaknesses.

Each type of chart is only suitable for a certain scenario, and they shouldn't be mixed up. Presenting dropped-out customer details for marketing scatter plots is a good example of this. A scatter plot is suitable for visualizing a categorical dataset with numeric values; you will be exploring this further in the following exercise.

To present your data in the best way possible, you should choose the right graph for the right data. In the following exercises, you will be introduced to various graph types and their suitability for different scenarios. You will also learn how to avoid plotting misleading charts.

You will plot each of these graphs in the following exercises and observe the changes in these graphs.

> **Note**
>
> These exercises require external libraries such as seaborn and matplotlib. Please refer to the *Preface* to find out how to install these libraries.
>
> In some installations of Jupyter, graphs do not show up automatically. Use the %matplotlib inline command at the beginning of your notebook to get around this.

Exercise 63 – drawing a scatter plot to study the data between ice cream sales versus temperature

In this exercise, you will get scatter plots as output while using sample data from an ice cream company to study the growth in the sale of ice creams against varying temperature data. Imagine that you have been assigned to analyze the sales of a particular ice cream outlet to study the effect of temperature on ice cream sales. Follow these steps:

1. Begin by opening a new Jupyter notebook file.

2. Enter the following code to import the matplotlib, seaborn, and numpy libraries with the following alias:

    ```
    import matplotlib.pyplot as plt
    import seaborn as sns
    import numpy as np
    ```

3. Prepare the dataset, as specified in the following code snippet:

    ```
    temperature = [14.2, 16.4, 11.9, 12.5, 18.9, 22.1, 19.4,
    23.1, 25.4, 18.1, 22.6, 17.2]
    sales = [215.20, 325.00, 185.20, 330.20, 418.60, 520.25,
    412.20, 614.60, 544.80, 421.40, 445.50, 408.10]
    ```

4. Plot the lists using the scatter plot:

    ```
    plt.scatter(temperature, sales, color='red')
    plt.show()
    ```

You will get the following output:

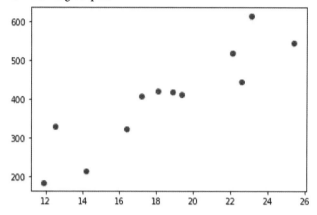

Figure 4.10 – A scatterplot containing the data of the ice cream temperature and sales data

Our plot looks fine, but only to our eyes. Anyone who views the chart will not have the context, so they won't understand what the chart is trying to tell them. Before we introduce other plots, it is useful for you to learn how to edit your plots and include additional information that will help your readers understand them.

5. Add a `title` command to your plot, as well as the *X*-axis (horizontal) and *Y*-axis (vertical) labels. Then, add the following lines before the `plt.show()` command:

```
plt.title('Ice-cream sales versus Temperature')
plt.xlabel('Sales')
plt.ylabel('Temperature')
plt.scatter(temperature, sales, color='red')
plt.show()
```

You will get the following output:

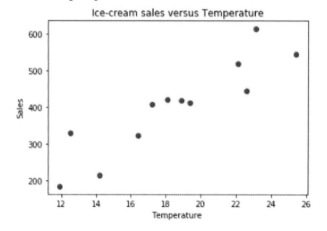

Figure 4.11 – Updated scatter plot of ice cream sales versus temperature

Our chart is now easier to understand. In this exercise, you used the sample ice cream sales versus temperature dataset and used the data to create a scatter plot that will be easier to understand for another user.

However, what if your dataset is time-based? In that case, you will usually use a line plot. Some examples of line plots include plotting heart rates or visualizing population growth against time or even the stock market. By creating a line plot, you can understand the trend and seasonality of data.

In the following exercise, you will be outputting the line chart, which corresponds to the time (that is, the number of days) and the price. For this, you will be plotting out stock prices.

Exercise 64 – drawing a line chart to find the growth in stock prices

In this exercise, you will be plotting the stock prices of a well-known company. You will be plotting this as a line chart that will be plotted as the number of days against the price growth. Follow these steps:

1. Open a new Jupyter notebook.

2. Enter the following code in a new cell to initialize our data as a list:

```
stock_price = [190.64, 190.09, 192.25, 191.79, 194.45,
196.45, 196.45, 196.42, 200.32, 200.32, 200.85, 199.2,
199.2, 199.2, 199.46, 201.46, 197.54, 201.12, 203.12,
203.12, 203.12, 202.83, 202.83, 203.36, 206.83, 204.9,
204.9, 204.9, 204.4, 204.06]
```

3. Now, use the following code to plot the chart, configure the chart title, and configure the titles of the axes:

```
import matplotlib.pyplot as plt
plt.plot(stock_price)
plt.title('Opening Stock Prices')
plt.xlabel('Days')
plt.ylabel('$ USD')
plt.show()
```

In the preceding code snippet, you added a title to the graph, as well as the number of days to the X-axis and the price to the Y-axis.

Execute the cell; you should see the following chart as the output:

Figure 4.12 – Line chart for opening stock prices

If you've noticed that the number of days in our line plot starts at 0, then you have sharp eyes. Usually, you start your axes at 0, but in this case, it represents the day, so you have to start at 1 instead.

4. You can fix this by creating a list that goes from 1 to 31, representing the days in March:

```
t = list(range(1, 31))
```

5. Plot this together with the data. You can also define the numbers on the *X*-axis using xticks:

```
plt.plot(t, stock_price, marker='.', color='red')
plt.xticks([1, 8, 15, 22, 28])
```

The complete code that contains the underlying changes is as follows:

```
stock_price = [190.64, 190.09, 192.25, 191.79, 194.45,
196.45, 196.45, 196.42, 200.32, 200.32, 200.85, 199.2,
199.2, 199.2, 199.46, 201.46, 197.54, 201.12, 203.12,
203.12, 203.12, 202.83, 202.83, 203.36, 206.83, 204.9,
204.9, 204.9, 204.4, 204.06]
t = list(range(1, 31))
import matplotlib.pyplot as plt
plt.title('Opening Stock Prices')
plt.xlabel('Days')
plt.ylabel('$ USD')
```

```
plt.plot(t, stock_price, marker='.', color='red')
plt.xticks([1, 8, 15, 22, 28])
plt.show()
```

You will get the following output:

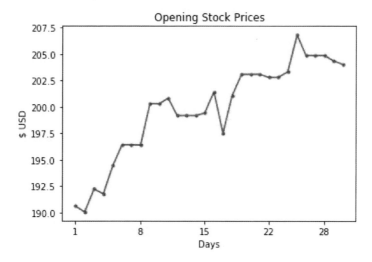

Figure 4.13 – Updated line chart with a customized line color, marker, and date range

In this exercise, you learned how to generate a line graph that displays the output based on time. In the next exercise, you will learn how to plot bar plots, which is another useful visualization for displaying categorical data.

Exercise 65 – plotting bar plot to grade students

A bar plot is a straightforward chart type. It is great for visualizing the count of items in different categories. When you get the final output for this exercise, you may think that histograms and bar plots look the same. But that's not the case. The main difference between a histogram and a bar plot is that there is no space between the adjacent columns in a histogram. Here, you will learn how to plot a bar graph.

In this exercise, you will draw bar charts to display the data of students and the corresponding bar plots as a visual output. Follow these steps:

1. Open a new Jupyter notebook file.

2. Type the following code into a new cell, to initialize the dataset:

```
grades = ['A', 'B', 'C', 'D', 'E', 'F']
students_count = [20, 30, 10, 5, 8, 2]
```

3. Plot the bar chart with our dataset and customize the `color` command:

```
import matplotlib.pyplot as plt
plt.bar(grades, students_count, color=['green', 'gray',
'gray', 'gray', 'gray', 'red'])
```

Execute the cell; you will get the following output:

```
Out[5]:  <BarContainer object of 6 artists>
```

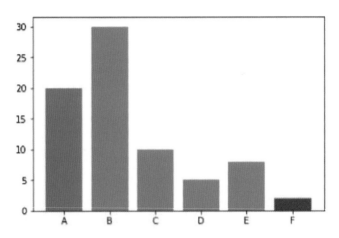

Figure 4.14 – Output showing the number of students without any labels on the plot

Here, you defined two lists: the `grades` list for storing the grades, which is used as the X-axis, and the `students_count` list for storing the number of students who score a respective grade, which is used as the Y-axis. Then, you used the `plt` plotting engine and the `bar` command to draw a bar chart.

4. Enter the following code to add the main title and the axis titles to our chart for ease of understanding. Again, use the `show()` command to display the rendered chart:

```
plt.title('Grades Bar Plot for Biology Class')
plt.xlabel('Grade')
plt.ylabel('Num Students')
plt.bar(grades, students_count, color=['green', 'gray',
'gray', 'gray', 'gray', 'red'])
plt.show()
```

Execute the cell; you will get the following chart as output:

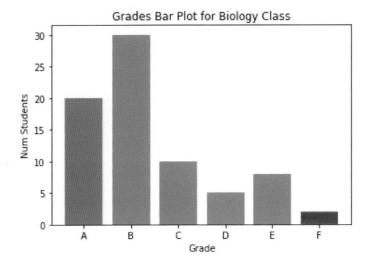

Figure 4.15 – Bar plot outputting the grade and number of students with labels

Sometimes, it is easier to use horizontal bars to represent relationships. What you have to do is change the bar function to `.barh`.

5. Enter the following code in a new cell and observe the output:

```
plt.barh(grades, students_count, color=['green', 'gray',
'gray', 'gray', 'gray', 'red'])
```

You will get the following output:

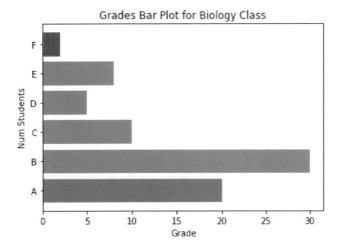

Figure 4.16 – Horizontal bar plots

In this exercise, you implemented a sample list of data and output that data as bar graphs; these bar graphs were shown as vertical bars and horizontal bars as well. This could vary, depending on your usage.

In the next exercise, you will be implementing pie charts, which many organizations use to pictorially classify their data. Pie charts are good for visualizing percentages and fractional data; for instance, the percentage of people who agree or disagree on some opinions, the fractional budget allocation for a certain project, or the results of an election.

However, a pie chart is often regarded as not a very good practice by many analysts and data scientists for the following reasons:

- Pie charts are often overused. Many people use pie charts without understanding why they should use them.

- A pie chart is not effective for comparison purposes when there are many categories.

- It is easier not to use a pie chart when the data can simply be presented using tables or even written words.

Exercise 66 – creating a pie chart to visualize the number of votes in a school

In this exercise, you will plot a pie chart of the number of votes for each of the three candidates in an election for club president. Follow these steps:

1. Open a new Jupyter notebook.

2. Type the following code into a new cell to set up our data:

```
# Plotting
labels = ['Monica', 'Adrian', 'Jared']
num = [230, 100, 98]   # Note that this does not need to
be percentages
```

3. Draw a pie chart by using the pie() method, and then set up colors:

```
import matplotlib.pyplot as plt
plt.pie(num, labels=labels, autopct='%1.1f%%',
colors=['lightblue', 'lightgreen', 'yellow'])
```

4. Add title and display the chart:

```
plt.title('Voting Results: Club President',
fontdict={'fontsize': 20})
plt.pie(num, labels=labels, autopct='%1.1f%%',
```

```
colors=['lightblue', 'lightgreen', 'yellow'])
plt.show()
```

You will get the following output:

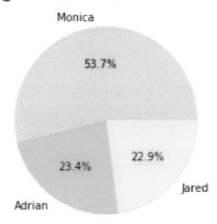

Figure 4.17 – Pie chart with three categories

Having completed this exercise, you are now able to generate data as a pie chart. This type of representation is the best visual aid that many organizations use when sorting out data.

Exercise 67 – generating a heatmap to visualize the grades of students

In this exercise, you will be implementing a heatmap visualization. Heatmaps are useful for showing the relationship between two categorical properties; for instance, the number of students who passed exams in three different classes. Follow these steps:

1. Open a new Jupyter notebook.

2. Type in the following code to define a heatmap function. First, you must prepare the plot:

```
def heatmap(data, row_labels, col_labels, ax=None, cbar_
kw={}, cbarlabel="", **kwargs):
    if not ax:
        ax = plt.gca()
    im = ax.imshow(data, **kwargs)
```

3. Now, define the color bar as `colorbar`, as shown in the following code:

```
cbar = ax.figure.colorbar(im, ax=ax, **cbar_kw)
cbar.ax.set_ylabel(cbarlabel, rotation=-90,
va="bottom")
```

4. Show all `ticks` and label them with their respective list entries:

```
ax.set_xticks(np.arange(data.shape[1]))
ax.set_yticks(np.arange(data.shape[0]))
ax.set_xticklabels(col_labels)
ax.set_yticklabels(row_labels)
```

5. Configure the horizontal axes for the labels to appear on top of the plot:

```
ax.tick_params(top=True, bottom=False,
                labeltop=True, labelbottom=False)
```

6. Rotate the tick labels and set their alignments:

```
plt.setp(ax.get_xticklabels(), rotation=-30,
ha="right",
            rotation_mode="anchor")
```

7. Turn off `spine` and create a white grid for the plot, as shown in the following code:

```
for edge, spine in ax.spines.items():
    spine.set_visible(False)
ax.set_xticks(np.arange(data.shape[1]+1)-.5,
minor=True)
ax.set_yticks(np.arange(data.shape[0]+1)-.5,
minor=True)
ax.grid(which="minor", color="w", linestyle='-',
linewidth=3)
ax.tick_params(which="minor", bottom=False,
left=False)
```

8. Return the heatmap:

```
return im, cbar
```

You can obtain this code directly from the `matplotlib` documentation. These heatmap functions help generate a heatmap.

9. Execute the cell, and, in the next cell, enter and execute the following code. You must define a numpy array to store our data and plot the heatmap using the functions defined previously:

```
import numpy as np
import matplotlib.pyplot as plt
data = np.array([
     [30, 20, 10,],
     [10, 40, 15],
     [12, 10, 20]
])
im, cbar = heatmap(data, ['Class-1', 'Class-2', 'Class-
3'], ['A', 'B', 'C'], cmap='YlGn', cbarlabel='Number of
Students')
```

As you can see, the heatmap is quite plain since it doesn't contain any textual information to help our readers understand the plot.

10. Now, let's continue and add another function that will help us annotate our heatmap visualization. Type and execute the following code in a new cell:

Exercise67.ipynb

```
def annotate_heatmap(im, data=None, valfmt="{x:.2f}",
                     textcolors=["black", "white"],
                     threshold=None, **textkw):
    import matplotlib
    if not isinstance(data, (list, np.ndarray)):
        data = im.get_array()
    if threshold is not None:
        threshold = im.norm(threshold)
    else:
        threshold = im.norm(data.max())/2.
    kw = dict(horizontalalignment="center",
              verticalalignment="center")
    kw.update(textkw)
    if isinstance(valfmt, str):
        valfmt = matplotlib.ticker.
StrMethodFormatter(valfmt)
```

11. In the new cell, type and execute the following code:

```
im, cbar = heatmap(data, ['Class-1', 'Class-2', 'Class-
3'], ['A', 'B', 'C'], cmap='YlGn', cbarlabel='Number of
Students')
texts = annotate_heatmap(im, valfmt="{x}")
```

This will annotate the heatmap and give us the following output:

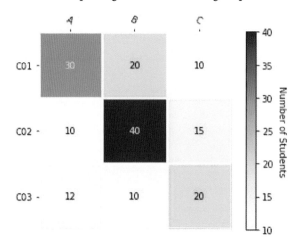

Figure 4.18 – Heatmap output from the sample data

Note that here, we put our data in a numpy array (np.array). This is because the methods we are going to call expect a numpy array.

Next, we plotted our heatmap using the heatmap method. We passed in our data, the row labels, ['Class-1', 'Class-2', 'Class-3'], and then our column labels, ['A', 'B', 'C']. We also passed in YlGn as cmap, which means we want to use the color yellow for small values, and the color green for big values. Then, we passed in cbarlabel as Number of Students to denote that the values we are plotting represent the number of students. Lastly, we annotated our heatmap with the data (30, 20, 10, and so on).

So far, you have learned how to visualize discrete categorical variables using heatmaps and bar plots. But what if you want to visualize a continuous variable? For example, instead of the grades of students, perhaps you want to plot the distribution of scores. For this type of data, you should use a density distribution plot, which we will cover in the next exercise.

Exercise 68 – generating a density plot to visualize the scores of students

In this exercise, you will be generating a density plot from a list of sample data. Follow these steps:

1. Begin by continuing from the previous Jupyter notebook file.

2. Enter the following code into a new cell, set up the data, and initialize the plot:

```
import seaborn as sns
data = [90, 80, 50, 42, 89, 78, 34, 70, 67, 73, 74, 80,
60, 90, 90]
sns.distplot(data)
```

Here, you have imported the seaborn module, which will be explained later in this exercise, and then created a list as data. sns.displot is used to plot the data as a density plot.

3. Configure the title and axes labels:

```
import matplotlib.pyplot as plt
plt.title('Density Plot')
plt.xlabel('Score')
plt.ylabel('Density')
sns.distplot(data)
plt.show()
```

You should get the following output:

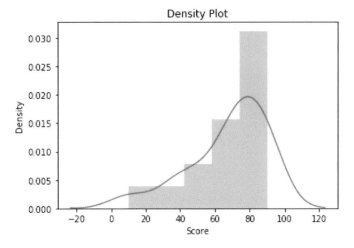

Figure 4.19 – Density plot output from the sample data

So far, in this exercise, you have used the seaborn library, which is a data visualization library based on matplotlib. It provides a high-level interface for drawing appealing visual graphs and supports chart types that do not come with matplotlib. For example, the seaborn library is used for density plots simply because it is not available in matplotlib.

In this exercise, you were able to implement and output the density plot graph, as shown in *Figure 4.19*, from the list sample data we inputted.

If you were to do this using matplotlib, you would need to write a separate function that calculates the density. To make things easier and create density plots, we can use seaborn. The line in the chart has been drawn using **kernel density estimation (KDE)**. KDE estimates the probability density function of a random variable, which, in this case, is the score of students.

In the next exercise, you will be implementing contour plots. Contour plots are suitable for visualizing large and continuous datasets. A contour plot is like a density plot with two features. In the following exercise, you will examine how to plot a contour plot using sample weight data.

Exercise 69 – creating a contour plot

In this exercise, you will be using a sample dataset containing the different weights of people to output a contour plot. Follow these steps:

1. Open a new Jupyter notebook.

2. Initialize the weight recording data using the following code in a new cell:

```
weight=[85.08,79.25,85.38,82.64,80.51,77.48,79.25,78.75,7
7.21,73.11,82.03,82.54,74.62,79.82,79.78,77.94,83.43,73.7
1,80.23,78.27,78.25,80.00,76.21,86.65,78.22,78.51,79.60,8
3.88,77.68,78.92,79.06,85.30,82.41,79.70,80.16,81.11,79.5
8,77.42,75.82,74.09,78.31,83.17,75.20,76.14]
```

3. Now, draw the plot using the following code. Execute the cell twice:

```
import seaborn as sns
sns.kdeplot(list(range(1,45)), weight, kind='kde',
cmap="Reds", )
```

4. Add legend, title, and axis labels to the plot:

```
import matplotlib.pyplot as plt
plt.legend(labels=['a', 'b'])
plt.title('Weight Dataset - Contour Plot')
plt.ylabel('height (cm)')
```

```
plt.xlabel('width (cm)')
sns.kdeplot(list(range(1,45)), weight, kind='kde',
cmap="Reds", )
```

5.   Execute this code; you will see the following output:

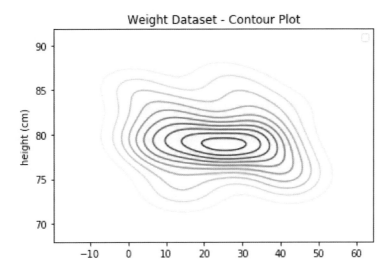

Figure 4.20 – The contour plot's output after using the weight dataset

In this exercise, you learned how to output a contour graph from a dataset.

Compare this with the scatter plot that we implemented in *Exercise 63 – drawing a scatter plot to study the data between ice cream sales versus temperature*. Which chart type do you think is easier for us to use to visualize the data?

Extending graphs

Sometimes, you will need to show multiple charts in the same figure for comparison purposes or to extend the depth of the story that you are telling. For instance, in an election, you want one chart that shows the percentage, and another chart that shows the actual votes. In this section, you will learn how to use subplots in `matplotlib`.

Note that the following code is shown in multiple plots. Follow these steps:

> **Note**
>
> We will use `ax1` and `ax2` to plot our charts now, instead of `plt`.

1. To initialize the figure and two axis objects, execute the following code:

```python
import matplotlib.pyplot as plt
# Split the figure into 2 subplots
fig = plt.figure(figsize=(8,4))
ax1 = fig.add_subplot(121) # 121 means split into 1 row ,
2 columns, and put in 1st part.
ax2 = fig.add_subplot(122) # 122 means split into 1 row ,
2 columns, and put in 2nd part.
```

2. The following code plots the first subplot, which is a pie chart:

```python
labels = ['Adrian', 'Monica', 'Jared']
num = [230, 100, 98] ax1.pie(num, labels=labels,
autopct='%1.1f%%', colors=['lightblue', 'lightgreen',
'yellow'])
ax1.set_title('Pie Chart (Subplot 1)')
```

3. Now, plot the second subplot, which is a bar chart:

```python
# Plot Bar Chart (Subplot 2)
labels = ['Adrian', 'Monica', 'Jared']
num = [230, 100, 98]
plt.bar(labels, num, color=['lightblue', 'lightgreen',
'yellow'])
ax2.set_title('Bar Chart (Subplot 2)')
ax2.set_xlabel('Candidate')
ax2.set_ylabel('Votes')
fig.suptitle('Voting Results', size=14)
```

This will produce the following output:

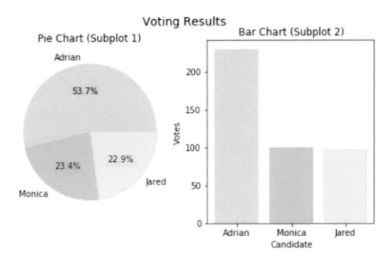

Figure 4.21 – Output showing a pie chart and a bar chart with the same data next to each other

> **Note**
>
> If you want to try out the previously mentioned code example, be sure to put all the code in a single input field in your Jupyter notebook for both outputs to be shown next to each another.

In the following exercise, you will be using `matplotlib` to output 3D plots.

Exercise 70 – generating 3D plots to plot a sine wave

Matplotlib supports 3D plots. In this exercise, you will plot a 3D sine wave using sample data. Follow these steps:

1. Open a new Jupyter notebook file.

2. Now, type the following code into a new cell and execute the code:

```
from mpl_toolkits.mplot3d import Axes3D
import numpy as np
import matplotlib.pyplot as plt
X = np.linspace(0, 10, 50)
```

```
Y = np.linspace(0, 10, 50)
X, Y = np.meshgrid(X, Y)
Z = (np.sin(X))
# Setup axis
fig = plt.figure(figsize=(7,5))
ax = fig.add_subplot(111, projection='3d')
```

Here, you imported the mplot3d package. The mplot3d package adds 3D plotting capabilities by supplying an axis object that can create a 2D projection of a 3D scene. Next, you must initialize the data and set up the drawing axis.

3.   Use the plot_surface() function to plot the 3D surface chart and configure the title and axes labels:

```
ax.plot_surface(X, Y, Z)
# Add title and axes labels
ax.set_title("Demo of 3D Plot", size=13)
ax.set_xlabel('X')
ax.set_ylabel('Y')
ax.set_zlabel('Z')
```

Note

Enter the preceding code in a single input field in your Jupyter notebook, as shown in *Figure 4.22*.

Execute the cell; you will get the following output:

```
In [10]:  from mpl_toolkits.mplot3d import Axes3D
          import numpy as np
          import matplotlib.pyplot as plt
          import seaborn as sns
          X = np.linspace(0, 10, 50)
          Y = np.linspace(0, 10, 50)
          X, Y = np.meshgrid(X, Y)
          Z = (np.sin(X))

          # Setup axis
          fig = plt.figure(figsize=(7,5))
          ax = fig.add_subplot(111, projection='3d')
          ax.plot_surface(X, Y, Z)

          # Add title and axes labels
          ax.set_title("Demo of 3D Plot", size=13)
          ax.set_xlabel('X')
          ax.set_ylabel('Y')
          ax.set_zlabel('Z')
```

```
Out[10]:  Text(0.5, 0, 'Z')
```

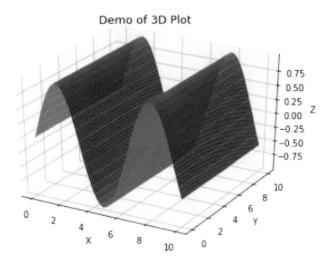

Figure 4.22 – A 3D plot of demo data using matplotlib

In this exercise, you implemented a very interesting feature provided by matplotlib known as the 3D plot, which is an added feature in Python visualizations.

The don'ts of plotting graphs

In newspapers, blogs, or social media, there are a lot of misleading graphs that make people misunderstand the actual data. We will look at some examples of this in this section and learn how to avoid them.

Manipulating the axis

Imagine that you have three students with three different scores from an exam. Now, you have to plot their scores on a bar chart. There are two ways to do this – the misleading way and the right way:

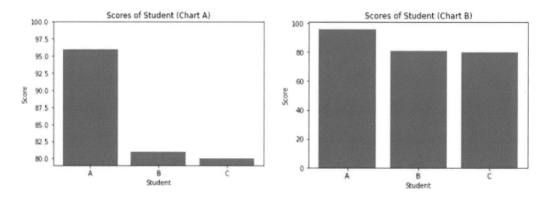

Figure 4.23 – Chart A (starts from 80) and Chart B (starts from 0)

Looking at **Chart A**, it will be interpreted that the score of student **A** is about 10 times higher than students **B** and **C**. However, that is not the case. The scores for the students are 96, 81, and 80, respectively. **Chart A** is misleading because the *Y*-axis ranges from 80 to 100. The correct *Y*-axis should range from 0 to 100, as in **Chart B**. This is simply because the minimum score a student can get is 0, and the maximum score a student can get is 100. The scores of students **B** and **C** are just slightly lower than student **A**.

Cherry picking data

Now, let's have a look at the opening stock prices:

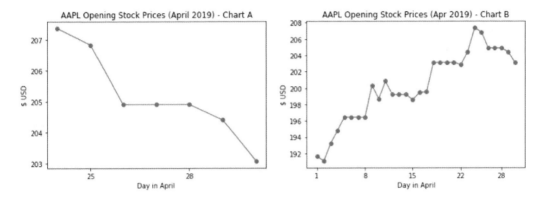

Figure 4.24 – Chart A (shows only 7 days) and Chart B (shows the entire month)

Chart A, whose title is **AAPL Opening Stock Prices (April 2019)**, shows a declining trend in Apple® stock prices. However, the chart is only showing the last 7 days of April, which means that the title of the chart is misleading. **Chart B** is the correct chart as it shows a whole month of stock prices. As you can see, cherry-picking the data can give people a different perception of the reality of the data.

Wrong graph, wrong context

Take a look at the following two graphs, which show a survey asking whether to demolish an old teaching building:

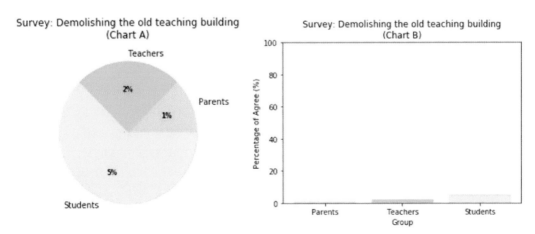

Figure 4.25 – A pie chart versus a column chart

Using the wrong graph can give readers the wrong context to understand the data. Here, **Chart A** uses a pie chart to make readers think that the students want to demolish the old teaching building. However, as shown in **Chart B**, the majority (95%) of the students voted to not demolish the old teaching building. A pie chart should only be used when every piece of the pie adds up to 100%. In this case, a bar chart is better at visualizing the data.

Activity 13 – visualizing the Titanic dataset using a pie chart and bar plots

Charts are not only useful visualization devices in presentations and reports; they also play a crucial role in **Exploratory Data Analysis (EDA)**. In this activity, you will learn how to explore a dataset using visualizations.

In this activity, you will be using the famous Titanic dataset. Here, you will focus on plotting the expected data. The steps to load the dataset will be covered later in this book.

> **Note**
>
> In this activity, we will be using the Titanic dataset. The `titanic_train.csv` dataset's CSV file has been uploaded to this book's GitHub repository and can be found at https://packt.live/31egRmb.

Follow these steps to complete this activity:

1. Load the CSV file.

   Open the file and read its content to load the data line by line into the `lines` variable, as shown in the following code snippet:

   ```
   import csv
   lines = []
   with open('titanic_train.csv', encoding="utf-8") as csv_
   file:
       csv_reader = csv.reader(csv_file, delimiter=',')
       for line in csv_reader:
           lines.append(line)
   ```

2. Prepare a data object that stores all the `passengers` details using the following variables:

   ```
   data = lines[1:]
   passengers = []
   headers = lines[0]
   ```

3. Extract the `survived`, `pclass`, `age`, and `gender` fields into their respective lists for the passengers who survived:

```
survived = [p['Survived'] for p in passengers]
pclass = [p['Pclass'] for p in passengers]
age = [float(p['Age']) for p in passengers if p['Age'] !=
'']
gender_survived = [p['Sex'] for p in passengers if
int(p['Survived']) == 1]
```

4. Based on this, your main goal and output will be to generate plots according to the following requirements:

    -   Visualize the proportion of passengers that survived the incident (in a pie chart)

    -   You will get the following output:

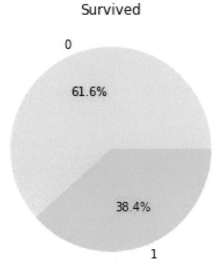

Figure 4.26 – A pie chart showing the survival rate of the passengers

    -   Compare the gender of passengers who survived the incident (in a bar plot)

You will get the following output:

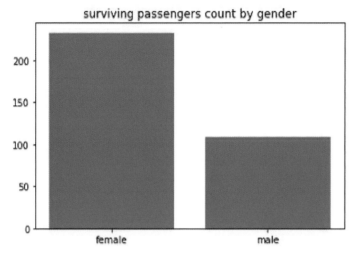

Figure 4.27 – A bar plot showing the variation in the gender of those who survived the incident

> **Note**
> The solution for this activity can be found in *Appendix* on GitHub.

Summary

In this chapter, you learned how to read and write to a text file using Python, followed by using assertions in defensive programming, which is a way of debugging your code. Finally, you explored different types of graphs and charts to plot data. We discussed the suitability of each plot for different scenarios and datasets while providing suitable examples along the way. We also discussed how to avoid plotting charts that could be misleading.

In the next chapter, you will learn how to use Python to write **Object-Oriented Programming** (**OOP**) code. This includes creating classes and instances, using `write` subclasses that inherit the property of the parent class, and extending functionalities using methods and properties.

5

Constructing Python – Classes and Methods

Overview

By the end of this chapter, you will be able to use and distinguish between class and instance attributes, use instance methods to perform calculations based on the instance attributes of an object, use static methods to write small utility functions to refactor code in a class to avoid repetition, use property setters to handle the assignment of values to computed properties and perform validation, and create classes that inherit methods and attributes from other classes.

Introduction

In *Chapter 4, Extending Python, Files, Errors, and Graphs*, you began to move beyond the basic and fundamental into writing defensive code and anticipating potential issues. In this chapter, you will be introduced to one of the cornerstones of **object-oriented programming** (**OOP**) – classes. Classes contain the definition of the objects we work with. All objects you work within OOP are defined by a class, either in your code or in a Python library. So far in this book, we have been using this method, but we have not discussed how to extend and customize the behavior of objects. In this chapter, you will start with objects you are familiar with and build on these by introducing the concept of classes.

Perhaps you have been working with a string object in Python. What exactly is a string? What sort of things can you do with strings? Are there things you'd like to be able to do with strings that Python's `string` object doesn't allow? Can you customize the behavior of this object somehow? This chapter will answer these questions by exploring classes. Writing classes will unlock a world of possibilities, in which you'll be able to elegantly modify and combine code from external sources to fit your requirements.

For example, say you find a third-party library for managing calendars that you want to incorporate into your organization's internal application. You will want to inherit classes from the library and override methods/properties in order to use the code as per your particular context. So, you can see how methods can come in handy.

Your code will become increasingly intuitive and readable, and your logic will be more elegantly encapsulated according to the **Don't Repeat Yourself** (**DRY**) principle, which will be explained later in the chapter.

We will be covering the following topics:

- Classes and objects
- Defining classes
- The __init__ method
- Methods
- Properties
- Inheritance

Technical requirements

You can find the code files used in this chapter on GitHub at `https://github.com/PacktPublishing/The-Python-Workshop-Second-Edition/tree/main/Chapter05`.

Classes and objects

Classes are fundamental to OOP languages such as Python. A class is simply a template for creating objects. Classes define an object's various properties and specify the things you can do with that object. So far in this book, you have been relying on classes defined in the Python standard library or built into the Python programming language itself. For example, in *Exercise 38 – finding the system date* of *Chapter 3, Executing Python – Programs, Algorithms, and Functions*, you used the `datetime` class to retrieve the current date. You will start off by exploring some more of the classes you've already been using. This can be performed in a Python shell or Jupyter notebook.

Create a new integer object called x in a Python console:

```
>>> x = 10
>>> x
10
```

You can see the class that x was created from by calling the `type` function:

```
>>> type(x)
<class 'int'>
```

The `integer` class doesn't just let you store a single number – the x object has other properties, too:

```
>>> x.bit_length()
```

You will get the following output:

4

This method computes the number of binary digits needed to represent x as a binary number (1010).

As you learned in *Chapter 3, Executing Python – Programs, Algorithms, and Functions*, you can also view the docstring to read about this object and its class:

```
>>> print(x.__doc__)
int([x]) -> integer
int(x, base=10) -> integer
```

Convert a number or string to an integer, or return 0 if no arguments are given. If x is a number, return x.__int__(). For floating point numbers, this truncates toward zero.

So, you can see that even the simplest objects in Python, such as strings, have many interesting properties and methods that can be used to retrieve information about the object or perform some computation with the object. When you reach a point in your programming where you want to customize the behavior of these methods, or perhaps create a new type of object entirely, you will need to start writing your own classes. For example, perhaps instead of a string object, you want a `name` object that has a string as its main property and also contains methods that allow you to translate the name into other languages.

Exercise 71 – exploring strings

Many of our examples and exercises so far have involved strings. In this exercise, you will go beyond the text that a string object can store and look at the other properties and methods available in this class.

The aim of the exercise is to demonstrate that the string objects you are already familiar with have many other methods and properties that you might not have been aware of. This exercise can be performed in a Jupyter notebook:

1. Define a new string:

```
my_str = 'hello World!'
```

2. Check what class our object has:

```
type(my_str)
```

You will get the following output:

```
str
```

3. View the docstring of the `str` class:

```
print(my_str.__doc__)
```

You will get the following output:

```
str(object='') -> str
str(bytes_or_buffer[, encoding[, errors]]) -> str

Create a new string object from the given object. If encoding or
errors is specified, then the object must expose a data buffer
that will be decoded using the given encoding and error handler.
Otherwise, returns the result of object.__str__() (if defined)
or repr(object).
encoding defaults to sys.getdefaultencoding().
errors defaults to 'strict'.
```

Figure 5.1 – The docstring of the str class

4. View the full list of properties and methods of `my_str`:

```
my_str.__dir__()
```

The output will be as follows:

```
['__repr__',
 '__hash__',
 '__str__',
 '__getattribute__',
 '__lt__',
 '__le__',
 '__eq__',
 '__ne__',
 '__gt__',
 '__ge__',
 '__iter__',
 '__mod__',
 '__rmod__',
 '__len__',
 '__getitem__',
 '__add__',
 '__mul__',
 '__rmul__',
 '__contains__',
 '__new__',
 'encode',
 'replace',
 'split',
 'rsplit',
 'join',
 'capitalize',
```

Figure 5.2 – A complete list of the properties and methods of my_str

5. You will see the results of a few of the preceding methods:

```
my_str.capitalize()
```

You will get the following output:

```
'Hello world!'
```

Now, let's get the output in uppercase:

```
my_str.upper()
```

Now the output will be as follows:

```
'HELLO WORLD!'
```

Now, let's get the output in lowercase without any spacing:

```
my_str.replace(' ', '')
```

The output changes to this:

```
'helloWorld!'
```

In this exercise, you explored the various properties of a string object in Python. The purpose here was to illustrate that you are already working with objects that don't just represent simple data types but have more complex definitions. We will now turn to creating templates to build our own custom objects using classes.

Defining classes

Built-in classes and classes imported from Python packages are sometimes sufficient for our requirements. However, often you want to invent a new type of object because there isn't an object in the standard libraries that has the properties/methods that you require. Remember that a class is like a template for creating a new object.

For example, create a new class called `Australian`:

```
class Australian:
    is_human = True
    enjoys_sport = True
```

You now have a new template for creating `Australian` objects (or people, if you prefer). Our code assumes that all new Australians will be human and enjoy sport.

You will firstly create a new object of `Australian`:

```
john = Australian()
```

Check the class of our Australian:

```
>>> type(john)
<class '__main__.Australian'>
```

You will also view some of John's attributes:

```
>>> john.is_human
```

```
True
```

```
>>> john.enjoys_sport
```

```
True
```

The `is_human` and `enjoys_sport` attributes are called class attributes. **Class attributes** do not change between objects of the same class. For example, let's create another Australian:

```
>>> ming = Australian()
```

Ming is also human and enjoys sport. We will soon learn about instance attributes, which can vary between objects created by a class.

Exercise 72 – creating a Pet class

The aim of this exercise is to create our first class. You will create a new class called `Pet`, with class attributes and a docstring. You will also create instances of this class:

1. Define a `Pet` class with two class attributes and a docstring:

    ```
    class Pet:
        """
        A class to capture useful information regarding my
    pets, just in case
        I lose track of them.
        """
        is_human = False
        owner = 'Michael Smith'
    ```

2. Create an instance of this class:

```
chubbles = Pet()
```

3. Check the is_human property of our new pet, chubbles:

```
chubbles.is_human
```

You will get the following output:

False

4. Check the owner:

```
chubbles.owner
print(chubbles.__doc__)
```

The output is as follows:

```
                    'Michael Smith'


A class to capture useful information regarding my pets, just incase
I lose track of them.
```

Figure 5.3 – Output showing that Chubbles is owned by Michael Smith
and output of a class to capture useful information

In this exercise, we created our first class and examined the properties of an object created with this new class.

The __init__ method

In *Exercise 72 – creating a Pet class*, you used the Pet class to create a Pet object called chubbles in the following manner:

```
chubbles = Pet()
```

Here, you'll explore more about what happens when you create objects from a class in this manner.

Python has a special method called __init__, which is called when you initialize an object from one of our class **templates**. For example, building on the previous exercise, suppose you wanted to specify the height of a pet. You would add an __init__ method as follows:

```
class Pet:
    """
    A class to capture useful information regarding my pets,
```

```
just in case
    I lose track of them.
    """
    def __init__(self, height):
        self.height = height


    is_human = False
    owner = 'Michael Smith'
```

The init method takes the height value and assigns it as an attribute of our new object. You can test this as follows:

```
chubbles = Pet(height=5)
chubbles.height
```

This will give us the following output:

```
out: 5
```

Exercise 73 – creating a Circle class

The aim of this exercise is to use the init method. You will create a new class called Circle with an init method that allows us to specify the radius and color of a new Circle object. You then use this class to create two circles:

1. Create a Circle class with a class attribute called is_shape:

    ```
    class Circle:
        is_shape = True
    ```

2. Add an init method to our class, allowing us to specify the radius and color of the specific circle:

    ```
    class Circle:
        is_shape = True


        def __init__(self, radius, color):
            self.radius = radius
            self.color = color
    ```

3. Initialize two new Circle objects with different radii and colors:

    ```
    first_circle = Circle(2, 'blue')
    second_circle = Circle(3, 'red')
    ```

Let's have a look at some of the attributes of the `Circle` objects:

```
first_circle.color
```
```
'blue'
```

```
second_circle.color
```
```
'red'
```

```
first_circle.is_shape
```
```
True
```

Figure 5.4 – Checking the attributes of our circles

In this exercise, you learned how to use the init method to set instance attributes.

> **Note**
>
> Any `Circle` objects created from our `Circle` class will always have `is_shape` = `True` but may have different radii and colors. This is because `is_shape` is a class attribute defined outside of the init method, and `radius` and `color` are instance attributes set in the init method.

Keyword arguments

As we learned in *Chapter 3, Executing Python – Programs, Algorithms, and Functions*, in the *Basic functions* section, there are two types of arguments that can go into functions – **positional** arguments and **keyword** arguments (`kwargs`). Remember that positional arguments are listed first and must be specified when calling a function, whereas keyword arguments are optional:

```
def function_name (thing, thang = 4)
                      ↓         ↓
                     arg      kwarg
```

Figure 5.5 – Args and kwargs

The examples so far in this chapter have just contained positional arguments. However, you may want to provide a default value for an instance attribute. For example, you can take your previous example and add a default value for `color`:

```
class Circle:
    is_shape = True
```

```
    def __init__(self, radius, color='red'):
        self.radius = radius
        self.color = color
```

Now, if you initialize a circle without specifying a color, it will default to red:

```
my_circle = Circle(23)
my_circle.color
```

You will get the following output:

```
'red'
```

Exercise 74 – the Country class with keyword arguments

The aim of this exercise is to use keyword arguments to allow optional instance attribute inputs to be specified in the init function.

You create a class called Country, where there are three optional attributes that can be passed into the init method:

1. Create the Country class with three keyword arguments to capture details about the Country object:

    ```
    class Country:
        def __init__(self, name='Unspecified',
    population=None, size_kmsq=None):
            self.name = name
            self.population = population
            self.size_kmsq = size_kmsq
    ```

2. Initialize a new Country, noting that the order of parameters does not matter because you are using named arguments:

    ```
    usa = Country(name='United States of America', size_
    kmsq=9.8e6)
    ```

> **Note**
>
> Here, e is shorthand for "10 to the power of" – for instance, 2e4 == 2 x 10 ^ 4 == 20,000.

3. Use the __dict__ method to view a list of the attributes of the usa object:

```
usa.__dict__
```

You will get the following output:

```
{'name': 'United States of America',
 'population': None,
 'size_kmsq': 9800000.0}
```

Figure 5.6 – Dictionary output of our usa object

In this exercise, you learned how keyword arguments can be used when initializing an object with a class.

Methods

You have already come across one special method, the init method. However, the power of classes will start to become more obvious to you as you begin writing your own custom methods. There are three types of methods you will explore in the following sections:

- Instance methods
- Static methods
- Class methods

Instance methods

Instance methods are the most common type of method you will need to use. They always take self as the first positional argument. The __init__ method discussed in the previous section is an example of an instance method.

Here is another example of an instance method, extending our Circle class from *Exercise 73 – creating a Circle class*:

```
import math
class Circle:
    is_shape = True

    def __init__(self, radius, color='red'):
        self.radius = radius
        self.color = color

    def area(self):
        return math.pi * self.radius ** 2
```

The `area` method will use the `radius` attribute of the circle to compute the area of the circle using the following formula, which you may recall from math classes:

$$Area = \pi * r^2$$

Figure 5.7 – A formula to calculate the area of a circle

You can now test the `area` method:

```
circle = Circle(3)
circle.area()
```

The output is as follows:

```
28.274333882308138
```

As you may have realized by now, `self` represents the instance (that is, the object) within the method. This is always the first positional argument of an instance method, and Python passes it to the function without you needing to do anything. So, in the preceding example, when you call the `area` function, behind the scenes, Python passes the circle object through as the first argument.

This is necessary because it allows you to access other attributes and methods of your `Circle` object within the method.

Note the elegance of being able to change the radius of our circle without needing to worry about updating the area.

For example, taking our previously defined `circle` object, let's change the radius from 3 to 2:

```
circle.radius = 2
circle.area()
```

Now you will get the output:

```
12.566370614359172
```

If you had set `area` as an attribute of `Circle`, you would need to update it each time the radius changed. However, writing it as a method where it is expressed as a function of the radius makes your code more maintainable.

Exercise 75 – adding an instance method to our Pet class

The aim of this exercise is to add our first instance method to a class in order to determine whether or not our pet should be considered tall.

You will continue and add an instance method to the `Pet` class created in *Exercise 72 – creating a Pet class*:

1. Start with your previous definition of `Pet`:

    ```
    class Pet:
        def __init__(self, height):
            self.height = height

        is_human = False
        owner = 'Michael Smith'
    ```

2. Add a new method that allows you to check whether your pet is tall or not, where your definition of tall is where `Pet` has a height of at least `50`:

    ```
    class Pet:
        def __init__(self, height):
            self.height = height

        is_human = False
        owner = 'Michael Smith'

        def is_tall(self):
            return self.height >= 50
    ```

3. Now, create a `Pet` object and check whether he is tall:

    ```
    bowser = Pet(40)
    bowser.is_tall()
    ```

    You will get the following output:

    False

4. Now, suppose that Bowser grows. Then, you need to update his height and check again whether he is tall:

    ```
    bowser.height = 60
    bowser.is_tall()
    ```

The output is as follows:

```
True
```

Adding arguments to instance methods

The preceding example showed an instance method that took only the positional `self` parameter. Often, you need to specify other inputs to compute your methods. For instance, in *Exercise 75 – Adding an instance method to our Pet class*, you hardcoded the definition of "tall" as any pet with a height greater than or equal to 50. Instead, you could allow that definition to be passed in via the method in the following manner:

```
class Pet:
    def __init__(self, height):
        self.height = height


    is_human = False
    owner = 'Michael Smith'


    def is_tall(self, tall_if_at_least):
        return self.height >= tall_if_at_least
```

You can then create a pet and check whether its height exceeds some arbitrary benchmark that you specify:

```
bowser = Pet(40)
bowser.is_tall(30)
```

You will get the following output:

```
True
```

Now, let's change the height to 50, as mentioned here:

```
bowser.is_tall(50)
```

The output now will be:

```
False
```

Exercise 76 – computing the size of our country

The aim of this exercise is to use a keyword argument in the context of an instance method.

You will create a `Country` class and add a method to calculate the area of a country in square miles:

1. Start with the following definition of `Country`, which allows the name, population, and size in square kilometers to be specified:

```
class Country:
    def __init__(self, name='Unspecified',
    population=None, size_kmsq=None):
        self.name = name
        self.population = population
        self.size_kmsq = size_kmsq
```

2. There are 0.621371 miles in a kilometer. Use this constant to write a method that returns the size in square miles. The class should now look like this:

```
class Country:
    def __init__(self, name='Unspecified',
    population=None, size_kmsq=None):
        self.name = name
        self.population = population
        self.size_kmsq = size_kmsq

    def size_miles_sq(self, conversion_rate=0.621371):
        return self.size_kmsq * conversion_rate ** 2
```

3. Create a new `Country` object and check the conversion:

```
algeria = Country(name='Algeria', size_kmsq=2.382e6)
algeria.size_miles_sq()
```

You will get the following output:

```
919694.772584862
```

4. Suppose someone told you that the conversion rate was incorrect, and that there are 0.6 miles in a kilometer. Without changing the default parameter, recalculate the size of Algeria in square miles using the new rate:

```
algeria.size_miles_sq(conversion_rate=0.6)
```

You will get the following output:

```
857520.0
```

In this exercise, you learned how to allow optional keyword arguments to be passed into instance methods to alter the calculation performed.

The __str__ method

Like __init__, the __str__ method is another special instance method that you need to know about. This is the method that is called whenever an object is rendered as a string.

For example, this is what is displayed when you print the object to the console. You can explore this in the context of your Pet class. Suppose you have a Pet class in which you can assign a height and name to the Pet instance:

```
class Pet
    def __init__(self, height, name):
        self.height = height
        self.name = name


    is_human = False
    owner = 'Michael Smith'
```

Now, you create a pet and print it to the console:

```
my_pet = Pet(30, 'Chubster')
print(my_pet)
```

The output will be as follows:

```
<__main__.Pet object at 0x0000018E1BBA5630>
```

Figure 5.8 – An unhelpful string representation of the Pet object

This is not a very helpful representation of our pet. So, we need to add __str__ method:

```
class Pet:
    def __init__(self, height, name):
        self.height = height
        self.name = name


    is_human = False
```

```
      owner = 'Michael Smith'

    def __str__(self):
        return f"{self.name} (height: {self.height} cm)"
```

Like any instance method, our __str__ method takes self as the first argument in order to access attributes and other methods of the Pet object. You can create another pet:

```
  my_other_pet = Pet(40, 'Rudolf')
  print(my_other_pet)
```

You will get the following output:

```
            Rudolf (height: 40 cm)
```

Figure 5.9 – A much nicer string representation of the object

This is a much nicer representation of our Pet object and makes it easier to quickly inspect objects without diving into the individual attributes. It also makes it easier for someone to import your code into their work and be able to understand what the various objects represent.

Exercise 77 – adding an __str__ method to the Country class

The aim of this exercise is to learn how to add string methods in order to give more helpful string representations of objects when printed to the console.

You extend the Country class from *Exercise 76 – computing the size of our country* by adding an __str__ method to customize how the object is rendered as a string:

1. Start with our previous definition of Country:

```
    class Country:
        def __init__(self, name='Unspecified',
    population=None, size_kmsq=None):
            self.name = name
            self.population = population
            self.size_kmsq = size_kmsq
```

2. Add a simple string method that returns the name of the country:

```
        def __str__(self):
            return self.name
```

3. Create a new country and test the string method:

```
chad = Country(name='Chad')
print(chad)
```

You will get the following output:

```
Chad
```

4. Now try adding a more complex string method that displays the other information regarding our country, but only if that information is available:

```
def __str__(self):
    label = self.name
    if self.population:
        label = f'{label}, population: {self.
population}'
    if self.size_kmsq:
        label = f'{label}, size_kmsq: {self.size_
kmsq}'
    return label
```

5. Create a new country and test the string method:

```
chad = Country(name='Chad', population=100)
print(chad)
```

The output is as follows:

```
Chad, population: 100
```

In this exercise, you learned how to add a string method to improve the string representation of objects when printed to the console.

Static methods

Static methods are similar to instance methods, except that they do not implicitly pass the positional `self` argument. Static methods aren't used as frequently as instance methods, so they only warrant a brief mention here. Static methods are defined using the `@staticmethod` decorator. Decorators allow us to alter the behavior of functions and classes.

Here is an example of a static method added to our `Pet` class:

```
class Pet:
    def __init__(self, height):
        self.height = height
```

```
    is_human = False
    owner = 'Michael Smith'

    @staticmethod
    def owned_by_smith_family():
        return 'Smith' in Pet.owner
nibbles = Pet(100)
nibbles.owned_by_smith_family()
```

You will get the following output:

```
True
```

The @staticmethod notation is how decorators are added to functions in Python. Technically, this is actually passing the owned_by_smith_family function to a higher-order function that alters its behavior. However, for now, just think of it as allowing us to avoid having the positional self argument. This method should not be written as an instance method, because it does not rely on any instance attributes of the Pet object – that is, the result will be the same for all pets created from the class. Of course, you could alternatively write this as a class attribute – that is, owned_by_smith_family = True.

However, generally, you prefer to avoid writing code that needs to be updated in two places when one piece of underlying information changes. If you changed the pet owner to Ming Xu, you would also need to remember to update the owned_by_smith_family attribute to False. The preceding implementation avoids this problem, as the owned_by_smith_family static method is a function of the current owner.

Exercise 78 – refactoring instance methods using a static method

Static methods are used to store utilities related to a class. In this exercise, you will create a Diary class and show how you can use a static method to apply the **DRY** principle (refer to *Chapter 3, Executing Python – Programs, Algorithms, and Functions*, which discussed *helper functions*) to refactor our code:

1. Create a simple Diary class that stores two dates:

    ```
    import datetime
    class Diary:
        def __init__(self, birthday, christmas):
            self.birthday = birthday
            self.christmas = christmas
    ```

2. Suppose you want to be able to view dates in a custom date format. Add two instance methods that print out the dates in the dd-mm-yy format:

```
def show_birthday(self):
    return self.birthday.strftime('%d-%b-%y')
def show_christmas(self):
    return self.christmas.strftime('%d-%b-%y')
```

3. Create a new `Diary` object and test one of the methods:

```
my_diary = Diary(datetime.date(2020, 5, 14), datetime.
date(2020, 12, 25))
my_diary.show_birthday()
```

The output will be as follows:

```
'14-May-20'
```

4. Imagine you had a more complex `Diary` class, where you needed to format dates in this custom manner throughout our code. You would have the `strftime('%d-%b-%y')` line appearing many times in your code. If someone came to you and asked you to update the display format throughout the entire code base, you would need to change the code in lots of places. Instead, you could create a `format_date` static method utility to store this logic once:

```
class Diary:
    def __init__(self, birthday, christmas):
        self.birthday = birthday
        self.christmas = christmas

    @staticmethod
    def format_date(date):
        return date.strftime('%d-%b-%y')

    def show_birthday(self):
        return self.format_date(self.birthday)
    def show_christmas(self):
        return self.format_date(self.christmas)
```

Now, if someone asks you to update the date format, there is a single location in the code that is your source of truth.

Class methods

The third type of method you will explore is class methods. Class methods are like instance methods, except that instead of the instance of an object being passed as the first positional `self` argument, the class itself is passed as the first argument. As with static methods, you use a decorator to designate a class method. For example, we can take our `Australian` class and add a class method:

```
class Australian:
    is_human = True
    enjoys_sport = True


    @classmethod
    def is_sporty_human(cls):
        return cls.is_human and cls.enjoys_sport
```

Note that the first positional argument of this method is `cls`, not `self`. You can call this method on the class itself:

```
Australian.is_sporty_human()
```

You will get the following output:

```
True
```

Alternatively, you can also call it on an instance of the class:

```
aussie = Australian()
aussie.is_sporty_human()
```

You will get the following output:

```
True
```

Another way class methods are used is to provide nice utilities for creating new instances.

For example, let's take our `Country` class, as defined earlier:

```
class Country:
    def __init__(self, name='Unspecified', population=None,
    size_kmsq=None):
        self.name = name
        self.population = population
        self.size_kmsq = size_kmsq
```

Suppose you want to avoid a situation where you create a country where people can specify the size in square miles rather than square kilometers. You could use a class method that takes the square mile input from the user and converts it into square kilometers, before initializing an instance of the class:

```python
@classmethod
def create_with_msq(cls, name, population, size_msq):
    size_kmsq = size_msq / 0.621371 ** 2
    return cls(name, population, size_kmsq)
```

Now, suppose that you want to create a `mexico` object and you know that it has an area of 760,000 square miles:

```python
mexico = Country.create_with_msq('Mexico', 150e6, 760000)
mexico.size_kmsq
```

The output is as follows:

```
1968392.1818017708
```

Exercise 79 – extending our Pet class with class methods

In this exercise, we will show two common uses of class methods in the context of our `Pet` class:

1. Start with the following definition of the `Pet` class:

    ```python
    class Pet:
        def __init__(self, height):
            self.height = height


        is_human = False
        owner = 'Michael Smith'
    ```

2. Add a class method that returns whether the pet is owned by a member of the `Smith` family:

    ```python
    @classmethod
    def owned_by_smith_family(cls):
        return 'Smith' in cls.owner
    ```

3. Now, suppose that you want a way of producing pets with various random heights. Perhaps you're performing some simulations regarding buying 100 pets, and you want to see what the average height might be. Firstly, import the `random` module:

    ```python
    import random
    ```

4. Next, add a class method that picks a random number from 0 to 100 and assigns it to the `height` property of a new pet:

```
@classmethod
def create_random_height_pet(cls):
    height = random.randrange(0, 100)
    return cls(height)
```

5. Lastly, you create 5 new pets and see what their heights are:

```
for I in range(5):
    pet = Pet.create_random_height_pet()
    print(pet.height)
```

The output is as follows:

```
99
61
26
92
53
```

In this exercise, you learned how class methods can be used to customize the creation of new objects and how to perform a basic calculation based on a class attribute.

> **Note**
>
> Your output may look different because these are random numbers between 0 and 100.

Properties

Properties are used to manage the attributes of objects. They are an important and powerful aspect of OOP but can be challenging to grasp at first. For example, suppose you have an object that has a `height` attribute and a `width` attribute. You might also want such an object to have an `area` property, which is simply the product of the `height` and `width` attributes. You would prefer not to save the area as an attribute of the shape because the area should update whenever the height or width changes. In this sort of scenario, you will want to use a property.

You will start by exploring the property decorator and then discuss the getter/setter paradigm.

The property decorator

The property decorator looks similar to the static methods and class methods that you have already encountered. It simply allows a method to be accessed as an attribute of an object, rather than it needing to be called like a function with ().

To understand the need for this decorator, consider the following class, which stores information about the temperature:

```
class Temperature:
    def __init__(self, celsius, fahrenheit):
        self.celsius = celsius
        self.fahrenheit = fahrenheit
```

Let's create a new temperature and check the fahrenheit attribute:

```
freezing = Temperature(0, 32)
freezing.fahrenheit
```

You will get the following output:

```
32
```

Now, suppose you decide it would be better to just store the temperature in Celsius and convert it to Fahrenheit when needed:

```
class Temperature:
    def __init__(self, celsius):
        self.celsius = celsius

    def fahrenheit(self):
        return self.celsius * 9 / 5 + 32
```

This is nicer because if the value of the temperature in Celsius is updated, you won't need to worry about updating fahrenheit as well:

```
my_temp = Temperature(0)
print(my_temp.fahrenheit())
my_temp.celsius = -10
print(my_temp.fahrenheit())
```

You will get the following output:

```
32.0
```

```
14.0
```

In the preceding code, you can see that you need to call the `fahrenheit` instance method with `()`, whereas when you were accessing the attribute before, no parentheses were necessary.

This could be a problem if the previous version of this code was being used elsewhere or by other people. All references to `fahrenheit` would have to have parentheses appended. Instead, you could turn `fahrenheit` into a property, which allows us to access it like an attribute, despite it being a method of the class. To do this, you simply add the `property` decorator:

```python
class Temperature:
    def __init__(self, celsius):
        self.celsius = celsius

    @property
    def fahrenheit(self):
        return self.celsius * 9 / 5 + 32
```

You can now access the `fahrenheit` property in the following manner:

```python
freezing = Temperature(100)
freezing.fahrenheit
```

The output will be as follows:

```
212.0
```

Exercise 80 – the full name property

The aim of this exercise is to use the property decorator to add object properties.

In this exercise, you create a `Person` class and learn how to use a property to display its full name:

1. Create a `Person` class with two instance attributes, the first and last names:

```python
class Person:
    def __init__(self, first_name, last_name):
        self.first_name = first_name
        self.last_name = last_name
```

2. Add a `full_name` property with the `@property` decorator:

```
@property
def full_name(self):
    return f'{self.first_name} {self.last_name}'
```

3. Create a `customer` object and test the `full_name` property:

```
customer = Person('Mar','Lo')
customer.full_name
```

You should get the following output:

```
'Mary Lo'
```

4. Suppose someone was using your code and decided to update the name of this customer in the following manner:

```
customer.full_name = 'Mary Schmid'
```

They would see the following error:

```
-------------------------------------------------------------------------
AttributeError                          Traceback (most recent call last)
<ipython-input-222-fef40f29f19e> in <module>
----> 1 customer.full_name = 'Mary Schmidt'

AttributeError: can't set attribute
```

Figure 5.10 – Trying to set a value of a property that doesn't support attribute setting

The following section introduces the concept of setters, which allow you to customize how input is handled when you try to assign attributes in this way.

The setter method

The `setter` method will be called whenever a user assigns a value to a property. This will allow us to write code so that a user doesn't need to think about which attributes of an object are stored as instance attributes, rather than computed by functions. Here is an example of what *Exercise 80 – the full name property* would look like if we added a full name setter:

```
class Person:
    def __init__(self, first_name, last_name):
        self.first_name = first_name
        self.last_name = last_name
```

```
@property
def full_name(self):
    return f'{self.first_name} {self.last_name}'

@full_name.setter
def full_name(self, name):
    first, last = name.split(' ')
    self.first_name = first
    self.last_name = last
```

Note the following conventions:

- The decorator should be the method name, followed by .setter
- It should take the value being assigned as a single argument (after self)
- The name of the setter method should be the same as the name of the property

Now you can create the same customer, but this time you can update their first and last names simultaneously by assigning a new value to the full_name property:

```
customer = Person('Mar','Lo')
customer.full_name = 'Mary Schmid'
customer.last_name
```

You should get the following output:

```
'Schmid'
```

Exercise 81 – writing a setter method

The aim of this exercise is to use a setter method to customize the way values are assigned to properties.

You will extend the Temperature class by allowing a user to assign a new value for fahrenheit directly to the property:

1. Let's start with the Temperature class from earlier:

```
class Temperature:
    def __init__(self, celsius):
        self.celsius = celsius
```

```
@property
def fahrenheit(self):
    return self.celsius * 9 / 5 + 32
```

2. Add an `@fahrenheit.setter` function that converts the `fahrenheit` value to Celsius and stores it in the `celsius` instance attribute:

```
@fahrenheit.setter
def fahrenheit(self, value):
    self.celsius = (value-- 32) * 5 / 9
```

3. Create a new temperature and check the `fahrenheit` property:

```
temp = Temperature(5)
temp.fahrenheit
```

The output is as follows:

```
41.0
```

4. Update the `fahrenheit` property and check the `celsius` attribute:

```
temp.fahrenheit = 32
temp.celsius
```

The output is as follows:

```
0.0
```

In this exercise, you wrote your first setter method, allowing you to customize how values are set to properties.

Validation via the setter method

Another common use of the setter method is to prevent a user from setting values that shouldn't be allowed. If you consider our previous example with the `Temperature` class, the minimum temperature theoretically possible is approximately -460 degrees Fahrenheit. It seems prudent to prevent people from creating temperatures that are lower than this value. You can update the setter method from the previous exercise as follows:

```
@fahrenheit.setter
def fahrenheit(self, value):
    if value < -460:
        raise ValueError('Temperatures less than -460F are
not possible')
    self.celsius = (value-- 32) * 5 / 9
```

Now, if the user attempts to update the temperature to an impossible value, the code will throw an exception:

```
temp = Temperature(5)
temp.fahrenheit = -500
```

You should get the following output:

```
---------------------------------------------------------------------
ValueError                                 Traceback (most recent call last)
<ipython-input-112-a59047203345> in <module>
      1 temp = Temperature(5)
----> 2 temp.fahrenheit = -500

<ipython-input-108-256b69371a35> in fahrenheit(self, value)
     10     def fahrenheit(self, value):
     11         if value < -460:
---> 12             raise ValueError('Temperatures less than -460F are not poss
ible')
     13         self.celcius = (value - 32) * 5 / 9

ValueError: Temperatures less than -460F are not possible
```

Figure 5.11 – Demonstrating validation as part of the setter property

We will now move on to our last topic of the chapter.

Inheritance

Class inheritance allows attributes and methods to be passed from one class to another. For example, suppose there is already a class available in a Python package that does almost everything you want. However, you just wish it had one extra method or attribute that would make it right for your purpose. Instead of rewriting the entire class, you could inherit the class and add additional properties, or change existing properties.

The DRY principle revisited

Remember the DRY principle: "*Every piece of knowledge or logic must have a single, unambiguous representation within a system.*" So far in this chapter, we have seen how classes allow us to more elegantly encapsulate logic about what objects represent. This has already moved us further along the path to writing clean, modularized code. Inheritance is the next step in this journey. Suppose we wanted to create two classes, one representing cats and the other, dogs.

Our `Cat` class may look like this:

```
class Cat:
    is_feline = True

    def __init__(self, name, weight):
        self.name = name
        self.weight = weight
```

Similarly, our `Dog` class would look the same, except that it would have a different value for the `is_feline` class attribute:

```
class Dog:
    is_feline = False

    def __init__(self, name, weight):
        self.name = name
        self.weight = weight
```

You can probably already see that this is a violation of the DRY principle. A lot of the preceding code is identical in the two classes. However, suppose that, in our program, cats and dogs are sufficiently different to require separate class definitions. You need a way to capture the common information about cats and dogs, without repeating it in both class definitions — enter inheritance.

Single inheritance

Single inheritance, also known as subclassing, involves creating a child class that inherits the attributes and methods of a single parent class. Taking the preceding example of cats and dogs, we can instead create a `Pet` class that represents all the common parts of the `Cat` and `Dog` classes:

```
class Pet:
    def __init__(self, name, weight):
        self.name = name
        self.weight = weight
```

The `Cat` and `Dog` classes can now be created by subclassing the parent class, `Pet`:

```
class Cat(Pet):
    is_feline = True
```

```
class Dog(Pet):
    is_feline = False
```

You can check whether this is working as expected:

```
my_cat = Cat('Kibbles', 8)
my_cat.name
```

You will get the following output:

```
'Kibbles'
```

Now, the logic in the init method is specified only once, and our Cat and Dog classes simply inherit it from the parent class, Pet. Now, if you decide to change the logic in the init method, you don't need to change it in two places, making our code easier to maintain. Likewise, it will be easier in the future to create different types of Pet classes. Additionally, you could create further subclasses of the Dog class if you wanted to create different types of Dog classes, depending on breed. You can show the structure of our classes as a hierarchy, much like a family tree:

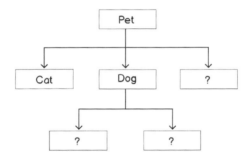

Figure 5.12 – Class inheritance

Exercise 82 – inheriting from the Person class

The goal of this exercise is to see how methods and attributes are inherited by child classes from parent classes.

In this exercise, you will create a Baby class and an Adult class, which will both inherit from a common Person class:

1. Start with the following Person class definition, which takes first and last names as inputs in the init function:

    ```
    class Person:
        def __init__(self, first_name, last_name):
    ```

```
                self.first_name = first_name
                self.last_name = last_name
```

2. Create a `Baby` class that inherits from `Person`, and add a `speak` instance method:

```
class Baby(Person):
    def speak(self):
        print('Blah blah blah')
```

3. Do the same for an `Adult` class:

```
class Adult(Person):
    def speak(self):
        print('Hello, my name is %s' % self.first_name)
```

4. Create a `Baby` and an `Adult` object, and make them speak:

```
jess = Baby('Jessie', 'Mcdonald')
tom = Adult('Thomas', 'Smith')
jess.speak()
tom.speak()
```

You will get the following output:

```
Blah blah blah
Hello, my name is Thomas
```

Figure 5.13 – Our baby and adult speaking

In this exercise, you learned how to inherit attributes and methods between classes.

Subclassing classes from Python packages

In our examples so far, you have written the parent class ourselves. However, often, the reason for subclassing is that a class already exists in a third-party package, and you just want to extend the functionality of that class with a few custom methods.

For example, suppose you wanted to have an integer object where you could check whether it was divisible by another number. You could create your own integer class and add a custom instance method, as follows:

```
class MyInt(int):
    def is_divisible_by(self, x):
        return self % x == 0
```

You could then use this class to create integer objects that have this useful method:

```
a = MyInt(8)
a.is_divisible_by(2)
```

The output is as follows:

```
True
```

Exercise 83 – subclassing the datetime.date class

The aim of this exercise is to show how you can inherit from classes in external libraries.

In this exercise, you create your own custom date class by inheriting from the datetime module. You add our own custom method that allows you to increment the date by a given number of days:

1. Import the datetime module:

    ```
    import datetime
    ```

2. Create a MyDate class that inherits from datetime.date. Create an add_days instance method that uses a timedelta object to increment the date:

    ```
    class MyDate(datetime.date):
        def add_days(self, n):
            return self + datetime.timedelta(n)
    ```

3. Create a new object using the MyDate class, and try out your custom add_days method:

    ```
    d = MyDate(2019, 12, 1)
    print(d.add_days(40))
    print(d.add_days(400))
    ```

    You should get the following output:

    ```
    2020-01-10
    2021-01-04
    ```

    Figure 5.14 – Adding days to a date

In this exercise, you learned how to inherit from classes in external libraries. This will often be useful, as external libraries may get you 90% of the way to solving the problem, but they're rarely built exactly for your own use case.

Overriding methods

When inheriting classes, you often do so in order to change the behavior of a class, not just to extend the behavior. The custom methods or attributes you create on a child class can be used to override the method or attribute that was inherited from the parent.

For example, suppose the following `Person` class was provided by a third-party library:

```python
class Person:
    def __init__(self, first_name, last_name):
        self.first_name = first_name
        self.last_name = last_name

    @property
    def full_name(self):
        return f'{self.first_name} {self.last_name}'

    @full_name.setter
    def full_name(self, name):
        first, last = name.split(' ')
        self.first_name = first
        self.last_name = last
```

Perhaps you are using this class but have problems when setting the names of people whose full names consist of three parts:

```python
my_person = Person('Mary', 'Smith')
my_person.full_name = 'Mary Anne Smith'
```

You will get the following output:

```
--------------------------------------------------------------------
ValueError                                Traceback (most recent call last)
<ipython-input-146-9604ddbc3006> in <module>
      1 my_person = Person('Mary', 'Smith')
----> 2 my_person.full_name = 'Mary Anne Smith'

<ipython-input-142-a8f3417079a7> in full_name(self, name)
     10     @full_name.setter
     11     def full_name(self, name):
---> 12         first, last = name.split(' ')
     13         self.first_name = first
     14         self.last_name = last

ValueError: too many values to unpack (expected 2)
```

Figure 5.15 – Failing to set a property

Suppose that in cases where there are three or more names that make up a full name, you want to assign the first part of the name to the first_name attribute and the rest of the names to the last_name attribute. You could subclass Person and override the method, as follows:

1. Start by creating a BetterPerson class that inherits from Person:

    ```
    class BetterPerson(Person):
    ```

2. Add a full name property that combines the first and last names:

    ```
    @property
    def full_name(self):
        return f'{self.first_name} {self.last_name}'
    ```

3. Add full_name.setter to first split the full name into its components, then set the first name equal to the first part of the name, and set the last name equal to the second part of the name. The code also deals with cases where there are more than two components to the name, and it puts everything except the first name into the last name:

    ```
    @full_name.setter
    def full_name(self, name):
        names = name.split(' ')
        self.first_name = names[0]
        if len(names) > 2:
            self.last_name = ' '.join(names[1:])
        elif len(names) == 2:
            self.last_name = names[1]
    ```

4. Now, create a BetterPerson instance and see it in action:

    ```
    my_person = BetterPerson('Mary', 'Smith')
    my_person.full_name = 'Mary Anne Smith'
    print(my_person.first_name)
    print(my_person.last_name)
    ```

    The output is as follows:

    ```
    Mary
    Anne Smith
    ```

Calling the parent method with super()

Suppose the parent class has a method that is almost what you want it to be, but you need to make a small alteration to the logic. If you override the method as you did previously, you'll need to specify the entire logic of the method again, which may become a violation of the DRY principle. When building an application, you often require code from third-party libraries, and some of this code can be quite complex. If a certain method has 100 lines of code, you wouldn't want to include all that code in your repository in order to simply change one of those lines.

For example, suppose you have the following Person class:

```python
class Person:
    def __init__(self, first_name, last_name):
        self.first_name = first_name
        self.last_name = last_name

    def speak(self):
        print('Hello, my name is', self.first_name)
```

Now, suppose you want to create a subclass to make the person say more things in the speak method. One option would be to do so as follows:

```python
class TalkativePerson(Person):
    def speak(self):
        print('Hello, my name is', self.first_name)
        print('It is a pleasure to meet you!')
john = TalkativePerson('John', 'Tomic')
john.speak()
```

The output will be as follows:

```
Hello, my name is John
It is a pleasure to meet you!
```

Figure 5.16 – Our talkative person speaking

This implementation is okay, though it isn't ideal that you've copied the Hello, my name is John line from the Person class. All you wanted to do was add additional things for TalkativePerson to say; you didn't need to change the way they say their name. Perhaps the Person class will be updated in the future to say something slightly different, and you want the TalkativePerson class to also reflect those changes. This is where the super() method comes in handy. super() allows you to access the parent class without explicitly referring to it by name. In the preceding example, you can use super() as follows:

```
class TalkativePerson(Person):
    def speak(self):
        super().speak()
        print('It is a pleasure to meet you!')
john = TalkativePerson('John', 'Tomic')
john.speak()
```

You will get the following output:

```
Hello, my name is John
It is a pleasure to meet you!
```

Figure 5.17 – Using the super() method to write cleaner code

The super() method allows you to access the parent class, Person, and call the corresponding speak method. Now, if any updates were made to the Person class's speak method, it would be reflected in what our TalkativePerson says as well.

Exercise 84 – overriding methods using super()

The aim of this exercise is to learn how to override methods using the super function. We will subclass our previously created Diary class and show how super can be used to modify the behavior of a class without unnecessarily repeating code:

1. Import the datetime module:

```
import datetime
```

2. Start with the Diary class, as defined previously:

```
class Diary:
    def __init__(self, birthday, christmas):
        self.birthday = birthday
        self.christmas = christmas

    @staticmethod
    def format_date(date):
    return date.strftime('%d-%b-%y')
```

```
        def show_birthday(self):
            return self.format_date(self.birthday)
        def show_christmas(self):
            return self.format_date(self.christmas)
```

3. Suppose you're unhappy with the fact that the hardcoded date time format is in the `format_`
    `date` method, and you would prefer a custom format that could be specified for each `diary`
    object separately. One temptation would be to simply copy the whole class and start making
    modifications. However, when dealing with more complex classes, this is almost never a good
    option. Instead, let's subclass `Diary` and start by allowing it to be initialized with a custom
    `date_format` string:

```
    class CustomDiary(Diary):
        def __init__(self, birthday, christmas, date_format):
            self.date_format = date_format
            super().__init__(birthday, christmas)
```

4. You also want to override the `format_date` method to use your new `date_format` attribute:

```
        def format_date(self, date):
            return date.strftime(self.date_format)
```

5. Now, when you create `diary` objects, each object can have a different string representation
    of the dates:

```
    first_diary = CustomDiary(datetime.date(2018,1,1),
    datetime.date(2018,3,3), '%d-%b-%Y')
    second_diary = CustomDiary(datetime.date(2018,1,1),
    datetime.date(2018,3,3), '%d/%m/%Y')
    print(first_diary.show_birthday())
    print(second_diary.show_christmas())
```

You will get the following output:

```
01-Jan-2018
03/03/2018
```

Figure 5.18 – Viewing our diary dates

In this exercise, you learned how to override methods using the `super` function. This allows you to
more carefully override methods in the parent classes you inherit from.

Multiple inheritances

You often think of inheritance as allowing us to reuse common methods and attributes between related child classes. For example, a typical class structure could look like this:

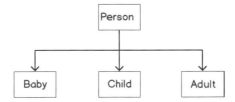

Figure 5.19 – Single inheritance

Each child class inherits from a single parent class, `Person`.

However, it's also possible to inherit from more than one parent class. Often, there are elements of multiple classes that you want to combine to create a new class. For example, you might combine an `Adult` class with a `Calendar` class to make an `OrganizedAdult` class:

Figure 5.20 – Multiple inheritance

Exercise 85 – creating a consultation appointment system

Suppose you are running a hospital and building a consultation appointment system. You want to be able to schedule appointments for various types of patients.

In this exercise, you will start with the previously defined `Adult` and `Baby` classes and create `OrganizedAdult` and `OrganizedBaby` classes by inheriting from a second parent class, `Calendar`:

1. Import the `datetime` module:

    ```
    import datetime
    ```

2. Start with the Baby and Adult classes, as defined previously:

```python
class Person:
    def __init__(self, first_name, last_name):
        self.first_name = first_name
        self.last_name = last_name
class Baby(Person):
    def speak(self):
        print('Blah blah blah')
class Adult(Person):
    def speak(self):
        print('Hello, my name is', self.first_name)
```

3. Create a Calendar class that you can use to help the adults and babies become more organized:

```python
class Calendar:
    def book_appointment(self, date):
        print('Booking appointment for date', date)
```

4. Create OrganizedBaby and OrganizedAdult classes that inherit from multiple parent classes:

```python
class OrganizedAdult(Adult, Calendar):
    pass
class OrganizedBaby(Baby, Calendar):
    pass
```

> **Note**
> If you want to define a class without adding or customizing its methods/attributes, you simply write pass.

5. Create some objects from your new classes and test their methods:

```python
andres = OrganizedAdult('Andres', 'Gomez')
boris = OrganizedBaby('Boris', 'Bumblebutton')
andres.speak()
boris.speak()
boris.book_appointment(datetime.date(2018,1,1))
```

The output is as follows:

```
Hello, my name is Andres
Blah blah blah
Booking appointment for date 2018-01-01
```

Figure 5.21 – Booking an appointment

6. Suppose you wanted to warn a user when they try to book an appointment with a baby. You could override the book_appointment method, using the super() method, to run the book_appointment method on the Calendar class:

```
class OrganizedBaby(Baby, Calendar):
    def book_appointment(self, date):
        print('Note that you are booking an appointment
with a baby.')
        super().book_appointment(date)
```

7. Now, test whether it works:

```
boris = OrganizedBaby('Boris', 'Bumblebutton')
boris.book_appointment(datetime.date(2018,1,1))
```

The output is as follows:

```
Note that you are booking an appointment with a baby.
Booking appointment for date 2018-01-01
```

Figure 5.22 – Booking an appointment with a baby

Note that it's not always necessary to use inheritance when building your classes. If you only have one child class, having a parent class is often unnecessary. In fact, your code may be more readable if it's all stored in one class. Sometimes, the job of a good programmer is to consider the future and answer the question, *"Will it become useful at some point to have built this with multiple inherited classes?"* Answering this question simply becomes easier with experience.

Method resolution order

Suppose you were inheriting from two parent classes, both of which have a method of the same name. Which would be used when calling the method on the child class? Which would be used when calling it via super()? You should find this out through an example. Suppose you have Dog and Cat classes, and you combine them to make a monstrosity, DogCat:

```python
class Dog:
    def make_sound(self):
        print('Woof!')

class Cat:
    def make_sound(self):
        print('Miaw!')
class DogCat(Dog, Cat):
    pass
```

What sort of sounds would such a creature make?

```python
my_pet = DogCat()
my_pet.make_sound()
```

You will get the following output:

```
Woof!
```

So, you can see that Python first checks for the existence of the make_sound method on the Dog class, and since it is implemented, you don't end up calling the make_sound method of the Cat class. Simply, Python reads from left to right in the list of classes. If you switched the order of Dog and Cat, our DogCat would miaw:

```python
class DogCat(Cat, Dog):
    pass
my_pet = DogCat()
my_pet.make_sound()
```

You should get the following output:

```
Miaw!
```

Suppose you wanted to override the method on DogCat and use the super() method. The same method resolution order would apply:

```
class DogCat(Dog, Cat):
    def make_sound(self):
        for i in range(3):
            super().make_sound()
my_pet = DogCat()
my_pet.make_sound()
```

You will get the following output:

```
Woof!

Woof!

Woof!
```

Activity 14 – creating classes and inheriting from a parent class

Suppose you are writing a computer game where the graphics are made up of various types of shapes. Each shape has certain properties, such as the number of edges, area, and color. The shapes also behave in different ways. You want to be able to customize the way each shape behaves independently, while also not duplicating any code between the definition of each shape.

The aim of this activity is to create classes that can be used to represent a rectangle and a square. These two classes will inherit from a parent class called Polygon. The Rectangle and Square classes will have a property for computing the number of sides, the perimeter, and the area of the shape. Let's see the steps:

1. Add a num_sides property to the Polygon class that returns the number of sides.

2. Add a perimeter property to the Polygon class.

3. Add docstring to the Polygon class.

4. Add a __str__ method to the Polygon class that represents the polygon as "*polygon with X sides*," where X is the actual number of sides of the Polygon instance.

5. Create a child class called Rectangle, which accepts two arguments from the user in the init method: height and width.

6. Add an area property to Rectangle.

7. Create a Rectangle object and check the computation of the area and perimeter.

    You will get the following output:

    ```
    (5, 12)
    ```

8. Create a child class called `Square` that inherits from `Rectangle`. You should only take one argument from the user when initializing a square.

9. Create a `Square` object and check the computation of the area and perimeter. You will get the following output:

```
(25, 20)
```

> **Note**
>
> The solution for this activity can be found in *Appendix* on GitHub.

Summary

In this chapter, you have begun your journey into a cornerstone of OOP – classes. You learned how classes allow you to write more elegant, reusable, and DRY code. You learned about the importance of and distinction between class and instance attributes, and how to set them in class definition. You also explored various types of methods and when to use them. You explored the concept of a property and the Pythonic implementation of getters and setters. Lastly, you learned how to share methods and attributes between classes via single and multiple inheritance.

In the next chapter, you will explore the Python standard library and the various tools you can avail yourself of before needing to turn to third-party modules.

6

The Standard Library

Overview

By the end of this chapter, you will be able to utilize Python's Standard Library to write efficient code, create and manipulate files by interacting with the OS filesystem, evaluate dates and times efficiently without falling into the most common mistakes, and set up applications with logs to facilitate future troubleshooting.

Introduction

In the previous chapters, you saw how we can create our own classes by incorporating logic and data. Yet, you often don't need to do that—you can rely on the Standard Library's functions and classes to do most of the work.

The Python Standard Library consists of modules that are available on all implementations of the language. Every Python installation will have access to these without the need for any further steps for the modules defined in the Standard Library.

While other famous languages don't have a standard library, others have what seems to be an extensive set of tooling and functionality. Python goes a step further by including a vast number of basic utilities and protocol implementations as part of the default installation of the interpreter.

Standard libraries are useful and perform tasks such as unzipping files, speaking with other processes and the OS on your computer, processing HTML, and even printing graphics on the screen. A program that sorts a list of music files according to their artists can be written in a few lines when you use the correct modules of the Standard Library.

In this chapter, you will look at the importance of the Standard Library and how it can be used in our code to write faster and better Python with fewer keystrokes. You will walk through a subset of the modules, covering them in detail on a user level.

We will be covering the following topics in detail:

- The importance of the Standard Library
- Working with dates and times
- Interacting with the OS
- Using the `subprocess` module
- Logging in Python
- Using collections in Python
- Using `functools`

Technical requirements

The code files for this chapter are available on GitHub at `https://github.com/PacktPublishing/The-Python-Workshop-Second-Edition/tree/main/Chapter06`.

The importance of the Standard Library

Python is often described as coming with *batteries included*, which is usually a reference to its Standard Library. The Python Standard Library is vast, unlike any other language in the tech world. The Python Standard Library includes modules to connect to a socket; that is, one to send emails, one to connect to SQLite, one to work with the locale module, or one to encode and decode JSON and XML.

It is also renowned for including modules such as `turtle` and `tkinter`, graphical interfaces that most users probably don't use anymore, but they have proven useful when Python is taught in schools and universities.

It even includes **Integrated Development and Learning Environment** (**IDLE**), a Python-integrated development environment. It is not widely used as there are either other packages within the Standard Library that are used more often or external tools to substitute them. These libraries are divided into high-level modules and lower-level modules:

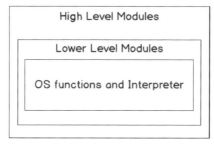

Figure 6.1 – Graphical representation of the types of standard libraries

Let's discuss each in detail.

High-level modules

The Python Standard Library is truly vast and diverse, providing a *toolbelt* for the user that can be used to write most of their trivial programs. You can open an interpreter and run the following code snippet to print graphics on the screen. This can be executed on the Python terminal:

```
>>> from turtle import Turtle, done
>>> turtle = Turtle()
>>> turtle.right(180)
>>> turtle.forward(100)
>>> turtle.right(90)
>>> turtle.forward(50)
>>> done()
```

This code uses the `turtle` module, which can be used to print the output on the screen, as shown in *Figure 6.2*:

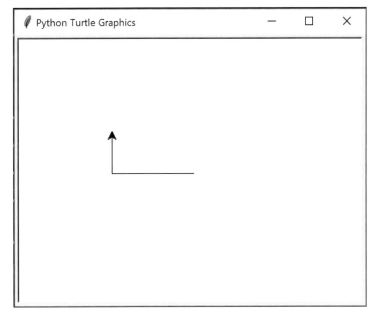

Figure 6.2 – Example of output screen when using turtle

This output will look like the trail of a turtle that follows when the cursor is moved. The `turtle` module allows the user to interact with the cursor and leave a trail as it keeps moving. It has functions to move around the screen and print as it advances.

Here is a detailed explanation of the `turtle` module code snippet:

1. It creates a turtle in the middle of the screen.

2. It then rotates it 180 degrees to the right.

3. It moves forward 100 pixels, painting as it walks.

4. It then rotates to the right once again, this time by 90 degrees.

5. It then moves forward 50 pixels once again.

6. It ends the program using `done()`.

You can go ahead and explore and input different values, playing around a bit with the `turtle` module and checking the different outputs you get, before you dive further into this chapter.

The `turtle` module you worked on is an example of one of the high-level modules that the Standard Library offers.

Other examples of high-level modules include the following:

- `difflib`: To check the differences line by line across two blocks of text

- `re`: For regular expressions, which will be covered in *Chapter 7, Becoming Pythonic*

- `sqlite3`: To create and interact with SQLite databases

- Multiple data compressing and archiving modules, such as `gzip`, `zipfile`, and `tarfile`

- `xml`, `json`, `csv`, and `config` parser: For working with multiple file formats

- `sched`: To schedule events in the Standard Library

- `argparse`: For the straightforward creation of command-line interfaces

Now, you will use another high-level module, `argparse`, as an example and see how it can be used to create a command-line interface that echoes words passed in and, optionally, capitalizes them in a few lines of code. This can be executed in the Python terminal:

```python
import argparse
parser = argparse.ArgumentParser()
parser.add_argument("message", help="Message to be echoed")
parser.add_argument("-c", "--capitalize", action="store_true")
args = parser.parse_args()
if args.capitalize:
        print(args.message.capitalize())
    else:
        print(args.message)
```

This code example creates an instance of the `ArgumentParser` class, which helps you to create command-line interface applications.

It then defines two arguments, as shown in the highlighted lines (using `parser.add_argument`: `message` and `capitalize`).

Note that `capitalize` can also be referred to as `-c`, and we make it a Boolean flag option by changing the default action to `store_true`. At that point, you can just call `parse_args`, which will take the arguments passed in the command line, validate them, and expose them as attributes of `args`.

The code then takes the input message and chooses whether to capitalize it based on the flag.

You can now interact with this file, named `echo.py`, as shown in the output in *Figure 6.3*:

```
mcorcherojim at PF11AY8S in ~
$ python3.7 echo.py --help
usage: echo.py [-h] [-c] message

positional arguments:
  message            Message to be echoed

optional arguments:
  -h, --help         show this help message and exit
  -c, --capitalize
mcorcherojim at PF11AY8S in ~
$ python3.7 echo.py hello --capitalize
Hello
```

Figure 6.3 – Example help message of an argparse script

> **Note**
>
> We will be using this capitalize tool in *Exercise 87 – extending the echo.py example.*

Lower-level modules

The Standard Library also contains multiple lower-level modules that users rarely interact with. These lower-level modules are outside that of the Standard Library. Good examples are the different internet protocol modules, text formatting and templating, interacting with C code, testing, serving HTTP sites, and so on. The Standard Library comes with low-level modules to satisfy the needs of users in many of those scenarios, but you will usually see Python developers relying on libraries such as `jinja2`, `requests`, `flask`, `cython`, and `cffi` that are built on top of the low-level Standard Library module as they provide a nicer, simpler, more powerful interface. It is not that you cannot create an extension with the C API or `ctypes`, but `cython` allows you to remove a lot of the boilerplate, whereas the Standard Library requires you to write and optimize the most common scenarios.

Finally, there is another type of low-level module, which extends or simplifies the language. Notable examples of these are the following:

- `asyncio`: To write asynchronous code

- `typing`: To type hint

- `contextvar`: To save state based on the context

- `contextlib`: To help with the creation of context managers

- `doctest`: To verify code examples in documentation and docstrings

- `pdb` and `bdb`: To access debugging tools

There are also modules such as `dis`, `ast`, and `code` that allow the developer to inspect, interact, and manipulate the Python interpreter and the runtime environment, but those aren't required by most beginner and intermediate developers.

Knowing how to navigate the Standard Library

Getting to know the Standard Library is key for any intermediate/advanced developer, even if you don't know how to use all the modules. Knowing what the library contains and when modules can be used provides any developer with a boost in speed and quality when developing Python applications.

> **Note**
>
> Once Python beginners master the basic syntax of the language, they are usually encouraged to take the Standard Library tour in the Python documentation (`https://docs.python.org/3/tutorial/stdlib.html`).

While developers from other languages may try to implement everything on their own from scratch, experienced Python programmers will always first ask themselves, "*How can I do this with the Standard Library?*", since using the code in the Standard Library brings multiple benefits, which will be explained later in the chapter.

The Standard Library makes code simpler and easier to understand. By using modules such as `dataclasses`, you can write code that would otherwise take hundreds of lines to create by yourself and would most likely include bugs.

The `dataclass` module allows you to create value semantic types with fewer keystrokes by providing a decorator that can be used in a class, which will generate all the required boilerplate to have a class with the most common methods.

> **Note**
>
> Value semantic types represent the classes of the data that they hold. Objects can be easily copied by attributes and printed, and can then be compared using these attributes.

Exercise 86 – using the dataclass module

In this exercise, you will create a class to hold data for a geographical point. This is a simple structure with two coordinates, x and y.

These coordinate points, x and y, are used by other developers who need to store geographical information. They will be working daily with these points, so they need to be able to create them with an easy constructor and be able to print them and see their values—converting them into a dictionary to save them into their database and share it with other people.

This exercise can be performed in the Jupyter notebook:

1. Import the dataclass module:

   ```
   import dataclasses
   ```

   This line brings the dataclasses module to the local namespace, allowing us to use it.

2. Define dataclass:

   ```
   @dataclasses.dataclass
   class Point:
       x: int
       y: int
   ```

   With these four lines, you have defined dataclass by its most common methods. You can now see how it behaves differently from a standard class.

3. Create an instance, which is the data for a geographical point:

   ```
   p = Point(x=10, y=20)
   print(p)
   ```

   The output will be as follows:

   ```
   Point(x=10, y=20)
   ```

4. Now, compare the data points with another Point object:

   ```
   p2 = Point(x=10, y=20)
   p == p2
   ```

The output will be as follows:

```
True
```

5.   Serialize the data:

```
dataclasses.asdict(p)
```

The output will be as follows:

```
{'x': 10, 'y': 20}
```

You now know how to use data classes to create value semantic types!

> **Note**
>
> Even if developers might be tempted to implement methods by themselves because they seem trivial, there are many edge cases that modules such as dataclass already take account of, such as what happens if __eq__ receives an object of a different type or a subclass of it.

The dataclasses module is part of the Standard Library, so most experienced users will understand how a class decorated with a dataclass decorator will behave compared to a custom implementation of those methods. This would require either further documentation to be written, or for users to fully understand all the code in all classes that are manually crafting those methods.

Moreover, using the battle-tested code that the Standard Library provides is also key to writing an efficient and robust application. Functions such as sort in Python use a custom sorting algorithm known as timsort. This is a hybrid stable sorting algorithm derived from merge sort and insertion sort, and will usually result in better performance results and fewer bugs than any algorithm that a user could implement in a limited amount of time.

Exercise 87 – extending the echo.py example

In this exercise, you will be using the previously mentioned capitalize tool with help messages and a variable number of arguments.

After the creation of the capitalize tool that you saw earlier in this topic, you can implement an enhanced version of the echo tool in Linux, which is used in some embedded systems that have Python. You will use the previous code for capitalize and enhance it to have a nicer description. This will allow the echo command to repeat the word passed in and to take more than one word.

When you execute the code, it should generate the following `help` message:

```
mariocj89 at DESKTOP-9B6VH3A in ~/workspace
$ python3.7 echo.py -h
usage: echo.py [-h] [-c] [--repeat REPEAT] message [message ...]

Prints out the words passed in, capitalizes them if required and repeat them
in as many lines as requested.

positional arguments:
  message              Messages to be echoed

optional arguments:
  -h, --help           show this help message and exit
  -c, --capitalize
  --repeat REPEAT
```

Figure 6.4 – Expected output from the help command

It should produce the following output when running with these arguments:

```
mariocj89 at DESKTOP-9B6VH3A in ~/workspace
$ python3.7 echo.py hello packt reader --repeat=3 -c
Hello Packt Reader
Hello Packt Reader
Hello Packt Reader
```

Figure 6.5 – Expected output of running the Exercise 87 script

Let's resolve the steps for this exercise:

1. The first step is to add a description to the `echo` command. We will start by adding a description to the `echo.py` script command. You can do so by passing it as an argument to the `ArgumentParser` class:

    ```
    parser = argparse.ArgumentParser(description="""
    Prints out the words passed in, capitalizes them if
    required
    and repeats them in as many lines as requested.
    """)
    ```

    The description passed in as an argument of the `ArgumentParser` class will be used as the `help` message when the user either runs the tools incorrectly or asks for help on how to use the tool.

> **Note**
> Notice how you can split the description into multiple lines to easily format our code, but the output appears as if all lines were together.

2. The next step is to allow multiple messages rather than a single message. You can do so by using the `nargs` keyword argument when adding a positional parameter:

```
parser.add_argument("message", help="Messages to be
echoed", nargs="+")
```

By passing `nargs="+"`, you tell `argparse` that we require at least one `message` to be passed in. Other options include ? for optional, and * for 0 or more. You can also use any natural number to require a specific number of parameters.

3. Finally, you need to add a new option with a default value to control the number of times the message is repeated. We will do so by adding a `repeat` flag with a `default` value:

```
parser.add_argument("-repeat", type=int, default=1)
```

This adds a new option, `repeat`, which allows us to pass an integer that defaults to 1, and that will control the number of times the words are repeated.

> **Note**
> Notice how you pass a type, which is just a callable. This will be used to transform and validate the argument passed in, and you indicate what the default value is if a user does not specify the option. Alternatively, you could have marked it as `required=True` to force the user to always pass a value.

Altogether, the code and implementation will be as shown in the following code snippet:

```
import argparse
parser = argparse.ArgumentParser(description="""
Prints out the words passed in, capitalizes them if
required
and repeat them in as many lines as requested.
""")
parser.add_argument("message", help="Messages to be
echoed", nargs="+")
parser.add_argument("-c", "--capitalize", action="store_
true")
parser.add_argument("--repeat", type=int, default=1)
args = parser.parse_args()
if args.capitalize:
```

```
        messages = [m.capitalize() for m in args.message]
    else:
        messages = args.message
    for _ in range(args.repeat):
        print(" ".join(messages))
```

You just created a CLI application that allows you to echo messages with an intuitive interface. You can now use the `argparse` module to create any other CLI application.

Quite often, the Standard Library in Python has answers to developers' most common questions. By having a general knowledge of the different modules in Python and always questioning what can be used from the Standard Library, you will write better Python code that uses easy-to-read, well-tested, and efficient utilities.

Working with dates and times

Many programs will need to deal with dates and times, and Python comes with multiple modules to help you handle those effectively. The most common module is the `datetime` module. The `datetime` module comes with three types that can be used to represent dates, times, and timestamps. There are also other modules, such as the `time` module or the `calendar` module, which can be used for some other use cases.

`datetime.date` can be used to represent any date between the years 1 and 9999. For any date/time outside of this range, you would need to use more specialized libraries, such as the `astropy` library.

You can create a `datetime.date` object by passing the year, month, and day, or get today by just calling `datetime.date.today()`:

```
import datetime
datetime.date.today()
```

The output is as follows:

datetime.date(2019, 4, 20)

Figure 6.6 – Representation of a date object

The output format for `time` is similar; it takes the hour, minute, second, and microsecond. All of them are optional and are initialized at 0 if not provided. This can also be created with `tzinfo`, but you will see more about that attribute in the `datetime.datetime` section.

Within the datetime module, you have what is probably the most frequently used class, the datetime.datetime class. It can represent a combination of a date and a time, and it actually inherits from datetime.date. But before you start to explore the datetime class within the datetime module, you need to better understand the concept of time and how you represent it.

There are usually two kinds of **time** that you need to represent. They are commonly referred to as timestamps and wall time.

The first, timestamps, can be seen as a unique point in time independent of any human interpretation of it. It is an absolute point in the line of time that is not relative to any geographical location or country. This is used for astronomical events, log records, and the synchronization of machines, among other things.

The second, wall time, refers to the time *on the wall* at a specific location. This is the time humans use, and you synchronize your time using it. This time is the "legal" time as it is dictated by the country and is related to a time zone. This is used for meetings, flight schedules, working hours, and so on. The interval of time can change at any point due to legislation. As an example, think of countries that observe **daylight saving time (DST)** and change their standard clock accordingly.

> **Note**
> If you need to work extensively with time, it is important to read about UTC and the history of how you measure time to avoid more complex issues, but you will go through a quick overview of good practices when handling time in this topic to avoid the most common mistakes.

When you are working with wall time, you just need to treat datetime.datetime objects as a mere combination of a date and a time at a location. But you should usually attach a time zone to it to be more precise and get proper semantics for time comparison and basic arithmetic. The two most commonly used libraries to handle time zones are pytz and dateutil.

You must use dateutil when using wall times; pytz has a time model that will lead the inexperienced user to make mistakes more often than not. To create a datetime with a time zone, you just need to pass it through the tzinfo argument:

```
import datetime
from dateutil import tz
datetime.datetime(1989, 4, 24, 10, 11,
                       tzinfo=tz.gettz("Europe/Madrid"))
```

This creates a datetime with that time zone information attached.

Exercise 88 – comparing datetime across time zones

The goal of this exercise is to create two different `datetime` instances and compare them when they are in different time zones:

1. Import the `datetime` and `tz` modules from `dateutil`:

    ```
    import datetime
    from dateutil import tz
    ```

> **Note**
>
> `dateutil` is not a module from the Standard Library, though it is the one recommended by the Standard Library.

2. Create the first `datetime` object for `Madrid`:

    ```
    d1 = datetime.datetime(1989, 4, 24, hour=11,
                            tzinfo=tz.gettz("Europe/
    Madrid"))
    ```

    With this line, you create a `datetime` object for April 24, 1989, at 11 a.m. in Madrid.

3. Create the second `datetime` object for `Los_Angeles`:

    ```
    d2 = datetime.datetime(1989, 4, 24, hour=8,
                            tzinfo=tz.gettz("America/Los_
    Angeles"))
    ```

    This creates a `datetime` object that seems to have a difference of 3 hours less and a different time zone.

4. Now, compare them:

    ```
    print(d1.hour > d2.hour)
    print(d1 > d2)
    ```

    The output is as follows:

    ```
                              True
                              False
    ```

    Figure 6.7 – Output when comparing the conditions for the time zones

When you compare the two `datetime` objects, you can see that even though the first `datetime` object has a higher hour than the second (that is, the first is at `11` and the second is at `8`), the first is not greater, and is, therefore, later than the second, as the time zone is different, and 8 in Los Angeles happens after 11 in Madrid.

5.   You can convert datetime from one time zone to another. You should do that to see what time the second datetime object would show if it was in Madrid:

```
d2_madrid = d2.astimezone(tz.gettz("Europe/Madrid"))
print(d2_madrid.hour)
```

The output is as follows:

```
17
```

It is 5 p.m. Now, it is obvious that the second datetime object is later than the first.

At other times, you might work just with timestamps, with time not related to any location. The easiest way to do this is to use UTC, with 0 as the offset. **UTC** is **Coordinated Universal Time** and is a system that provides a universal way of coordinating time across locations—you have most likely already used it. It is *the most common standard* for the time. The time zones you saw in the previous exercises define offsets from UTC that allow the library to identify what time corresponds to time from one location to another.

To create a datetime object with an offset of 0, also known as a datetime object in UTC, you can use datetime.timezone.utc as the tzinfo argument. This will then represent an absolute point in the line of time. You can safely add, subtract, and compare datetime objects without any issues when using UTC. On the other hand, if you use any specific time zone, you should be aware that nations might change the time at any point, which could make any of your calculations invalid.

You now know how to create datetimes, compare them, and convert them across time zones. This is a common exercise when developing applications that deal with time.

In the next exercise, you'll look at the time delta between two datetime objects. Here, the delta is the difference.

Exercise 89 – calculating the time delta between two datetime objects

In this exercise, you will subtract two datetime objects to calculate the delta between the two timestamps.

Quite often, when you work with datetime, what really matters is the difference between them, that is, the delta in time between two specific dates. Here, you will find out the difference in seconds between two important events that happened in your company, one on February 25, 2019, at 10:50, and the other on February 26 at 11:20. Both these times are in UTC. This exercise can be performed in a Jupyter notebook:

1.   Import the datetime module:

```
import datetime as dt
```

Quite often, developers import the datetime module through an alias, dt. This is done in many code bases to differentiate the datetime module from the datetime class.

2. Create two datetime objects as follows:

```
d1 = dt.datetime(2019, 2, 25, 10, 50,
                 tzinfo=dt.timezone.utc)
d2 = dt.datetime(2019, 2, 26, 11, 20,
                 tzinfo=dt.timezone.utc)
```

We created two datetime objects as dt.datetime, and you now have two datetime objects.

3. You can subtract two datetime object to get a time delta back or add a time delta to datetime.

Adding two datetime makes no sense, and the operation will, therefore, output an error with an exception. Hence, you subtract the two datetime to get the delta:

```
d2 - d1
```

The output is as follows:

```
datetime.timedelta(days=1, seconds=1800)
```

Figure 6.8 – Output with the delta between two days and seconds

4. You can see that the delta between the two datetime is 1 day and 1,800 seconds, which can be translated to the total number of seconds by calling total_seconds in the time delta object that the subtraction returns:

```
td = d2 - d1
td.total_seconds()
```

The output is as follows:

```
88200.0
```

5. It happens quite often that you need to send datetime objects in formats such as JSON or others that do not support native datetimes. A common way to serialize datetime is by encoding them in a string using the ISO 8601 standard.

This can be done by using isoformat, which will output a string, and parsing them with the fromisoformat method, which takes a datetime serialized to a string with isoformat and transforms it back to a datetime:

```
d1 = dt.datetime.now(dt.timezone.utc)
d1.isoformat()
```

The output is as follows:

```
'2019-04-21T12:38:49.117769+00:00'
```

Figure 6.9 – Output with datetime serialized to a string with isoformat and back to datetime

Another module that you use when dealing with time is the `time` module. In the `time` module, you can get the Unix time through `time.time`. This will return the number of seconds since the Unix epoch is without leap seconds. This is known as **Unix time** or **POSIX time**.

You are encouraged to read about leap seconds if you need to develop highly time-sensitive applications, but Python offers no time support for them. The `time` and `datetime` modules just use the system clock, which will not count leap seconds.

But what happens in an instance where a leap second occurs is up to the OS admin. Some companies slow down time around leap seconds, while others just skip them by making a second take two seconds in the real world. If you need to figure this out in your workplace, you will need to check with your OS admin how the NTP servers are configured to act in leap seconds. Luckily, you know well in advance when the next leap second will happen, as the **International Earth Rotation and Reference Systems Service** (`https://packt.live/2oKYtUR`) publishes leap seconds at least 8 weeks in advance.

You now understand the basics of time arithmetic and know how to calculate the time delta between two timestamps.

Exercise 90 – calculating the Unix epoch time

In this exercise, you will use the `datetime` and `time` modules to calculate Unix epoch time.

If you can just look it up, you can also calculate the Unix epoch. As `time.time` gives us the number of seconds since the epoch, you can create a time delta with it and subtract it from a `datetime` object you've created. You will see how to perform that in this exercise.

This exercise can be performed in a Jupyter notebook:

1. Import the `time` and `datetime` modules and get them to the current namespace:

    ```
    import datetime as dt
    import time
    ```

2. Get the current time. You use both `datetime` and `time` to do this:

    ```
    time_now = time.time()
    datetime_now = dt.datetime.now(dt.timezone.utc)
    ```

> **Note**
>
> You use the UTC time zone when getting time with `datetime`. This is necessary because `time.time` returns Unix time, which uses `epoch` that is in UTC.

3. You can now calculate the epoch by subtracting `datetime` and a time delta, which you get from the current time since you said that these are the number of seconds since the epoch:

```
epoch = datetime_now - dt.timedelta(seconds=time_now)
print(epoch)
```

The output is as follows:

```
1970-01-01 00:00:00.000052+00:00
```

Figure 6.10 – Calculating the epoch

The result is the Unix epoch — January 1, 1970.

Having completed this exercise, you know how to use the `time` and `datetime` modules to get the output as the Unix epoch time, as shown in *Figure 6.10*, and to use `timedelta` to represent intervals.

There is one more module that is sometimes used in combination with `datetime`, which is the `calendar` module. The `calendar` module provides additional information about calendar years, that is, how many days there are in a month. This can also be used to output calendars such as the Unix function.

Now, have a look at an example where you create a calendar and get all of the days in a month as follows:

```
import calendar
c = calendar.Calendar()
list(c.itermonthdates(2019, 2))
```

The output is as follows:

```
datetime.date(2019, 1, 28),
datetime.date(2019, 1, 29),
datetime.date(2019, 1, 30),
datetime.date(2019, 1, 31),
datetime.date(2019, 2, 1),
datetime.date(2019, 2, 2),
```

Figure 6.11 – Output showing month 1 and its days as a calendar

> **Note**
>
> Though the function returns all date instances for all the weeks in the month, if you want to get only the days that belong to the specific month, you need to filter them:

```
list(d for d in c.itermonthdates(2019, 2)
        if d.month == 2)
```

You will get the following output:

```
datetime.date(2019, 2, 1),
datetime.date(2019, 2, 2),
datetime.date(2019, 2, 3),
datetime.date(2019, 2, 4),
datetime.date(2019, 2, 5),
```

Figure 6.12 – Output showing month 2 and its days as a calendar

> **Note**
>
> Bear in mind that when working with `datetime`, there are some basic assumptions that you might make that will cause bugs in your code. For instance, assuming a year will have 365 days will cause problems for 29 February, or assuming that a day has 24 hours when any international traveler can tell you that this isn't the case. A detailed table on the wrong assumptions of time and its reasoning is mentioned in *Appendix* on GitHub.

If you need to work with dates and times, make sure to always use well-tested libraries such as `dateutil` from the Standard Library, and consider using a good testing library such as `freezegun` to validate your assumptions. You'd be surprised to discover the endless number of bugs that computer systems have when exposed to time quirks.

To know more about time, you first need to understand how the system clock works. For example, your computer clock is not like a clock on the wall; it uses the **Network Time Protocol** (**NTP**) to coordinate with other connected computers. NTP is one of the oldest internet protocols still in use. Time is really hard to measure, and the most efficient way to do so is by using atomic clocks. The NTP creates a hierarchy of clocks and synchronizes them periodically. A good exercise is to disable the NTP sync on your computer for a day and check how your system clock deviates from the internet by running the NTP manually.

Handling dates and times properly is extremely difficult. For simple applications, you should be fine with a basic level of understanding, but otherwise, further reading and more specialized libraries will be needed. In Python, we have the `datetime` module as the key to handling date and time, which also contains the `timezone.utc` time zone. There are also `time` and `calendar` modules, which can be used when we need to measure with UNIX time and to get calendar information, respectively.

Activity 15 – calculating the time elapsed to run a loop

You are part of an IT department, and you are asked to inspect an application that outputs random numbers but with a delay. In order to investigate this delayed output, you check the code as there have been updates to the application where the development team has added a new line of code to get a list of random numbers. You are asked to confirm this by checking the time it takes to run that line of code using the time module.

> **Note**
>
> To perform this activity, you can just record the time by using time.time to compute the difference in time since, before, and after the function. If you want to be more precise and use the time in nanoseconds, you can use time_ns.

You will see in the section about profiling in *Chapter 9, Practical Python – Advanced Topics*, how to measure performance in a more precise way.

This was the line of code that was added in by the development team:

```
l = [random.randint(1, 999) for _ in range(10 * 3)]
```

While it is possible to run the code and use time.time to calculate the elapsed time, is there any better function in the time module to do this?

Follow these steps:

1. Record the time before running the previously mentioned code line with the time.time function.
2. Record the time after running the same code with the time.time function.
3. Find the difference between the two.
4. Repeat the steps using time.time_ns.

    The output is as follows:

    ```
    187500
    ```

> **Note**
>
> The solution for this activity can be found in *Appendix* on GitHub.

Now we know how to handle date and time effectively with Python.

Interacting with the OS

One of the most common uses of Python is to write code that interacts with the OS and its filesystem. Whether you are working with files or you just need some basic information about the OS, this topic will cover the essentials of how to do it in a multiplatform way through the os, sys, platform, and pathlib modules of the Standard Library.

OS information

There are three key modules that are used to inspect the runtime environment and the OS. The os module enables miscellaneous interfaces with the OS. You can use it to inspect environment variables or to get other user and process-related information. This, combined with the platform module (which contains information about the interpreter and the machine where the process is running) and the sys module (which provides you with helpful system-specific information) will usually provide you with all the information that you need about the runtime environment.

Exercise 91 – inspecting the current process information

The goal of this exercise is to use the Standard Library to report information about the running process and the platform on your system:

1. Import the os, platform, and sys modules:

    ```
    import platform
    import os
    import sys
    ```

2. To get basic process information such as Process id and Parent id, you can use the os module:

    ```
    print("Process id:", os.getpid())
    print("Parent process id:", os.getppid())
    ```

    The output is as follows:

    ```
    Process id: 13244
    Parent process id: 8792
    ```

    Figure 6.13 – The expected output showing the process ID and the parent process ID of the system

    This gives us the process ID and the parent process ID. This constitutes a basic step when you try to perform any interaction with the OS that involves your process and is the best way to uniquely identify the running process. You can try restarting the kernel or the interpreter and see how the pid value changes, as a new process ID is always assigned to a running process in the system.

3. Now, get the `platform` and Python interpreter information:

```
print("Machine network name:", platform.node())
print("Python version:", platform.python_version())
print("System:", platform.system())
```

The output is as follows:

```
Machine network name: PF11AY8S
Python version: 3.7.0
System: Windows
```

Figure 6.14 – The expected output showing the network name, Python version, and the system type

These functions of the module platform can be used to ascertain the information of the computer where your Python code is running, which is useful when you are writing code that might be specific to the machine or system information.

4. Get the Python path and the arguments passed to the interpreter:

```
print("Python module lookup path:", sys.path)
print("Command to run Python:", sys.argv)
```

This will give us a list of paths where Python will look for modules and the command line that was used to start the interpreter as a list of arguments.

5. Get the username through an environment variable:

```
print("USERNAME environment variable:",
os.environ["USER"])
```

The output is as follows:

```
USERNAME environment variable: CorcheroMario
```

Figure 6.15 – The expected output showing the username environment variable

The `environ` attribute of the `os` module is `dict` that maps the environment variable name to its values. The keys are the name of the environment variables, and the value is the one that it was set to initially. It can be used to read and set environment variables, and it has the methods that you would expect `dict`. You can use `os.environ.get(varname, default)` to provide a default value if a variable was not set, and `pop` to remove items or just assign a new value. There are also two other methods, `getenv` and `putenv`, which can be used to get and set environment variables, but using `os.environ` as `dict` is more readable.

This is just a small peek into these three modules and some of the attributes and functions that they provide. Further and more specialized information can be found in the modules, and you are encouraged to explore the modules when any specific runtime information is needed.

Having completed this exercise, you learned how to use multiple modules such as os and platform to query information about the environment that can be used to create programs that interact with it.

Using pathlib

Another useful module is pathlib. Even though many of the actions that are performed with pathlib can be done with os.path, the pathlib library offers a much better experience, which you'll go into more detail on later.

The pathlib module provides a way to represent and interact with filesystem paths.

A path object of the module, which is the basic util of the module, can just be created with its default argument to start a relative path to the current working directory:

```
import pathlib
path = pathlib.Path()
print(repr(path))
```

You will get the following output:

```
WindowsPath('.')
```

> **Note**
>
> You can get and change the current working directory with os.getcwd() and os.chdir(), respectively.

You will get either a PosixPath or WindowsPath function of the platform you are running on.

You can use the string representation of a path at any time to be used in the functions that accept a string as a path; this can be done by calling str(path).

The `path` objects can be joined with just a forward slash (`/`), which feels really natural and easy to read, as shown in the following code snippet:

```
import pathlib
path = pathlib.Path(".")
new_path = path / "folder" / "folder" / "example.py"
```

You can now perform multiple operations on those `path` objects. One of the most common ones is to call `resolve` in the resulting object, which will make the path absolute and resolve all `..` references. As an example, paths such as `./my_path/` will be resolved to paths such as `/current/workspace/my_path`, which start with the root filesystem.

Some of the most common operations to perform on a path are the following:

- `exists`: Checks whether the path exists in the filesystem and whether it is a file or a directory.
- `is_dir`: Checks whether the path is a directory.
- `is_file`: Checks whether the path is a file.
- `iterdir`: Returns an iterator with `path` objects to all the files and directories contained within the `path` object.
- `mkdir`: Creates a directory in the path indicated by the `path` object.
- `open`: Opens a file in the current path, similar to running `open` and passing the string representation of the path. It returns a `file` object that can be operated like any other.
- `read_text`: Returns the content of the file as a Unicode string. If the file is in binary format, the `read_bytes` method should be used instead.

Finally, a key function of `Path` objects is **glob**. This allows you to specify a set of filenames by using wildcards. The main character used to do so is `*`, which matches any character in the path level. `**` matches any name but crossing directories. This means that `"/path/*"` will match any file in `"path" whilst "/path/**"` and will match any file within its path and any of its directories.

You will look at this in the next exercise.

Exercise 92 – using the glob pattern to list files within a directory

In this exercise, you will learn how to list the files of an existing source tree. This is a key part of developing any application that works with a filesystem.

You are given the following file and folder structure, which you have in the GitHub repository:

Figure 6.16 – Initial folder structure

1. Create a path object for the current path:

```
import pathlib
p = pathlib.Path("")
```

> **Note**
>
> You could also use pathlib.Path.cwd() and get an absolute path directly.

2. Next, we will find all files in the directory with the txt extension. You can start by listing all such files by using glob:

```
txt_files = p.glob("*.txt")
print("*.txt:", list(txt_files))
```

The output is as follows:

```
*.txt: [WindowsPath('path-exercise/file_a.txt')]
```

Figure 6.17 – Output showing the file with the .txt extension

This lists all the files in the current location that end with txt, which, in this case, is only file_a.txt. Folders within other directories are not listed, as the single star, *, does not cross directories and if there was another file not ending in txt, it would not be included either.

Note how you need to transform txt_files into a list. This is needed as glob returns an iterator and you want to print the list. This is useful since, when you are listing files, there might be an endless number of files.

If you wanted to list all of the text files in any folder within the path, no matter the number of subdirectories, you could use the double star syntax, **:

```
print("**/*.txt:", list(p.glob("**/*.txt")))
```

The output is as follows:

```
**/*.txt: [WindowsPath('path-exercise/file_a.txt'), WindowsP
ath('path-exercise/folder_1/file_b.txt'), WindowsPath('path-
exercise/folder_2/folder_3/file_d.txt')]
```

Figure 6.18 – Output showing all the files in all the folders

This lists all files that end with .txt within any folder in the current path described by the path object, p.

This lists not only folder_1/file_b.txt and folder_2/folder_3/file_d.txt but also file_a.txt, which is not within any folder, as ** matches within any number of nested folders, including 0.

> **Note**
> folder_1/file_c.py won't be listed, however, as it does not match the ending we provided in glob.

3. If you wanted to list all files one level deep within a subdirectory only, you could use the following glob pattern:

```
print("*/*:", list(p.glob("*/*")))
```

The output is as follows:

```
*/*: [WindowsPath('path-exercise/folder_1/file_b.txt'), Wind
owsPath('path-exercise/folder_1/file_c.py'), WindowsPath('pa
th-exercise/folder_2/folder_3')]
```

Figure 6.19 – Output showing the files within a subdirectory

This will list both files within folder_1 and folder_2/folder_3, which is also a path. If you wanted to get only files, you could filter each of the paths by checking the is_file method, as mentioned previously:

```
print("Files in */*:", [f for f in p.glob("*/*") if f.is_
file()])
```

The output is as follows:

```
Files in */*: [WindowsPath('path-exercise/folder_1/file_b.tx
t'), WindowsPath('path-exercise/folder_1/file_c.py')]
```

Figure 6.20 – Output showing the files within folder_1, folder_2, and folder_3

This will not include paths that are no longer a file.

> **Note**
>
> There is also another module that is worth mentioning, which contains high-level functions for file and folder operations, shutil. With shutil, it is possible to recursively copy, move, or delete files.

You now know how to list files within a tree based on their attributes or extensions.

Listing all hidden files in your home directory

In Unix, *hidden* files are those that start with a **dot**. Usually, those files are not listed when you list files with tools such as ls unless you explicitly ask for them. You will now use the pathlib module to list all hidden files in your home directory. The code snippet indicated here will show exactly how to list these hidden files:

```
import pathlib
p = pathlib.Path.home()
print(list(p.glob(".*")))
```

The pathlib docs find the function that gives us the home directory, and then we use the glob pattern to match any file starting with a dot. In the next topic, we will be using the subprocess module.

Using the subprocess module

Python is really useful in situations where we need to start and communicate with other programs on the OS.

The subprocess module allows us to start a new process and communicate with it, bringing to Python all the available tools installed on your OS through an easy-to-use API. The subprocess module can be seen by calling any other program from your shell.

This module has gone through some work to modernize and simplify its API, and you might see code using subprocess in ways different from those shown in this topic.

The subprocess module has two main APIs: the subprocess.run call, which manages everything from you passing the right arguments, and subprocess.Popen, a lower-level API that is available for more advanced use cases. You are going to cover only the high-level API, subprocess.run, but if you need to write an application that requires something more complex, as we have previously seen with the Standard Library, go through the documentation (available at https://docs.python.org/3/library/subprocess.html) and explore the APIs for more complex use cases.

> **Note**
>
> The following examples have been run on a Linux system, but subprocess can be used on Windows as well; it will just need to call Windows programs. You can use dir instead of ls, for example.

Now you will see how you can call the Linux system `ls` by using subprocess and listing all the files:

```
import subprocess
subprocess.run(["ls"])
```

This will just create a process and run the `ls` command. If the `ls` command is not found (in Windows, for example), running this command will fail and raise an exception.

> **Note**
>
> The return value is an instance of `CompletedProcess`, but the output of the command is sent to standard output in the console.

If you want to be able to capture and see the output that our process produced, you need to pass the `capture_output` argument. This will capture `stdout` and `stderr` and make it available in the `completedProcess` instance returned by run:

```
result = subprocess .run(["ls"], capture_output=True)
print("stdout: ", result.stdout)
print("stderr: ", result.stderr)
```

The output is as follows:

```
stdout:   b'subprocess-examples.ipynb\n'
stderr:   b''
```

Figure 6.21 – Output showing the subprocess module

> **Note**
>
> The `stdout` and `stderr` result is a byte string. If you know that the result is text, you can pass the `text` argument to have it decoded.

Now, let's omit `stderr` from the output as you know it is empty, as shown in *Figure 6.21*:

```
result = subprocess .run(
        ["ls"],
        capture_output=True, text=True
    )
print("stdout: \n", result.stdout)
```

The output is as follows:

stdout:
subprocess-examples.ipynb

Figure 6.22 – Output showing the subprocesses using stdout

You can also pass more arguments, such as `-l`, to have the files listed with details:

```
result = subprocess.run(
        ["ls", "-l"],
        capture_output=True, text=True
    )
print("stdout: \n", result.stdout)
```

The output is as follows:

```
stdout:
 total 4
-rwxrwxrwx 1 mcorcherojim mcorcherojim 1957 Apr 19 17:14 subprocess-examples.ipynb
```

Figure 6.23 – Output showing the files listed in detail using -l

The first thing that usually surprises users when using `suprocess.run` is that the command that needs to be passed in to run is a list of strings. This is for convenience and security. Many users will jump into using the shell argument, which will make passing the command arguments as a string work but there are security concerns. When doing so, you are basically asking Python to run our command in the system shell, and you are, therefore, responsible for escaping the characters as needed. Imagine for a moment that you accept user input, and you are going to pass it to the `echo` command. A user would then be able to pass `hacked; rm -rf /` as the argument for `echo`.

> **Note**
> Do not run the `hacked; rm -rf /` command as that will delete everything from the system.

By using the semicolon, the user can mark the end of a shell command and start their own, which will delete all of your root! Additionally, when your arguments have spaces or any other shell character, you have to escape them accordingly. The simplest and safest way to use `subprocess.run` is to pass all tokens one by one as a list of strings, as shown in the examples here.

In some situations, you might want to inspect the return code that our return process has returned. In those situations, you can just check the `returncode` attribute in the returning instance of `subprocess.run`:

```
result = subprocess.run(["ls", "non_existing_file"])
print("rc: ", result.returncode)
```

The output is as follows:

```
rc: 2
```

If you wanted to make sure that our command succeeded without always having to check that the return code was 0 after running, you could use the `check=True` argument. This will raise errors if the program reported any:

```
result = subprocess.run(
    ["ls", "non_existing_file"],
    check=True
)
print("rc: ", result.returncode)
```

The output is as follows:

```
---------------------------------------------------------------
CalledProcessError                       Traceback (most recent call last)
<ipython-input-31-36d3d0f47957> in <module>()
----> 1 result = subprocess .run(["ls", "non_existing_file"], check=True)
      2 print("rc: ", result.returncode)

/usr/local/lib/python3.7/subprocess.py in run(input, capture_output, timeout, check, *popenargs, **kwargs)
    479         if check and retcode:
    480             raise CalledProcessError(retcode, process.args,
--> 481                                 output=stdout, stderr=stderr)
    482     return CompletedProcess(process.args, retcode, stdout, stderr)
    483

CalledProcessError: Command '['ls', 'non_existing_file']' returned non-zero exit status 2.
```

Figure 6.24 – The result of running subprocess on a failed command

This is a great way to call other programs in which we just want them to be executed to have a look at the error, such as calling batch processing scripts or programs. The exceptions raised in those situations contain information such as the command that was run, the output if it was captured, and the return code.

The subprocess.run function also has some other interesting arguments that are helpful in some more special situations. As an example, if you are using subprocess.call with a program that expects any input through stdin, you can pass such input via the stdin argument. You can also pass a timeout for how many seconds you should wait for the program to finish. If the program does not return by that time, it will be terminated and, once finished, a timeout exception will be raised to inform us of the failure.

Processes created with the subprocess.run method will inherit the environment variables from the current process.

sys.executable is a string giving the absolute path of the executable binary for the Python interpreter on systems. If Python is unable to retrieve the real path to its executable process, sys.executable will be an empty string or None.

> **Note**
> The -c option on the Python interpreter is for running code inline. You will be using this option in *Activity 16 – testing Python code*.

You will see how you can customize child processes in the following exercise.

Exercise 93 – customizing child processes with env vars

As part of an auditing tool, you are asked to print our environment variables by using the subprocess module, without relying on the Python os.environ variable. However, you have to do so while concealing our server name, as our manager does not want to show this information to our clients.

In this exercise, you will call other apps in the OS while changing the environment variables of the parent process. You will see how you can change environment variables when using subprocess:

1. Import the subprocess module into the current namespace:

    ```
    import subprocess
    ```

    You can also bring just the run command by running subprocess by importing run, but by importing this module itself, we can see the module name when we are calling run. Otherwise, you wouldn't know where run was coming from. Additionally, subprocess defines some constants that are used for some arguments on the advanced use of Popen. By importing subprocess, you have all those available.

2. You can run the env Unix command, which will list the process environment variables in stdout:

    ```
    result = subprocess.run(
        ["env"],
        capture_output=True,
    ```

```
    text=True
)
print(result.stdout)
```

You pass `capture_output` and `text` to be able to read the `stdout` result in a Unicode string. You can confirm that the process indeed has a list of environment variables already set; those match the ones of the parent process:

```
SHELL_TITLE=PF11AY8S | Started: 2019-04-19T04:44:27 UTC
TERM=xterm-color
SHELL=/bin/bash
HISTSIZE=100000
SERVER=PF11AY8S
DOCKER_HOST=localhost:2375
```

Figure 6.25 – Output showing the environment variables using env

3. If you wanted to customize the environment variables that our subprocess has, you could use the env keyword of the `subprocess.run` method:

```
result = subprocess.run(
    ["env"],
    capture_output=True,
    text=True,
    env={"SERVER": "OTHER_SERVER"}
)
print(result.stdout)
```

The output is as follows:

```
SERVER=OTHER_SERVER
```

Figure 6.26 – Output showing a different set of environment variables

4. Now, we'll modify the default set of variables. Most of the time, you just want to modify or add one variable, not just replace them all. Therefore, what we did in the previous step is too radical, as tools might require environment variables that are always present in the OS.

    To do so, you will have to take the current process environment and modify it to match the expected result. We can access the current process environment variables via `os.environ` and copy them via the `copy` module, though you can also use the `dict` expansion syntax with the keys that you want to change to modify it, as shown in the following example:

```
import os
result = subprocess.run(
```

```
        ["env"],
        capture_output=True,
        text=True,
        env={**os.environ, "SERVER": "OTHER_SERVER"}
    )
    print(result.stdout)
```

The output is as follows:

```
SHELL_TITLE=PF11AY8S | Started: 2019-04-19T04:44:27 UTC
TERM=xterm-color
SHELL=/bin/bash
HISTSIZE=100000
SERVER=OTHER_SERVER
DOCKER_HOST=localhost:2375
```

Figure 6.27 – Modifying the default set of environment variables

You can see that you now have the same environments in the process created with subprocess as those in the current process, but that you have modified SERVER.

You can use the subprocess module to create and interact with other programs installed on our OS. The subprocess.run function and its different arguments make it easy to interact with different kinds of programs, check their output, and validate their results. There are also more advanced APIs available through the subprocess.Popen call if they are needed.

Activity 16 – testing Python code

A company that receives small Python code snippets from its clients with basic mathematical and string operations has realized that some of the operations crash their platform. There is some code sent by clients that causes the Python interpreter to abort as it cannot compute it.

This is an example:

```
compile("1" + "+1" * 10 ** 6, "string", "exec")
```

You are therefore asked to create a small program that can run the requested code and check whether it will crash without breaking the current process. This can be done by running the same code with subprocess and the same interpreter version that is currently running the code.

To get this code, you need to do the following:

1. Find out the executable of our interpreter by using the sys module.

2. Use subprocess to run the code with the interpreter that you used in the previous step.

3. Use the -c option of the interpreter to run code inline.

4. Check whether the result code is -11, which corresponds to an abort in the program.

> **Note**
> The solution for this activity can be found in *Appendix* on GitHub.

In the following topic, you will be using logging, which plays a major part in the life of a developer.

Logging in Python

Setting up an application or a library to log is not just good practice; it is a key task of a responsible developer. It is as important as writing documentation or tests. Many people consider logging the **runtime documentation**, the same way developers read the documentation when interacting with the DevOps source code, and other developers will use the log traces when the application is running.

Hardcore logging advocates state that debuggers are extremely overused, and people should rely more on logging, using both info and trace logs to troubleshoot their code in development.

The idea is that if you are not able to troubleshoot your code with the highest level of verbosity in development, then you may have issues in production that you won't be able to figure out the root issue of. In this part, we will cover how logging works and how to configure it to not fall into those kinds of issues.

Using logging

Logging is the best way to let the users of the running application know which state the process is in and how it is processing its work. It can also be used for auditing or troubleshooting client issues. There is nothing more frustrating than trying to figure out how your application behaved last week and having no information at all about what happened when it faced an issue.

You should also be careful about what information we log. Many companies will require users to never log information such as credit cards or any sensitive user data. While it is possible to conceal such data after it is logged, it is better to be mindful when we log it.

You might wonder what is wrong with just using `print` statements, but when you start to write large-scale applications or libraries, you realize that just using `print` does nothing to instrument an application. By using the `logging` module, you also get the following:

- **Multithreading support**: The logging module is designed to work in multithreaded environments. This is needed when using multiple threads as, otherwise, the data that you log will get interleaved, as can happen with `print`.

- **Categorization through multiple levels of logging**: When using `print`, there is no way to transmit the importance of the log trace being emitted. By using logging, we can choose the category that we want to log under to transmit its importance.

- **Separation of concerns between instrumentation and configuration**: There are two different users of the logging library: those who just emit and those who configure the logging stack. The logging library separates those nicely, allowing libraries and applications to just instrument their code with logs at different levels, and the final user to configure the logging stack at will.

- **Flexibility and configurability**: The logging stack is easily extensible and configurable. There are many types of handlers, and it is trivial to create new classes that extend its functionality. There is even a cookbook on how to extend the logging stack in the Standard Library documentation.

The main class you interact with when using the logging library is `logger`. It can be used to emit logs in any category. You usually create `loggers` objects by getting them through the `logging.getLogger(<logger name>)` factory method.

Once you have a `logger` object, you can call the different logging methods that match the different default categories in which you are able to log:

- `debug`: Fine-grained messages that are helpful for debugging and troubleshooting applications, usually enabled in development. As an example, a web server will log the input payload when receiving a request at this level.

- `info`: Coarse-grained informational messages that highlight the progress of an application. As an example, a web server will emit the requests being handled at this level without details of the data being received.

- `warning`: Messages that inform the user of a potentially harmful situation in the application or library. In our example of a web server, this will happen if you fail to decode an input JSON payload because it is corrupted. Note that while it might feel like an error and it might be for the whole system, if you own the frontend as well, the issue is not in the application handling the request; it is in the process sending it. Therefore, a warning might help notify the user of such an issue, but it is not an error. The error should be reported to the client as an error response, and the client should handle it as appropriate.

- `error`: Used for situations where an error has taken place but the application can continue to function properly. Logging an error usually means there is an action that needs to be carried out by a developer in the source code that logged it. Logging errors commonly happen when you capture an exception and have no way of handling it effectively. It is quite common to set up alerts in connection with errors to inform the DevOps or developer that an error situation took place. In our web server application, this might happen if you fail to encode a response or an exception is raised that was not expected when handling the request.

- `fatal`: Fatal logs indicate that there has been an error situation that compromises the current stability of the program, and, quite often, the process is restarted after a fatal message is logged. A fatal log means that the application needs an operator to take action urgently, compared to an error that a developer is expected to handle. A common situation is when the connection to a database is lost, or any other resource that is key for the application is no longer reachable.

Logger object

Loggers have a hierarchy of names split by a dot. For example, if you ask for a logger named my.logger, you are creating a logger that is a child of my, which is a child of the root logger. All top-level loggers "inherit" from the root logger.

You can get the root logger by calling getLogger without arguments or by logging directly with the logging module. A common practice is to use __name__ as the logger module. This makes your logging hierarchy follow your source code hierarchy. Unless you have a strong reason not to do that, use __name__ when developing libraries and applications.

Exercise 94 – using a logger object

The goal of this exercise is to create a logger object and use four different methods that allow us to log in the categories mentioned earlier in the *Logging in Python* section:

1. Import the logging module:

   ```
   import logging
   ```

2. Create a logger object:

   We can now get a logger object through the getLogger factory method:

   ```
   logger = logging.getLogger("logger_name")
   ```

   This logger object will be the same everywhere, and you call it with the same name.

3. Log with different categories:

   ```
   logger.debug("Logging at debug")
   logger.info("Logging at info")
   logger.warning("Logging at warning")
   logger.error("Logging at error")
   logger.fatal("Logging at fatal")
   ```

   The output is as follows:

   ```
   Logging at warning
   Logging at error
   Logging at fatal
   ```

Figure 6.28 – The output of running logging

By default, the logging stack will be configured to log records on level warning and above (error and critical), which explains why you only see those levels being printed to the console. You will see later how to configure the logging stack to include other levels, such as info. Use files or a different format to include further information.

4. Include information when logging:

```
system = "moon"
for number in range(3):
    logger.warning("%d errors reported in %s", number,
system)
```

Usually, when you log, you don't pass just a string but also some variable or information that helps us with the current state of the application:

```
0 errors reported in moon
1 errors reported in moon
2 errors reported in moon
```

Figure 6.29 – The output of running warning logs

> **Note**
>
> You use Python standard string interpolation, and you pass the remainder of the variables as attributes. %d is used to format numbers, while %s is used for strings. The string interpolation format also has syntax to customize the formatting of numbers or to use the repr of an object.

After this exercise, you now know how to use the different logger methods to log in different categories depending on the situation. This will allow you to properly group and handle your application messages.

Logging in warning, error, and fatal categories

You should be mindful when you log in the warning, error, and fatal categories. If there is something worse than an error, it is two errors. Logging an error is a way of informing the system of a situation that needs to be handled, and if you decide to log an error and raise an exception, you are basically duplicating the information. As a rule of thumb, following these two pieces of advice is key to an application or library that logs errors effectively:

*   Never ignore an exception that transmits an error silently. If you handle an exception that notifies you of an error, log that error.

*   Never raise and log an error. If you are raising an exception, the caller has the ability to decide whether it is truly an error situation, or whether they were expecting the issue to occur. They can then decide whether to log it following the previous rule, to handle it, or to re-raise it.

A good example of where the user might be tempted to log an error or warning is in the library of a database when a constraint is violated. From the library perspective, this might look like an error situation, but the user might be trying to insert it without checking whether the key was already in the table. The user can therefore just try to insert and ignore the exception, but if the library code logs a warning when such a situation happens, the warning or error will just spew the log files without a valid reason. Usually, a library will rarely log an error unless it has no way of transmitting the error through an exception.

When you are handling exceptions, it is quite common to log them and the information they come with. If you want to include the exception and trace back the full information, you can use the `exc_info` argument in any of the methods that we saw before:

```
try:
    int("nope")
except Exception:
    logging.error("Something bad happened", exc_info=True)
```

The output is as follows:

```
ERROR:root:Something bad happened
Traceback (most recent call last):
  File "<ipython-input-8-adcdec9cc60b>", line 2, in <module>
    int("nope")
ValueError: invalid literal for int() with base 10: 'nope'
```

Figure 6.30 – Example output when logging an exception with exc_info

The error information now includes the message you passed in, but also the exception that was being handled with the traceback. This is common and so useful that there is a shortcut for it. You can call the `exception` method to achieve the same as using `error` with `exc_info`:

```
try:
    int("nope")
except Exception:
    logging.exception("Something bad happened")
```

The output is as follows:

```
ERROR:root:Something bad happened
Traceback (most recent call last):
  File "<ipython-input-9-39a74a45c693>", line 2, in <module>
    int("nope")
ValueError: invalid literal for int() with base 10: 'nope'
```

Figure 6.31 – Example output when logging an exception with the exception method

Now, you will review two common bad practices with the `logging` module.

The first one is greedy string formatting. You might see some linters complain about formatting a string by the user rather than relying on the `logging` module's string interpolation. This means that `logging.info("string template %s", variable)` is preferred over `logging.info("string template {}".format(variable))`. This is the case since if you perform the string interpolation with the format, you will be doing it no matter how we configure the logging stack. If the user who configures the application decides that they don't need to print out the logs in the information level, you will have to perform interpolation when it wasn't necessary:

```
# prefer
logging.info("string template %s", variable)
# to
logging.info("string template {}".format(variable))
```

> **Note**
> Linters are programs that detect code style violations, errors, and suggestions for the user.

The other, more important, bad practice is capturing and formatting exceptions when it's not really needed. Often, you see developers capturing broad exceptions and formatting them manually as part of a log message. This is not only a boilerplate but also less explicit. Compare the following two approaches:

```
d = dict()
# Prefer
try:
    d["missing_key"] += 1
except Exception:
    logging.error("Something bad happened", exc_info=True)
# to
try:
    d["missing_key"] += 1
except Exception as e:
    logging.error("Something bad happened: %s", e)
```

The output is as follows:

```
ERROR:root:Something bad happened
Traceback (most recent call last):
  File "<ipython-input-18-997c7c2a8b8d>", line 5, in <module>
    d["missing_key"] += 1
KeyError: 'missing_key'
ERROR:root:Something bad happened: 'missing_key'
```

Figure 6.32 – Example output difference of exc_info versus logging an exception string

The output in the second approach will only print the text of the exception, without further information. We don't know whether it was a key error, nor where the issue appeared. If the exception was raised without a message, we would just get an empty message. Additionally, if logging an error, use an exception, and you won't need to pass `exc_info`.

Configuring the logging stack

Another part of the `logging` library is the functions to configure it, but before diving into how to configure the logging stack, you should understand its different parts and the role they play.

You've already seen `logger` objects, which are used to define the logging messages that need to be generated. There are also the following classes, which take care of the process of processing and emitting a log:

- **Log records**: This is the object that is generated by the logger and contains all the information about the log, including the line where it was logged, the level, the template, and arguments, among others.

- **Formatters**: These take log records and transform them into strings that can be used by handlers that output to streams.

- **Handlers**: These are the ones that actually emit the records. They frequently use a formatter to transform records into strings. The Standard Library comes with multiple handlers to emit log records into `stdout`, `stderr`, `files`, `sockets`, and so on.

- **Filters**: Tools to fine-tune log record mechanisms. They can be added to both handlers and loggers.

If the functionality that is already provided by the Standard Library is not enough, you can always create your own kind of classes that customize how the logging process is performed.

> **Note**
>
> The `logging` library is truly flexible. If you are interested in doing so, read through the logging cookbook in the Python official documentation to see some examples at `https://docs.python.org/3/howto/logging-cookbook.html`.

Armed with this knowledge, there are multiple ways to configure all of the elements of the logging stack. You can do so by plugging together all the classes manually with code, passing `dict` via `logging.config.dictConfig`, or through an `ini` file with `logging.config.iniConfig`.

Exercise 95 – configuring the logging stack

In this exercise, you will learn how to configure the logging stack through multiple methods to output log messages to `stdout`.

You want to configure the logging stack to output logs to the console, which should look like this:

```
INFO: Hello logging world
```

Figure 6.33 – Outputting logs to the console

> **Note**
>
> The background is white, which means the output went to `stdout` and not `stderr`, as in the previous examples. Make sure to restart the kernel or interpreter every time prior to configuring the logging stack.

You will see how you can configure it with code, with a dictionary, with `basicConfig`, and with a `config` file:

1. Open a new Jupyter notebook.
2. Start with configuring the code.

    The first way to configure the stack is by manually creating all the objects and plugging them together:

    ```
    import logging
    import sys
    root_logger = logging.getLogger()
    handler = logging.StreamHandler(sys.stdout)
    formatter = logging.Formatter("%(levelname)s: %(message)s")
    handler.setFormatter(formatter)
    root_logger.addHandler(handler)
    root_logger.setLevel("INFO")
    logging.info("Hello logging world")
    ```

The output will be as follows:

```
INFO: Hello logging world
```

In this code, you get a handle of the root logger in the third line by calling `getLogger` without any arguments. You then create a stream handler, which will output to `sys.stdout` (the console) and a formatter to configure how we want the logs to look. Finally, you just need to bind them together by setting the formatter in the handler and the handler in the logger. You set the level in the logger, though you could also configure it in the handler.

3.   Restart the kernel on Jupyter and now use `dictConfig` to achieve the same configuration:

Exercise95.ipynb

```python
import logging
from logging.config import import dictConfig
dictConfig({
    "version": 1,
    "formatters": {
        "short":{
            "format": "%(levelname)s: %(message)s",
        }
    },
    "handlers": {
        "console": {
            "class": "logging.StreamHandler",
            "formatter": "short",
            "stream": "ext://sys.stdout",
        "level": "DEBUG",
        }
    },
    "loggers": {
        "": {
            "handlers": ["console"],
            "level": "INFO"
        }
    }
})
logging.info("Hello logging world")
```

> **Note**
>
> If the previous link does not render, use `https://nbviewer.jupyter.org/`.

The output will be as follows:

```
INFO: Hello logging world
```

The dictionary configuring the logging stack is identical to the code in *step 1*. Many of the configuration parameters that are passed in as strings can also be passed as Python objects. For example, you can use `sys.stdout` instead of the string passed to the `stream` option, or `logging.INFO` rather than `INFO`.

> **Note**
>
> The code in *step 3* is identical to the code in *step 2*; it just configures it in a declarative way through a dictionary.

4. Now, again, restart the kernel on Jupyter and use `basicConfig` as mentioned in the following code snippet:

```python
import sys
import logging
logging.basicConfig(
    level="INFO",
    format="%(levelname)s: %(message)s",
    stream=sys.stdout
)
logging.info("Hello there!")
```

The output will be as follows:

```
INFO: Hello there!
```

The logging stack comes with a utility function, `basicConfig`, which can be used to perform some basic configurations, such as the one we're performing here, as mentioned in the code snippet that follows.

5. Another way to configure the logging stack is by using an `ini` file. We require an `ini` file, as follows:

```
logging-config.ini
[loggers]
keys=root
[handlers]
```

```
keys=console_handler
[formatters]
keys=short
[logger_root]
level=INFO
handlers=console_handler
[handler_console_handler]
class=StreamHandler
```

> **Note**
> If this code does not render, use `https://nbviewer.jupyter.org/`.

You can then load it with the following code:

```
import logging
from logging.config import fileConfig
fileConfig("logging-config.ini")
logging.info("Hello there!")
```

The output will be as follows:

INFO: Hello there!

All applications should configure the logging stack only once, ideally at startup. Some functions, such as `basicConfig`, will not run if the logging stack has already been configured.

You now know all of the different ways to configure an application's logging stack. This is one of the key parts of creating an application.

In the next topic, you will learn about collections.

Using collections in Python

You read about built-in collections in *Chapter 2, Python Structures*. You saw `list`, `dict`, `tuple`, and `set`, but sometimes, those collections are not enough. The Python Standard Library comes with modules and collections that provide a number of advanced structures that can greatly simplify our code in common situations. Now, you will explore how you can use `Counter`, `defaultdict`, and `ChainMap`.

The counter class

Counter is a class that allows us to count **hashable** objects. It has **keys** and **values** as a dictionary (it actually inherits from dict) to store objects as keys and the number of occurrences in values. A Counter object can be created either with the list of objects that you want to count or with a dictionary that already contains the mapping of objects to their count. Once you have a counter instance created, you can get information about the count of objects, such as getting the most common ones or the count of a specific object.

Exercise 96 – counting words in a text document

In this exercise, you will use a counter to count the occurrences of words in the text document at https://packt.live/2O0aXWs:

1. Get the list of words from https://packt.live/2O0aXWs, which is our source data:

```
import urllib.request
url = 'https://www.w3.org/TR/PNG/iso_8859-1.txt'
response = urllib.request.urlopen(url)
words = response.read().decode().split()
len(words)   # 858
```

Here, you are using urllib, another module within the Standard Library, to get the contents of the URL of https://packt.live/2O0aXWs. You can then read the content and split it based on spaces and break lines. You will be using words to play with the counter.

2. Now, create a counter:

```
import collections
word_counter = collections.Counter(words)
```

This creates a counter with the list of words passed in through the word list. You can now perform the operations you want on the counter.

> **Note**
>
> As this is a subclass of the dictionary, you can perform all the operations that you can also perform on the dictionary.

3. Get the five most common words:

```
for word, count in word_counter.most_common(5):
    print(word, "-", count)
```

You can use the `most_common` method on the counter to get a list of tuples with all the words and the number of occurrences. You can also pass a limit as an argument that limits the number of results:

```
LETTER - 114
SMALL - 58
CAPITAL - 56
WITH - 55
SIGN - 21
```

Figure 6.34 – Getting the five most common words as output

4. Now, explore occurrences of some words, as shown in the following code snippet:

```
print("QUESTION", "-", word_counter["QUESTION"])
print("CIRCUMFLEX", "-", word_counter["CIRCUMFLEX"])
print("DIGIT", "-", word_counter["DIGIT"])
print("PYTHON", "-", word_counter["PYTHON"])
```

You can use the counter to explore the occurrences of specific words by just checking them with a key. Now, check for QUESTION, CIRCUMFLEX, DIGIT, and PYTHON:

```
QUESTION - 2
CIRCUMFLEX - 11
DIGIT - 10
PYTHON - 0
```

Figure 6.35 – Output exploring the occurrences of some words

Note how you can just query the counter with a key to get the number of occurrences. Something else interesting to note is that when you query for a word that does not exist, you get 0. Some users might have expected `KeyError`.

In this exercise, you just learned how to get a text file from the internet and perform some basic processing operations, such as counting the number of words.

The defaultdict class

Another class that is considered to create simpler-to-read code is the `defaultdict` class. This class behaves like `dict` but allows you to provide a factory method to be used when a key is missing. This is extremely useful in multiple scenarios where you edit values, especially if you know how to generate the first value, such as when you are building a cache or counting objects.

In Python, whenever you see code like the following code snippet, you can use `defaultdict` to improve the code quality:

```
d = {}
def function(x):
    if x not in d:
        d[x] = 0 # or any other initialization
    else:
        d[x] += 1 # or any other manipulation
```

Some people will try to make this more Pythonic by using **EAFP** (easier to ask forgiveness than permission) over **LBYL** (look before you leap), which handles the failure rather than checking whether it will succeed:

```
d = {}
def function(x):
    try:
        d[x] += 1
    except KeyError:
        d[x] = 1
```

While this is indeed the preferred way to handle this code according to Python developers, as it better conveys the information that the main part of the logic is the successful case, the correct solution for this kind of code is `defaultdict`. Intermediate to advanced Python developers will immediately think of transforming that code into a default `dict` and then comparing how it looks:

```
import collections
d = collections.defaultdict(int)
def function(x):
    d[x] += 1
```

The code becomes trivial, and it is identical to what you saw in the two previous examples. `defaultdict` is created with a factory method that will just call `int ()` if the key is missing, which returns 0 and is incremented by one. It is a simply beautiful piece of code. But note that `defaultdict` can be used in other ways; the function passed to its constructor is a callable `factory` method. You use `int` not as a type, but as a function that is called. In the same way, you could pass `list`, `set`, or any callable you want to create.

Exercise 97 – refactoring code with defaultdict

In this exercise, you will learn how to refactor code and simplify it by using `defaultdict`:

```python
_audit = {}
def add_audit(area, action):
    if area in _audit:
        _audit[area].append(action)
    else:
        _audit[area] = [action]


def report_audit():
    for area, actions in _audit.items():
        print(f"{area} audit:")
        for action in actions:
            print(f"- {action}")
        print()
```

The code template mentioned earlier in this exercise keeps an audit of all the actions that are performed in a company. They are split by area and the dictionary that was used. You can clearly see in the `add_audit` function the pattern we spoke about before. You will see how you can transform that into simpler code by using `defaultdict` and how it could be later extended in a simpler way:

1. We will start by running the code that keeps an audit of all the actions, as mentioned previously. First, run the code to see how it behaves. Before doing any refactoring, you should understand what you are trying to change, and ideally, have tests for it:

```python
add_audit("HR", "Hired Sam")
add_audit("Finance", "Used 1000£")
add_audit("HR", "Hired Tom")
report_audit()
```

You should get the following output:

```
HR audit:
- Hired Sam
- Hired Tom

Finance audit:
- Used 1000£
```

Figure 6.36 – Output showing the code keeping an audit of the changes

You can see that this works as expected, and you can add items to the audit and report them.

2. Introduce a default `dict`. You can change `dict` for `defaultdict` and just create a list whenever you try to access a key that does not exist. This will need to be done only in the `add_audit` function. As `report_audit` uses the object as a dictionary and `defaultdict` is a dictionary, you don't need to change anything in that function. You will see how it will look in the following code snippet:

```
import collections
_audit = collections.defaultdict(list)
def add_audit(area, action):
    _audit[area].append(action)


def report_audit():
    for area, actions in _audit.items():
        print(f"{area} audit:")
        for action in actions:
            print(f"- {action}")
        print()
```

> **Note**
>
> The `add_audit` function has become a single line. It just appends an action to an area.

When a key is not found in the _audit object, `defaultdict` just calls the `list` method, which returns an empty list. The code could not be any simpler.

What about if you are asked to log the creation of an area in the audit? Basically, whenever a new area is created in our `audit` object, it is to have an element present. The developer that initially wrote the code claims that it was easier to change with the old layout, without using `defaultdict`.

3. Use the `add_audit` function to create the first element. The code without `defaultdict` for `add_audit` will be as follows:

```
def add_audit(area, action):
    if area not in _audit:
        _audit[area] = ["Area created"]
    _audit[area].append(action)
```

The code change performed in `add_audit` is much more complex than the one you will have to perform in your function with `defaultdict`.

With `defaultdict`, you just need to change the factory method from being a list to being a list with the initial string:

```
import collections
_audit = collections.defaultdict(lambda: ["Area
created"])
def add_audit(area, action):
    _audit[area].append(action)


def report_audit():
    for area, actions in _audit.items():
        print(f"{area} audit:")
        for action in actions:
            print(f"- {action}")
        print()
```

And it is still simpler than without `defaultdict`:

```
add_audit("HR", "Hired Sam")
add_audit("Finance", "Used 1000£")
add_audit("HR", "Hired Tom")
report_audit()
```

You should get the following output:

```
HR audit:
- Area created
- Hired Sam
- Hired Tom

Finance audit:
- Area created
- Used 1000£
```

Figure 6.37 – Output with a function to create the first element

At the end of this exercise, you now know how to use `defaultdict` with multiple different factory methods. This is useful when writing **Pythonic** code and simplifying existing code bases.

The ChainMap class

Another interesting class in the collection's module is ChainMap. This is a structure that allows you to combine lookups for multiple mapping objects, usually dictionaries. It can be seen as a multilevel object; the user can see the front of it with all the keys and all the mappings, but the keys that map on the frontend hide the mappings on the backend.

Say you want to create a function that returns the menu our users will have at a restaurant; the function just returns a dictionary with the different types of elements of the lunch and their values. You want to allow our users to customize any part of the lunch, but you also want to provide some defaults. This can easily be done with ChainMap:

```python
import collections
_defaults = {
    "appetizers": "Hummus",
    "main": "Pizza",
    "dessert": "Chocolate cake",
    "drink": "Water",
}
def prepare_menu(customizations):
    return collections.ChainMap(customizations, _defaults)
def print_menu(menu):
    for key, value in menu.items():
        print(f"As {key}: {value}.")
```

> **Note**
>
> You have a dictionary that provides you with the defaults, and you are combining it with the user's customizations by using ChainMap. The order is important, as it makes the user's dictionary values appear before the defaults and, if desired, you can also have more than two dictionaries, which might be useful for other use cases.

You will now see how ChainMap behaves when you pass in different values:

```python
menu1 = prepare_menu({})
print_menu(menu1)
```

The output is as follows:

```
As appetizers: Hummus.
As main: Pizza.
As dessert: Chocolate cake.
As drink: Water.
```

Figure 6.38 – ChainMap outputting different values

If the user passes in no customization, you get the default menu. All keys and values are taken from the _default dictionary that we provided:

```
menu3 = prepare_menu({"side": "French fries"})
print_menu(menu3)
```

The output is as follows:

```
As appetizers: Hummus.
As main: Pizza.
As dessert: Chocolate cake.
As drink: Water.
As side: French fries.
```

Figure 6.39 – Output with no customization, that is, the default menu

When a user passes a dictionary that changes one of the keys that is present in the _default dictionary, the value of the second dictionary is shadowed by the first one. You can see how the drink is now Red Wine rather than Water:

```
menu2 = prepare_menu({"drink": "Red Wine"})
print_menu(menu2)
```

The output is as follows:

```
As appetizers: Hummus.
As main: Pizza.
As dessert: Chocolate cake.
As drink: Red Wine.
```

Figure 6.40 – The value of the dictionary changed, changing the drink to red wine

Users can also pass in new keys, which will be reflected in ChainMap.

You might be tempted to think that this is just an over-complication of using the dictionary constructor and that the same could be achieved with an implementation such as the following one:

```python
def prepare_menu(customizations):
    return {**customizations, **_defaults}
```

But the semantics are different. That implementation would create a new dictionary, which would not allow changes to the user's customizations or the defaults. Say you wanted to change the defaults after you have created some menus; we can do this with the ChainMap implementation since the returned object is just a view of multiple dictionaries:

```python
_defaults["main"] = "Pasta"
print_menu(menu3)
```

The output is as follows:

```
As appetizers: Hummus.
As main: Pasta.
As dessert: Chocolate cake.
As drink: Water.
As side: French fries.
```

Figure 6.41 – Output with changed default values

> **Note**
>
> You were able to change the main dish. Changes in any of dict that is part of ChainMap are visible when interacting with it.

The different classes in the collection modules allow the developer to write better code by using more appropriate structures. With the knowledge you have gained in this topic, try to explore others, such as deque or basic skeletons, to build your own containers. Using these classes effectively in many situations is what differentiates an experienced Python programmer from a beginner.

Using functools

The final module of the Standard Library you are going to look at allows constructs with a minimal amount of code. In this topic, you are going to see how to use lru_cache and partial.

Caching with functools.lru_cache

Often, you have a function that is heavy to compute, in which you just want to cache results. Many developers will create their own caching implementation by using a dictionary, but that is error-prone and adds unnecessary code to our project. The `functools` module comes with a decorator — that is, `functools.lru_cache`, which is provided exactly for these situations. It is a recently used cache, with `max_size` that is provided when the code is constructed. This means that you can specify a number of input values that you want to cache as a maximum to limit the memory this function can take, or it can grow indefinitely. Once you reach the maximum number of different inputs that we want to cache, the input that was the least recently used will be thrown away in favor of a new call.

Additionally, the decorator provides some new methods in the function that can be used to interact with the cache. We can use `cache_clear` to remove all of the previous hits saved in `cache` or `cache_info` to get information about the **hits** and **misses**, to allow us to tune it if needed. The original function information is also offered for inspection, as with any properly decorated function, through the `__wrapped__` decorator.

It is important to keep in mind that the LRU cache should be used only in functions. This is useful if we just want to reuse existing values or the side effect will not happen. As an example, we should not use the cache on a function that writes something into a file or sends a package to an endpoint, as those actions will not be performed once the function is called again with the same input, which is the main purpose of the cache.

Lastly, for the cache to be usable in a function, all objects being passed need to be hashable. This means that `integers`, `frozensets`, `tuples`, and so on are allowed, but not modifiable objects, such as `dicts`, `sets`, or `lists`.

Exercise 98 – using lru_cache to speed up our code

In this exercise, you will see how to configure a function to use cache with `functools` and to reuse the results from previous calls to speed up the overall process.

You use the `lru` cache function of the `functools` module to reuse values that a function has already returned without having to execute them again.

We will start with a function that is mentioned in the following code snippet, which simulates taking a long time to compute, and we will see how we can improve this:

```
import time
def func(x):
    time.sleep(1)
    print(f"Heavy operation for {x}")
    return x * 10
```

If we call this function twice with the same arguments, we will be executing the code twice to get the same result:

```
print("Func returned:", func(1))
print("Func returned:", func(1))
```

The output is as follows:

```
Heavy operation for 1
Func returned: 10
Heavy operation for 1
Func returned: 10
```

Figure 6.42 – Output showing the same arguments by calling the function twice

We can see this in the output and the print within the function, which happens twice. This is a clear improvement in performance as once the function is executed, future executions are practically free. Now, we will improve the performance in the steps that follow:

1. Add the lru cache decorator to the func function:

```
import functools
import time
@functools.lru_cache()
def func(x):
    time.sleep(1)
    print(f"Heavy operation for {x}")
    return x * 10
```

When we execute the function for the same input, we now see that the code is executed only once, but we still get the same output from the function:

```
print("Func returned:", func(1))
print("Func returned:", func(1))
print("Func returned:", func(2))
```

The output is as follows:

```
Heavy operation for 1
Func returned: 10
Func returned: 10
Heavy operation for 2
Func returned: 20
```

Figure 6.43 – Output showing the code being executed once but with the same output

Note

`Heavy operation` only happens once for 1. We are also calling 2 here to show that the value is different based on its input, and, since 2 was not cached before, it has to execute the code for it.

This is extremely useful; with just one line of code, we have at hand a fully working implementation of an LRU cache.

2. The cache comes with a default size of 128 elements, but this can be changed if needed, through the `maxsize` argument:

```
import functools
import time
@functools.lru_cache(maxsize=2)
def func(x):
    time.sleep(1)
    print(f"Heavy operation for {x}")
    return x * 10
```

By setting it to 2, we are sure that only two different inputs will be saved. We can see this by using three different inputs and calling them in reverse order later:

```
print("Func returned:", func(1))
print("Func returned:", func(2))
print("Func returned:", func(3))
print("Func returned:", func(3))
print("Func returned:", func(2))
print("Func returned:", func(1))
```

The output is as follows:

```
Heavy operation for 1
Func returned: 10
Heavy operation for 2
Func returned: 20
Heavy operation for 3
Func returned: 30
Func returned: 30
Func returned: 20
Heavy operation for 1
Func returned: 10
```

Figure 6.44 – Output with a changed cache size

The cache successfully returned the previous values for the second call of 2 and 3, but the result for 1 was destroyed once 3 arrived, since we limited the size to two elements only.

3. Sometimes, the functions you want to cache are not in our control to change. If you want to keep both versions, that is, a cached and an uncached one, we can achieve this by using the `lru_cache` function just as a function and not as a decorator, as decorators are just functions that take another function as an argument:

```python
import functools
import time
def func(x):
    time.sleep(1)
    print(f"Heavy operation for {x}")
    return x * 10
cached_func = functools.lru_cache()(func)
```

Now, we can use either `func` or its cached version, `cached_func`:

```python
print("Cached func returned:", cached_func(1))
print("Cached func returned:", cached_func(1))
print("Func returned:", func(1))
print("Func returned:", func(1))
```

The output is as follows:

```
Heavy operation for 1
Cached func returned: 10
Cached func returned: 10
Heavy operation for 1
Func returned: 10
Heavy operation for 1
Func returned: 10
```

Figure 6.45 – Output with the lru_cache function

We can see how the cached version of the function did not execute the code in the second call, but the uncached version did.

You just learned how to use `functools` to cache the values of a function. This is a really quick way to improve the performance of your application when applicable.

Adapting functions with partial

Another often used function in `functools` is `partial`. This allows us to adapt existing functions by providing values for some of their arguments. It is like binding arguments in other languages, such as C++ or JavaScript, but this is what you would expect from a Python function. The `partial` function can be used to remove the need for specifying positional or keyword arguments, which makes it useful when we need to pass a function that takes arguments as a function that does not take them. Have a look at some examples.

You will use a function that just takes three arguments and prints them:

```
def func(x, y, z):
    print("x:", x)
    print("y:", y)
    print("z:", z)
func(1, 2, 3)
```

The output is as follows:

```
x: 1
y: 2
z: 3
```

Figure 6.46 – The output, which simply prints the arguments

You can use `partial` to transform this function to take fewer arguments. This can be done in two ways, mainly, by passing the arguments as a keyword, which is more expressive (as shown next), or through positional arguments:

```
import functools
new_func = functools.partial(func, z='Wops')
new_func(1, 2)
```

The output is as follows:

```
x: 1
y: 2
z: Wops
```

Figure 6.47 – Using partial to transform the output

You can call `new_func` without passing the `z` argument, as you have provided a value through the `partial` function. The `z` argument will always be set to the value provided when the function was created through the partial call.

If you decide to use `positional` only, the number of arguments you pass will bind from left to right, which means that if you only pass one argument, the `x` argument should no longer be provided:

```
import functools
new_func = functools.partial(func, 'Wops')
new_func(1, 2)
```

The output is as follows:

```
x: Wops
y: 1
z: 2
```

Figure 6.48 – Output with positional arguments

Exercise 99 – creating a print function that writes to stderr

By using `partial`, you can also rebind the optional arguments to a different default, allowing us to change the default value that the function has. You will see how you can repurpose the `print` function to create a `print_stderr` function that just writes to `stderr`.

In this exercise, you will create a function that acts like `print`, but the output is `stderr` rather than `stdout`:

1. To start, you need to explore the arguments that `print` takes. You will call `help` on `print` to see what the documentation offers:

    ```
    help(print)
    ```

    The output is as follows:

    ```
    Help on built-in function print in module builtins:

    print(...)
        print(value, ..., sep=' ', end='\n', file=sys.stdout, flush=False)

        Prints the values to a stream, or to sys.stdout by default.
        Optional keyword arguments:
        file:  a file-like object (stream); defaults to the current sys.stdout.
        sep:   string inserted between values, default a space.
        end:   string appended after the last value, default a newline.
        flush: whether to forcibly flush the stream.
    ```

    Figure 6.49 – Output with print arguments.

The argument that you are interested in is `file`, which allows us to specify the stream you want to write to.

2. Now, print the default value for the optional argument, `file`, which is `sysstdout`, but you can pass `sys.stderr` to get the behavior you are looking for:

```
import sys
print("Hello stderr", file=sys.stderr)
```

The output is as follows:

```
Hello stderr
```

Figure 6.50 – Print to stderr output

As you are printing to `stderr`, the output appears in red as expected.

3. You can use `partial` to specify arguments to be passed and create a new function. You will bind `file` to `stderr` and see the output:

```
import functools
print_stderr = functools.partial(print, file=sys.stderr)
print_stderr("Hello stderr")
```

The output is as follows:

```
Hello stderr
```

Figure 6.51 – Print to stderr output through partial

Great! This works as expected; we now have a function that has changed the default value for the optional `file` argument.

Activity 17 – using partial on class methods

Even though `partial` is an extremely useful and versatile function of the `functools` module, it seems to fail when we try to apply it to a `class` method.

To begin with, you are working in a company that models superheroes. You are asked to fix the following code snippet, as the previous developer attempted to use `functools.partial` to create the `reset_name` function but it does not seem to work well. Explore `functools` to make the following code snippet work without errors by creating `partial` on a `class` method:

In this activity, you will explore the `partial` module to see how `partial` can be used in more advanced use cases. This activity can be performed on the Jupyter notebook:

```python
import functools
if __name__ == "__main__":
    class Hero:
        DEFAULT_NAME = "Superman"
        def __init__(self):
            self.name = Hero.DEFAULT_NAME

        def rename(self, new_name):
            self.name = new_name


        reset_name = functools.partial(rename, DEFAULT_NAME)


        def __repr__(self):
            return f"Hero({self.name!r})"
```

When we try to use `partial` in this class, to create the `reset_name` method, something seems to not work. Make the following succeed by modifying the way we used `partial` previously:

```python
if __name__ == "__main__":
    hero = Hero()
    assert hero.name == "Superman"
    hero.rename("Batman")
    assert hero.name == "Batman"
    hero.reset_name()
    assert hero.name == "Superman"
```

Follow these steps:

1. Run the code and see what error it outputs.

2. Check for alternatives for `functools.partial` by running `help(functools)`.

3. Use `functools.partialmethod` to implement the new class.

Note

The solution for this activity can be found in *Appendix* on GitHub.

Summary

You have looked at multiple modules in the Standard Library and how they help you write well-tested and easier-to-read code. However, there are still many more modules to explore and understand in order to use them effectively though. We have learned that Python comes with *batteries included*, through its vast Standard Library, and that in many situations, the utilities it provides are extended through an advanced API. By having the mindset of checking how things can be solved with the Standard Library before trying to write your own code, you can become a better Python programmer.

Now that you have some knowledge of the Standard Library, you will start to look more deeply into how to make our code easier to read for Python programmers, usually known as Pythonic code. While using the Standard Library as much as possible is a good start, there are some other tips and tricks that we will look at in *Chapter 7, Becoming Pythonic*.

7
Becoming Pythonic

Overview

By the end of this chapter, you will be able to write succinct, readable expressions for creating lists; use Python comprehensions with lists, dictionaries, and sets; use `collections.defaultdict` to avoid exceptions when using dictionaries; write iterators to enable Pythonic access to your data types; explain how generator functions are related to iterators and write them to defer complex calculations; use the `itertools` module to succinctly express complex sequences of data; and use the `re` module to work with regular expressions in Python.

Introduction

Python is not just a programming language – it is made up of a community of programmers who use, maintain, and enjoy the Python programming language. As with any community, its members have shared cultures and values. The values of the Python community are well summarized in Tim Peter's document *The Zen of Python (PEP 20)* (`https://peps.python.org/pep-0020/`), which includes this statement, among others:

"There should be one – and preferably only one – obvious way to do it."

The Python community has a long history of friendly rivalry with another community of programmers centered around the Perl programming language. Perl was designed around the idea that *There Is More Than One Way To Do It* (TIMTOWTDI, which is pronounced *Tim Toady*). While Tim Peter's line in *PEP 20* is a dig at Perl, it also introduces the idea of Pythonicity.

Code is Pythonic if it works the way that a Python programmer would expect it to work. Sometimes, writing Pythonic code is easy and entails doing the simplest thing that could work. However, if you are writing a class, data structure, or module that will be used by other programmers, then sometimes, you must go the extra mile so that they will be able to do the simplest thing that could work. Hopefully, your module will have more users than writers, and this is the correct trade-off to make.

In the previous chapter, you were introduced to the different standard libraries, and you also learned how logging could be useful when it comes to handling data. This chapter introduces a few of the Python language and library features that are particularly Pythonic. You explored how collections worked in the previous chapter. Now, you will add to this knowledge by exploring collection comprehensions that work with lists, sets, and dictionaries. Iterators and generators allow you to add list-like behavior to your code so that it can be used in a more Pythonic way. You will also examine some of the types and functions in Python's standard library that make advanced use of collections easier to write, and easier to understand.

Having these tools at your disposal will make it easier for you to read, write, and understand Python code. In the current world of open source software, and with data scientists sharing their code through Jupyter notebooks, Pythonic code is your gateway to membership in the global Python community.

In this chapter, we will cover the following topics:

- Using list comprehensions
- Set and dictionary comprehensions
- Using `defaultdict` to get default values
- Creating custom iterators
- Leveraging itertools
- Lazy evaluations with generators
- Using regular expressions

Technical requirements

You can find the code files for this chapter on GitHub at https://github.com/PacktPublishing/The-Python-Workshop-Second-Edition/tree/main/Chapter07.

Using list comprehensions

List comprehensions are a flexible, expressive way of writing Python expressions to create sequences of values. They make iterating over the input and building the resulting list implicit so that program authors and readers can focus on the important features of what the list represents. It is this concision that makes list comprehensions a Pythonic way of working with lists or sequences.

List comprehensions are built out of bits of Python syntax we have already seen. They are surrounded by square brackets ([]), which signify Python symbols for a literal list. They contain `for` elements in a list, which is how Python iterates over members of a collection. Optionally, they can filter elements out of a list using the familiar syntax of the `if` expression.

Exercise 100 – introducing list comprehensions

In this exercise, you will be writing a program that creates a list of cubes of whole numbers from 1 to 5. This example is trivial because we're focusing more on how you can build a list than on the specific operations that are done to each member of the list.

Nonetheless, you may need to do this sort of thing in the real world, such as if you were to write a program to teach students about functions by graphing those functions. That application might require a list of *x* coordinates that generates a list of *y* coordinates so that it can plot a graph of the function. First, you will explore what this program looks like using the Python features you have already seen. Follow these steps:

1. Open a Jupyter notebook and type in the following code:

```
cubes = []
for x in [1,2,3,4,5]:
        cubes.append(x**3)
print(cubes)
```

You will get the following output:

```
[1, 8, 27, 64, 125]
```

Understanding this code involves keeping track of the state of the cube's variable, which starts as an empty list, and of the x variable, which is used as a cursor to keep track of the program's position in the list. This is all irrelevant to the task at hand, which is to list the cubes of each of these numbers. It will be better – more Pythonic, even – to remove all the irrelevant details. Luckily, list comprehensions allow us to do that.

2. Now, write the following code, which replaces the previous loop with a list comprehension:

```
cubes = [x**3 for x in [1,2,3,4,5]]
print(cubes)
```

You will get the following output:

```
[1, 8, 27, 64, 125]
```

This says, *"For each member in the [1,2,3,4,5] list, call it x, calculate the x**3 expression, and put that in the list cubes."* This list can be any list-like object, such as a range.

3. Now, you can make this example even simpler by writing the following:

```
cubes = [x**3 for x in range(1,6)]
print(cubes)
```

You will get the following output:

```
[1, 8, 27, 64, 125]
```

Now, the code is as short and succinct as it can be. Rather than telling you the recipe that the computer follows to build a list of the cubes of the numbers 1, 2, 3, 4, and 5, it tells you that it calculates the cube of x for every x starting from 1 and smaller than 6. This is the essence of Pythonic coding: reducing the gap between what you say and what you mean when you tell the computer what it should do.

A list comprehension can also filter its inputs when building a list. To do this, you must add an `if` expression to the end of the comprehension, where the expression can be any test of an input value that returns `True` or `False`. This is useful when you want to transform some of the values in a list while ignoring others. As an example, you could build a photo gallery of social media posts by making a list of thumbnail images from photos found in each post, but only when the posts are pictures, not text status updates.

4. You want to get Python to shout the names of the Monty Python cast, but only those whose name begins with T. Enter the following Python code into a notebook:

```
names = ["Graham Chapman", "John Cleese", "Terry
Gilliam", "Eric Idle", "Terry Jones"]
```

5. The preceding code shows the names you are going to use. Now, enter the following list comprehension to filter only those that start with "T" and operate on them:

```
print([name.upper() for name in names if name.
startswith("T")])
```

You will get the following output:

```
['TERRY GILLIAM', 'TERRY JONES']
```

By completing this exercise, you have created a filter list using list comprehension.

Exercise 101 – using multiple input lists

All the examples you have seen so far build one list out of another by performing an expression on each member of the list. You can define comprehension over multiple lists by defining a different element name for each of the lists.

> **Note**
>
> Monty Python is the name of an Anglo-American comedy group known for their TV show "Monty Python's Flying Circus" (BBC, 1969), as well as films such as "Monty Python and the Holy Grail" (1975), stage shows, and albums. The group has achieved international popularity, especially among the computer science community. The Python language was named after the group. The term *spam*, now used for unsolicited email and other unwanted digital communications, also comes from a Monty Python sketch in which a café humorously insists on serving tinned meat (or spam) with everything. Other jokes, scenarios, and names taken from the group are often found in examples and even official Python documentation. So, if you ever encounter strange names or odd situations when going through tutorials, now you know why.

To show how this works, in this exercise, you will be multiplying the elements of two lists together. The Spam Café in *Monty Python's Flying Circus* (refer to the preceding note) famously served a narrow range of foodstuffs mostly centered around a processed meat product. You will use ingredients from its menu to explore multiple-list comprehension. Follow these steps:

1. Enter the following code into a Jupyter notebook:

    ```
    print([x*y for x in ['spam', 'eggs', 'chips'] for y in
    [1,2,3]])
    ```

    The output is as follows:

    ```
    ['spam', 'spamspam', 'spamspamspam', 'eggs', 'eggseggs', 'eggseggseggs', 'chips', 'chipschips', 'chipschipschips']
    ```

    Figure 7.1 – The output printing the elements of two lists together

    Inspecting the result shows that the collections are iterated in a nested fashion, with the rightmost collection on the inside of the nest and the leftmost on the outside. Here, if x is set to spam, then x*y is calculated with y being equal to each of the values of 1, 2, and then 3 before x is set to eggs, and so on.

2. Reverse the order of the lists:

    ```
    print([x*y for x in [1,2,3] for y in ['spam', 'eggs',
    'chips']])
    ```

    The output is as follows:

    ```
    ['spam', 'eggs', 'chips', 'spamspam', 'eggseggs', 'chipschips', 'spamspamspam', 'eggseggseggs', 'chipschipschips']
    ```

    Figure 7.2 – The output with the reverse order of the list

    Swapping the order of the lists changes the order of the results in the comprehension. Now, x is initially set to 1, then y to each of spam, eggs, and chips, before x is set to 2, and so on. While the result of multiplication does not depend on its order (for instance, the results of 'spam'*2 and 2*'spam' are the same, namely, spamspam), the fact that the lists are iterated in a different order means that the same results are computed in a different sequence.

    For instance, the same list could be iterated multiple times in a list comprehension – the lists for x and y do not have to be different:

    ```
    numbers = [1,2,3]
    print([x**y for x in numbers for y in numbers])
    ```

    The output is as follows:

    ```
    [1, 1, 1, 2, 4, 8, 3, 9, 27]
    ```

In the following activity, you will be creating fixtures for a chess tournament featuring four players. You will be using list comprehension and filters to find the best fixture.

Activity 18 – building a chess tournament

In this activity, you will use a list comprehension to create the fixtures for a chess tournament. Fixtures are strings of the form "player 1 versus player 2." Because there is a slight advantage to playing as white, you also want to generate the "player 2 versus player 1" fixture so that the tournament is fair. But you do not want people playing against themselves, so you should also filter out fixtures such as "player 1 versus player 1."

Follow these steps to complete this activity:

1. Open a Jupyter notebook.

2. Define the list of player names: `Magnus Carlsen`, `Fabiano Caruana`, `Yifan Hou`, and `Wenjun Ju`.

3. Create a list comprehension that uses this list of names twice to create tournament fixtures in the correct format.

4. Add a filter to the comprehension so that no player is pitted against themselves.

5. Print the list of tournament fixtures.

    You should get the following output:

```
['Magnus Carlsen vs. Fabiano Caruana', 'Magnus Carlsen vs. Yifan Hou', 'Magnus Carlsen vs. Wenjun Ju', 'Fabiano Caruana vs.
Magnus Carlsen', 'Fabiano Caruana vs. Yifan Hou', 'Fabiano Caruana vs. Wenjun Ju', 'Yifan Hou vs. Magnus Carlsen', 'Yifan H
ou vs. Fabiano Caruana', 'Yifan Hou vs. Wenjun Ju', 'Wenjun Ju vs. Magnus Carlsen', 'Wenjun Ju vs. Fabiano Caruana', 'Wenju
n Ju vs. Yifan Hou']
```

Figure 7.3 – The expected output showing the tournament fixtures

> **Note**
> The solution for this activity can be found in *Appendix* on GitHub.

Set and dictionary comprehensions

List comprehensions are handy ways in which to concisely build sequences of values in Python. Other forms of comprehension are also available, which you can use to build other collection types. A set is an unordered collection: you can see what elements are in a set, but you cannot index into a set nor insert an object at a particular location in the set because the elements are not ordered. An element can only be present in a set once, whereas it could appear in a list multiple times.

Sets are frequently useful in situations where you want to quickly test whether an object is in a collection but do not need to track the order of the objects in the collection. For example, a web service might keep track of all of the active session tokens in a set so that when it receives a request, it can test whether the session token corresponds to an active session.

A dictionary is a collection of pairs of objects, where one object in the pair is called the key, and the other is called the value. In this case, you associate a value with a particular key, and then you can ask the dictionary for the value associated with that key. Each key may only be present in a dictionary once, but multiple keys may be associated with the same value. While the name "dictionary" suggests a connection between terms and their definitions, dictionaries are commonly used as indices (and, therefore, dictionary comprehension is often used to build an index). Going back to the web service example, different users of the service could have different permissions, thus limiting the actions that they can perform. The web service could construct a dictionary in which the keys are session tokens, and the values represent user permissions. This is so that it can quickly tell whether a request associated with a given session is permissible.

The syntax for both set and dictionary comprehensions looks very similar to list comprehension, with the square brackets (`[]`) simply replaced by curly braces (`{}`). The difference between the two is how the elements are described. For a set, you need to indicate a single element; for example, `{ x for x in ... }`. For a dictionary, you need to indicate a pair containing the key and the value; for example, `{ key:value for key in... }`.

Exercise 102 – using set comprehensions

The difference between a list and a set is that the elements in a list have an order, while those in a set do not. This means that a set cannot contain duplicate entries: an object is either in a set or not.

In this exercise, you will be changing a set comprehension into a set. Follow these steps:

1. Enter the following comprehension code into a notebook to create a list:

    ```
    print([a + b for a in [0,1,2,3] for b in [4,3,2,1]])
    ```

    The output is as follows:

    ```
    [4, 3, 2, 1, 5, 4, 3, 2, 6, 5, 4, 3, 7, 6, 5, 4]
    ```

2. Now, create a set by changing the outer square brackets in the comprehension to curly braces:

    ```
    print({a+b for a in [0,1,2,3] for b in [4,3,2,1]})
    ```

    The output is as follows:

    ```
    {1, 2, 3, 4, 5, 6, 7}
    ```

Notice that the set created in *step 2* is much shorter than the list created in *step 1*. The reason for this is that the set does not contain duplicate entries – try counting how many times the number 4 appears in each collection. It's in the list four times (because 0 + 4 = 4, 1 + 3 = 4, 2 + 2 = 4, and 3 + 1 = 4), but sets don't retain duplicates, so there's only one instance of the number 4 in the set. If you just removed the duplicates from the list produced in *step 1*, you'd have a list of [4, 3, 2, 1, 5, 6, 7]. Sets don't preserve the order of their elements either, so the numbers appear in a different order in the set created in *step 2*. The fact that the numbers in the set appear in numerical order is due to the implementation of the set type in Python.

Exercise 103 – using dictionary comprehensions

Curly-brace comprehension can also be used to create a dictionary. The expression on the left-hand side of the for keyword in the comprehension should contain a comprehension. You write the expression that will generate the dictionary keys to the left of the colon and the expression that will generate the values to the right. Note that a key can only appear once in a dictionary.

In this exercise, you will create a lookup dictionary of the lengths of the names in a list and print the length of each name. Follow these steps:

1. Enter the following list of names of Monty Python stars in a notebook:

    ```
    names = ["Eric", "Graham", "Terry", "John", "Terry"]
    ```

2. Use a comprehension to create a lookup dictionary of the lengths of the names:

    ```
    print({k:len(k) for k in ["Eric", "Graham", "Terry",
    "John", "Terry"]})
    ```

    The output will be:

    ```
    {'Eric': 4, 'Graham': 6, 'Terry': 5, 'John': 4}
    ```

    Figure 7.4 – A lookup dictionary equaling the length of the names in the list

Notice that the entry for Terry only appears once, because dictionaries cannot contain duplicate keys. Here, you created an index of the length of each name, keyed by name. An index like this could be useful in a game, where it could work out how to lay out the score table for each player without repeatedly having to recalculate the length of each player's name.

Activity 19 – building a scorecard using dictionary comprehensions and multiple lists

You are the backend developer for a renowned college. Management has asked you to build a demo scorecard for their students based on the marks they have achieved in their exams.

Your goal in this activity is to use dictionary comprehension and lists in Python to build a demo scorecard for four students in the college.

Follow these steps to complete this activity:

1. Create two separate lists: one for the names of the students and another for their scores.

2. Create a dictionary comprehension that iterates over the numbers in a range of the same length as the lists of names and scores. The comprehension should create a dictionary where, for the ith number in the range, the key is the ith name, and the value is the ith score.

3. Print out the resulting dictionary to make sure it's correct.

   Here the output will be:

   ```
   {'Vivian': 70, 'Racheal': 82, 'Tom': 80, 'Adrian': 79}
   ```

   Figure 7.5 – A dictionary indicating the names and scores as a key-value pair

> **Note**
> The solution for this activity can be found in *Appendix* on GitHub.

Using defaultdict to get default values

The built-in dictionary type considers it to be an error when you try to access the value for a key that doesn't exist. It will raise a `KeyError`, which you have to handle; otherwise, your program will crash. Often, that's a good idea. If the programmer doesn't get the key correct, it could indicate a typo or a misunderstanding of how the dictionary is used.

It's often a good idea, but not always. Sometimes, it's reasonable that a programmer doesn't know what the dictionary contains; whether it's created from a file supplied by the user or the content of a network request, for example. In situations like this, any of the keys the programmer expects could be missing, but handling `KeyError` instances everywhere is tedious, repetitive, and makes the intent of the code harder to see.

For these situations, Python provides the `collections.defaultdict` type. It works like a regular dictionary, except that you can give it a function that creates a default value to use when a key is missing. Rather than raise an error, it calls that function and returns the result.

Exercise 104 – adopting a default dict

In this exercise, you will be using a regular dictionary that raises a `KeyError` when you try to access a missing key. Follow these steps:

1. Create a dictionary for `john`:

   ```
   john = {'first_name': 'John', 'surname': 'Cleese'}
   ```

   Attempt to use a `middle_name` key that was not defined in the dictionary:

   ```
   john['middle_name']
   ```

Let's see the output:

```
-----------------------------------------------------------------------
KeyError                                   Traceback (most recent call last)
<ipython-input-1-63d140c09c07> in <module>
      1 john = { 'first_name': 'John', 'surname': 'Cleese' }
----> 2 john['middle_name']

KeyError: 'middle_name'
```

Figure 7.6 – The output showing KeyError: 'middle_name'

2. Now, import `defaultdict` from `collections` and wrap the dictionary in `defaultdict`:

```
from collections import defaultdict
safe_john = defaultdict(str, john)
```

The first argument is the type constructor for a string, so missing keys will appear to have the empty string as their value.

3. Attempt to use a key that was not defined via the wrapped dictionary:

```
print(safe_john['middle_name'])
```

Now you will get the following output:

```
' '
```

No exception is triggered at this stage; instead, an empty string is returned. The first argument to the constructor of `defaultdict`, called `default_factory`, can be any callable (that is, function-like) object. You can use this to compute a value based on the key or return a default value that is relevant to your domain.

4. Create a `defaultdict` that uses a lambda as its `default_factory`:

```
from collections import defaultdict
courses = defaultdict(lambda: 'No!')
courses['Java'] = 'This is Java'
```

This dictionary will return the value from the lambda on any unknown key.

5. Access the value at an unknown key in this new dictionary:

```
print(courses['Python'])
```

```
'No!'
```

6. Access the value at a known key in this new dictionary:

```
print(courses['Java'])
```

The output will be as follows:

```
This is Java
```

The benefit of the default dictionary is that in situations where you know it is likely that expected keys will be missing from a dictionary, you can work with default values and not have to sprinkle your code with exception-handling blocks. This is another example of Pythonicity: if what you mean is "*use the value for the "foo" key, but if that doesn't exist, then use "bar" as the value,*" then you should write that, rather than "*use the value for the "foo" key, but if you get an exception and the exception is KeyError, then use "bar" as the value.*"

Default dicts are great for working with untrusted input, such as a file chosen by the user or an object received over the network. A network service shouldn't expect any input it gets from a client to be well formatted. If it treats the data, it receives a request as a JSON object. It should be ready for the data to not be in JSON format. If the data is JSON, the program should not expect all of the keys defined by the API to have been supplied by the client. The default dict gives you a concise way to work with such under-specified data.

Creating custom iterators

The Pythonic secret that enables comprehensions to find all of the entries in a list, range, or other collection is an iterator. Supporting iterators in your classes opens them up for use in comprehensions, for...in loops, and anywhere that Python works with collections. Your collection must implement a method called __iter__(), which returns the iterator.

The iterator itself is also a Python object with a simple contract. It must provide a single method, __next__(). Each time __next__() is called, the iterator returns the next value in the collection. When the iterator reaches the end of the collection, __next__() raises StopIteration to signal that the iteration should terminate.

If you've used exceptions in other programming languages, you may be surprised by this use of an exception to signal a fairly commonplace situation. After all, plenty of loops reach an end, so it's not exactly an exceptional circumstance. Python is not so dogmatic about exceptions, favoring simplicity and expressiveness over universal rules-lawyering.

Once you've learned the techniques to build iterators, the applications are limitless. Your collections or collection-like classes can supply iterators so that programmers can work with them using Pythonic collection techniques such as comprehensions. For example, an application that stores its data model in a database can use an iterator to retrieve each row that matches a query as a separate object in a loop or comprehension. A programmer can say, "*For each row in the database, do this to the row,*" and treat it like a list of rows, when your data model object is secretly running a database query each time the iterator's __next__() method is called.

Exercise 105 – the simplest iterator

The easiest way to provide an iterator for your class is to use one from another object. If you are designing a class that controls access to its collection, then it might be a good idea to let programmers iterate over your object using the collection's iterator. In this case, just have __iter__() return the appropriate iterator.

In this exercise, you will be coding an `Interrogator` who asks awkward questions to people on a quest. It takes a list of questions in its constructor. Follow these steps to write the program that prints these questions:

1. Enter the constructor into a notebook:

```
class Interrogator:
    def __init__(self, questions):
        self.questions = questions
```

Using an `Interrogator` in a loop probably means asking each of its questions in sequence. The easiest iterator that can achieve this is the iterator that collects questions.

2. Therefore, to implement the __iter__() method to return that object, add the __iter__() method:

```
def __iter__(self):
    return self.questions.__iter__()
```

Now, you can create a list of questions, give them to an `Interrogator`, and use that object in a loop.

3. Create a list of questions:

```
questions = ["What is your name?", "What is your quest?",
"What is the average airspeed velocity of an unladen
swallow?"]
```

4. Create an `Interrogator`:

```
awkward_person = Interrogator(questions)
```

5. Now, use this `Interrogator` in a for loop:

```
for question in awkward_person:
    print(question)
```

Now the output will be:

```
What is your name?
What is your quest?
What is the average airspeed velocity of an unladen swallow?
```

Figure 7.7 – The list of questions asked using Interrogator

On the face of it, you've done nothing more than add a level of interaction between the `Interrogator` class and the collection of questions. From an implementation perspective, that's exactly right. However, from a design perspective, what you've done is much more powerful. You've designed an `Interrogator` class that programmers can ask to iterate over its questions, without having to tell the programmer anything about how `Interrogator` stores its questions. While it's just forwarding a method call to a list object today, you could change that tomorrow to use a SQLite3 database or a web service call, and programmers using the `Interrogator` class will not need to change anything.

For a more complicated case, you need to write your own iterator. The iterator must implement a `__next__()` method, which returns the next element in the collection or raises `StopIteration` when it gets to the end.

Exercise 106 – a custom iterator

In this exercise, you'll implement a classical-era algorithm called the Sieve of Eratosthenes. To find prime numbers between 2 and an upper bound value, n, first, you must list all of the numbers in that range. Now, 2 is a prime, so return that. Then, remove 2 from the list, and all multiples of 2, and return the new lowest number (which will be 3). Continue until there are no more numbers left in the collection. Every number that gets returned using this method is a successively higher prime. It works because any number you find in the collection to return did not get removed at an earlier step, so it has no lower prime factors other than itself.

First, build the architecture of the class. Its constructor needs to take the upper bound value and generate the list of possible primes. The object can be its own iterator so that its `__iter__()` method will return itself. Follow these steps:

1. Define the `PrimesBelow` class and its initializer:

    ```
    class PrimesBelow:
        def __init__(self, bound):
            self.candidate_numbers = list(range(2,bound))
    ```

2. Implement the `__iter__()` method to return itself:

    ```
    def __iter__(self):
        return self
    ```

The main body of the algorithm is in the __next__() method. With each iteration, it finds the next lowest prime. If there isn't one, it raises StopIteration. If there is one, it sieves that prime number and its multiples from the collection and then returns the prime number.

3. Define the __next__() method and the exit condition. If there are no remaining numbers in the collection, then the iteration can stop:

```
def __next__(self):
    if len(self.candidate_numbers) == 0:
        raise StopIteration
```

4. Complete the implementation of __next__() by selecting the lowest number in the collection as the value for next_prime and removing any multiples of that number before returning the new prime:

```
next_prime = self.candidate_numbers[0]
self.candidate_numbers = [x for x in self.
candidate_numbers if x % next_prime != 0]
    return next_prime
    return next_prime
```

5. Use an instance of this class to find all the prime numbers below 100:

```
primes_to_a_hundred = [prime for prime in
PrimesBelow(100)]
print(primes_to_a_hundred)
```

The output is as follows:

```
[2, 3, 5, 7, 11, 13, 17, 19, 23, 29, 31, 37, 41, 43, 47, 53, 59, 61, 67, 71, 73, 79, 83, 89, 97]
```

Figure 7.8 – The output indicating all prime numbers below 100

This exercise demonstrates that by implementing an iterative algorithm as a Python iterator, you can treat it like a collection. The program does not build the collection of all of the prime numbers: you did that yourself in *step 5* by using the PrimesBelow class, but otherwise, PrimesBelow was generating one number at a time, whenever you called the __next()__ method. This is a great way to hide the implementation details of an algorithm from a programmer. Whether you give them a collection of objects to iterate over or an iterator that computes each value as it is requested, programmers can use the results in the same way.

Exercise 107 – controlling the iteration

You do not have to use an iterator in a loop or comprehension. Instead, you can use the `iter()` function to get its argument's iterator object, and then pass that to the `next()` function to return successive values from the iterator. These functions call through to the `__iter__()` and `__next__()` methods, respectively. You can use them to add custom behavior to an iteration or to gain more control over the iteration.

In this exercise, you will print the prime numbers below 5. An error should be raised when the object runs out of prime numbers. To do this, you will use the `PrimesBelow` class you created in the previous exercise. Follow these steps:

1. Get the iterator for a `PrimesBelow` instance. `PrimesBelow` is the class you created in *Exercise 106 – a custom iterator*, so if you still have the notebook you created for that exercise, you can enter this code in a cell at the end of that notebook:

    ```
    primes_under_five = iter(PrimesBelow(5))
    ```

2. Repeatedly use `next()` with this object to generate successive prime numbers:

    ```
    next(primes_under_five)
    ```

    The output will be as follows:

    2

    Now, run this code once again:

    ```
    next(primes_under_five)
    ```

    The output will be as follows:

    3

3. When the object runs out of prime numbers, the subsequent use of `next()` raises the `StopIteration` error:

    ```
    next(primes_under_five)
    ```

    You will get the following output:

    ```
    ---------------------------------------------------------------
    NameError                               Traceback (most recent call last)
    <ipython-input-1-c81778c59ded> in <module>
    ----> 1 primes_under_five = iter(PrimesBelow(5))
          2 next(primes_under_five)
          3 2
          4 next(primes_under_five)
          5 3

    NameError: name 'PrimesBelow' is not defined
    ```

Figure 7.9 – The StopIteration error is thrown when the object runs out of prime numbers

Being able to step through an iteration manually is incredibly useful in programs that are driven by a sequence of inputs, including a command interpreter. You can treat the input stream as an iteration over a list of strings, where each string represents a command. Call next() to get the next command, work out what to do, and then execute it. Then, print the result, and go back to next() to await the subsequent command. When StopIteration is raised, the user has no more commands for your program, and it can exit.

Leveraging itertools

Iterators are useful for describing sequences, such as Python lists and ranges, and sequence-like collections, such as your data types, which provide ordered access to their contents. Iterators make it easy to work with these types in a Pythonic way. Python's library includes the itertools module, which has a selection of helpful functions for combining, manipulating, and otherwise working with iterators. In this section, you will use a couple of helpful tools from the module. There are plenty more available, so be sure to check out the official documentation for itertools.

One of the important uses of itertools is in dealing with infinite sequences. There are plenty of situations in which a sequence does not have an end: everything from infinite series in mathematics to the event loop in a graphical application. A graphical user interface is usually built around an event loop in which the program waits for an event (such as a key press, a mouse click, a timer expiring, or something else) and then reacts to it. The stream of events can be treated as a potentially infinite list of event objects, with the program taking the next event object from the sequence and doing its reaction work. Iterating over such a sequence with either a Python for..in loop or a comprehension will never terminate. There are functions in itertools for providing a window onto an infinite sequence; the following exercise will look at one of those.

Exercise 108 – using infinite sequences and takewhile()

An alternative algorithm to the Sieve of Eratosthenes for generating prime numbers is to test each number in sequence – to see whether it has any divisors other than itself. This algorithm uses a lot more time than the Sieve in return for a lot less space.

In this exercise, you will be implementing a better algorithm that uses less space than the Sieve to generate prime numbers. Follow these steps:

1. Enter the following iterator algorithm into a notebook:

Exercise108.ipynb

```
class Primes:
    def __init__(self):
        self.current = 2
    def __iter__(self):
        return self
    def __next__(self):
        while True:
            current = self.current
            square_root = int(current ** 0.5)
            is_prime = True
        if square_root >= 2:
            for i in range(2, square_root + 1):
                if current % i == 0:
                    is_prime = False
                    break
        self.current += 1
        if is_prime:
            return current
```

> **Note**
> If this code does not render, please enter the URL `https://nbviewer.jupyter.org/`.

> **Note**
> The class you just entered is an iterator, but the `__next__()` method never raises a `StopIteration` error. This means it never exits. Even though you know that each prime number it returns is bigger than the previous one, a comprehension doesn't know that, so you can't simply filter out large values.

2. Enter the following code to get a list of primes that are lower than 100:

```
[p for p in Primes() if p < 100]
```

Because the iterator never raises `StopIteration`, this program will never finish. You'll have to force it to exit.

3.   Click on the **Stop** button in the Jupyter notebook.

The output will be:

```
----------------------------------------------------------------
KeyboardInterrupt                          Traceback (most recent call last)
<ipython-input-23-afd3c871a33d> in <module>()
----> 1 [p for p in Primes() if p < 100]

<ipython-input-23-afd3c871a33d> in <listcomp>(.0)
----> 1 [p for p in Primes() if p < 100]

<ipython-input-22-c1ad65bf0095> in __next__(self)
     11                 if square_root >= 2:
     12                     for i in range(2, square_root + 1):
---> 13                         if current % i == 0:
     14                             is_prime = False
     15                             break

KeyboardInterrupt:
```

Figure 7.10 – Iterator forced to exit

To work with this iterator, `itertools` provides the `takewhile()` function, which wraps the iterator in another iterator. You can also supply `takewhile()` with a Boolean function, and its iteration will take values from the supplied iterator until the function returns `False`, at which time it raises `StopIteration` and stops. This makes it possible to find prime numbers below 100 from the infinite sequence entered previously.

4.   Use `takewhile()` to turn the infinite sequence into a finite one:

```
import itertools
print([p for p in itertools.takewhile(lambda x: x<100,
Primes())])
```

You will get the following output:

```
[2, 3, 5, 7, 11, 13, 17, 19, 23, 29, 31, 37, 41, 43, 47, 53, 59, 61, 67, 71, 73, 79, 83, 89, 97]
```

Figure 7.11 – Using the takewhile() function to produce a finite sequence

Surprisingly, it's also useful to be able to turn a finite sequence into an infinite one.

Exercise 109 – turning a finite sequence into an infinite one, and back again

In this exercise, you will consider a turn-based game, such as chess. The person playing white makes the first move. Then, the person playing black takes their turn. Then white. Then black. Then white, black, white, and so on until the game ends. If you had an infinite list of white, black, white, black, white, and so on, then you could always look at the next element to decide whose turn it is. Follow these steps:

1. Enter the list of players into a notebook:

    ```
    import itertools
    players = ['White', 'Black']
    ```

2. Use the `cycle` function of `itertools` to generate an infinite sequence of turns:

    ```
    turns = itertools.cycle(players)
    ```

    To demonstrate that this has the expected behavior, you'll want to turn it back into a finite sequence so that you can view the first few members of the `turns` iterator. You can use `takewhile()` for that and, here, combine it with the `count()` function from `itertools`, which produces an infinite sequence of numbers.

3. List the players who take the first 10 turns in a chess game:

    ```
    countdown = itertools.count(10, -1)
    print([turn for turn in itertools.takewhile(lambda
    x:next(countdown)>0, turns)])
    ```

    You will get the following output:

```
['White', 'Black', 'White', 'Black', 'White', 'Black', 'White', 'Black', 'White', 'Black']
```

Figure 7.12 – Using the takewhile() function to list the players who take the first 10 turns in the chess game

This is the "round-robin" algorithm for allocating actions (in this case, making a chess move) to resources (in this case, the players), and has many more applications than board games. A simple way to do load balancing between multiple servers in a web service or a database application is to build an infinite sequence of the available servers and choose one in turn for each incoming request.

Lazy evaluations with generators

A function that returns a value does all of its computation and gives up control to its caller, which supplies that value. This is not the only possible behavior for a function. Instead, it can yield a value, which passes control (and the value) back to the caller but leaves the function's state intact. Later, it can yield another value, or finally return to indicate that it is done. A function that yields is called a generator.

Generators are useful because they allow a program to defer or postpone calculating a result until it's required. Finding the successive digits of π, for example, is hard work, and it gets harder as the number of digits increases. If you wrote a program to display the digits of π, you might calculate the first 1,000 digits. Much of that effort will be wasted if the user only asks to see the first 10 digits. Using a generator, you can put off the expensive work until your program requires the results.

A real-world example of a situation where generators can help is when dealing with I/O. A stream of data coming from a network service can be represented by a generator that yields the available data until the stream is closed when it returns the remaining data. Using a generator allows the program to pass control back and forth between the I/O stream when data is available, and the caller where the data can be processed.

Python internally turns generator functions into objects that use the iterator protocol (such as ___ iter___, ___next___, and the StopIteration error), so the work you put into understanding iterations in the previous section means you already know what generators are doing. There is nothing you can write for a generator that could not be replaced with an equivalent iterator object. However, sometimes, a generator is easier to write or understand. Writing code that is easier to understand is the definition of Pythonicity.

Exercise 110 – generating a Sieve

In this exercise, you will be rewriting the Sieve of Eratosthenes as a generator function and comparing it with the result of the iterator version. Follow these steps:

1. Rewrite the Sieve of Eratosthenes as a generator function that yields its values:

```
def primes_below(bound):
    candidates = list(range(2,bound))
    while(len(candidates) > 0):
        yield candidates[0]
        candidates = [c for c in candidates if c %
candidates[0] != 0]
```

2. Confirm that the result is the same as the iterator version:

```
[prime for prime in primes_below(100)]
```

The output is as follows:

```
[2, 3, 5, 7, 11, 13, 17, 19, 23, 29, 31, 37, 41, 43, 47, 53, 59, 61, 67, 71, 73, 79, 83, 89, 97]
```

Figure 7.13 – The output indicating all prime numbers below 100

That's all there is to generators – they're just a different way of expressing an iterator. They do, however, communicate a different design intention; namely, that the flow of control is going to pass back and forth between the generator and its caller.

The answer to *Why does Python provide both the iterator and the generator?* is found at the end of this exercise. They do the same thing, but they expose different design intentions. The PEP in which generators were introduced (https://www.python.org/dev/peps/pep-0255/) contains more details in the *Motivations* and *Q&A* sections for students who would like to dig deeper.

Activity 20 – using random numbers to find the value of Pi

The Monte Carlo method is a technique that is used to approximate a numerical solution using random numbers. Named after the famous casino, chance is at the core of Monte Carlo methods. They use random sampling to obtain information about a function that will be difficult to calculate deterministically. Monte Carlo methods are frequently used in scientific computation to explore probability distributions and in other fields, including quantum physics and computational biology. They're also used in economics to explore the behavior of financial instruments under different market conditions. There are many applications for the Monte Carlo principle.

In this activity, you'll use a Monte Carlo method to find an approximate value for π. Here's how it works: two random numbers, (x, y), somewhere between (0, 0) and (1, 1), represent a random point in a square positioned at (0, 0) with sides whose length are 1:

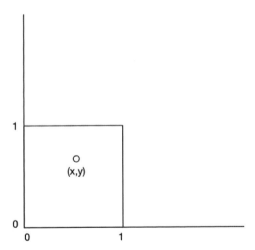

Figure 7.14 – A random point in a square with its side as unit 1

Using Pythagoras' Theorem, if the value of $$\sqrt{x^2 + y^2}$$ is less than 1, then the point is also in the top-right corner of a circle centered at (0,0) with a radius of -1:

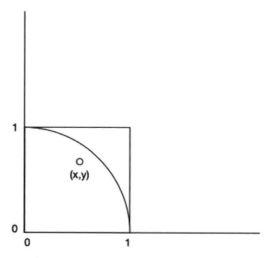

Figure 7.15 – Applying Pythagoras' Theorem to locate the point concerning the circle segment

Generate lots of points, count how many are within the circle segment, and divide the number of points within the circle by the total number of points generated. This gives you an approximation of the area of the circle segment, which should be π/4. Multiply the result by 4, and you have an approximate value of π. Data scientists often use this technique to find the area under more complex curves that represent probability distributions.

Write a generator to yield successive estimates of π. Follow these steps:

1. Define your generator function.

2. Set the total number of points, and the number within the circle segment, to 0.

3. Do the following substeps 10,000 times:

    I.   Generate two numbers between 0 and 1, using Python's random.random() function.

    II. Add 1 to the total number of points.

    III. Use math.sqrt() to find out how far the point represented by the numbers is from (0,0).

    IV. If the distance is less than 1, add 1 to the number of points within the circle.

    V.   Calculate your estimate for π: 4 * (points within the circle) / (total points generated).

    VI. If you have generated a multiple of 1,000 points, yield the approximate value for π. If you have generated 10,000 points, return the value.

4. Inspect the successive estimates of π and check how close they are to the true value (math.pi).

Note that because this activity uses random numbers, you may not get the exact results shown here:

```
[3.236, 3.232, 3.2106666666666666, 3.206, 3.1824, 3.1633333333333336, 3.1582857142857144, 3.1645, 3.1577777777777776]
[0.0944073464102071, 0.09040734641020709, 0.06907401307687344, 0.06440734641020684, 0.04080734641020678, 0.0217406797435404
36, 0.016693060695921247, 0.022907346410206753, 0.016185124187984457]
```

Figure 7.16 – A generator yielding successive estimates of π

> **Note**
>
> The solution for this activity can be found in *Appendix* on GitHub.

Using regular expressions

Regular expressions (or regexes) are a domain-specific programming language that defines a grammar for expressing efficient and flexible string comparisons. Introduced in 1951 by Stephen Cole Kleene, regular expressions have become a popular tool for searching and manipulating text. As an example, if you're writing a text editor and you want to highlight all web links in a document and make them clickable, you might search for strings that start with HTTP or HTTPS, then those that contain : //, and then those that contain some collection of printable characters, until you stop finding printable characters (such as a space, newline, or the end of the text), and highlight everything up to the end. With standard Python syntax, this will be possible, but you will end up with a very complex loop that will be difficult to get right. Using regexes, you match against `https?://\S+`.

This section will not teach you the full regular expression syntax – there are better resources for doing that. For example, check out *Mastering Python Regular Expressions* (`https://packt.live/2ISz4zs`) by Félix López and Victor Romero. This section will teach you how to use Python's `re` module to work with the regular expressions in Python. That said, some small amount of regex syntax will be useful, so let's examine the features that are used in regular expressions, as seen in the preceding URL:

- Most characters match their own identities, so `h` in a regex means "match exactly the letter h."

- Enclosing characters in square brackets can mean choosing between alternates, so if we thought a web link might be capitalized, we could start with `[Hh]` to mean "match either H or h." In the body of the URL, we want to match against any non-whitespace characters, and rather than write them all out, we can use the `\S` character class. Other character classes include `\w` (word characters), `\W` (non-word characters), and `\d` (digits).

- Two quantifiers are used. `?` means "0 or 1 time," so `s?` means "match if the text does not have `s` at this point or has it exactly once." The quantifier, `+`, means "1 or more times," so `\S+` says "one or more non-whitespace characters." There is also a quantifier, `*`, meaning "0 or more times."

The following are additional regex features that you will use in this chapter:

- Parentheses, (), introduce a numbered sub-expression, sometimes called a "capture group." They are numbered from 1, in the order that they appear in the expression.

- A backslash followed by a number refers to a numbered sub-expression, as described previously. As an example, \1 refers to the first sub-expression. These can be used when replacing text that matches the regex or to store part of a regex to use later in the same expression. Because of the way that backslashes are interpreted by Python strings, this is written as \\1 in a Python regex.

Regular expressions have various uses throughout software development since so much software deals with text. Validating user input in a web application, searching for and replacing entries in text files, and finding interesting events in application log files are all uses that regular expressions can be put to in a Python program.

Exercise 111 – matching text with regular expressions

In this exercise, you'll use the Python re module to find instances of repeated letters in a string.

The regex you will use is (\w)\\1+. (\w) searches for a single character from a word (that is, any letter or the underscore character, _) and stores that in a numbered sub-expression, \1. Then, \\1+ uses a quantifier to find one or more occurrences of the same character. Follow these steps to use this regex:

1. Import the re module:

```
import re
```

2. Define the string that you will search for, and the pattern by which to search:

```
title = "And now for something completely different"
pattern = "(\w)\\1+"
```

3. Search for the pattern and print the result:

```
print(re.search(pattern, title))
```

You will get the following output:

```
<re.Match object; span=(35, 37), match='ff'>
```

Figure 7.17 – Searching for a string using the re module

The re.search() function finds matches anywhere in the string: if it doesn't find any matches, it will return None. If you were only interested in whether the beginning of the string matched the pattern, you could use re.match(). Similarly, modifying the search pattern to start with the beginning-of-line marker (^) achieves the same aim as re.search("^(\w)\\1+", title).

Exercise 112 – using regular expressions to replace text

In this exercise, you'll use a regular expression to replace occurrences of a pattern in a string with a different pattern. Follow these steps:

1. Define the text to search:

```
import re
description = "The Norwegian Blue is a wonderful parrot.
This parrot is notable for its exquisite plumage."
```

2. Define the pattern to search for, and its replacement:

```
pattern = "(parrot)"
replacement = "ex-\\1"
```

3. Substitute the replacement for the search pattern using the re.sub() function:

```
print(re.sub(pattern, replacement, description))
```

You will get the following output:

```
The Norwegian Blue is a wonderful ex-parrot. This ex-parrot is notable for its exquisite plumage.
```

Figure 7.18 – Replacing occurrences of a repeating pattern in the string

The replacement refers to the capture group, "\1", which is the first expression in the search pattern to be surrounded by parentheses. In this case, the capture group is the whole word parrot. This lets you refer to the word parrot in the replacement without having to type it out again.

Activity 21 – finding a winner for The X-Files

At your online retail company, your manager has had an idea for a promotion. There is a whole load of old "The X-Files" DVDs in the warehouse, and she has decided to give one away for free to any customer whose name contains the letter *x*.

In this activity, you will be using Python's re module to find winning customers. The *x* could be capitalized if it's their initial, or lowercase if it's in the middle of their name, so you must use the [Xx] regular expression to search for both cases. Follow these steps:

1. Create a list of customer names. The customers are Xander Harris, Jennifer Smith, Timothy Jones, Amy Alexandrescu, Peter Price, and Weifung Xu.

2. Create a list comprehension using this list of names. Use the comprehension to filter only names where a search for the [Xx] regex is successful.

3.   Print the list of matching names. You should get the following output:

```
['Xander Harris', 'Amy Alexandrescu', 'Weifung Xu']
```

Figure 7.19 – The winner's list, indicating the presence of "Xx" in a customer name

> **Note**
> The solution for this activity can be found in *Appendix* on GitHub.

Summary

In this chapter, you learned how even though there is often more than one way to do something in Python, there is often a "Pythonic" way. The Pythonic way is succinct and easy to understand, leaving out boilerplate code and extraneous information to focus on the task at hand. Comprehensions are a Pythonic tool for manipulating collections, including lists, sets, and dictionaries. Comprehensions are powered by iterators, which can be written as classes or as generator functions that yield the iterated values. The Python library includes useful functions for working with iterators, including infinite sequences expressed as iterators.

In the next chapter, you'll move past the details of the Python language and into how to work as a professional Python programmer. You'll learn how to debug your Python code, write unit tests, and document, package, and share your Python code with other coders.

8

Software Development

Overview

By the end of this chapter, you will be able to troubleshoot issues in Python applications, explain why testing in software development is important, write test scenarios in Python to validate code, create a Python package that can be published to the **Python Package Index** (**PyPI**), write and publish documentation on the web, and create a Git repository and manage your source code versions.

Introduction

Software development goes beyond writing code. In *Chapter 7, Becoming Pythonic*, you were introduced to the idea of being Pythonic. When we write software as professionals, we expect the code to be up to a certain standard and to be able to manage and distribute that code in a way that can be easily consumed by other developers.

In this chapter, you will go through the various concepts and tools that allow you to elevate the level of your source code and applications. You will examine Python tools that every Python developer uses for testing, writing documentation, packaging their code, and version control, as well as learning about techniques that allow us to debug issues that occur in existing code. Additionally, you will write tests to validate your assumptions and implementations of your code. These are all concepts and tools that are key to any successful developer in any company, as they allow developers to develop and collaborate effectively. Finally, you will cover some basics about using Git to manage your source code versions.

We will be covering the following topics:

- How to debug
- Automated testing
- Creating a **Package Installer for Python** (**pip**) package
- Creating documentation the easy way
- Source code management

Technical requirements

You can find this chapter's code file on GitHub at `https://github.com/PacktPublishing/ The-Python-Workshop-Second-Edition/tree/main/Chapter08`.

How to debug

Sooner or later in your development, you will reach a point where you see your program behave differently than you initially expected. In situations such as these, you usually look back at the source code and try to understand what is different between your expectations and the code or inputs that are being used. To facilitate that process, there are multiple methods (in general, and some that are specific to Python) that you can use to try to "debug" or "troubleshoot" the issue.

Usually, the first action of an experienced developer, when frustration arises from unexpected results in their code, is to look at the logs or any other output that the application produces. A good starting point is trying to increase the logging verbosity, as discussed in *Chapter 6, The Standard Library*. If you are not able to troubleshoot the problem with just logs, it usually means that you should look back at how you are instructing your application to log its state and activity, producing what are known as traces, as there might be a good opportunity to improve it.

The next step in verifying the **inputs and outputs** (**I/Os**) of the program is to receive and verify the log. The usual next step in Python is to use the `pdb` Python debugger.

The `pdb` module and its **command-line interface** (**CLI**) tool allow you to navigate through the code as it runs and ask questions about the state of the program, its variables, and the flow of execution. It is similar to other tools, such as `gdb`, but it is at a higher level and is designed for Python.

There are two main ways to start `pdb`. You can just run the tool and feed it with a file or use the `breakpoint` command.

As an example, take a look at the following file:

```
# This is a comment
this = "is the first line to execute"
def secret_sauce(number):
    if number <= 10:
        return number + 10
    else:
        return number - 10
def magic_operation(x, y):
    res = x + y
    res *= y
```

```
        res /= x
        res = secret_sauce(res)
        return res
    print(magic_operation(2, 10))
```

When you begin executing the script with pdb, it works like this:

```
python3.10 -m pdb magic_operation.py
> [...]Lesson08/1.debugging/magic_operation.py(3)<module>()
-> this = "is the first line to execute"
(Pdb)
```

It will stop on the first line of the Python code to execute and give you a prompt to interact with pdb.

The first line shows you which current file you are in at the moment, while the final line shows you the pdb prompt (pdb), which tells you which debugger you are running and that it is waiting for input from the user.

Another way to start pdb is to change the source code to do this. At any point in the code, you can write `import pdb;pdb.set_trace()` for earlier versions of Python to tell the Python interpreter that you want to start a debugging session at that point. If you are using Python 3.7 or a later version, you can use `breakpoint()`.

If you execute the `magic_operation_with_breakpoint.py` file attached in the book's GitHub repository, which has `breakpoint()` in one of its lines, you will see that the debugger starts for you where you requested it.

When you are running things in an **integrated development environment** (**IDE**) or code in a large application, you could achieve the same effect by using the operations that we will demonstrate later, but just dropping that line in the file is by far the simplest and fastest way, as illustrated here:

```
$ python3.10 magic_operation_with_breakpoint.py
```

> [...]/Lesson08/1.debugging/magic_operation_with_breakpoint.py(7)secret_sauce()

-> if number <= 10:

(Pdb)

At this point, you can get a list of all the commands by running `help`, or you can get more information about a specific command by running the `help` command. The most commonly used commands are presented here:

- `break filename:linenumber`: This sets a breakpoint in the specified line. It ensures that you will stop the code at that point when other commands are running by continuing the execution. Breakpoints can be set in any file included in the standard library. If you want to set a breakpoint in a file that is part of a module, you can do so by just using its full path within the Python path. For example, to stop the debugger in the `parser` module, which is part of the **Hypertext Markup Language (HTML)** package of the standard library, you would perform `b html/parser:50` to stop the code on line *50* of the file.

- `break`: You can request to stop the code when a specific function is called. If the function is in the current file, you can pass the function name. If the function is imported from another module, you will have to pass the full function specification—for example, `html.parser.HTMLParser.reset`—to stop at the `reset` function of the `HTMLParser` class of `html.parser`.

- `break without arguments`: This lists all the current breakpoints that are set in the current state of the program.

- `continue`: This continues the execution until a breakpoint is found. This is quite useful when you start a program, set breakpoints in all lines of code or functions you want to inspect, and then just let it run until it stops at any of those.

- `where`: This prints a stack trace with the current line of execution where the debugger stopped. It is useful to know what called this function or to be able to move around the stack.

- `down` and `up`: These two commands allow you to move around in the stack. If you are in a function call, you can use `up` to move to the caller of the function and inspect the state in that frame, or you can use `down` to go deeper in the stack after you have moved up.

- `list`: This displays 11 lines of code from the point where the execution stopped for the first time to when it is called. Successive calls to `list` will display the following lines in batches of 11. To start again from where the execution stopped, use `list.`

- `longlist`: This shows the source code of the current function in the current frame that is being executed.

- `next`: This executes the line and moves to the following one.

- `step`: This executes the current line and stops at the first opportunity within the function being executed. This is useful when you don't want to just execute a function but want to step through it.

- `p`: This prints the value of an expression. It is useful for checking the content of variables.

- `pp`: This allows you to pretty print an expression. It is useful when you are trying to print long structures.

- run/restart: This restarts the program, keeping all the breakpoints still set. It is useful if you have passed an event you expected to see.

Many functions have shortcuts; for example, you can use b instead of break, c or cont instead of continue, l instead of list, ll for longlist, and so on.

There are other functions not covered here; pdb comes with a broad toolbox. Use help to learn about all the different functions and how to use them.

Exercise 113 – debugging a salary calculator

In this exercise, you will use the skills you learned to use pdb to debug an application that is not working as expected.

This is a salary calculator. Your company is using this to calculate the salary increase that will be given to our employees year after year, and a manager has reported that she is getting a 20% raise when the rulebook seems to suggest that she should be getting a 30% raise.

You are just told that the manager's name is Rose, and you will find that the code for the salary raise calculation looks like this:

Exercise113.py

```
3 def _manager_adjust(salary, rise):
4     if rise < 0.10:
5         # We need to keep managers happy.
6         return 0.10
7
8     if salary >= 1_000_000:
9         # They are making enough already.
10         return rise - 0.10
11
12
13 def calculate_new_salary(salary, promised_pct, is_manager,
is_good_year):
14     rise = promised_pct
15     # remove 10% if it was a bad year
16     if not is_good_year:
```

> **Note**
>
> If you read this code on GitHub, it is quite convoluted and difficult to read, but it applies different raises depending on factors such as whether the person is a manager, whether it was a good year, and the person's current salary. The aim here is to provide you with a complex code structure so that you can debug it by following the steps mentioned in this exercise. This could be very helpful in your everyday developer life as well when you are provided with a bunch of code and you need to find a way to debug it.

The following steps will help you complete this exercise:

1. The first step is to fully understand the issue, evaluate whether there is an issue with the source code, and get all the possible data. You need to ask the user who reported the error, and you need to ask yourself common questions such as the following:

   - Which version of the software were they using?

   - When did the error happen for the first time?

   - Has it worked before?

   - Is it an intermittent failure or can the user consistently reproduce it?

   - What was the input of the program when the issue manifested?

   - What is the output and what would be the expected output?

   - Do you have any logs or any other information to help you debug the issue?

   In this instance, you get to know that this happened with the last version of our script, and the person who reported it could reproduce it. It seems to be happening only to Rose, but that might be related to the arguments she is providing.

   For instance, she reported that her current salary is **United States dollars** (**USD**) $1,000,000. She was told she would get a 30% raise, and even if she is aware that managers earning that much get a penalty of 10%, as the company had a good year and she was a high earner, she was expecting a 10% bonus, which should amount to 30%. But she saw that her new salary was $1,200,000, rather than $1,300,000.

   You can translate this into the following arguments:

   - `salary`: 1,000,000

   - `promised_pct`: 0.30

   - `is_manager`: True

   - `is_good_year`: True

   The expected output was 1,300,000, and the output she reported was 1,200,000.

   You don't have any logs about the execution, as the code was not instrumented with this capability.

2. The next step in your debugging investigation is to confirm that you can reproduce the issue (this will be done by running the `calculate_new_salary` function and the known arguments). If you are not able to reproduce it, then it means that some of the input or assumptions that either you or the user made were incorrect, and you should go back to *step 1* for clarification.

    In this scenario, trying to reproduce the issue is easy—you need to run the function with the known arguments, like so:

    ```
    rose_salary = calculate_new_salary(1_000_000, 0.30, True,
    True)
    print("Rose's salary will be:", rose_salary)
    ```

    The output will look like this:

    ```
    1200000
    ```

    This effectively returns `1200000` rather than `1,300,000`, and you know from the **human resources (HR)** guidelines that she should be getting the latter. Indeed, something starts to look suspicious.

3. In some situations, it is helpful to try with other inputs to see how the program behaves before even running the debugger. This can give you some extra information. You know that there are special rules for people who earn a million dollars or more, so what happens if you raise that number to, say, $2,000,000?

    Consider the following:

    ```
    rose_salary = calculate_new_salary(2_000_000, 0.30, True,
    True)
    print("Rose's salary will be:", rose_salary)
    ```

    You see that now, the output is `2,400,000`. The raise was 20% rather than 30%. There is something wrong in the code.

    You can also try changing the percentage, so let's try that with a promised initial raise of 40%, like so:

    ```
    rose_salary = calculate_new_salary(1_000_000, 0.40, True,
    True)
    print("Rose's salary will be:", rose_salary)
    ```

    The output will look like this:

    ```
    Rose's salary will be: 1400000
    ```

    Interestingly, she would get a 40% raise because there is no penalty applied.

    From just trying out different inputs, you have seen what is special about Rose's situation is her 30% increase. When you start to debug things in the following step, you will see that you should keep an eye on the code that interacts with the promised percentage, as the initial salary change did not make a difference.

4. Start the debugger by firing up pdb and set up a breakpoint in your `calculate_new_salary` function, like so:

    ```
    $ python3.10 -m pdb salary_calculator.py
    ```

    > /Lesson08/1.debugging/salary_calculator.py(1)<module>()

    -> """Adjusts the salary rise of an employ"""

    (Pdb) b calculate_new_salary

    Breakpoint 1 at /Lesson08/1.debugging/salary_calculator.py:13

    (Pdb)

5. Now, run `continue` or `c` to ask the interpreter to run until the function is executed, like so:

    ```
    (Pdb) c
    ```

    The output will look like this:

    > /Lesson08/1.debugging/salary_calculator.py(14)calculate_new_salary()

    -> rise = promised_pct

    (Pdb)

6. Run the `where` command in order to get information about how you got to this point, like so:

    ```
    (Pdb) where
    ```

    The output will look like this:

    /usr/local/lib/python3.10/bdb.py(585)run()

    -> exec(cmd, globals, locals)

    <string>(1)<module>()

    /Lesson08/1.debugging/salary_calculator.py(34)<module>()

    -> rose_salary = calculate_new_salary(1_000_000, 0.30, True, True)

    > /Lesson08/1.debugging/salary_calculator.py(14)calculate_new_salary()

    -> rise = promised_pct

    (Pdb)

    See how pdb tells you that you are on line *14* of the `salary_calculator` file and this function was executed as it was called from line *34* with the arguments that are displayed on the screen.

Note

You can use up here if you want to go to the stack frame where the function was executed. This is the line of code with the state that the program was in when the function was called.

When you can pinpoint the issue to a part of the program, you can go step by step, running the code and checking whether your expectations match what the result of running that line gives you.

An important step here is to think about what you expect to happen before you run the line. This might seem to make it take longer to debug the program, but it will pay off because if there is a result that appears to be correct, but it is not, it will be easier to detect whether you expected the result rather than just confirming whether it was right *a posteriori*. Let's do this in your program.

7. Run the l command to confirm where you are in the program and args to print the arguments of the function, as follows:

    ```
    (Pdb) l
    ```

Note

The output from the debugger and the input that you provide is mentioned next.

You will get the following output:

```
(Pdb) l
  9                 # They are making enough already.
 10                 return rise - 0.10
 11
 12
 13 B    def calculate_new_salary(salary, promised_pct, is_manager, is_good_year):
 14 ->        rise = promised_pct
 15
 16             # remove 10% if it was a bad year
 17             if not is_good_year:
 18                 rise -= 0.01
 19             else:
```

Figure 8.1 – Listing the pdb output

Use args to print the arguments of the function, as follows:

```
(Pdb) args
```

You will get the following output:

```
(Pdb) args
salary = 1000000
promised_pct = 0.3
is_manager = True
is_good_year = True
```

Figure 8.2 – args output (continued)

You are effectively on the first line of the code, and the arguments are what you expected. You could also run `ll` to get the whole function printed.

8. Advance the lines of code by using n to move one line at a time, like so:

```
(Pdb) n
```

You will get the following output:

> /Lesson08/1.debugging/salary_calculator.py(17)calculate_new_salary()

-> if not is_good_year:

(Pdb) n

> /Lesson08/1.debugging/salary_calculator.py(23)calculate_new_salary()

-> if is_manager:

(Pdb) n

> /Lesson08/1.debugging/salary_calculator.py(24)calculate_new_salary()

-> rise = _manager_adjust(salary, rise)

Next, check on whether it was a good year. As the variable is `True`, it does not get into the branch and jumps to line *23*. As Rose is a manager, this does get into that branch, where it will perform the manager adjustment.

9. Print the value of the raise before and after the `_manager_adjust` function is called by running `p rise`.

You can run `step` to get into the function, but the error is unlikely to be there, so you can print the current raise before and after executing the function. You know that, as she is earning a million dollars, her pay should be adjusted, and therefore, the rise should be `0.2` after executing it. The code is illustrated here:

```
(Pdb) p rise
0.3
(Pdb) n
> /Lesson08/1.debugging/salary_calculator.py(27)
calculate_new_salary()
```

```
-> if rise >= 0.20:
(Pdb) p rise
```

0.19999999999999998

The adjusted raise is 0.199999999999999998 rather than 0.20, so what is going on here? There is clearly an issue within the _manager_adjust function. You will have to restart the debugging and investigate it.

10. You can then continue to the second execution and print the lines and arguments at that point by running c, c, ll, and args, as follows:

```
(Pdb) b _manager_adjust
Breakpoint 2 at /Lesson08/1.debugging/salary_calculator.
py:3
(Pdb) restart
```

The output will look like this:

```
Restarting salary_calculator.py with arguments:
        salary_calculator.py
> /Lesson08/1.debugging/salary_calculator.py(1)<module>()
-> """Adjusts the salary rise of an employ"""
(Pdb) c
> /Lesson08/1.debugging/salary_calculator.py(14)
calculate_new_salary()
-> rise = promised_pct
(Pdb) c
> /Lesson08/1.debugging/salary_calculator.py(4)_manager_
adjust()
-> if rise < 0.10:
(Pdb) ll
3 B def _manager_adjust(salary, rise):
4 -> if rise < 0.10:
5 # We need to keep managers happy.
6 return 0.10
7
8 if salary >= 1_000_000:
9 # They are making enough already.
10 return rise - 0.10
(Pdb) args
salary = 1000000
```

```
    rise = 0.3
    (Pdb)
```

You see the input is what you expected (0.3), but you know the output is not. Rather than 0.2, you are getting 0.19999999999999998. Let's walk through this function code to understand what is happening. By running n three times until the end of the function, you can then use rv to see the returned value, as follows:

```
(Pdb) n
> /Lesson08/1.debugging/salary_calculator.py(8)_manager_
adjust()
-> if salary >= 1_000_000:
(Pdb) n
> /Lesson08/1.debugging/salary_calculator.py(10)_manager_
adjust()
-> return rise - 0.10
(Pdb) n
--Return--
> /Lesson08/1.debugging/salary_calculator.py(10)_manager_
adjust()->0.19999999999999998
-> return rise - 0.10
(Pdb) rv
```

0.19999999999999998

You found the error: when we are subtracting 0.10 from 0.30, the result is not 0.20 as you might have expected. It is that weird number, 0.19999999999999998, due to the loose precision of float numbers. This is a well-known issue in computer science. We should not rely on floats for equality comparison if we need fraction numbers; we should use the decimal module instead, as we have seen in previous chapters.

In this exercise, you have learned how to identify errors when you perform debugging. You can now start to think about how to fix these errors and propose solutions to your colleagues.

Now, let's take a look at an activity to debug a Python code application.

Activity 22 – debugging sample Python code for an application

Consider the following scenario: you have a program that creates a picnic basket for you. The baskets are created in a function that depends on whether the user wants a healthy meal and whether they are hungry. You provide a set of initial items in the basket, but users can also customize this via a parameter.

A user reported that they got more strawberries than expected when creating multiple baskets. When asked for more information, they said that they tried to create a healthy basket for a non-hungry person first, and a non-healthy basket for a hungry person with just "tea" in the initial basket. Those two baskets were created correctly, but when the third basket was created for a healthy person who was also hungry, the basket appeared with one more strawberry than expected.

In this activity, you need to run the reproducers mentioned on GitHub and check for the error in the third basket. Once you have found the error with the basket, you need to debug the code and fix the error.

The following table provides a summary of the preceding scenario:

Health?	Hungry?	Initial Basket	Output
True	False	-	['orange', 'apple', 'strawberry']
False	True	["tea"]	['tea', 'jam', 'sandwich']
True	True	-	['orange', 'apple', 'strawberry', 'strawberry', 'sandwich']

Figure 8.3 – Summary table of the problem

There is a reproducer in the code example, so continue the debugging from there, and figure out where the issue is in the code.

Take a look at the following steps:

1. First, write test cases with the inputs provided in the preceding table.
2. Next, confirm whether the error report is genuine.
3. Then, run the reproducers in the code file and confirm the error in the code.
4. Finally, fix the code with the simple logic of if and else.

   You will get the following output:

```
In [6]: print("First basket:", create_picnic_basket(True, False))
        First basket: ['orange', 'apple', 'strawberry']

In [7]: print("Second basket:", create_picnic_basket(False, True, ["tea"]))
        Second basket: ['tea', 'jam', 'sandwich']

In [8]: print("Third basket:", create_picnic_basket(True, True))
        Third basket: ['orange', 'apple', 'strawberry', 'sandwich']
```

Figure 8.4 – Expected output from the basket

> **Note**
> The solution for this activity can be found in *Appendix* on GitHub.

In the next topic, you will be learning about automated testing.

Automated testing

Even though we explored and learned how to debug applications when errors are reported, we would prefer not to have to find errors in our applications. To increase the chances of having a bug-free code base, most developers rely on automated testing.

At the beginning of their careers, most developers will just manually test their code as they develop it. By just providing a set of inputs and verifying the output of the program, we can get a basic level of confidence that our code "works", but this quickly becomes tedious and does not scale as the code base grows and evolves. Automated testing allows us to record a series of steps and stimuli that we perform in our code and have a series of expected outputs recorded.

This is extremely efficient to reduce the number of bugs in our code base, because not only are we verifying the code, but we are also implementing it, and we keep a record of all those verifications for future modifications of the code base.

The amount of test lines that you write for each line of code really depends on each application. There are notorious cases, such as SQLite, where orders-of-magnitude more lines of tests are needed than lines of code, which greatly improves confidence in the software and allows quick release of new versions as features are added without needing the extensive **quality assurance (QA)** that other systems might require.

Automated testing is similar to the QA process that we see in other engineering fields. It is a key step of all software development and should be taken into account when developing a system.

Additionally, having automated tests also helps you to troubleshoot, as you have a set of test scenarios that you can adapt to simulate the user's input and environment and keep what is known as a regression test. This is a test that is added when an issue is detected, to ensure that the issue never happens again.

Test categorization

One of the first things to think about when writing an automated test is "*What are we verifying?*", and that would depend on the "*level*" of testing that you are doing. There is a lot of literature about how to categorize different test scenarios in the functions that they validate and the corresponding dependencies they have. It is not the same to write a test that just validates a simple Python function in our source code as it is to write something that validates an accounting system that connects to the internet and sends emails. To validate large systems, it is common to create different types of tests. They are usually known as the following:

- **Unit tests**: These are tests that just validate a small part of your code. Usually, they just validate a function with specific inputs within one of your files and only depend on code that has already been validated with other unit tests.

- **Integration tests**: These are more coarse-grained tests that will either validate interactions between different components of your code base (known as integration tests without environment) or the interactions between your code and other systems and the environment (known as integration tests with the environment).

- **Functional or end-to-end (E2E) tests**: These are usually really high-level tests that depend on the environment and often on external systems that validate the solution with inputs as the user provides them.

Say that you were to test the workings of Twitter, using the tests you are familiar with. In that case, the following would apply:

- A unit test would verify one of the functions, which will check whether a tweet body is shorter than a specific length

- An integration test would validate that, when a tweet is injected into the system, the trigger to other users is called

- An E2E test is one that ensures that, when a user writes a tweet and clicks **Send**, they can then see it on their home page

Software developers tend to prefer unit tests as they don't have external dependencies and are more stable and faster to run. The further we go into more coarse-grained tests, the more we'll come across what the user will perform, but both integration and E2E tests usually take much longer to run as the dependencies need to be set up, and they are usually flakier because—for example—the email server might not be working on that day, meaning we would be unable to run our tests.

> **Note**
>
> This categorization is a simplification of many experts working in the field. If you are interested in the different levels of testing and getting the right balance of tests, then a good place to start is the famous **Testing Pyramid**.

Test coverage

Something that generates debate across the community is test coverage. When you write tests for our code, you start to exercise it and begin to hit different code paths. As you write more tests, you cover more and more of the code that you are testing. The percentage of code that you test is known as **test coverage**, and developers will argue that different percentages are "the right amount." Getting to 100% coverage might seem an unnecessary task, but it proves to be quite useful in large code bases that need to perform tasks such as migrating from Python 2 to Python 3. However, this all depends on how much you are willing to invest in testing your application, and each developer might target a different number for each of the projects that they run.

Moreover, something important to remember is that 100% coverage does not mean that your code does not have bugs. You can write tests that exercise your code but do not properly validate it, so be mindful of falling into the trap of just writing tests to hit the coverage target. Tests should be written to exercise the code with inputs that will be provided by users and try to find edge cases that can uncover issues with the assumptions that you made at the time that you wrote it, and not just to hit a number.

Writing tests in Python with unit testing

The Python standard library comes with a `unittest` module to write test scenarios and validate your code. Usually, when you are creating tests, you create a file for the test to validate the source code of another file. In that file, you can create a class that inherits from `unittest.TestCase` and has method names that contain the word `test` to be run on execution. You can record expectations through functions such as `assertEquals` and `assertTrue`, which are part of the base class, and you can, therefore, access them.

Exercise 114 – checking sample code with unit testing

In this exercise, you will write and run tests for a function that checks whether a number is divisible by another. This will help you to validate the implementation and potentially find any existing bugs. Proceed as follows:

1. Create an `is_divisible` function that checks whether a number is divisible by another. Save this function in a file named `sample_code`.

    This function is also provided in the `sample_code.py` file. The file just has a single function that checks whether a number is divisible by another, as illustrated in the following code snippet:

    ```
    def is_divisible(x, y):
        if x % y == 0:
            return True
        else:
            return False
    ```

2. Create a `test` file that will include the test cases for our function. Then, add the skeleton for a test case, as follows:

```python
import unittest
from sample_code import is_divisible
class TestIsDivisible(unittest.TestCase):
    def test_divisible_numbers(self):
        pass
if __name__ == '__main__':
    unittest.main()
```

This code imports the function to test, `is_divisible`, and the `unittest` module. It then creates the common boilerplate to start writing tests: a class that inherits from `unittest.TestCase` and two final lines that allow you to run the code and execute the tests.

3. Now, write the test code, as follows:

```python
    def test_divisible_numbers(self):
        self.assertTrue(is_divisible(10, 2))
        self.assertTrue(is_divisible(10, 10))
        self.assertTrue(is_divisible(1000, 1))
    def test_not_divisible_numbers(self):
        self.assertFalse(is_divisible(5, 3))
        self.assertFalse(is_divisible(5, 6))
        self.assertFalse(is_divisible(10, 3))
```

You now write the code for your tests by using the `self.assertX` methods. There are different kinds of methods for different kinds of asserts. For example, `self.assertEqual` will check whether the two arguments are equal or fail otherwise. You will use `self.assertTrue` and `self.assertFalse`. With this, you can create the preceding tests.

4. Run the test, like so:

```
python3.10 test_unittest.py -v
```

Run the test by executing it with a Python interpreter. By using `-v`, you get extra information about the test names as the tests are running.

You should get the following output:

```
test_divisible_numbers (__main__.TestIsDivisible) ... ok
test_not_divisible_numbers (__main__.TestIsDivisible) ... ok

----------------------------------------------------------------------
Ran 2 tests in 0.016s

OK
```

Figure 8.5 – Unit test run output

5. Now, add more complex tests, as follows:

```python
def test_dividing_by_0(self):
    with self.assertRaises(ZeroDivisionError):
        is_divisible(1, 0)
```

By adding a test when you pass 0, you want to check whether it will raise an exception.

The `assertRaises` context manager will validate that the function raises the exception passed in within the context.

So, there you go: you have a test suite with the standard library `unittest` module.

Unit testing is a great tool for writing automated tests, but the community seems to generally prefer to use a third-party tool named `pytest`, which allows the user to write tests by just having plain functions in their function and by using Python's `assert` keyword.

This means that rather than using `self.assertEquals(a, b)`, you can just do `assert a == b`. Additionally, `pytest` comes with some enhancements, such as capturing output, modular fixtures, or user-defined plugins. If you plan to develop any test suite that is bigger than a few tests, consider checking for `pytest`.

Writing a test with pytest

Even if a unit test is part of the standard library, it is more common to see developers use `pytest` to run and write the test. You can refer to the `pytest` package website for more information about how to write and run tests with it: `https://docs.pytest.org/en/latest/`.

Have a look at the following code snippet:

```python
from sample_code import is_divisible
import pytest
def test_divisible_numbers():
    assert is_divisible(10, 2) is True
    assert is_divisible(10, 10) is True
```

```
        assert is_divisible(1000, 1) is True
    def test_not_divisible_numbers():
        assert is_divisible(5, 3) is False
        assert is_divisible(5, 6) is False
        assert is_divisible(10, 3) is False
    def test_dividing_by_0():
        with pytest.raises(ZeroDivisionError):
            is_divisible(1, 0)
```

This code creates three test cases by using `pytest`. The main difference is that by having a class that has `assert` methods within it, you can create free functions and use the `assert` keyword of Python itself. This also gives you more explicit error reports when they fail.

In the next section, let's take a look at creating pip packages.

Creating a pip package

When you are working with Python code, you need to differentiate between the **source code tree**, the **source distributions** (**sdists**), and a **binary distribution** (wheels, for example, which are explained ahead). The folder where you work on the code is known as the source code tree, which is essentially how it is presented in the folder. This also contains Git files, configuration files, and others. The sdist is a way to package your code so that it can be executed and installed on any machine—it just contains all the source code without any development-related files. A binary distribution is similar to a sdist, but it comes with the files ready to be installed on the system—there is no execution needed in the client host. Wheels are a particular standard for binary distributions that replace the old format, Python eggs. When we consume Python wheels, we just get a file that is ready to be installed without the need of any compilation or build step, just ready to be consumed. This is especially useful for Python packages with C extensions.

When you want to distribute your code to users, you need to create sdists or binary distributions and then upload them to a repository. The most common Python repository is PyPI, which allows users to install packages by using pip.

PyPI is an official package repository maintained by the **Python Software Foundation** (**PSF**) that contains Python packages. Anyone can publish packages to it, and many Python tools usually default to consume packages from it. The most common way to consume from PyPI is through pip, which is maintained by the **Python Packaging Authority** (**PyPA**). This is the recommended tool for consuming Python packages.

The most common tool to package your source code is `setuptools`. With `setuptools`, you can create a `setup.py` file that contains all the information about how to create and install the package. `Setuptools` comes with a method named `setup`, which should be called with all the **metadata** that you want to create a package with.

Here's some example boilerplate code that could be copied and pasted when creating a package:

```python
import setuptools
setuptools.setup(
    name="packt-sample-package",
    version="1.0.0",
    author="Author Name",
    author_email="author@email.com",
    description="packt example package",
    long_description="This is the longer description and will
appear in the web.",
    py_modules=["packt"],
    python_requires=">=3.7",
    classifiers=[
        "Programming Language :: Python :: 3",
        "Operating System :: OS Independent",
    ],
)
```

Take special note of the following parameters:

- `name`: The name of the package in PyPA. It is a good practice to have it match your library or file import name.

- `version`: A string that identifies the version of the package.

- `py_modules`: A list of Python files to package. You can also use the `package` keyword to target full Python packages—we will explore how to do this in the next exercise.

You can now create a sdist by running the following command:

```
python3.10 setup.py sdist
```

This will generate a file in the `dist` folder, which is ready to be distributed to PyPI.

If you have the `wheel` package installed, you can also run the following command to create a wheel:

```
python3.10 setup.py bdist_wheel
```

Once you have this file generated, you can install `twine`, which is the tool recommended by PyPA for uploading packages to PyPI. With `twine` installed, you just need to run the following command:

```
twine upload dist/*
```

You can test your package by installing any of the artifacts in the dist folder.

Usually, you won't just have a single file to distribute, but a whole set of files within a folder, which makes a Python package. In those situations, there is no need to write all the files within the folder one by one—you can just use the following line instead of the py_module option:

```
packages=setuptools.find_packages(),
```

This will find and include all the packages in the directory where the setup.py file is.

Exercise 115 – creating a distribution that includes multiple files within a package

In this exercise, you are going to create your own package that can contain multiple files and upload them to the test version of PyPI:

1. Create a virtual environment and install twine and setuptools.

   Start by creating a virtual environment with all the dependencies that you need.

   Make sure you are in an **empty** folder to start, and then execute the following code:

   ```
   python3.10 -m venv venv
   . venv/bin/activate
   python3.10 -m pip install twine setuptools
   ```

   You now have all the dependencies you need to create and distribute your package.

2. Create the actual package source code.

   You will create a Python package named john_doe_package.

   Note, please change this to your first and last name. Here's the code you'll need:

   ```
   mkdir john_doe_package
   touch john_doe_package/__init__.py
   echo "print('Package imported')" > john_doe_package/code.py
   ```

   The second line will create a Python file, which you will package within the Python package.

   This is a basic Python package that just contains an init file and another file named code—you can add as many files as desired. The __init__ file marks the folder as a Python package.

3. Add the `setup.py` file.

    You need to add a `setup.py` file at the top of your source tree to indicate how your code should be packaged. Add a `setup.py` file, like so:

    ```
    import setuptools
    setuptools.setup(
        name="john_doe_package",
        version="1.0.0",
        author="Author Name",
        author_email="author@email.com",
        description="packt example package",
        long_description="This is the longer description and
    will appear in the web.",
        packages=setuptools.find_packages(),
        python_requires=">=3.7",
        classifiers=[
            "Programming Language :: Python :: 3",
            "Operating System :: OS Independent",
        ],
    )
    ```

    The previously mentioned code is a function call where you pass all the metadata.

    Be sure to change `john_doe_package` to the name of your own package.

4. Create a distribution by calling the `setup.py` file, like so:

    `python3.10 setup.py sdist`

    This will create a sdist. You can test it out by installing it locally, like so:

    ```
    cd dist && python3.10 -m pip install *
    ```

5. Upload to the PyPI test, as follows:

    ```
    twine upload -repository-url=https://test.pypi.org/
    legacy/ dist/*
    ```

    The last step is to upload the file to the test version of PyPI.

    To run this step, you need an account in `TestPyPI`. Go to `https://test.pypi.org/account/register/` to create one.

Once created, you can run the following command to upload the package to the web:

```
$ twine upload --repository-url=https://test.pypi.org/legacy/ dist/*
Uploading distributions to https://test.pypi.org/legacy/
Enter your username: mariocj89
Enter your password:
Uploading john_doe_package-1.0.0.tar.gz
100%|
```

Figure 8.6 – Uploading with the twine output

This will prompt you for the username and password that you used to create your account. Once this is uploaded, you can go to `https://packt.live/2qj1o7N`, click on your **project**, and you should be able to see the following on the **PyPI** web page:

Figure 8.7 – Sample uploaded package website

You just published your first package. In this exercise, you learned how to create a Python package, package it, and upload it to PyPI.

Adding more information to your package

So, you have seen how to create a really simple package. When you create a package, you should also include a README file that can be used to generate a description of the project and is part of the sdist. This file gets packaged by default.

Consider exploring the different attributes that can be used with `setuptools.setup`. By having a look through the documentation, you can find a lot of useful metadata that might be appropriate for your package.

Additionally, to facilitate testing, many people consider it to be good practice to place all the source code of your package within an `src` directory. This is done to prevent the Python interpreter from automatically finding your package as it is part of the current working directory, as Python adds the current working directory to the Python path. If your package contains any logic about the data files that are packaged with your code, you should really use the `src` directory, as it will force you to work against the installed version of your package, rather than the source directory tree.

PyPA has recently created a guide on how to package projects, which contains further details than those discussed in this book.

> **Note**
>
> If you need to package multiple applications, consider having a look through `https://packaging.python.org/tutorials/packaging-projects/`.

Creating documentation the easy way

A critical part of all software that is distributed across the world is documentation. Documentation allows the users of your code to be able to understand how to call the different functions that we provide without having to read the code. There are multiple levels of documentation that you are going to explore in this topic. You will see how to write documentation that can be consumed in the console and on the web. In the purpose and size of our project, you should consider how broad your documentation should be and what kind of instructions and information it should contain.

Using docstrings

In Python, documentation is part of the language. When you declare a function, you can use docstrings to document its interface and behavior. Docstrings can be created by having a triple-quoted string block just after the function signature. This content is not only available to the reader but also to the user of the **application programming interface (API)**, as it is part of a `__doc__` attribute of the function, class, or module. It is the content that will be provided if we call the `help` function in the object passed. As an example, take a look at the contents of the `__doc__` attribute of the `print` function here:

```
print(print.__doc__)
```

You will get the result as:

```
print(value, ..., sep=' ', end='\n', file=sys.stdout, flush=False)

Prints the values to a stream, or to sys.stdout by default.
Optional keyword arguments:
file:  a file-like object (stream); defaults to the current sys.stdout.
sep:   string inserted between values, default a space.
end:   string appended after the last value, default a newline.
flush: whether to forcibly flush the stream.
```

Figure 8.8 – print documentation

It is the same content as calling `help(print)`. You can create your own function with a `__doc__` attribute, as follows:

```
>>>def example():
    """Prints the example text"""
    print("Example")
>>>example.__doc__
'Prints the example text'
```

You can now use `help` in your function by executing `help(example)` ", which will result in the following text:

```
Help on function example in module __main__:

example()
    Prints the example text
```

Figure 8.9 – Help content in the example module

Docstrings usually contain a title with a short description of the function and a body with further information about what it does in detail. Additionally, you can also document all the parameters the function takes, including its types, the return type, and whether it raises any exceptions. This is all really useful information for your users and even for yourself when you have to use the code at a later time.

Using Sphinx

Using docstrings to document APIs is useful, but quite often, you need something more. You want to generate a website with guides and other information about your library. In Python, the most common way to do this is via **Sphinx**. Sphinx allows you to generate documentation in multiple formats—such as **Portable Document Format** (**PDF**), **electronic publication** (**EPUB**), or HTML—easily from **reStructuredText** (**RST**) with some markup. Sphinx also comes with multiple plugins, and some of them are useful for Python, such as generating API documentation from docstrings or allowing you to view code behind the API implementation.

Once installed via pip, it comes with two main CLI scripts, which the user interacts with: `sphinx-build` and `sphinx-quickstart`. The first is used to build the documentation on an existing project with Sphinx configuration, while the second can be used to quickly bootstrap a project.

When you bootstrap a project, Sphinx will generate multiple files for you, and the most important ones are listed here:

- `conf.py`: This contains all the user configurations for generating documentation. This is the most common place to look for configuration parameters when you want to customize something from the Sphinx output.

- `Makefile`: An easy-to-use makefile that can be used to generate documentation with a simple `make html` command. There are other targets that can be useful, such as the one to run `doctests`.

- `index.rst`: The main entry point for our documentation.

Usually, most projects create a folder named `docs` within their source tree root to contain everything related to the documentation and Sphinx. This folder can then refer to the source code by either installing it or by adding it to the path in their configuration file.

If you are not familiar with RST, it is best to have a quick look through `https://www.sphinx-doc.org/en/master/usage/restructuredtext/basics.html`. It has a short explanation of the different special syntaxes you can find in RST, which will be translated into special HTML tags such as `links`, `anchors`, `tables`, `images`, and others.

On top of this, Sphinx is easily extendable via plugins. Some of them are part of the default distribution when you install Sphinx. Plugins allow you to extend the functionality to do things such as automatically creating documentation for your modules, classes, and functions by just writing a single directive.

Finally, there are multiple themes available when you generate documentation with Sphinx—these are all configurable in `conf.py`. Quite often, you can find more Sphinx themes available on PyPI, which can be just installed easily via pip.

Exercise 116 – documenting a divisible code file

In this exercise, you are going to document the `divisible.py` module that you created in the testing topic from *Exercise 114 – checking sample code with unit testing* using Sphinx. Proceed as follows:

1. Create a folder structure.

    First, create an empty folder with just the `divisible.py` module and another empty folder named `docs`. The `divisible.py` module should contain the following code:

    ```
    def is_divisible(x, y):
        if x % y == 0:
            return True
        else:
            return False
    ```

2. Run the `sphinx-quickstart` tool.

    Make sure you have Sphinx installed (otherwise, run `python3.10 -m pip install sphinx --user`) and run `sphinx-quickstart` within the `docs` folder. You can leave all the functions with the default value by pressing return when prompted, except for the following:

    - **Project name:** `divisible`

    - **Author name:** Write your name here

- **Project release**: 1.0.0

- **Autodoc**: y

- **Intersphinx**: y

With these options, you are ready to start a project that can be easily documented and generate HTML output with Sphinx. Additionally, you have enabled two of the most common plugins: `autodoc`, which we will use to generate documentation out of the code, and `intersphinx`, which allows you to reference other Sphinx projects, such as the Python standard library.

3. Build the documentation for the first time.

Building the documentation is easy—just run `make html` within the `docs` directory to generate the HTML output of your documentation. You can now open the `index.html` file in your browser within the `docs/build/html` folder.

You should get the following output:

Figure 8.10 – First documentation output with Sphinx

It's not a lot of content, but it's quite impressive for the amount of code you have written.

4. Configure Sphinx to find your code.

The next step is to generate and include documentation from your Python source code. The first thing that you will have to do to be able to do that is to edit the `conf.py` file within the `docs` folder and uncomment these three lines:

```
# import os
# import sys
# sys.path.insert(0, os.path.abspath('.'))
```

Once uncommented, the last line should be changed to this since you have your divisible source code one level above your code:

```
sys.path.insert(0, os.path.abspath('..'))
```

A better alternative to this would be to make sure your package is installed when running Sphinx—this is a more extended method, but a simpler solution.

Last but not least, you are going to use another plugin, called `napoleon`. This allows you to format your functions by using the `napoleon` syntax. To do so, add the following line in the list of extensions within the `conf.py` file, within the `extensions` variable, after `'sphinx.ext.autodoc'`:

```
'sphinx.ext.napoleon',
```

You can read https://www.sphinx-doc.org/en/master/usage/extensions/napoleon.html for more information about the `napoleon` syntax for Sphinx.

5. Generate documentation from the source code.

    Adding the documentation from a module to Sphinx is really simple—you can just add the following two lines to your `index.rst` file:

    ```
    ..  automodule:: divisible
        :members:
    ```

Once those two lines are added, run `make html` again and check whether an error is generated. If no error appears, then you are all set. You have configured Sphinx to bring the documentation from docstrings to your RST file.

6. Add docstrings.

    To give Sphinx something to work with, add a docstring at the module level and one docstring for the function that you defined.

    Our `divisible.py` file should now look like this:

    ```python
    """Functions to work with divisibles"""
    def is_divisible(x, y):
        """Checks if a number is divisible by another
        Arguments:
            x (int): Divisor of the operation.
            y (int): Dividend of the operation.
        Returns:
            True if x can be divided by y without reminder,
            False otherwise.
        Raises:
            :obj:'ZeroDivisionError' if y is 0.
        """
        if x % y == 0:
            return True
        else:
            return False
    ```

You are using the `napoleon`-style syntax to define the different arguments that your function takes, what it can return, and the exception it raises.

Note that you use a special syntax to reference the exception that it raises. This will generate a link to the definition of the object.

If you run `make html` again, you should get the following output:

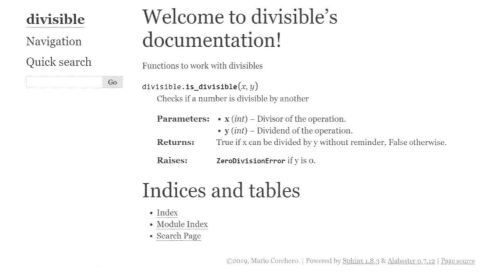

Figure 8.11 – HTML documentation output with docstring

You can now distribute your documentation to your users. Note that it will always be up to date as you are generating it from the source code.

More complex documentation

In the previous exercise, you examined simple documentation for a really small module. Most libraries also include tutorials and guides along with their API documentation. Check Django, flask, or CPython as examples, as they are all generated with Sphinx.

Note that if you intend your library to be used extensively and successfully, then documentation will be a key part of it. When you want to document how an API behaves, you should use just the plain API documentation that you generated before. However, there is also room to create small guides for specific features or tutorials to walk users through the most common steps to start a project.

Additionally, there are tools such as `readthedocs` that greatly simplify the generation and hosting of documentation. You can take the project that we just generated and connect it to `readthedocs` through its **user interface** (**UI**) to have your documentation hosted on the web and automatically regenerated every time you update the master branch of your project.

Source code management

When you work with code, you need a way in which to keep a picture of how your code evolves and how changes are being applied to different files. For instance, say that, by mistake, you make changes to your code that suddenly break it, or you start to make changes and just want to go back to the previous version. Many people start by just copying their source code into different folders and naming it with a timestamp based on checkpoints they make in different phases of the project. This is the most rudimentary approach to version control.

Version control is the system by which you keep control of code as it evolves over time. Developers have been suffering for long enough to create a piece of software that can do this job efficiently, and one of the most popular tools to do this is Git. **Git** is a **distributed version control system** that allows developers to manage their code locally as it evolves, look at the history, and easily collaborate with other developers. Git is used for managing some of the biggest projects around the world, such as the Windows kernel, CPython, Linux, or Git itself; however, at the same time, Git is really useful and versatile for small projects as well.

Repository

A repository is an isolated workspace where you can work with your changes and have Git record them and track their history. One repository can contain as many files and folders as you want, with all of them tracked by Git.

There are two ways to create a repository: you can either clone an existing repository by using `git clone <url of the repository>`, which will bring a local copy of a repository into your current path, or you can create a repository from an existing folder with `git init`, which will just mark the folder as a repository by creating the necessary files.

Once you have a repository locally created, you can start to work with your version control system by issuing different commands to indicate whether you want to add changes, check previous versions, or more.

Commit

A `commit` object is the history of your repository. Each repository has many commits: one for every time you use `git commit`. Each of those commits will contain the commit title, the person who added the commit to the repository, the author of the changes, the dates when the commit and the changes were made, an **identifier** (**ID**) that is represented by a hash, and the hash of the parent commit. With this, you can create a tree of all the commits within the repository, which allows you to see the history of your source code. You can see the content of any commit by running `git show <commit sha>`.

When you run `git commit`, you create a commit from all the changes that you have in the staging area. An editor will open, which includes some meta-information such as the title and the commit body. You can see a representation of this in the following screenshot:

Figure 8.12 – Git commands showing how they interact with the repository and the staging area

> **Note**
>
> A good guide on how to write good commit messages can be found here: `https://packt.live/33zARRV`. We suggest that you take a look after finishing this book.

Staging area

When you are working locally and making changes to your files and source code, Git will report that those changes happened, and they are not saved. By running `git status`, you can see which files were modified. If you decide that you want to save those changes in the staging area in preparation for a commit, you can add them with the `git add <path>` command. It can be used in files or folders to add all files within that folder. Once they are added to the staging area, the next `git commit` command will save the changes in the repository through a `commit` object.

Sometimes, you don't want to add all the content of a file to the staging area, just part of it. For this use case, both `git commit` and `git add` have an option to guide you through the different changes in the file and allow you to select which ones you want to add. This is through the `-p` option, which will ask you for each of the changed chunks within your code and which ones you want to add.

Undoing local changes

When you are working on a file, you can run `git diff` to see all the changes that have been made locally but are not yet part of the staging area or a commit. Sometimes, you realize you want to undo your changes and come back to the version you have saved in the staging area or in the last commit. You can do this by checking out of the file by running `git checkout <path>`. This applies to both files and folders.

If instead, you want to revert your repository to a previous commit in history, you can do this by running `git reset <commit sha>`.

History

As we mentioned before, the repository has a commit history. This includes all the commits that have been performed before. You can see them by running `git log`, which will present you with the title, body, and some other information. The most important part of each of these entries is the `sha` hash of the commit, which uniquely represents each of the commits.

Ignoring files

When you work with your source code, you may find that, by running your program or any other action, you have files in your repository that you don't want Git to track. In that scenario, you can use a special file that has to be placed at the top of the directory and named `.gitignore`, which can list all the files in **global (glob)** patterns that you don't want Git to track. This is especially handy for adding things such as IDE-generated files, compiled Python files, and more.

Exercise 117 – making a change in CPython using Git

In this exercise, you are going to change a file in the local `CPython` repository by cloning the repository and working on your local copy. For the sake of the exercise, you will just add your name to the list of authors of the project.

> **Note**
> The repository will be on your local PC, so no one will see the changes—don't worry.

You begin by first installing `Git`. That is the first step to installing the tool itself. You can install it on Windows via `https://git-scm.com/download/win`, or on Unix by following the instructions at `https://git-scm.com/book/en/v2/Getting-Started-Installing-Git`.

If you are running on Windows, follow this exercise by using `git-shell` for Windows. On Unix, just use your preferred terminal. Then, proceed as follows:

1. Begin by cloning the `cpython` repository.

    As we mentioned before, you can create a repository by simply cloning it. You can clone the `cpython` source code by running the following command:

    ```
    git clone https://github.com/python/cpython.git
    ```

    This will create a folder named `cpython` in the current workspace. Don't worry; it is normal for it to take a few minutes, as CPython has a lot of code and long history. You will then see the following output:

```
$ git clone https://github.com/python/cpython.git
Cloning into 'cpython'...
remote: Enumerating objects: 1, done.
remote: Counting objects: 100% (1/1), done.
remote: Total 745673 (delta 0), reused 0 (delta 0), pack-reused 745672
Receiving objects: 100% (745673/745673), 277.17 MiB | 2.38 MiB/s, done.
Resolving deltas: 100% (599013/599013), done.
Checking connectivity... done.
Checking out files: 100% (4134/4134), done.
```

Figure 8.13 – git clone output of CPython

2. Edit the `Misc/ACKS` file and confirm the changes.

    You can now add your name to the `Misc/ACKS` file. To do this, just open the file in that path and add your name in alphabetical order and your surname.

    Check the changes by running `git status`. This command will show you whether there are any changed files, as illustrated here:

```
$ git status
On branch master
Your branch is up-to-date with 'origin/master'.
Changes not staged for commit:
  (use "git add <file>..." to update what will be committed)
  (use "git checkout -- <file>..." to discard changes in working directory)

        modified:   Misc/ACKS

no changes added to commit (use "git add" and/or "git commit -a")
```

Figure 8.14 – git status output

Note how it gives you instructions on how to proceed if you want to add the changes to the staging area in preparation for a commit or to reset them. Let's check the content of the changes by running `git diff`. Here's the output:

```
$ git diff
diff --git a/Misc/ACKS b/Misc/ACKS
index ec5b017..f38f40b 100644
--- a/Misc/ACKS
+++ b/Misc/ACKS
@@ -326,6 +326,7 @@ David M. Cooke
 Jason R. Coombs
 Garrett Cooper
 Greg Copeland
+Mario Corchero
 Ian Cordasco
 Aldo Cortesi
 Mircea Cosbuc
```

Figure 8.15 – git diff output

This provides you with a nice output that indicates the changes in the lines. Green with a plus sign means that a line was added, while red with a minus sign means a line was removed.

3. Now, commit the changes. Once you are happy with the changes that you have made, let's add those to the staging area by running `git add Misc/ACKS`, which will move the file into the staging area, allowing you to then commit them at any time by running `git commit`. When you run `git commit`, an editor will open to create a commit. Add a title and body (separated by an empty line), as illustrated in the following screenshot:

```
Add Mario Corchero to Misc/ACKS file

Adds my name as I am experimenting how to user git.
# Please enter the commit message for your changes. Lines starting
# with '#' will be ignored, and an empty message aborts the commit.
# On branch master
# Your branch is up-to-date with 'origin/master'.
#
# Changes to be committed:
#       modified:   Misc/ACKS
#
```

Figure 8.16 – Commit message output example

When you close the editor and save, the commit should be created, as illustrated here:

```
$ git commit
[master 6bdb37c] Add Mario Corchero to Misc/ACKS file
 1 file changed, 1 insertion(+)
```

Figure 8.17 – git commit output

You have created your first commit. You can check the contents of it by running `git show`, as illustrated here:

```
$ git show
commit 6bdb37c2ec16bc7a8a3fd518754518e76b8b12d1
Author: Mario Corchero <mariocj89@gmail.com>
Date:   Tue May 14 22:11:40 2019 +0100

    Add Mario Corchero to Misc/ACKS file

    Adds my name as I am experimenting how to user git.

diff --git a/Misc/ACKS b/Misc/ACKS
index ec5b017..f38f40b 100644
--- a/Misc/ACKS
+++ b/Misc/ACKS
@@ -326,6 +326,7 @@ David M. Cooke
 Jason R. Coombs
 Garrett Cooper
 Greg Copeland
+Mario Corchero
 Ian Cordasco
 Aldo Cortesi
 Mircea Cosbuc
```

Figure 8.18 – Git showing the output

> **Note**
>
> This was an introduction to Git. If you plan to use Git daily, check out the *Pro Git* book. This is a free book (at `https://packt.live/35EoBS5`) that will guide you on how to use Git.

In this chapter, you have learned multiple skills on how to develop software professionally, many not specific to Python, that will ideally help you in your career going forward.

Summary

In this chapter, you have seen that software development is more than just writing code in Python. When you want to elevate your code further than a simple script on your computer, you need to know how to troubleshoot, distribute, document, and test it. The Python ecosystem provides you with tools to do all of these things. You have learned how to troubleshoot code using pdb and have followed steps on how to identify and narrow down a problem by inspecting logs and the input. You have also learned how to write automated tests and about the importance of these.

You saw how you can package your code to be distributed across the internet, how you can also document those packages to make them easier to use and consume by your final users, and, finally, how to use Git to manage changes as your code evolves.

In the next chapter, we will touch on some more advanced topics; some of them build on top of what you just learned. You will explore things such as how to take the code you just wrote and have it processed from package to production, how to use Git to collaborate with other members of the team through GitHub, and how to profile your code when you suspect that it is not as fast as it could be.

Practical Python – Advanced Topics

Overview

By the end of this chapter, you will be able to write Python collaboratively as a member of a team; use `conda` to document and set up the dependencies for your Python programs; use Docker to create reproducible Python environments for running your code; write programs that take advantage of multiple cores in modern computers; write scripts that can be configured from the command line and explain the performance characteristics of your Python programs; and use tools to make your programs faster.

Introduction

In this chapter, you'll continue the shift that started in *Chapter 8, Software Development*, away from an individual focus on learning the syntax of the Python language toward becoming a contributing member of a Python development team. Solving complex problems in large projects needs expertise from multiple contributors, so it's very common to work on code with one or more colleagues in a developer community. Having already seen how to use `git` version control in *Chapter 8, Software Development*, you'll apply that knowledge in this chapter to working with teams. You'll be using GitHub, branches, and `pull` requests in order to keep your project in sync.

Moving on, when you deliver a certain project in the IT world, at some point, you'll want to deliver your code to your customers or stakeholders. An important part of the deployment process is making sure that the customer's system has the libraries and modules that your software needs and also the same versions that you were developing against. For this, you'll learn how to use `conda` to create baseline Python environments with particular libraries present and how to replicate those environments on another system.

Next, you will look at Docker, which is a popular way to deploy software to internet servers and cloud infrastructures. You'll learn how to create a container that includes your conda environment and your Python software and how to run the containerized software within Docker.

Finally, you'll learn some useful techniques for developing real-world Python software. These include learning how to take advantage of parallel programming, how to parse command-line arguments, and how to profile your Python code to discover and fix performance problems.

Here's a list of topics that we will cover:

- Developing collaboratively
- Dependency management
- Deploying code into production
- Multiprocessing
- Parsing command-line arguments in scripts
- Performance and profiling
- Profiling

Technical requirements

You can find the code files for this chapter on GitHub at https://github.com/PacktPublishing/The-Python-Workshop-Second-Edition/tree/main/Chapter09.

You will need the following things set up on your systems to follow the exercises in this chapter:

- Anaconda (installation instructions covered in this book's *Preface*)
- Docker (installation instructions covered in this book's *Preface*)
- pypy (available at https://pypy.org/download.html – check for a version compatible with Python 3.11)

Developing collaboratively

In *Chapter 8, Software Development*, you used git to keep track of the changes you made to your Python project. At its heart, membership in a programming team involves multiple people sharing their changes through git and ensuring that they are incorporating everybody else's changes when doing their own work.

There are many ways for people to work together using `git`. The developers of the Linux kernel each maintain their own repository and share potential changes over email, which they each choose whether to incorporate or not. Large companies, including Facebook and Google, use *trunk-based development*, in which all changes must be made on the main branch, usually called the *master*.

A common workflow popularized by support in the GitHub user interface is the `pull` request.

In the `pull` request workflow, you maintain your repository as `fork` in GitHub of the canonical version from which software releases are made, often referred to as `upstream` or `origin`. You make a small collection of related changes, each representing progress toward a single bug fix or new feature, in a named branch on your own repository, which you push to your hosted repository with `git push`. When you are ready, you submit a `pull` request to the `upstream` repository. The team reviews these changes together in the `pull` request and you add any further work needed to the branch. When the team is happy with the `pull` request, a supervisor or another developer merges it upstream, and the changes are *pulled* into the canonical version of the software.

The advantage of the `pull` request workflow is that it's made easy by the user interface in applications such as Bitbucket, GitHub, and GitLab. The disadvantage comes from keeping those branches around while the `pull` request is being created and is under review. It's easy to fall behind as other work goes into the `upstream` repository, leaving your branch out of date and introducing the possibility that your change will conflict with some other changes, and those conflicts will need a resolution.

To deal with fresh changes and conflicts as they arise, rather than as a huge headache when it's time to merge the `pull` request, you use `git` to fetch changes from the upstream repository, and either merge them into your branch or rebase your branch on the up-to-date upstream revision. Merging combines the history of commits on two branches and rebasing reapplies commits so that they start at the tip of the branch you are rebasing against. Your team should decide which of these approaches it prefers.

Exercise 118 – writing Python on GitHub as a team

In this exercise, you will learn how to host code on GitHub, make a `pull` request, and then approve changes to the code. To make this exercise more effective, you can collaborate with a friend:

1. If you don't have an account already, create one at `https://github.com`.

2. Log into `https://github.com/` and create a new repository by clicking **New**:

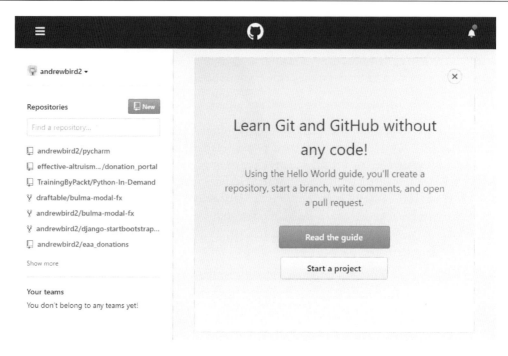

Figure 9.1 – The GitHub home page

3. Give the repository an appropriate name, such as python-demo, and click **Create repository**.

4. Now, click **Code** and you will be able to see the HTTPS URL; however, note that we will need the SSH URL. Hence, you will see **SSH** on the same tab, which you need to click on:

Figure 9.2 – Using the SSH URL on GitHub

5. Now, copy the SSH URL on GitHub. Then, using your local command prompt, such as CMD in Windows, clone the repository:

```
git clone git@github.com:andrewbird2/python-demo.git
```

> **Note**
>
> Your command will look slightly different from the preceding command because of the different username. You need to add your SSH URL after `git clone`. Note that you may also need to add an SSH key to your GitHub account for authentication. If so, follow the instructions here to add the SSH key: `https://packt.live/2qjhtKH`.

6. In your new `python-demo` directory, create a Python file. It doesn't matter what it contains; for instance, create a simple one-line `test.py` file, as shown in the following code snippet:

```
echo "x = 5" >> test.py
```

7. Let's use `commit` on our changes:

```
git add .
git commit -m "Initial"
git push origin master
```

You will get the following output:

```
Enumerating objects: 3, done.
Counting objects: 100% (3/3), done.
Writing objects: 100% (3/3), 223 bytes | 111.00 KiB/s, done.
Total 3 (delta 0), reused 0 (delta 0)
To github.com:andrewbird2/python-demo.git
 * [new branch]      master -> master
```

Figure 9.3 – Pushing our initial commit

At this point, if you are working with someone else, clone their repository, and perform the following steps on their code base to experience what collaboration feels like. If working alone, just proceed with your own repository.

8. Create a new branch called `dev`:

```
git checkout -b dev
```

You will get the following output:

```
(base) C:\Users\andrew.bird\python-demo>git checkout -b dev
Switched to a new branch 'dev'
```

Figure 9.4 – Creating a dev branch

9. Create a new file called hello_world.py. This can be done in a text editor or with the following simple command:

```
echo 'print("Hello World!")' >> hello_world.py
```

10. Now, use commit on the new file to the dev branch and push it to the created python-demo repository:

```
git add .
git commit -m "Adding hello_world"
git push --set-upstream origin dev
```

11. Go to the project repository in your web browser and click **Compare & pull request**:

Figure 9.5 – The home page of the repository on GitHub

12. Here, you can see a list of changes made to the dev branch that you created. You can also provide an explanation that someone else might read when reviewing your code before deciding whether or not it should be committed to the master branch:

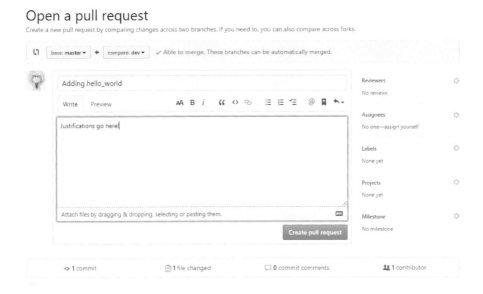

Figure 9.6 – Adding justifications to the code on GitHub

13. Click **Create pull request** to add the justifications on GitHub.

14. Now, if working with a partner, you should switch back to the original repository that you own and view their `pull` request. You can comment on it if you have any concerns regarding the `commit` request; otherwise, you can simply click **Merge pull request**:

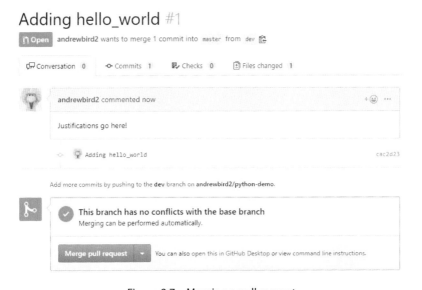

Figure 9.7 – Merging a pull request

You now understand how people can work together on the same repository on GitHub, reviewing and discussing each other's code before merging into the master branch. This comes in very handy as a developer when you want to have a single repository to store your code or help a fellow developer located somewhere else in the world. In the following section, you will look at dependency management.

Dependency management

In the IT world, most complex programs depend on libraries beyond the Python standard library. You may use numpy or pandas to deal with multidimensional data or matplotlib to visualize data in graphs (this will be covered in *Chapter 10, Data Analytics with pandas and NumPy*), or any number of other libraries available to Python developers.

Just like your own software, the libraries developed by other teams frequently change as bugs are fixed, features are added, and old code is removed or refactored, which is the process of restructuring existing code. That means it's important that your team uses the same version of a library so that it works in the same way for all of them.

Additionally, you want your customers or the servers where you deploy your software to use the same versions of the same libraries as well, so that everything works the same way on their computers, too.

There are multiple tools for solving this problem. These include pip, easy_install, brew, and conda, to name a few. You are already familiar with pip, and in some contexts, it suffices to use this package manager to keep track of dependencies.

For instance, try running pip freeze in the command prompt. You will get the following output:

```
(base) C:\Users\andrew.bird\Python-In-Demand>pip freeze
alabaster==0.7.12
anaconda-client==1.7.2
anaconda-navigator==1.9.6
anaconda-project==0.8.2
asn1crypto==0.24.0
astroid==2.1.0
astropy==3.1
atomicwrites==1.2.1
attrs==18.2.0
Babel==2.6.0
backcall==0.1.0
backports.os==0.1.1
```

Figure 9.8 – Output of pip freeze (truncated)

This package list could be saved to a text file with the following command: pip freeze > requirements.txt. This will create a file called requirements.txt, which will be similar to *Figure 9.9*:

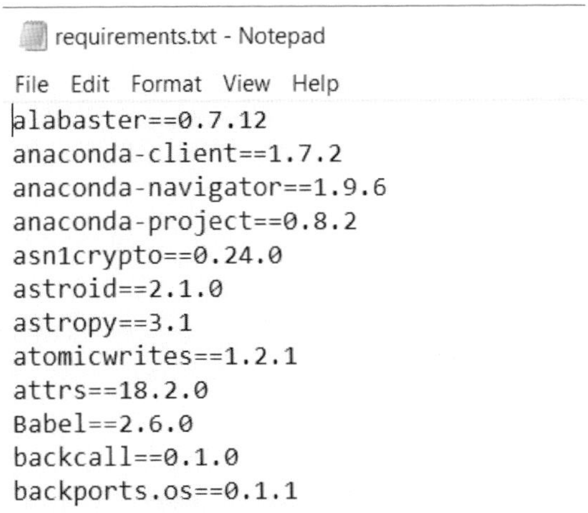

Figure 9.9 – Viewing requirements.txt in Notepad (truncated)

Now that you have the information about the packages, you can choose to install these packages on another machine or environment with the following command: `pip install -r requirements.txt`.

In this chapter, we will focus on `conda`, which provides a complete solution for dependency management. `conda` is particularly popular among data scientists and machine learning programmers. For instance, some dependencies in machine learning environments can't be managed by `pip`, as they might not be a simple Python package. `conda` takes care of these for us.

Virtual environments

In this chapter, you will use `conda` to create "virtual environments." When you code in Python, you have certain versions of certain packages installed. You're also using a specific version of Python itself, which is 3.10. However, what if you are working on two projects, with each requiring different versions of the packages? You would need to reinstall all of the packages when switching between these projects, which would be a hassle. Virtual environments address this problem. A virtual environment contains a set of particular packages for specific versions. By switching between virtual environments, you can switch between different packages and versions instantly. Typically, you will have a different virtual environment for each major project you are working on.

Exercise 119 – creating and setting up a conda virtual environment to install numpy and pandas

In this exercise, you'll create a virtual environment with `conda` and execute some simple code to import basic libraries. This exercise will be performed in the `conda` environment.

With conda installed on your system, you can create a new conda environment and include packages in it – for example, numpy:

1. Now, you should run the following command using the **Anaconda Prompt** program, which is now installed on your computer:

    ```
    conda create -n example_env numpy
    ```

    The output will be as follows:

```
(base) C:\Users\andrew.bird>conda create -n example_env numpy
Solving environment: done

==> WARNING: A newer version of conda exists. <==
  current version: 4.5.12
  latest version: 4.7.10

Please update conda by running

    $ conda update -n base -c defaults conda


## Package Plan ##

  environment location: C:\Users\andrew.bird\AppData\Local\conda\conda\envs\example_env

  added / updated specs:
    - numpy


The following packages will be downloaded:
```

Figure 9.10 – Creating a new conda environment (truncated)

> **Note**
> If you are asked to enter y/n by the prompt, you need to enter y to proceed further.

2. Activate the conda environment:

    ```
    conda activate example_env
    ```

    You can add other packages to the environment with conda install.

3. Now, add pandas to the example_env environment:

    ```
    conda install pandas
    ```

The output will be as follows:

```
(example_env) C:\Users\andrew.bird>conda install pandas
Solving environment: done


==> WARNING: A newer version of conda exists. <==
  current version: 4.5.12
  latest version: 4.7.10

Please update conda by running

    $ conda update -n base -c defaults conda



## Package Plan ##

  environment location: C:\Users\andrew.bird\AppData\Local\conda\conda\envs\example_env

  added / updated specs:
    - pandas


The following packages will be downloaded:
```

Figure 9.11 – The pandas output (truncated)

4. Next, open a Python terminal within the virtual environment by typing in `python` and then verify that you can import `pandas` as `numpy` as expected:

```
python
import pandas as pd
import numpy as np
```

5. Now, exit the Python terminal in the virtual environment using the `exit()` method:

```
exit()
```

6. Finally, deactivate the virtual environment:

```
conda deactivate
```

> **Note**
> You may have noticed the $ sign in the prompts. While working on the prompt, you need to ignore the $ sign. The $ sign is just to mention that the command will be executed on the terminal.

In this exercise, you created your first virtual environment using conda, installed packages such as numpy and pandas, and ran simple Python code to import libraries.

Saving and sharing virtual environments

Now, suppose you have built an application that relies on various Python packages. You now decide that you want to run the application on a server, so you want a way of setting up the same virtual environment on the server as you have running on your local machine. As you previously encountered with pip freeze, the metadata defining a conda environment can be easily exported to a file that can be used to recreate an identical environment on another computer.

Exercise 120 – sharing environments between a conda server and your local system

In this exercise, you will export the metadata of our example_env conda environment, which you created in *Exercise 119 – creating and setting up a conda virtual environment to install numpy and pandas*, to a text file and learn how to recreate the same environment using this file.

This exercise will be performed on the conda environment command line:

1. Activate your example environment for example_env:

   ```
   conda activate example_env
   ```

2. Now, export the environment to a text file:

   ```
   conda env export > example_env.yml
   ```

   The env export command produces the text metadata (which is mainly just a list of Python package versions) and the > example_env.yml part of the command stores this text in a file. Note that the .yml extension is a special easy-to-read file format that is usually used to store configuration information.

3. Now, use deactivate on that environment and remove it from conda:

   ```
   conda deactivate
   conda env remove --name example_env
   ```

4. You no longer have an example_env environment, but you can recreate it by importing the example_env.yml file you created earlier in the exercise:

   ```
   conda env create -f example_env.yml
   ```

You have now learned how to save your environment and create an environment using the saved file. This approach can be used when transferring your environment between your personal computers when collaborating with another developer or even when deploying code to a server.

Deploying code into production

You now have all of the pieces to get your code onto another computer and get it running. You can use `pip` (covered in *Chapter 8, Software Development*) to create a package and `conda` to create a portable definition of the environment needed for your code to run. These tools still give users a few steps to follow to get up and running and each step adds effort and complexity that may put them off.

A common tool for one-command setup and installation of software is **Docker**. Docker is based on Linux container technologies. However, because the Linux kernel is open source, developers have been able to make it so that Docker containers can run on both Windows and macOS. Programmers create Docker images, which are Linux filesystems containing all of the code, tools, and configuration files necessary to run their applications. Users download these images and use Docker to execute them or deploy the images into networks using `docker-compose`, Docker Swarm, Kubernetes, and similar tools.

You prepare your program for Docker by creating a Dockerfile file that tells Docker what goes into your image. In the case of a Python application, that's Python and your Python code.

Firstly, you need to install Docker.

> **Note**
> The installation steps for Docker are mentioned in the book's *Preface*.

Note that after installing, you may need to restart your computer.

To test Docker, run the `hello-world` application to confirm that Docker is correctly configured. `hello-world` is a simple Docker application that comes as part of the standard library of Docker apps:

```
docker run hello-world
```

You will get the following output:

```
(base) C:\Users\andrew.bird\Python-In-Demand>
(base) C:\Users\andrew.bird\Python-In-Demand>docker run hello-world

Hello from Docker!
This message shows that your installation appears to be working correctly.

To generate this message, Docker took the following steps:
 1. The Docker client contacted the Docker daemon.
 2. The Docker daemon pulled the "hello-world" image from the Docker Hub.
    (amd64)
 3. The Docker daemon created a new container from that image which runs the
    executable that produces the output you are currently reading.
 4. The Docker daemon streamed that output to the Docker client, which sent it
    to your terminal.

To try something more ambitious, you can run an Ubuntu container with:
 $ docker run -it ubuntu bash

Share images, automate workflows, and more with a free Docker ID:
 https://hub.docker.com/

For more examples and ideas, visit:
 https://docs.docker.com/get-started/
```

Figure 9.12 – Running hello-world with Docker

You have successfully installed and run Docker on your local machine.

Exercise 121 – Dockerizing your Fizzbuzz tool

In this exercise, you'll use Docker to create an executable version of a simple Python script that creates a sequence of numbers. However, instead of printing 3 or multiples of 3, it will print Fizz, and multiples of 5 will print Buzz.

This exercise will be performed in the docker environment:

1. Create a new directory called my_docker_app and use cd to go into this directory, as shown in the following commands:

    ```
    mkdir my_docker_app
    cd my_docker_app
    ```

2. Within this directory, create an empty file called Dockerfile. You can create this with Jupyter Notebook or your favorite text editor. Ensure this file does not have any extensions, such as .txt.

3. Now, add the first line to your `Dockerfile`:

    ```
    FROM python:3
    ```

    This line tells it to use a system that has Python 3 installed. Specifically, this is going to use a Python image built on top of a minimal Linux distribution called Alpine. More details about this image can be found at `https://packt.live/32oNn6E`.

4. Next, create a `fizzbuzz.py` file in the `my_docker_app` directory with the following code:

    ```python
    for num in range(1,101):
        string = ""
        if num % 3 == 0:
            string = string + "Fizz"
        if num % 5 == 0:
            string = string + "Buzz"
        if num % 5 != 0 and num % 3 != 0:
            string = string + str(num)
        print(string)
    ```

5. Now, add a second line to your `Dockerfile` file. This line tells Docker to include the `fizzbuzz.py` file in the application:

    ```
    ADD fizzbuzz.py /
    ```

6. Finally, add the command that Docker must run:

    ```
    CMD [ "python", "./fizzbuzz.py" ]
    ```

7. Your `Dockerfile` file should look as follows:

    ```
    FROM python:3
    ADD fizzbuzz.py /
    CMD [ "python", "./fizzbuzz.py" ]
    ```

> **Note**
>
> This Docker output file will be saved locally on your system. You shouldn't try to access these kinds of files directly.

8. Now, build your Docker image. You will name it `fizzbuzz_app`:

    ```
    $ docker build -t fizzbuzz_app .
    ```

    This command created an `image` file on your system that contains all of the information required to execute your code in a simple Linux environment.

9. Now, you can run your program inside Docker:

    ```
    docker run fizzbuzz_app
    ```

    The output will be as follows:

Figure 9.13 – Running your program inside Docker (truncated)

You can see the full list of Docker images available on your system by running `docker images`. This list should include your new `fizzbuzz_app` application.

Finally, suppose your `fizzbuzz` file imported a third-party library as part of the code. For example, perhaps it used the `pandas` library (it shouldn't need to). In this case, our code would break, because the installation of Python within the Docker image does not contain the `pandas` package.

10. To fix this, you can simply add a `pip install pandas` line to our `Dockerfile` file. Our updated `Dockerfile` file will look as follows:

    ```
    FROM python:3
    ADD fizzbuzz.py /
    RUN pip install pandas
    CMD [ "python", "./fizzbuzz.py" ]
    ```

In this exercise, you installed and deployed your first application with Docker. In the following section, we will look at multiprocessing.

Running code in parallel with multiprocessing

It's common to need to execute more than one thing in parallel in a modern software system. Machine learning programs and scientific simulations benefit from using the multiple cores available in a modern processor, dividing their work up between concurrent threads operating on parallel hardware. Graphical user interfaces and network servers do their work in the background, leaving a thread available to respond to user events or new requests.

As a simple example, suppose your program had to execute three steps: **A**, **B**, and **C**. These steps are not dependent on each other, meaning they can be completed in any order. Usually, you would simply execute them in order, as follows:

Figure 9.14 – Processing with a single thread

However, what if you could do all of these steps at the same time, rather than waiting for one to complete before moving on to the next one? Our workflow would look as follows:

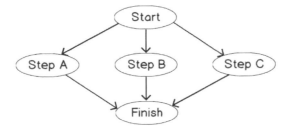

Figure 9.15 – Multithreaded processing

This has the potential to be a lot faster if you have the infrastructure to execute these steps at the same time. That is, each step will need to be executed by a different thread.

Python itself uses multiple threads to do some work internally, which puts some limits on the ways in which a Python program can do multiprocessing. The three safest ways to work are as follows:

- Find a library that solves your problem and handles multiprocessing for you (which has been carefully tested)

- Launch a new Python interpreter by running another copy of your script as a completely separate process

- Create a new thread within the existing interpreter to do some work concurrently

The first of these is the easiest and the most likely to be a success. The second is fairly simple and imposes the most overhead on your computer, as the operating system is now running two independent Python scripts. The third is very complicated, easy to get wrong, and still creates a lot of overhead, as Python maintains a **Global Interpreter Lock (GIL)**, which means that only one thread at a time can interpret a Python instruction. A quick rule of thumb to choose between the three approaches is to always pick the first one. If a library doesn't exist to address your needs, then pick the second. If you absolutely need to share memory between the concurrent processes, or if your concurrent work is related to handling I/O, then you can choose the third carefully.

Multiprocessing with execnet

It's possible to launch a new Python interpreter with the standard library's `subprocess` module. However, doing so leaves a lot of work up to you about what code to run and how to share data between the "parent" and "child" Python scripts.

An easier interface is the `execnet` library. `execnet` makes it very easy to launch a new Python interpreter running some given code, including versions such as Jython and IronPython, which integrate with the Java virtual machine and .NET common language runtime, respectively. It exposes an asynchronous communication channel between the parent and child Python scripts, so the parent can send data that the child works on and get on with its own thing until it's ready to receive the result. If the parent is ready before the child is finished, then the parent waits.

Exercise 122 – working with execnet to execute a simple Python squaring program

In this exercise, you'll create a `squaring` process that receives x over an `execnet` channel and responds with x**2. This is much too small a task to warrant multiprocessing, but it does demonstrate how to use the library.

This exercise will be performed on a Jupyter notebook:

1. First, install `execnet` using the `pip` package manager:

    ```
    $ pip install execnet
    ```

2. Now, write the `square` function, which receives numbers on a channel and returns their square:

    ```python
    import execnet
    def square(channel):
        while not channel.isclosed():
            number = channel.receive()
            number_squared = number**2
            channel.send(number_squared)
    ```

> **Note**
>
> Due to the way `execnet` works, you need to type the following examples into a Jupyter notebook. You cannot type them into the interactive >>> prompt.

The `while not channel.isclosed()` statement ensures that we only proceed with the calculation if there is an open channel between the parent and child Python processes. `number = channel.receive()` takes the input from the parent process that you want to use `square` on. It is then squared in the `number_squared = number**2` code line. Lastly, you send the squared number back to the parent process with `channel.send(number_squared)`.

3. Now, set up a `gateway` channel to a remote Python interpreter running that function:

    ```python
    gateway = execnet.makegateway()
    channel = gateway.remote_exec(square)
    ```

A `gateway` channel manages the communication between the parent and child Python processes. The channel is used to actually send and receive data between the processes.

4. Now, send some integers from our parent process to the child process, as shown in the following code snippet:

    ```python
    for i in range(10):
        channel.send(i)
        i_squared = channel.receive()
        print(f"{i} squared is {i_squared}")
    ```

You will get the following output:

```
0 squared is 0
1 squared is 1
2 squared is 4
3 squared is 9
4 squared is 16
5 squared is 25
6 squared is 36
7 squared is 49
8 squared is 64
9 squared is 81
```

Figure 9.16 – The results passed back from the child Python processes

Here, you loop through 10 integers, send them through the `square` channel, and then receive the result using the `channel.receive()` function.

5.   When you are done with the remote Python interpreter, close the `gateway` channel to cause it to quit:

```
gateway.exit()
```

In this exercise, you learned how to use `execnet` to pass instructions between Python processes. In the following section, you will be looking at multiprocessing with the `multiprocessing` package.

Multiprocessing with the multiprocessing package

The `multiprocessing` module is built into Python's standard library. Similar to `execnet`, it allows you to launch new Python processes. However, it provides an API that is lower level than `execnet`. This means that it's harder to use than `execnet`, but affords more flexibility. An `execnet` channel can be simulated by using a pair of multiprocessing queues.

Exercise 123 – using the multiprocessing package to execute a simple Python program

In this exercise, you will use the `multiprocessing` module to complete the same task as in *Exercise 122 – working with execnet to execute a simple Python squaring program*:

1.   Create a new text file called `multi_processing.py`.

2.   Now, use `import` for the `multiprocessing` package:

```
import multiprocessing
```

3. Create a `square_mp` function that will continuously monitor the queue for numbers, and when it sees a number, it will take it, square it, and place it in the outbound queue:

```python
def square_mp(in_queue, out_queue):
    while(True):
        n = in_queue.get()
        n_squared = n**2
        out_queue.put(n_squared)
```

4. Finally, add the following block of code to `multi_processing.py`:

```python
if __name__ == '__main__':
    in_queue = multiprocessing.Queue()
    out_queue = multiprocessing.Queue()
    process = multiprocessing.Process(target=square_mp,
    args=(in_queue, out_queue))
    process.start()
    for i in range(10):
        in_queue.put(i)
        i_squared = out_queue.get()
        print(f"{i} squared is {i_squared}")
    process.terminate()
```

Recall that the `if name == '__main__'` line simply avoids executing this section of code if the module is being imported elsewhere in your project. In comparison, `in_queue` and `out_queue` are both queue objects through which data can be sent between the parent and child processes. Within the following loop, you can see that you add integers to `in_queue` and get the results from `out_queue`. If you look at the preceding `square_mp` function, you can see how the child process will get its values from the `in_queue` object and pass the result back into the `out_queue` object.

5. Execute your program from the command line as follows:

```
python multi_processing.py
```

The output will be as follows:

```
(base) C:\Users\andrew.bird\Python-In-Demand\Lesson09>python multi_processing.py
0 squared is 0
1 squared is 1
2 squared is 4
3 squared is 9
4 squared is 16
5 squared is 25
6 squared is 36
7 squared is 49
8 squared is 64
9 squared is 81

(base) C:\Users\andrew.bird\Python-In-Demand\Lesson09>
```

Figure 9.17 – Running our multiprocessing script

In this exercise, you learned how to pass tasks between our parent and child Python processes using the multiprocessing package and you found the square of a set of numbers.

Multiprocessing with the threading package

Whereas multiprocessing and execnet create a new Python process to run your asynchronous code, threading simply creates a new thread within the current process. Therefore, it uses fewer operating resources than other alternatives. Your new thread shares all its memory, including global variables, with the creating thread. The two threads are not truly concurrent, because the GIL means only one Python instruction can be running at once across all threads in a Python process.

Finally, you cannot terminate a thread, so unless you plan to exit your whole Python process, you must provide the thread function with a way to exit. In the following exercise, you'll use a special signal value sent to a queue to exit the thread.

Exercise 124 – using the threading package

In this exercise, you will use the threading module to complete the same task of squaring numbers as in *Exercise 122 – working with execnet to execute a simple Python squaring program*:

1. In a Jupyter notebook, use import for the threading and queue modules:

    ```
    import threading
    import queue
    ```

2. Create two new queues to handle the communication between our processes, as shown in the following code snippet:

```
in_queue = queue.Queue()
out_queue = queue.Queue()
```

3. Create the function that will watch the queue for new numbers and return squared numbers. The if n == 'STOP' line allows you to terminate the thread by passing STOP into the in_queue object:

```
def square_threading():
    while True:
        n = in_queue.get()
        if n == 'STOP':
            return
        n_squared = n**2
        out_queue.put(n_squared)
```

4. Now, create and start a new thread:

```
thread = threading.Thread(target=square_threading)
thread.start()
```

5. Loop through 10 numbers, pass them into the in_queue object, and receive them from the out_queue object as the expected output:

```
for i in range(10):
    in_queue.put(i)
    i_squared = out_queue.get()
    print(f"{i} squared is {i_squared}")
in_queue.put('STOP')
thread.join()
```

The output will be as follows:

```
0 squared is 0
1 squared is 1
2 squared is 4
3 squared is 9
4 squared is 16
5 squared is 25
6 squared is 36
7 squared is 49
8 squared is 64
9 squared is 81
```

Figure 9.18 – Output from the threading loop

In this exercise, you learned how to pass tasks between our parent and child Python processes using the threading package. In the following section, you will look at parsing command-line arguments in scripts.

Parsing command-line arguments in scripts

Scripts often need input from their user in order to make certain choices about what the script does or how it runs. For instance, consider a script to train a deep learning network used for image classification. A user of this script will want to tell it where the training images are and what the labels are, and may want to choose what model to use, the learning rate, where to save the trained model configuration, and other features.

It's conventional to use command-line arguments; that is, values that the user supplies from their shell or their own script when running your script. Using command-line arguments makes it easy to automate using the script in different ways and will be familiar to users who have experience using the Unix or Windows command shells.

Python's standard library module for interpreting command-line arguments, argparse, supplies a host of features, making it easy to add argument handling to scripts in a fashion that is consistent with other tools. You can make arguments required or optional, have the user supply values for certain arguments, or define default values. argparse creates usage text, which the user can read using the --help argument, and checks the user-supplied arguments for validity.

Using argparse is a four-step process. First, you create a parser object. Second, you add arguments your program accepts to the parser object. Third, tell the parser object to parse your script's argv (short for argument vector – the list of arguments that were supplied to the script on launch); it checks them for consistency and stores the values. Finally, use the object returned from the parser object in your script to access the values supplied in the arguments.

To run all of the exercises in this section, later on, you will need to type the Python code into the .py files and run them from your operating system's command line, not from a Jupyter notebook.

Exercise 125 – introducing argparse to accept input from the user

In this exercise, you'll create a program that uses argparse to take a single input from the user called flag. If the flag input is not provided by the user, its value is False. If it is provided, its value is True. This exercise will be performed in a Python terminal:

1. Create a new Python file called argparse_demo.py.

2. Import the argparse library:

    ```
    import argparse
    ```

3. Create a new parser object, as shown in the following code snippet:

    ```
    parser = argparse.ArgumentParser(description="Interpret a
    Boolean flag.")
    ```

4. Add an argument that will allow the user to pass through the -flag argument when they execute the program:

    ```
    parser.add_argument('--flag', dest='flag', action='store_
    true', help='Set the flag value to True.')
    ```

    The store_true action means that the parser will set the value of the argument to True if the flag input is present. Otherwise, it will set the value to False. The exact opposite can be achieved using the store_false action.

5. Now, call the parse_args() method, which executes the actual processing of the arguments:

    ```
    arguments = parser.parse_args()
    ```

6. Now, print the value of the argument to see whether it worked:

    ```
    print(f"The flag's value is {arguments.flag}")
    ```

7. Execute the file with no arguments supplied; the value of arguments.flag should be False:

    ```
    python argparse_example.py
    ```

    The output will be as follows:

    ```
    (base) C:\Users\andrew.bird\Python-In-Demand\Lesson09>python argparse_demo.py
    The flag's value is False
    ```

    Figure 9.19 – Running argparse_demo with no arguments

8. Run the script again with the `--flag` argument to set it to `True`:

```
python argparse_demo.py –flag
```

The output will be as follows:

```
(base) C:\Users\andrew.bird\Python-In-Demand\Lesson09>python argparse_demo.py --flag
The flag's value is True

(base) C:\Users\andrew.bird\Python-In-Demand\Lesson09>
```

Figure 9.20 – Running argparse_demo with the --flag argument

9. Now, enter the following code and see the `help` text that `argparse` extracted from the description and the `help` text you supplied:

```
python argparse_demo.py –help
```

You will get the following output:

```
(base) C:\Users\andrew.bird\Python-In-Demand\Lesson09>python argparse_demo.py --help
usage: argparse_demo.py [-h] [--flag]

Interpret a Boolean flag.

optional arguments:
  -h, --help  show this help message and exit
  --flag      Set the flag value to True.
```

Figure 9.21 – Viewing the help text of argparse_demo

You have successfully created a script that allows an argument to be specified when it is executed. You can probably imagine how useful this can often be.

Positional arguments

Some scripts have arguments that are fundamental to their operation. For example, a script that copies a file always needs to know the **source** and **destination** files. It would be inefficient to repetitively type out the names of the arguments, for instance, `python copyfile.py --source infile --destination outfile`, every time you used the script.

You can use positional arguments to define arguments that the user does not name but are always provided in a particular order. The difference between a positional and a named argument is that a named argument starts with a hyphen (`-`), such as `--flag` in *Exercise 125 – introducing argparse to accept input from the user*. A positional argument does **not** start with a hyphen.

Exercise 126 – using positional arguments to accept source and destination inputs from a user

In this exercise, you will create a program that uses `argparse` to take two inputs from the user: `source` and `destination`.

This exercise will be performed in a Python terminal:

1. Create a new Python file called `positional_args.py`.

2. Import the `argparse` library:

    ```
    import argparse
    ```

3. Create a new `parser` object:

    ```
    parser = argparse.ArgumentParser(description="Interpret
    positional arguments.")
    ```

4. Add two arguments for the `source` and `destination` values:

    ```
    parser.add_argument('source', action='store', help='The
    source of an operation.')
    parser.add_argument('dest', action='store', help='The
    destination of the operation.')
    ```

5. Call the `parse_args()` method, which executes the actual processing of `arguments`:

    ```
    arguments = parser.parse_args()
    ```

6. Now, print the value of `arguments` so that you can see whether it worked:

    ```
    print(f"Picasso will cycle from {arguments.source} to
    {arguments.dest}")
    ```

7. Now, execute the file while using this script with no arguments, which causes an error because it expects two `positional` arguments:

    ```
    python positional_args.py
    ```

    The output now will be as follows:

    ```
    (base) C:\Users\andrew.bird\Python-In-Demand\Lesson09>python positional_args.py
    usage: positional_args.py [-h] source dest
    positional_args.py: error: the following arguments are required: source, dest
    ```

    Figure 9.22 – Running the script with no arguments specified

8. Try running the script and specifying two locations as the source and destination positional arguments:

> **Note**
>
> The arguments are supplied on the command line with no names or leading hyphens.

```
$ python positional_args.py Chichester Battersea
```

The output is as follows:

```
(base) C:\Users\andrew.bird\Python-In-Demand\Lesson09>python positional_args.py Chichester Battersea
Picasso will cycle from Chichester to Battersea
```

Figure 9.23 – Successfully specifying two positional arguments

In this exercise, you learned how to parameterize your scripts by accepting positional arguments using the `argparse` Python package.

Performance and profiling

Python is not often thought of as a high-performance language, although it really should be. The simplicity of the language and the power of its standard library mean that the time from idea to result can be much shorter than in other languages with better runtime performance.

However, we have to be honest. Python is not among the fastest-running programming languages in the world and sometimes, that's important. For instance, if you're writing a web server application, you need to be able to handle as many network requests as are being made, and with timeliness that satisfies the users making the requests.

Alternatively, if you're writing a scientific simulation or a deep learning inference engine, then the simulation or training time can completely dwarf the programmer time (which is your time) spent writing the code. In any situation, reducing the time spent running your application can decrease the cost, whether measured in dollars on your cloud hosting bill or in milliamp-hours on your laptop battery.

Changing your Python environment

You'll learn how to use some of Python's timing and profiling tools later on in this section. Before that, you can consider whether you even need to do that. Taligent, an object-oriented software company in the 1990s, had a performance saying: *"There is no code faster than no code."* You can generalize that idea as follows:

There is no work that can be done faster than doing no work.

The fastest way to speed up your Python program can often be to simply use a different Python interpreter. You saw earlier in this chapter that multithreaded Python is slowed down by GIL, which means that only one Python thread can execute a Python instruction at any time in a given process. The Jython and IronPython environments, targeting the Java virtual machine and .NET common language runtime, do not have GIL, so they may be faster for multithreaded programs, but there are also two Python implementations that are specifically designed to perform better, so we'll look to those for assistance in later sections.

PyPy

We will now look at another Python environment in more detail. It's called pypy and Guido van Rossum (Python's creator) has said, "*If you want your code to run faster, you should probably just use PyPy.*"

PyPy's secret is **just-in-time** (**JIT**) compilation, which compiles the Python program to a machine language, such as Cython, but does it while the program is running rather than once on the developer's machine, as with **ahead-of-time** (**AOT**) compilation. For a long-running process, a JIT compiler can try different strategies to compile the same code and find the ones that work best in the program's environment. The program will quickly get faster until the best version the compiler can find is running. Take a look at PyPy in the following exercise.

Exercise 127 – using PyPy to find the time to get a list of prime numbers

In this exercise, you will be executing a Python program to get a list of prime numbers using milliamp-hours, but remember that you are more interested in checking the amount of time needed to execute the program using pypy.

This exercise will be performed in a Python terminal:

1. First, run the pypy3 command, as shown in the following code snippet:

```
pypy3
Python 3.6.1 (dab365a465140aa79a5f3ba4db784c4af4d5c195,
Feb 18 2019, 10:53:27)
[PyPy 7.0.0-alpha0 with GCC 4.2.1 Compatible Apple LLVM
10.0.0 (clang-1000.11.45.5)] on darwin
Type "help", "copyright", "credits" or "license" for more
information.
And now for something completely different: ''release 1.2
upcoming''
>>>>
```

Note that you may find it easier to navigate to the folder with the `pypy3.exe` file and run the preceding command, instead of following the installation instructions to create a symlink.

2. Press *Ctrl + D* to exit `pypy`.

You're going to use the program from *Chapter 7, Becoming Pythonic*, again, which finds prime numbers using the *Sieve of Eratosthenes method*. There are two changes that you will introduce here: firstly, find prime numbers up to 1,000 to give the program more work to do; secondly, instrument it with Python's `timeit` module so that you can see how long it takes to run. `timeit` runs a Python statement multiple times and records how long it takes. Tell `timeit` to run your Sieve of Eratosthenes 10,000 times (the default is 100,000 times, which takes a very long time).

3. Create an `eratosthenes.py` file and enter the following code:

```python
import timeit
class PrimesBelow:
    def __init__(self, bound):
        self.candidate_numbers = list(range(2,bound))
    def __iter__(self):
        return self
    def __next__(self):
        if len(self.candidate_numbers) == 0:
            raise StopIteration
        next_prime = self.candidate_numbers[0]
        self.candidate_numbers = [x for x in self.candidate_numbers if x % next_prime != 0]
        return next_prime
print(timeit.timeit('list(PrimesBelow(1000))',
setup='from __main__ import PrimesBelow', number=10000))
```

4. Run the file with the regular Python interpreter:

`python eratosthenes.py`

You will get the following output:

```
(base) C:\Users\andrew.bird\Python-In-Demand\Lesson09>python eratosthenes.py
17.597791835
```

Figure 9.24 – Executing with the regular Python interpreter

The number will be different on your computer, but that's `17.6` seconds to execute the `list(PrimesBelow(1000))` statement 10,000 times, or 1,760 µs per iteration. Now, run the same program using pypy instead of CPython:

```
$ pypy3 eratosthenes.py
```

You will get the following output:

```
4.81645076300083
```

Here, it is 482 µs per iteration.

In this exercise, you will have noticed that it only takes 30% of the time to run our code in pypy as it took in Python. You really can get a significant performance boost with very little effort, just by switching to pypy.

Cython

A Python module can be compiled to C with a wrapper, which means it is still accessible from other Python code. Compiling code simply means it is taken from one language and put into another. In this case, the compiler takes Python code and expresses it in the C programming language. The tool that does this is called Cython and it often generates modules with lower memory use and execution time than if they're left as Python.

> **Note**
>
> The standard Python interpreter, the one you've almost certainly been using to complete the exercises and activities in this course, is sometimes called **CPython**. This is confusingly similar to **Cython**, but the two are actually different projects.

Exercise 128 – adopting Cython to find the time taken to get a list of prime numbers

In this exercise, you will install Cython, and, as mentioned in the previous exercise, you will find a list of prime numbers, although you are more interested in knowing the amount of time it takes to execute the code using Cython.

This exercise will be performed on the command line:

1. Firstly, install cython, as shown in the following code snippet:

    ```
    $ pip install cython
    ```

2.　Now, go back to the code you wrote for *Exercise 8 – displaying strings*, and extract the class for iterating over primes using the Sieve of Eratosthenes into a file, `sieve_module.py`:

```
class PrimesBelow:
    def __init__(self, bound):
        self.candidate_numbers = list(range(2,bound))
    def __iter__(self):
        return self
    def __next__(self):
        if len(self.candidate_numbers) == 0:
            raise StopIteration
        next_prime = self.candidate_numbers[0]
        self.candidate_numbers = [x for x in self.
candidate_numbers if x % next_prime != 0]
        return next_prime
```

3.　Compile that into a C module using `Cython`. Create a file called `setup.py` with the following contents:

```
from distutils.core import setup
from Cython.Build import cythonize
setup(
    ext_modules = cythonize("sieve_module.py")
)
```

4.　Now, on the command line, run `setup.py` to build the module, as shown in the following code snippet:

```
$ python setup.py build_ext --inplace
```

The output will look different if you're on Linux or Windows, but you should see no errors:

```
running build_ext
building 'sieve_module' extension
creating build
creating build/temp.macosx-10.7-x86_64-3.7
gcc -Wno-unused-result -Wsign-compare -Wunreachable-code
-DNDEBUG -g -fwrapv -O3 -Wall -Wstrict-prototypes -I/
Users/leeg/anaconda3/include -arch x86_64 -I/Users/leeg/
anaconda3/include -arch x86_64 -I/Users/leeg/anaconda3/
include/python3.7m -c sieve_module.c -o build/temp.
macosx-10.7-x86_64-3.7/sieve_module.o
```

```
gcc -bundle -undefined dynamic_lookup -L/Users/leeg/
anaconda3/lib -arch x86_64 -L/Users/leeg/anaconda3/
lib -arch x86_64 -arch x86_64 build/temp.macosx-
10.7-x86_64-3.7/sieve_module.o -o /Users/leeg/Nextcloud/
Documents/Python Book/Lesson_9/sieve_module.cpython-37m-
darwin.so
```

5. Now, import the `timeit` module and use it in a script called `cython_sieve.py`:

```
import timeit
print(timeit.timeit('list(PrimesBelow(1000))',
setup='from sieve_module import PrimesBelow',
number=10000))
```

6. Run this program to see the timing:

```
$ python cython_sieve.py
```

The output will be as follows:

```
3.830873068
```

Here, it is 3.83 seconds, so 383 μs per iteration. That's a little over 40% of the time taken by the CPython version, but the `pypy` Python was still able to run the code faster. The advantage of using Cython is that you are able to make a module that is compatible with CPython, so you can make your module code faster without needing to make everybody else switch to a different Python interpreter to reap the benefits.

Profiling code

Having exhausted the minimum-effort options for improving your code's performance, it's time to actually put some work in if you need to go faster. There's no recipe to follow to write fast code: if there were, we could have taught you that in the previous chapter and there wouldn't need to be a section on performance now. Of course, speed also isn't the only performance goal – you might want to reduce memory use or increase the number of simultaneous operations that can be in flight – but programmers often use "performance" as a synonym for "reducing time to completion," and that's what you'll investigate here.

Improving performance is a scientific process: you observe how your code behaves, hypothesize about a potential improvement, make the change, and then observe it again and check that you really did improve things. Good tool support exists for the observation steps in this process and you'll look at one of these tools now: `cProfile`.

`cProfile` is a module that builds an execution profile of your code. Every time your Python program enters or exits a function or other callable, `cProfile` records what it is and how long it takes. It's then up to you to work out how you could spend less time doing that. Remember to compare a profile recorded before your change with one recorded after to make sure you improved things! As you'll see in the next exercise, not all "optimizations" actually make your code faster, and careful measurement and thought are needed to decide whether the optimization is worth pursuing and retaining. In practice, cProfile is often used when trying to understand why code is taking longer than expected to execute. For example, you might write an iterative calculation that suddenly takes 10 minutes to compute after scaling to 1,000 iterations. With cProfile, you might discover that this is due to some inefficient function in the pandas library, which you could potentially avoid to speed up your code.

Profiling with cProfile

The goal of this example is to learn how to diagnose code performance using cProfile. In particular, to understand which parts of your code are taking the most time to execute.

This is a pretty long example, and the point is not to make sure that you type in and understand the code but to understand the process of profiling, consider changes, and observe the effects those changes have on the profile. This example will be performed on the command line:

1. Start with the code you wrote in *Chapter 7, Becoming Pythonic*, to generate an infinite series of prime numbers:

```python
class Primes:
    def __init__(self):
        self.current = 2
    def __iter__(self):
        return self
    def __next__(self):
        while True:
            current = self.current
            square_root = int(current ** 0.5)
            is_prime = True
            if square_root >= 2:
                for i in range(2, square_root + 1):
                    if current % i == 0:
                        is_prime = False
                        break
            self.current += 1
            if is_prime:
                return current
```

2. You'll remember that you had to use `itertools.takewhile()` to turn this into a finite sequence. Do so to generate a large list of primes and use `cProfile` to investigate its performance:

```
import cProfile
import itertools
cProfile.run('[p for p in itertools.takewhile(lambda x:
x<10000, Primes())]')
```

You will get the following output:

```
     2466 function calls in 0.021 seconds

Ordered by: standard name

ncalls  tottime  percall  cumtime  percall filename:lineno(function)
     1    0.000    0.000    0.000    0.000 <ipython-input-1-5aedc56b5f71>:2(__init__)
     1    0.000    0.000    0.000    0.000 <ipython-input-1-5aedc56b5f71>:4(__iter__)
  1230    0.020    0.000    0.020    0.000 <ipython-input-1-5aedc56b5f71>:6(__next__)
  1230    0.000    0.000    0.000    0.000 <string>:1(<lambda>)
     1    0.001    0.001    0.021    0.021 <string>:1(<listcomp>)
     1    0.000    0.000    0.021    0.021 <string>:1(<module>)
     1    0.000    0.000    0.021    0.021 {built-in method builtins.exec}
     1    0.000    0.000    0.000    0.000 {method 'disable' of '_lsprof.Profiler' objects}
```

Figure 9.25 – Investigating performance with cProfile

The __next__() function is called most often, which is not surprising, as it is the iterative part of the iteration. It also takes up most of the execution time in the profile. So, is there a way to make it faster?

One hypothesis is that the method does a lot of redundant divisions. Imagine that the number 101 is being tested as a prime number. This implementation tests whether it is divisible by 2 (no), then 3 (no), and then 4, but 4 is a multiple of 2, so you know it isn't divisible by 2.

3. As a hypothesis, change the __next__() method so that it only searches the list of known prime numbers. You know that if the number being tested is divisible by any smaller numbers, at least one of those numbers is itself prime:

```
class Primes2:
    def __init__(self):
        self.known_primes=[]
        self.current=2
    def __iter__(self):
        return self
    def __next__(self):
        while True:
            current = self.current
```

```
                        prime_factors = [p for p in self.known_primes
            if current % p == 0]
                    self.current += 1
                    if len(prime_factors) == 0:
                        self.known_primes.append(current)
                    return current
        cProfile.run('[p for p in itertools.takewhile(lambda x:
        x<10000, Primes2())]')
```

The output will be as follows:

```
23708 function calls in 0.468 seconds

Ordered by: standard name

ncalls  tottime  percall  cumtime  percall filename:lineno(function)
 10006    0.455    0.000    0.455    0.000 <ipython-input-2-c6ffd796f813>:10(<listcomp>)
     1    0.000    0.000    0.000    0.000 <ipython-input-2-c6ffd796f813>:2(__init__)
     1    0.000    0.000    0.000    0.000 <ipython-input-2-c6ffd796f813>:5(__iter__)
  1230    0.011    0.000    0.466    0.000 <ipython-input-2-c6ffd796f813>:7(__next__)
  1230    0.000    0.000    0.000    0.000 <string>:1(<lambda>)
     1    0.001    0.001    0.468    0.468 <string>:1(<listcomp>)
     1    0.000    0.000    0.468    0.468 <string>:1(<module>)
     1    0.000    0.000    0.468    0.468 {built-in method builtins.exec}
 10006    0.001    0.000    0.001    0.000 {built-in method builtins.len}
  1230    0.000    0.000    0.000    0.000 {method 'append' of 'list' objects}
     1    0.000    0.000    0.000    0.000 {method 'disable' of '_lsprof.Profiler' objects}
```

Figure 9.26 – It took longer this time!

Now, __next()__ isn't the most frequently called function in the profile, but that's not a good thing. Instead, you've introduced a list comprehension that gets called even more times, and the whole process takes 30 times longer than it used to.

4.   One thing that changed in the switch from testing a range of factors to the list of known primes is that the upper bound of tested numbers is no longer the square root of the candidate prime. Going back to thinking about testing whether 101 is prime, the first implementation tested all numbers between 2 and 10. The new one tests all primes from 2 to 97 and is therefore doing more work. Reintroduce the square root upper limit using takewhile to filter the list of primes:

```
class Primes3:
    def __init__(self):
        self.known_primes=[]
        self.current=2
    def __iter__(self):
        return self
    def __next__(self):
```

```
            while True:
                current = self.current
                sqrt_current = int(current**0.5)
                potential_factors = itertools.
        takewhile(lambda x: x < sqrt_current, self.known_primes)
                prime_factors = [p for p in potential_factors
        if current % p == 0]
                self.current += 1
                if len(prime_factors) == 0:
                    self.known_primes.append(current)
                    return current
        cProfile.run('[p for p in itertools.takewhile(lambda x:
        x<10000, Primes3())]')
```

The output will be as follows:

```
        291158 function calls in 0.102 seconds

Ordered by: standard name

ncalls  tottime  percall  cumtime  percall filename:lineno(function)
267345    0.023    0.000    0.023    0.000 <ipython-input-3-10d4133c7618>:11(<lambda>)
 10006    0.058    0.000    0.081    0.000 <ipython-input-3-10d4133c7618>:12(<listcomp>)
     1    0.000    0.000    0.000    0.000 <ipython-input-3-10d4133c7618>:2(__init__)
     1    0.000    0.000    0.000    0.000 <ipython-input-3-10d4133c7618>:5(__iter__)
  1265    0.018    0.000    0.100    0.000 <ipython-input-3-10d4133c7618>:7(__next__)
  1265    0.000    0.000    0.000    0.000 <string>:1(<lambda>)
     1    0.001    0.001    0.102    0.102 <string>:1(<listcomp>)
     1    0.000    0.000    0.102    0.102 <string>:1(<module>)
     1    0.000    0.000    0.102    0.102 {built-in method builtins.exec}
 10006    0.001    0.000    0.001    0.000 {built-in method builtins.len}
  1265    0.000    0.000    0.000    0.000 {method 'append' of 'list' objects}
     1    0.000    0.000    0.000    0.000 {method 'disable' of '_lsprof.Profiler' objects}
```

Figure 9.27 – Getting faster this time

5. Much better. Well, much better than `Primes2` anyway. This still takes seven times longer than the original algorithm. There's still one trick to try. The biggest contribution to the execution time is the list comprehension as highlighted in the previous code. By turning that into a `for` loop, it's possible to break the loop early by exiting as soon as a prime factor for the candidate prime is found:

```
class Primes4:
    def __init__(self):
        self.known_primes=[]
        self.current=2
```

```
        def __iter__(self):
            return self
        def __next__(self):
            while True:
                current = self.current
                sqrt_current = int(current**0.5)
                potential_factors = itertools.
    takewhile(lambda x: x < sqrt_ current, self.known_primes)
                is_prime = True
                for p in potential_factors:
                    if current % p == 0:
                        is_prime = False
                        break
                self.current += 1
                if is_prime == True:
                    self.known_primes.append(current)
                    return current
cProfile.run('[p for p in itertools.takewhile(lambda x:
x<10000, Primes4())]')
```

The output will be as follows:

```
    64802 function calls in 0.033 seconds

Ordered by: standard name

ncalls  tottime  percall  cumtime  percall filename:lineno(function)
 61001    0.007    0.000    0.007    0.000 <ipython-input-4-4f9e19e7ebde>:11(<lambda>)
     1    0.000    0.000    0.000    0.000 <ipython-input-4-4f9e19e7ebde>:2(__init__)
     1    0.000    0.000    0.000    0.000 <ipython-input-4-4f9e19e7ebde>:5(__iter__)
  1265    0.024    0.000    0.032    0.000 <ipython-input-4-4f9e19e7ebde>:7(__next__)
  1265    0.000    0.000    0.000    0.000 <string>:1(<lambda>)
     1    0.001    0.001    0.033    0.033 <string>:1(<listcomp>)
     1    0.000    0.000    0.033    0.033 <string>:1(<module>)
     1    0.000    0.000    0.033    0.033 {built-in method builtins.exec}
  1265    0.000    0.000    0.000    0.000 {method 'append' of 'list' objects}
     1    0.000    0.000    0.000    0.000 {method 'disable' of '_lsprof.Profiler' objects}
```

Figure 9.28 – An even faster output

Once again, the result is better than the previous attempt, but it is still not as good as the "naive" algorithm. This time, the biggest contribution to the runtime is the lambda expression on line 11. This tests whether one of the previously found primes is smaller than the square root of the candidate number. There's no way to remove that test from this version of the algorithm. In other words, surprisingly, in this case, doing too much work to find a prime number is faster than finding the minimum work necessary and doing just that.

6. In fact, the good news is that our effort has not been wasted. I don't recommend running this yourself unless the instructor says it's time for a coffee break, but if you increase the number of primes your iterator searches for, there will come a point where the "optimized" algorithm will outpace the "naive" implementation:

```
cProfile.run('[p for p in itertools.takewhile(lambda x:
x<10000000, Primes())]')
```

You will get the following output:

```
         1329166 function calls in 147.528 seconds

   Ordered by: standard name

   ncalls  tottime  percall  cumtime  percall filename:lineno(function)
        1    0.000    0.000    0.000    0.000 <ipython-input-1-5aedc56b5f71>:2(__init__)
        1    0.000    0.000    0.000    0.000 <ipython-input-1-5aedc56b5f71>:4(__iter__)
   664580  146.901    0.000  146.901    0.000 <ipython-input-1-5aedc56b5f71>:6(__next__)
   664580    0.101    0.000    0.101    0.000 <string>:1(<lambda>)
        1    0.514    0.514  147.516  147.516 <string>:1(<listcomp>)
        1    0.011    0.011  147.528  147.528 <string>:1(<module>)
        1    0.000    0.000  147.528  147.528 {built-in method builtins.exec}
        1    0.000    0.000    0.000    0.000 {method 'disable' of '_lsprof.Profiler' objects}
```

Figure 9.29 – The result of the naive implementation

Now, we can run the same with the alternative implementation:

```
cProfile.run('[p for p in itertools.takewhile(lambda x:
x<10000000, Primes4())]')
```

You will get the following output:

```
         317503134 function calls in 106.236 seconds

   Ordered by: standard name

      ncalls  tottime  percall  cumtime  percall filename:lineno(function)
   315507795   24.815    0.000   24.815    0.000 <ipython-input-4-4f9e19e7ebde>:11(<lambda>)
           1    0.000    0.000    0.000    0.000 <ipython-input-4-4f9e19e7ebde>:2(__init__)
           1    0.000    0.000    0.000    0.000 <ipython-input-4-4f9e19e7ebde>:5(__iter__)
      665111   80.611    0.000  105.523    0.000 <ipython-input-4-4f9e19e7ebde>:7(__next__)
      665111    0.114    0.000    0.114    0.000 <string>:1(<lambda>)
           1    0.583    0.583  106.221  106.221 <string>:1(<listcomp>)
           1    0.015    0.015  106.236  106.236 <string>:1(<module>)
           1    0.000    0.000  106.236  106.236 {built-in method builtins.exec}
      665111    0.097    0.000    0.097    0.000 {method 'append' of 'list' objects}
           1    0.000    0.000    0.000    0.000 {method 'disable' of '_lsprof.Profiler' objects}
```

Figure 9.30 – The result of the optimized implementation

By the end of this example, you were able to find the best-optimized method to run the code. This decision was made possible by observing the amount of time needed to run the code, allowing us to tweak the code to address inefficiencies. In the following activity, you will put all of these concepts together.

Activity 23 – generating a list of random numbers in a Python virtual environment

You work for a sports betting website and want to simulate random events in a particular betting market. In order to do so, your goal will be to create a program that is able to generate long lists of random numbers using multiprocessing.

In this activity, the aim is to create a new Python environment, install the relevant packages, and write a function using the threading library to generate a list of random numbers.

Here are the steps:

1. Create a new conda environment called my_env.

2. Activate the conda environment.

3. Install numpy in your new environment.

4. Install and run a Jupyter notebook from within your virtual environment.

5. Create a new Jupyter notebook and import libraries such as numpy, cProfile, itertools, and threading.

6. Create a function that uses the numpy and threading libraries to generate an array of random numbers. Recall that when threading, we need to be able to send a signal for the while statement to terminate. The function should monitor the queue for an integer that represents the number of random numbers it should return. For example, if the number 10 was passed into the queue, it should return an array of 10 random numbers.

7. Next, add a function that will start a thread and put integers into the in_queue object. You can optionally print the output by setting the show_output argument to True. Make this function loop through the integers 0 to n, where n can be specified when the function is called. For each integer between 0 and n, it will pass the integer into the queue, and receive the array of random numbers.

8. Run the numbers on a small number of iterations to test and see the output.

You will get the following output:

```
[]
[0.78155881]
[0.61671875 0.96379795]
[0.52748128 0.69182391 0.11764897]
[0.89243527 0.75566451 0.88089298 0.15782374]
[0.1140009  0.25980504 0.88632411 0.08730527 0.17493792]
[0.41370041 0.01167654 0.60758276 0.73804504 0.73648781 0.29094613
]
[0.8317736  0.57914287 0.01291246 0.61011878 0.91729392 0.50898183
 0.24640681]
[0.4475645  0.94036652 0.69823962 0.37459892 0.15512432 0.15115215
 0.65882522 0.77908825]
[0.42420881 0.7135031  0.22843178 0.20624473 0.32533328 0.86108686
 0.46407033 0.81794371 0.98958707]
```

Figure 9.31 – The expected sample output

9. Rerun the numbers with a large number of iterations and use `cProfile` to view a breakdown of what is taking time to execute.

Note

The solution for this activity can be found in *Appendix* on GitHub.

With this, we conclude this chapter on advanced topics for Python.

Summary

In this chapter, you have seen some of the tools and skills needed to transition from being a Python programmer to a Python software engineer. You have learned how to collaborate with other programmers using `Git` and GitHub, how to manage dependencies and virtual environments with `conda`, and how to deploy Python applications using Docker. We have explored multiprocessing and investigated tools and techniques used for improving the performance of your Python code. These new skills leave you better equipped to handle the messy real world of collaborative teams working on large problems in production environments. These skills are not just academic, but are essential tools for any aspiring Python developer to familiarize themselves with.

The next chapter will introduce the part of the book dedicated to using Python for data science. You will learn about popular libraries for working with numerical data and techniques for importing, exploring, cleaning up, and analyzing real-world data.

10

Data Analytics with pandas and NumPy

Overview

By the end of this chapter, you will be able to use NumPy to perform statistics and speed up matrix computations; use pandas to view, create, analyze, and modify DataFrames; organize and modify data using `read`, `transpose`, `loc`, `iloc`, and `concatenate`; clean data by deleting or manipulating NaN values and coercing column types; visualize data by constructing, modifying, and interpreting histograms and scatter plots; generate and interpret statistical models using pandas and statsmodels, and solve real-world problems using data analytics techniques.

Introduction

In *Chapter 9, Practical Python – Advanced Topics*, you learned how to use GitHub to collaborate with team members. You also used `conda` to document and set up the dependencies for Python programs and `docker` to create reproducible Python environments to run our code.

We will now shift gears to data science. Data science is booming like never before. Data scientists have become among the most sought-after practitioners in the world today. Most leading corporations have data scientists to analyze and explain their data.

Data analytics focuses on the analysis of big data. As each day goes by, there is more data than ever before – far too much for any human to analyze by sight. Leading Python developers such as Wes McKinney and Travis Oliphant addressed this gap by creating specialized Python libraries – in particular, pandas and NumPy – to handle big data.

Taken together, pandas and NumPy are masterful at handling big data. They are built for speed, efficiency, readability, and ease of use.

pandas provides you with a unique framework to view and modify data. It handles all data-related tasks such as creating DataFrames, importing data, scraping data from the web, merging data, pivoting, concatenating, and more.

NumPy, short for Numerical Python, is more focused on computation. NumPy interprets the rows and columns of pandas DataFrames as matrices in the form of NumPy arrays. When computing descriptive statistics such as the mean, median, mode, and quartiles, NumPy is blazingly fast.

Another key player in data analysis is Matplotlib, a graphing library that handles scatter plots, histograms, regression lines, and more, all of which you were introduced to in *Chapter 4, Extending Python, Files, Errors, and Graphs*. The importance of data graphs cannot be overstated since most non-technical professionals use them to interpret results.

We will be looking at the following topics in this chapter:

- NumPy and basic stats
- Matrices
- The pandas library
- Working with big data
- Null values
- Creating statistical graphs

Let's start!

Technical requirements

The code files for this chapter are available on GitHub at `https://github.com/PacktPublishing/The-Python-Workshop-Second-Edition/tree/main/Chapter10`.

NumPy and basic stats

NumPy is designed to handle big data swiftly. It includes the following essential components according to the NumPy documentation:

- A powerful n-dimensional array object
- Sophisticated (broadcasting) functions
- Tools for integrating C/C++ and Fortran code
- Useful linear algebra, Fourier transform, and random number capabilities

You will be using NumPy going forward. Instead of using lists, you will use NumPy arrays, which are basic elements of the NumPy package. NumPy arrays are designed to handle arrays of any dimension.

Numpy arrays can be indexed easily and can have many types of data, such as `float`, `int`, `string`, and `object`, but the types must be consistent to improve speed.

Exercise 129 – converting lists into NumPy arrays

In this exercise, you will convert a list into a `numpy` array. The following steps will enable you to complete this exercise:

1. Open a new Jupyter Notebook.

2. Then, you need to import `numpy`:

```
import numpy as np
```

3. Now, you must create a list for `test_scores` and confirm the type of data:

```
test_scores = [70,65,95,88]
type(test_scores)
```

The output will be as follows:

```
list
```

> **Note**
>
> Now that `numpy` has been imported, you can access all `numpy` methods, such as `numpy` arrays. Type `np.` and then press *Tab* on your keyboard to see the breadth of options. You are looking for an array.

4. Now, you must convert the list of marks into a `numpy` array and check the array's `type`. Enter the code shown in the following code snippet:

```
scores = np.array(test_scores)
type(scores)
```

The output will be as follows:

```
numpy.ndarray
```

In this exercise, you converted a list of test score marks into a NumPy array. You will find the mean using these values within the NumPy array in the following exercise.

One of the most common statistical measures is the mean. Traditionally thought of as the average, the mean of a list is the sum of each entry divided by the number of entries. In NumPy, the mean may be computed using the `.mean` method.

Exercise 130 – calculating the mean of the test score

In this exercise, you will use the `numpy` array you created to store our test scores from the previous exercise, and you will calculate the mean of `scores`. The following steps will enable you to complete this exercise:

1. Continue working in the same Jupyter Notebook from the previous exercise.

2. Now, to find the "average" of `scores`, you can use the `mean` method, as shown here:

```
scores.mean()
```

The output will be as follows:

```
79.5
```

> **Note**
> The word "average" is in quotation marks. This is not an accident. The mean is only one kind of average. Another kind of average is the median.

Given our test scores of 70, 65, 95, and 88, the "average" is 79.5, which is the expected output. In this exercise, you were able to use the `mean` function of NumPy and find the average of `scores`. In the following exercise, you will find the median using NumPy.

The median is the number in the middle. Although not necessarily the best measure of test averages, it's an excellent measure of income average because it is robust to outliers, unlike the mean, as you will see in the next exercise.

Exercise 131 – finding the median from a collection of income data

In this exercise, you will be finding the median from a collection of income data for a neighborhood and help a millionaire decide whether he should build his dream house in the neighborhood based on the income data. The `median` function here is a method of `numpy`.

The following steps will enable you to complete this exercise:

1. Open a new Jupyter Notebook.

2. Now, you need to import the `numpy` package as np, then create a `numpy` array and assign various pieces of `income` data, as shown in the following code snippet:

```
import numpy as np
income = np.array([75000, 55000, 88000, 125000, 64000,
97000])
```

3. Next, you must find the mean of the income data:

    ```
    income.mean()
    ```

    The output will be as follows:

    ```
    84000
    ```

    So far, so good. `84000` is the average `income` on your block.

4. Now, say the millionaire decides to build his dream house on the vacant corner lot. He adds a salary of 12 million dollars. Append the value of 12 million dollars to the current array and find the new mean:

    ```
    income = np.append(income, 12000000)
    income.mean()
    ```

    The output will be as follows:

    ```
    1786285.7142857143
    ```

    The new average income is 1.7 million dollars. Okay. Nobody makes close to 1.7 million dollars on the block, so it's not a representative average. This is where the median comes into play.

> **Note**
>
> Here, the median is not a method of `np.array`, but a method of `numpy` (the mean may be computed in the same way, as a method of `numpy`).

5. Now, to find the `median` function from the `income` values, you can use the following code:

    ```
    np.median(income)
    ```

    The output will be as follows:

    ```
    88000
    ```

This result says that half of the neighborhood residents make more than 88,000, and half of the blocks make less. This would give the millionaire a fair idea of the neighborhood. In this particular case, the median is a much better estimation of average income than the mean.

In the next section, you will be covering skewed data and outliers.

Skewed data and outliers

Something about the 12 million salary does not sit right. It's nowhere near anyone else's income. In statistics, there is an official terminology for this: you say that the data is skewed by an outlier of 12,000,000. In particular, the data is right-skewed since 12,000,000 is far to the right of every other data point.

Right-skewed data pulls the mean away from the median. If the mean greatly exceeds the median, this is clear evidence of right-skewed data. Similarly, if the mean is much less than the median, this is clear evidence of left-skewed data.

Unfortunately, there is no universal way to compute individual outliers. There are some general methods, including box plots, which you will check out later in *Exercise 146 – creating box plots*. For now, just keep in mind that outliers are far removed from other data points, and they skew the data.

Standard deviation

The standard deviation is a precise statistical measure of how spread out data points are. In the following exercise, you will find the standard deviation.

Exercise 132 – finding the standard deviation from income data

In this exercise, you will use the income data from *Exercise 131 – finding the median from a collection of income data*, to find the standard deviation of the dataset.

The following steps will enable you to complete this exercise:

1. Continue with the previous Jupyter Notebook.

2. Now, check the standard deviation using the `std()` method, as shown in the following code snippet:

```
income.std()
```

The output will be as follows:

```
4169786.007331644
```

As you can see, the standard deviation here is a huge number, which is 4 million. Although the standard deviation generally represents how far data points are expected to be from one another on average, the incomes are not 4 million away from each other.

Now, try to find the standard deviation of the `test_scores` data from *Exercise 129 – converting lists into NumPy arrays*.

3. Assign the `test_scores` list value once again:

```
test_scores = [70,65,95,88]
```

4. Now, convert this list into a numpy array:

```
scores = np.array(test_scores)
```

5. Now, find the standard deviation of `test_scores` using the `std()` method:

    ```
    scores.std()
    ```

    The output will be as follows:

    ```
    12.379418403139947
    ```

In this exercise, you observed that the income data is so skewed that the standard deviation of 4 million is practically meaningless. However, the 12.4 standard deviation of the test scores is meaningful; the mean test score of 79.5 with a standard deviation of 12.4 means that you can expect the scores to be about 12 points away from the mean on average.

Finding the min, max, and sum

What if you need to find the maximum, minimum, or sum of the `numpy` arrays?

You can find the maximum of an `np.array` array using the `max()` method, the minimum using the `min()` method, and the sum using the `sum()` method, as shown in the following example.

To find the maximum, enter the following code:

```
test_scores = [70,65,95,88]
np_scores = np.array(test_scores)
scores.max()
```

The output will be as follows:

```
95
```

To find the minimum, enter the following code:

```
scores.min()
```

The output will be as follows:

```
65
```

To find the sum, enter the following code:

```
scores.sum()
```

The output will be as follows:

```
318
```

In this example, you learned how to compute the max, min, and sum of a NumPy array. Although the range is not provided as a method, you can compute the range by taking the max minus the min.

Now, let's see how NumPy arrays can work together in matrices.

Matrices

Data is generally composed of rows, and each row contains the same number of columns. Data is often represented as a two-dimensional grid containing lots of numbers. It can also be interpreted as a list of lists, or a NumPy array of NumPy arrays.

In mathematics, a matrix is a rectangular array of numbers defined by the number of rows and columns. It is standard to list rows first, and columns second. For instance, a 2 x 3 matrix consists of 2 rows and 3 columns, whereas a 3 x 2 matrix consists of 3 rows and 2 columns.

Here is a 4 x 4 matrix:

$$\begin{bmatrix} 9 & 13 & 5 & 2 \\ 1 & 11 & 7 & 6 \\ 3 & 7 & 4 & 1 \\ 6 & 0 & 7 & 10 \end{bmatrix}$$

Figure 10.1 – Matrix representation of a 4 x 4 matrix

Exercise 133 – working with matrices

NumPy has several methods for creating matrices or n-dimensional arrays. One option is to place random numbers between 0 and 1 into each entry.

In this exercise, you will implement various `numpy` matrix methods and observe the outputs (recall that `random.seed` will allow us to reproduce the same numbers, but it's okay if you want to generate your own).

The following steps will enable you to complete this exercise:

1. Begin with a new Jupyter Notebook.

2. Now, generate a random 5 x 5 matrix, as shown in the following code snippet:

```
import numpy as np
np.random.seed(seed=60)
random_square = np.random.rand(5,5)
random_square
```

The output will be as follows:

```
array([[0.30087333, 0.18694582, 0.32318268, 0.66574957, 0.5669708 ],
       [0.39825396, 0.37941492, 0.01058154, 0.1703656 , 0.12339337],
       [0.69240128, 0.87444156, 0.3373969 , 0.99245923, 0.13154007],
       [0.50032984, 0.28662051, 0.22058485, 0.50208555, 0.63606254],
       [0.63567694, 0.08043309, 0.58143375, 0.83919086, 0.29301825]])
```

Figure 10.2 – A random 5 x 5 matrix being generated

In the preceding code, you used `random.seed`. Every time you run the script with `random.seed(seed=60)`, you will get the same sequence of values.

This matrix is very similar in composition to the DataFrames that you will be working with to analyze big data in this and the next two chapters.

Now, find the rows and columns of the generated matrix using indexing. The standard syntax is `random_square[row, column]`. If you omit the column entry, all columns will be selected.

3. Find the first row and first column of the matrix:

    ```
    random_square[0]
    ```

    The output will be as follows. It consists of all the columns and the first row:

    ```
    array([0.30087333, 0.18694582, 0.32318268, 0.66574957,
    0.5669708 ])
    ```

4. Now, to find the values of all the rows, and the first column of the matrix, enter the following code snippet:

    ```
    random_square[:,0]
    ```

    The output is as follows. It consists of all the rows and the first column only:

    ```
    array([0.30087333, 0.18694582, 0.32318268, 0.66574957,
    0.5669708 ])
    ```

5. Now, you must find individual entries by specifying the value of the matrix using the `random_square[row, column]` syntax.

    Find the first entry in the matrix by entering the following code:

    ```
    random_square[0,0]
    ```

    The output, which shows the entry in the first row and first column, will be as follows:

    ```
    0.30087333004661876
    ```

    We can find the first entry in another way:

    ```
    random_square[0][0]
    ```

The output will be as follows:

```
0.30087333004661876
```

Find the entry in the second row, third column:

```
random_square[2,3]
```

The output will be as follows:

```
0.9924592256795676
```

6. Now, to find the mean values of the matrix, you must find the mean of the entire matrix, individual rows, and columns using the `square.mean()` method, as shown in the following code.

    Here is the mean entry of the matrix:

    ```
    random_square.mean()
    ```

    The output will be as follows:

    ```
    0.42917627159618377
    ```

    Here is the mean entry of the first row:

    ```
    random_square[0].mean()
    ```

    The output will be as follows:

    ```
    0.4087444389228477
    ```

    Here is the mean entry of the last column:

    ```
    random_square[:,-1].mean()
    ```

    The output will be as follows:

    ```
    0.35019700684996913
    ```

In this exercise, you created a random 5 x 5 matrix, accessed rows, columns, and entries, and found various means of the matrix.

Computation time for large matrices

Let's see how long it takes to generate a matrix with 10 million entries and compute the mean:

```
%%time
np.random.seed(seed=60)
big_matrix = np.random.rand(100000, 100)
big_matrix.mean()
```

The output will be as follows:

```
CPU times: user 75.3 ms, sys: 8.14 ms, total: 83.5 ms
Wall time: 81.4 ms

0.5001355519953301
```

Figure 10.3 – Computation time for a matrix with 10 million entries

Your time will be different than ours, but it should be in the order of milliseconds. It takes much less than a second to generate a matrix of 10 million entries and compute its mean.

In the next exercise, you will use various NumPy arrays, including ndarray and numpy.ndarray, a (usually fixed-size) multidimensional array container of items of the same type and size.

Exercise 134 – creating an array to implement NumPy computations

In this exercise, you will generate a new matrix and perform mathematical operations on it, which will be covered later in this exercise. Unlike traditional lists, NumPy arrays allow each member of the list to be manipulated with ease. The following steps will enable you to complete this exercise:

1. Open a new Jupyter Notebook.

2. Now, import numpy and create an ndarray containing all values between 1 and 100 using arange:

    ```
    import numpy as np
    np.arange(1, 101)
    ```

    The output will be as follows:

```
array([  1,   2,   3,   4,   5,   6,   7,   8,   9,  10,  11,  12,  13,
        14,  15,  16,  17,  18,  19,  20,  21,  22,  23,  24,  25,  26,
        27,  28,  29,  30,  31,  32,  33,  34,  35,  36,  37,  38,  39,
        40,  41,  42,  43,  44,  45,  46,  47,  48,  49,  50,  51,  52,
        53,  54,  55,  56,  57,  58,  59,  60,  61,  62,  63,  64,  65,
        66,  67,  68,  69,  70,  71,  72,  73,  74,  75,  76,  77,  78,
        79,  80,  81,  82,  83,  84,  85,  86,  87,  88,  89,  90,  91,
        92,  93,  94,  95,  96,  97,  98,  99, 100])
```

Figure 10.4 – Showing ndarray with values between 1 to 100

3. Reshape the array to 20 rows and 5 columns:

    ```
    np.arange(1, 101).reshape(20,5)
    ```

The output will be as follows:

```
array([[  1,   2,   3,   4,   5],
       [  6,   7,   8,   9,  10],
       [ 11,  12,  13,  14,  15],
       [ 16,  17,  18,  19,  20],
       [ 21,  22,  23,  24,  25],
       [ 26,  27,  28,  29,  30],
       [ 31,  32,  33,  34,  35],
       [ 36,  37,  38,  39,  40],
       [ 41,  42,  43,  44,  45],
       [ 46,  47,  48,  49,  50],
       [ 51,  52,  53,  54,  55],
       [ 56,  57,  58,  59,  60],
       [ 61,  62,  63,  64,  65],
       [ 66,  67,  68,  69,  70],
       [ 71,  72,  73,  74,  75],
       [ 76,  77,  78,  79,  80],
       [ 81,  82,  83,  84,  85],
       [ 86,  87,  88,  89,  90],
       [ 91,  92,  93,  94,  95],
       [ 96,  97,  98,  99, 100]])
```

Figure 10.5 – Output with the reshaped array of 20 rows and 5 columns

4. Now, define mat1 as a 20 x 5 array between 1 and 100 and then subtract 50 from mat1, as shown in the following code snippet:

```
mat1 = np.arange(1, 101).reshape(20,5)
mat1 - 50
```

The output will be as follows:

```
array([[-49, -48, -47, -46, -45],
       [-44, -43, -42, -41, -40],
       [-39, -38, -37, -36, -35],
       [-34, -33, -32, -31, -30],
       [-29, -28, -27, -26, -25],
       [-24, -23, -22, -21, -20],
       [-19, -18, -17, -16, -15],
       [-14, -13, -12, -11, -10],
       [ -9,  -8,  -7,  -6,  -5],
       [ -4,  -3,  -2,  -1,   0],
       [  1,   2,   3,   4,   5],
       [  6,   7,   8,   9,  10],
       [ 11,  12,  13,  14,  15],
       [ 16,  17,  18,  19,  20],
       [ 21,  22,  23,  24,  25],
       [ 26,  27,  28,  29,  30],
       [ 31,  32,  33,  34,  35],
       [ 36,  37,  38,  39,  40],
       [ 41,  42,  43,  44,  45],
       [ 46,  47,  48,  49,  50]])
```

Figure 10.6 – Output of subtracting values from the array

5. Now, multiply mat1 by 10 and observe the change in the output:

```
mat1 * 10
```

The output will be as follows:

```
array([[  10,   20,   30,   40,   50],
       [  60,   70,   80,   90,  100],
       [ 110,  120,  130,  140,  150],
       [ 160,  170,  180,  190,  200],
       [ 210,  220,  230,  240,  250],
       [ 260,  270,  280,  290,  300],
       [ 310,  320,  330,  340,  350],
       [ 360,  370,  380,  390,  400],
       [ 410,  420,  430,  440,  450],
       [ 460,  470,  480,  490,  500],
       [ 510,  520,  530,  540,  550],
       [ 560,  570,  580,  590,  600],
       [ 610,  620,  630,  640,  650],
       [ 660,  670,  680,  690,  700],
       [ 710,  720,  730,  740,  750],
       [ 760,  770,  780,  790,  800],
       [ 810,  820,  830,  840,  850],
       [ 860,  870,  880,  890,  900],
       [ 910,  920,  930,  940,  950],
       [ 960,  970,  980,  990, 1000]])
```

Figure 10.7 – Output when you multiply mat1 by 10

6. Now, add mat1 to itself, as shown in the following code snippet:

```
mat1 + mat1
```

The output will be as follows:

```
array([[  2,   4,   6,   8,  10],
       [ 12,  14,  16,  18,  20],
       [ 22,  24,  26,  28,  30],
       [ 32,  34,  36,  38,  40],
       [ 42,  44,  46,  48,  50],
       [ 52,  54,  56,  58,  60],
       [ 62,  64,  66,  68,  70],
       [ 72,  74,  76,  78,  80],
       [ 82,  84,  86,  88,  90],
       [ 92,  94,  96,  98, 100],
       [102, 104, 106, 108, 110],
       [112, 114, 116, 118, 120],
       [122, 124, 126, 128, 130],
       [132, 134, 136, 138, 140],
       [142, 144, 146, 148, 150],
       [152, 154, 156, 158, 160],
       [162, 164, 166, 168, 170],
       [172, 174, 176, 178, 180],
       [182, 184, 186, 188, 190],
       [192, 194, 196, 198, 200]])
```

Figure 10.8 – Output of adding mat1 to itself

7. Now, multiply each entry in mat1 by itself:

```
mat1*mat1
```

The output will be as follows:

```
array([[    1,     4,     9,    16,    25],
       [   36,    49,    64,    81,   100],
       [  121,   144,   169,   196,   225],
       [  256,   289,   324,   361,   400],
       [  441,   484,   529,   576,   625],
       [  676,   729,   784,   841,   900],
       [  961,  1024,  1089,  1156,  1225],
       [ 1296,  1369,  1444,  1521,  1600],
       [ 1681,  1764,  1849,  1936,  2025],
       [ 2116,  2209,  2304,  2401,  2500],
       [ 2601,  2704,  2809,  2916,  3025],
       [ 3136,  3249,  3364,  3481,  3600],
       [ 3721,  3844,  3969,  4096,  4225],
       [ 4356,  4489,  4624,  4761,  4900],
       [ 5041,  5184,  5329,  5476,  5625],
       [ 5776,  5929,  6084,  6241,  6400],
       [ 6561,  6724,  6889,  7056,  7225],
       [ 7396,  7569,  7744,  7921,  8100],
       [ 8281,  8464,  8649,  8836,  9025],
       [ 9216,  9409,  9604,  9801, 10000]])
```

Figure 10.9 – Output of multiplying mat1 by itself

8. Now, take the dot product of mat1 and mat1.T, which is the equivalent of matrix multiplication:

```
np.dot(mat1, mat1.T)
```

The output will be as follows:

```
array([[   55,    130,    205,    280,    355,    430,    505,    580,    655,
          730,    805,    880,    955,   1030,   1105,   1180,   1255,   1330,
         1405,   1480],
       [  130,    330,    530,    730,    930,   1130,   1330,   1530,   1730,
         1930,   2130,   2330,   2530,   2730,   2930,   3130,   3330,   3530,
         3730,   3930],
       [  205,    530,    855,   1180,   1505,   1830,   2155,   2480,   2805,
         3130,   3455,   3780,   4105,   4430,   4755,   5080,   5405,   5730,
         6055,   6380],
       [  280,    730,   1180,   1630,   2080,   2530,   2980,   3430,   3880,
         4330,   4780,   5230,   5680,   6130,   6580,   7030,   7480,   7930,
         8380,   8830],
       [  355,    930,   1505,   2080,   2655,   3230,   3805,   4380,   4955,
         5530,   6105,   6680,   7255,   7830,   8405,   8980,   9555,  10130,
        10705,  11280],
       [  430,   1130,   1830,   2530,   3230,   3930,   4630,   5330,   6030,
         6730,   7430,   8130,   8830,   9530,  10230,  10930,  11630,  12330,
        13030,  13730],
       [  505,   1330,   2155,   2980,   3805,   4630,   5455,   6280,   7105,
         7930,   8755,   9580,  10405,  11230,  12055,  12880,  13705,  14530,
        15355,  16180],
       [  580,   1530,   2480,   3430,   4380,   5330,   6280,   7230,   8180,
         9130,  10080,  11030,  11980,  12930,  13880,  14830,  15780,  16730,
        17680,  18630],
       [  655,   1730,   2805,   3880,   4955,   6030,   7105,   8180,   9255,
        10330,  11405,  12480,  13555,  14630,  15705,  16780,  17855,  18930,
        20005,  21080],
       [  730,   1930,   3130,   4330,   5530,   6730,   7930,   9130,  10330,
        11530,  12730,  13930,  15130,  16330,  17530,  18730,  19930,  21130,
        22330,  23530],
       [  805,   2130,   3455,   4780,   6105,   7430,   8755,  10080,  11405,
        12730,  14055,  15380,  16705,  18030,  19355,  20680,  22005,  23330,
        24655,  25980],
       [  880,   2330,   3780,   5230,   6680,   8130,   9580,  11030,  12480,
        13930,  15380,  16830,  18280,  19730,  21180,  22630,  24080,  25530,
        26980,  28430],
       [  955,   2530,   4105,   5680,   7255,   8830,  10405,  11980,  13555,
        15130,  16705,  18280,  19855,  21430,  23005,  24580,  26155,  27730,
        29305,  30880],
```

Figure 10.10 – Truncated output of the dot product of mat1 and mat1

In this exercise, you computed and added values to an n-dimensional array, after which you implemented different NumPy computations.

When it comes to data analysis, NumPy will make your life easier. The ease with which NumPy arrays may be mathematically combined, manipulated, and used to compute standard statistical measures such as the mean, median, and standard deviation makes them far superior to Python lists. They handle big data exceptionally well, and it's hard to imagine the world of data science without them. In the next section, we will be covering pandas, Python's state-of-the-art library for storing, retrieving, analyzing, and manipulating big data.

The pandas library

pandas is the Python library that handles data on all fronts. pandas can import data, read data, and display data in an object called a **DataFrame**. A DataFrame consists of rows and columns. It's designed to look good and perform fast computations to make sense of big data.

In the IT industry, pandas is widely used for data manipulation. It is also used for stock prediction, data storage and retrieval, statistical analysis, cleaning data, and general data science.

In the following exercises, you will begin working with DataFrames by creating them, accessing them, viewing them, and performing different computations on them.

Exercise 135 – using DataFrames to manipulate stored student test score data

In this exercise, you will create a **dictionary**, which is one way to create a pandas DataFrame. You will then manipulate this data as required. To use pandas, you must import pandas, which is universally imported as pd. The following steps will enable you to complete this exercise:

1. Begin by importing pandas as pd:

    ```
    import pandas as pd
    ```

    Now that you have imported pandas, you must create a DataFrame.

2. Create a dictionary of test scores called test_dict:

    ```
    # Create dictionary of test scores
    test_dict = {'Scotty':[63,75,88], 'Joy':[48,98,92],
    'Kamala': [87, 86, 85]}
    ```

3. Next, you must place test_dict into the DataFrame using the DataFrame method:

    ```
    # Create DataFrame
    df = pd.DataFrame(test_dict)
    ```

4. Now, you can display the Dataframe:

```
# Display DataFrame
df
```

The output will be as follows:

	Scotty	Joy	Kamala
0	63	48	87
1	75	98	86
2	88	92	85

Figure 10.11 – Output with the values added to the DataFrame

You can inspect the DataFrame visually. First, each dictionary key is listed as a column. Second, the rows are labeled with indices starting with 0 by default. Third, the visual layout is clear and legible.

Each column and row of the DataFrame is officially represented as a pandas **series**. A series is a one-dimensional ndarray.

5. Now, you must rotate the DataFrame, which is also known as a **transpose**, a standard pandas method. A transpose turns rows into columns and columns into rows. Copy the code shown in the following code snippet to perform a transpose on the DataFrame:

```
# Transpose DataFrame
df = df.T
df
```

The output will be as follows:

	0	1	2
Scotty	63	75	88
Joy	48	98	92
Kamala	87	86	85

Figure 10.12 – The output of the transpose on the DataFrame

In this exercise, you created a DataFrame that holds the values of testscores, and to finish, you transposed this DataFrame to get a rotated output. In the next exercise, you will rename column names and select data from the DataFrame, which is essential to working with pandas.

Exercise 136 – DataFrame computations with the student test score data

In this exercise, you will rename the columns of the DataFrame, and you will select some data to display. The steps are as follows:

1. Open a new Jupyter Notebook.

2. Import pandas as pd and enter the student value, as shown in *Exercise 135 – using DataFrames to manipulate stored student test score data*. After this, convert it into a DataFrame and transpose it:

```
import pandas as pd
# Create dictionary of test scores
test_dict = {'Scotty':[63,75,88], 'Joy':[48,98,92],
'Kamala': [87, 86, 85]}
# Create DataFrame
df = pd.DataFrame(test_dict)
df = df.T
```

3. Now, rename the columns to something more precise. You can use .columns on the DataFrame to rename the column names:

```
# Rename Columns
df.columns = ['Quiz_1', 'Quiz_2', 'Quiz_3']
df
```

The output will be as follows:

	Quiz_1	Quiz_2	Quiz_3
Scotty	63	75	88
Joy	48	98	92
Kamala	87	86	85

Figure 10.13 – Output with changed column names

4. Now, select a range of values from specific rows and columns. You will be using .iloc with the index number, which is a pandas method that uses the same [rows, columns] syntax as in NumPy arrays. This is shown in the following code as you select the first row:

```
# Access first row by index number
df.iloc[0]
```

The output will be as follows:

```
Quiz_1     63
Quiz_2     75
Quiz_3     88
Name: Scotty, dtype: int64
```

Figure 10.14 – Output displaying the first row of data as a pandas series

5. Now, select a column using its name, as shown in the following code snippet.

You can access columns by putting the column name in quotes, inside brackets:

```
# Access first column by name
df['Quiz_1']
```

The output will be as follows:

```
Scotty     63
Joy        48
Kamala     87
Name: Quiz_1, dtype: int64
```

Figure 10.15 – Output displaying the first column of data as a pandas series

6. Now, select a column using the dot (.) notation:

```
# Access first column using dot notation
df.Quiz_1
```

The output will be as follows:

```
Scotty     63
Joy        48
Kamala     87
Name: Quiz_1, dtype: int64
```

Figure 10.16 – The same output after selecting a column using dot notation

---

Note

There are limitations to using dot notation, so bracket quotations are often preferable.

In this exercise, you implemented and changed the column names of the DataFrame, and then used .iloc, column names, and dot notation to select columns and rows of data from the DataFrame.

In the next exercise, you will implement different computations on DataFrames.

Exercise 137 – more computations on DataFrames

In this exercise, you will use the same testscore data and perform more computations on the DataFrame. The following steps will enable you to complete this exercise:

1. Open a new Jupyter Notebook.

2. Import pandas as pd and enter the student value, as shown in *Exercise 136 – DataFrame computations with the student test score data*. After this, convert it into a DataFrame:

```
import pandas as pd
# Create dictionary of test scores
test_dict = {'Scotty':[63,75,88], 'Joy':[48,98,92],
'Kamala': [87, 86, 85]}
# Create DataFrame
df = pd.DataFrame(test_dict)
```

3. Now, begin by arranging the rows of the DataFrame, as shown in the following code snippet.

You can use the same bracket notation, [], for rows as for lists and strings:

```
# Limit DataFrame to first 2 rows
df[0:2]
```

The output will be as follows:

	Scotty	Joy	Kamala
0	63	48	87
1	75	98	86

Figure 10.17 – Output showing the DataFrame's first two rows only

4. Transpose the DataFrame and rename the columns Quiz_1, Quiz_2, and Quiz_3, as covered in *Exercise 136 – DataFrame computations with the student test score data*:

```
df = df.T
df
# Rename Columns
```

```
df.columns = ['Quiz_1', 'Quiz_2', 'Quiz_3']
df
```

The output will be as follows:

	Quiz_1	Quiz_2	Quiz_3
Scotty	63	75	88
Joy	48	98	92
Kamala	87	86	85

Figure 10.18 – DataFrame of quiz scores with column names updated

5. Now, define a new DataFrame from the first two rows and the last two columns only.

    You can choose the rows and columns by name first using the .loc notation, as shown in the following code snippet:

```
# Define new DataFrame - first 2 rows, last 2 columns
rows = ['Scotty', 'Joy']
cols = ['Quiz_2', 'Quiz_3']
df_spring = df.loc[rows, cols]
df_spring
```

The output will be as follows:

	Quiz_2	Quiz_3
Scotty	75	88
Joy	98	92

Figure 10.19 – Output of the new DataFrame showing two columns and two rows only by name

> **Note**
> When selecting rows and columns by index, use the .iloc notation. When selecting rows and columns by name, use the .loc notation.

6. Now, select the first two rows and the last two columns using index numbers.

    You can use `.iloc` to select rows and columns by index, as shown in the following code snippet:

    ```
    # Select first 2 rows and last 2 columns using index
    numbers
    df.iloc[[0,1], [1,2]]
    ```

    The output will be as follows:

	Quiz_2	Quiz_3
Scotty	75	88
Joy	98	92

Figure 10.20 – Same output of selecting the first two rows and last two columns using index numbers

    Now, add a new column to find the quiz average of our students.

    You can generate new columns in a variety of ways. One way is to use available methods such as the mean. In pandas, it's important to specify the axis. An axis of 0 represents the column, while an axis of 1 represents the rows.

7. Now, create a new column as the mean, as shown in the following code snippet:

    ```
    # Define new column as mean of other columns
    df['Quiz_Avg'] = df.mean(axis=1)
    df
    ```

    The output will be as follows:

	Quiz_1	Quiz_2	Quiz_3	Quiz_Avg
Scotty	63	75	88	75.333333
Joy	48	98	92	79.333333
Kamala	87	86	85	86.000000

Figure 10.21 – Adding a new Quiz_Avg column to the output

    A new column can also be added as a list by choosing the rows and columns by name first.

8. Create a new column as a list, as shown in the following code snippet:

    ```
    df['Quiz_4'] = [92, 95, 88]
    df
    ```

The output will be as follows:

	Quiz_1	Quiz_2	Quiz_3	Quiz_Avg	Quiz_4
Scotty	63	75	88	75.333333	92
Joy	48	98	92	79.333333	95
Kamala	87	86	85	86.000000	88

Figure 10.22 – Output with a newly added column using lists

What if you need to delete the column you created? You can do so by using the `del` function. It's easy to delete columns in pandas using `del`.

9. Now, delete the `Quiz_Avg` column as it is not needed anymore:

```
del df['Quiz_Avg']
df
```

The output will be as follows:

	Quiz_1	Quiz_2	Quiz_3	Quiz_4
Scotty	63	75	88	92
Joy	48	98	92	95
Kamala	87	86	85	88

Figure 10.23 – Output after deleting the Quiz_Avg column

In this exercise, you implemented different ways to add and remove columns as per your requirements. In the next section, you will be looking at new rows and NaN, an official numpy designation that often appears in data analytics.

New rows and NaN

Say you have a new student who joins the class for the fourth quiz. What values should you put for the other three quizzes? The answer is NaN. This stands for **Not a Number**.

NaN is an official NumPy term. It can be accessed using np.NaN. It is case-sensitive, so the first and last *N*s must be capitalized and the middle *a* must be lowercase. In later exercises, you will look at different strategies for changing NaN.

Exercise 138 – concatenating and finding the mean with null values for our test score data

In this exercise, you will be concatenating and finding the mean with null values for the student `testscore` data you created in *Exercise 137 – more computations on DataFrames*, with four quiz scores. The following steps will enable you to complete this exercise:

1. Open a new Jupyter Notebook.

2. Import `pandas` and `numpy` and create a dictionary containing the `testscore` data to be transformed into a DataFrame, as shown in *Exercise 135 – using DataFrames to manipulate stored student test score data*:

```
import pandas as pd
# Create dictionary of test scores
test_dict = {'Scotty':[63,75,88], 'Joy':[48,98,92],
'Kamala': [87, 86, 85]}
# Create DataFrame
df = pd.DataFrame(test_dict)
# Transpose the DataFrame
df = df.T
df
# Rename Columns
df.columns = ['Quiz_1', 'Quiz_2', 'Quiz_3']
# Add Quiz 4
df['Quiz_4'] = [92, 95, 88]
df
```

The output will be as follows:

	Quiz_1	Quiz_2	Quiz_3	Quiz_4
Scotty	63	75	88	92
Joy	48	98	92	95
Kamala	87	86	85	88

Figure 10.24 – DataFrame output

3. Now, add a new row using the `.loc` notation by setting the index to `Adrian`, along with null values for the first three quizzes, but a score of 71 for the fourth quiz, as shown in the following code snippet:

```
import numpy as np
df.loc['Adrian'] = [np.NaN, np.NaN, np.NaN, 71]
df
```

The output will be as follows:

	Quiz_1	Quiz_2	Quiz_3	Quiz_4
Scotty	63.0	75.0	88.0	92.0
Joy	48.0	98.0	92.0	95.0
Kamala	87.0	86.0	85.0	88.0
Adrian	NaN	NaN	NaN	71.0

Figure 10.25 – Output with a new row added to the DataFrame

You can now compute the new mean, but you must skip the NaN values; otherwise, there will be no mean score for `Adrian`.

4. Find the `mean` value while ignoring NaN and use these values to create a new column named `Quiz_Avg`, as shown in the following code snippet:

```
df['Quiz_Avg'] = df.mean(axis=1, skipna=True)
df
```

The output will be as follows:

	Quiz_1	Quiz_2	Quiz_3	Quiz_4	Quiz_Avg
Scotty	63.0	75.0	88.0	92	79.50
Joy	48.0	98.0	92.0	95	83.25
Kamala	87.0	86.0	85.0	88	86.50
Adrian	NaN	NaN	NaN	71	71.00

Figure 10.26 – Output with the mean, which skips over null values

Notice that all values are floats (NaN is a float!). You can use df.dtypes to check the data types of the columns of the DataFrame.

Casting column types

Cast all the floats in Quiz_4 that you used in *Exercise 138 – concatenating and finding the mean with null values for our test score data*, as ints using the following code snippet:

```
df.Quiz_4.astype(int)
```

```
Scotty      92
Joy         95
Kamala      88
Adrian      71
Name: Quiz_4, dtype: int64
```

Note that to change the DataFrame itself, you must use df['Quiz_4']=df.Quiz_4.astype(int). Now, let's move on to the next topic, which is working with big data.

Working with big data

Now that you have been introduced to NumPy and pandas, you will use them to analyze real data of a much larger size. The phrase big data does not have an unambiguous meaning. Generally speaking, you can think of big data as data that is far too large to analyze by sight. It could contain tens of thousands, millions, billions, trillions, or even more rows of data.

Data scientists analyze data that exists in the cloud or online. One strategy to analyze real data is to download the data directly to your computer.

> **Note**
>
> It is recommended to create a new folder called Data to store all of the data that you will download for analysis. You can open your Jupyter Notebook in this same folder.

Downloading data

Data comes in many formats, and pandas is equipped to handle most of them. In general, when looking for data to analyze, it's worth searching for the keyword "dataset." A dataset is a collection of raw data that has been stored for others to access. Online, "data" is everywhere, whereas datasets are limited to data in its raw format.

You will start by examining the famous Boston Housing dataset from 1980, which is available in this book's GitHub repository.

This dataset can be found at `https://github.com/PacktPublishing/The-Python-Workshop-Second-Edition/tree/main/Datasets`.

If you have downloaded all of the GitHub files for this book to your computer, you already have the dataset in your files. Otherwise, you will need to download the dataset onto your local computer, as described in the next section.

Downloading the Boston Housing data from GitHub

Here are the steps to download the Boston Housing data:

1. Head to this book's GitHub repository at `https://github.com/PacktPublishing/The-Python-Workshop-Second-Edition` and download the dataset onto your local computer.

2. Move the downloaded dataset file into your data folder. It's useful to have a data folder to store all of your data.

3. Open a Jupyter Notebook in the same folder. Alternatively, if you open a Jupyter Notebook in your home directory, you can scroll to the `Data` folder on your Jupyter home page and create a new notebook from there:

Figure 10.27 – Jupyter Notebook filesystem with the new Data folder included

Reading data

Now that the data has been downloaded, and the Jupyter Notebook is open, you are ready to read the file. The most important part of reading a file is the extension. Our file is a `.csv` file. Therefore, you need a method for reading `.csv` files.

CSV stands for **Comma-Separated Values**. CSV files are a popular way of storing and retrieving data, and pandas handles them very well.

Here is a list of standard data files that pandas will read, along with the code for reading data:

type of file	code
csv files:	pd.read_csv('file_name')
excel files:	pd.read_excel('file_name')
feather files:	pd.read_feather('file_name')
html files:	pd.read_html('file_name')
json files:	pd.read_json('file_name')
sql database:	pd.read_sql('file_name')

Figure 10.28 – Standard data files that pandas can read

If the files are clean, pandas will read them properly. Sometimes, files are not clean, so you may need to change the function parameters. It's advisable to copy any errors and search for solutions online.

A further point of consideration is that the data should be read into a DataFrame. Pandas will convert the data into a DataFrame upon reading it, but you need to save the DataFrame as a variable.

> **Note**
>
> df is often used to store DataFrames, but it's not universal since you may be dealing with many DataFrames.

In the next exercise, you will be using the Boston Housing dataset and performing basic actions on the data.

Exercise 139 – reading and viewing the Boston Housing dataset

In this exercise, your goal is to read and view the Boston Housing dataset in your Jupyter Notebook. The following steps will enable you to complete this exercise:

1. Open a new Jupyter Notebook.

2. Import pandas as pd:

```
import pandas as pd
```

3. Now, choose a variable for storing the DataFrame and place the HousingData.csv file in the folder for this exercise. Then, run the following command:

```
df = pd.read_csv('HousingData.csv')
```

If no errors arise, the file has been read properly. Now, you can examine and view the file.

> **Note**
>
> If you are unable to access the data, you can use `housing_df = pd.read_csv('https://`
> `raw.githubusercontent.com/PacktWorkshops/The-Python-Workshop/`
> `master/Datasets/HousingData.csv')`. This is a special access point for raw CSV
> files that works in limited cases, with raw GitHub files being one of them.

4. Now, view the file by entering the following command:

```
df.head()
```

`.head` displays the first five rows of the DataFrame. You may view more rows by placing the number of your choice in parentheses.

The output will be as follows:

	CRIM	ZN	INDUS	CHAS	NOX	RM	AGE	DIS	RAD	TAX	PTRATIO	B	LSTAT	MEDV
0	0.00632	18.0	2.31	0.0	0.538	6.575	65.2	4.0900	1	296	15.3	396.90	4.98	24.0
1	0.02731	0.0	7.07	0.0	0.469	6.421	78.9	4.9671	2	242	17.8	396.90	9.14	21.6
2	0.02729	0.0	7.07	0.0	0.469	7.185	61.1	4.9671	2	242	17.8	392.83	4.03	34.7
3	0.03237	0.0	2.18	0.0	0.458	6.998	45.8	6.0622	3	222	18.7	394.63	2.94	33.4
4	0.06905	0.0	2.18	0.0	0.458	7.147	54.2	6.0622	3	222	18.7	396.90	NaN	36.2

Figure 10.29 – df.head() displaying the first five rows of the dataset

Before you perform operations on this dataset, you may be wondering what column names such as CRIM and ZN mean.

Here is a list of the columns, along with their meanings:

```
CRIM     per capita crime rate by town
ZN       proportion of residential land zoned for lots over 25,000 sq. ft.
INDUS    proportion of non-retail business acres per town
CHAS     Charles River dummy variable (= 1 if tract bounds river; 0 otherwise)
NOX      nitric oxide concentration (parts per 10 million)
RM       average number of rooms per dwelling
AGE      proportion of owner-occupied units built prior to 1940
DIS      weighted distances to five Boston employment centers
RAD      index of accessibility to radial highways
TAX      full-value property-tax rate per $10,000
PTRATIO  pupil-teacher ratio by town
LSTAT    % lower status of the population
MEDV     median value of owner-occupied homes in $1,000s
```

Figure 10.30 – Representation of the column values of the dataset

Now that you know what the columns in the dataset mean, you will perform operations on the DataFrame in the following exercise.

Exercise 140 – gaining data insights on the Boston Housing dataset

In this exercise, you will be performing some more advanced operations and using pandas methods to understand the dataset and get the desired insights. The following steps will enable you to complete this exercise:

1. Open a new Jupyter Notebook where your Boston Housing data is stored.

2. Import pandas, choose a variable where you will store the DataFrame, and read in the HousingData.csv file:

```
import pandas as pd
df = pd.read_csv('HousingData.csv')
```

3. Now, use the describe() method to display the key statistical measures of each column, including the mean, median, and quartiles, as shown in the following code snippet:

```
df.describe()
```

The truncated output will be as follows:

	CRIM	ZN	INDUS	CHAS	NOX	RM	AGE	DIS	RAD	TAX	PTRATIO	B
count	486.000000	486.000000	486.000000	486.000000	506.000000	506.000000	486.000000	506.000000	506.000000	506.000000	506.000000	506.000000
mean	3.611874	11.211934	11.083992	0.069959	0.554695	6.284634	68.518519	3.795043	9.549407	408.237154	18.455534	356.674032
std	8.720192	23.388876	6.835896	0.255340	0.115878	0.702617	27.999513	2.105710	8.707259	168.537116	2.164946	91.294864
min	0.006320	0.000000	0.460000	0.000000	0.385000	3.561000	2.900000	1.129600	1.000000	187.000000	12.600000	0.320000
25%	0.081900	0.000000	5.190000	0.000000	0.449000	5.885500	45.175000	2.100175	4.000000	279.000000	17.400000	375.377500
50%	0.253715	0.000000	9.690000	0.000000	0.538000	6.208500	76.800000	3.207450	5.000000	330.000000	19.050000	391.440000
75%	3.560263	12.500000	18.100000	0.000000	0.624000	6.623500	93.975000	5.188425	24.000000	666.000000	20.200000	396.225000
max	88.976200	100.000000	27.740000	1.000000	0.871000	8.780000	100.000000	12.126500	24.000000	711.000000	22.000000	396.900000

Figure 10.31 – The truncated output of descriptive statistics with df.describe()

In this output, you must review the meaning of each row:

- count: The number of rows with actual values.

- mean: The sum of each entry divided by the number of entries. It is often a good estimate of the average.

- std: The number of unit entries that are expected to deviate from the mean. It is a good measure of spread.

- min: The smallest entry in each column.

- 25%: The first quartile. 25% of the data has a value less than this number.

- 50%: The median. The halfway marker of the data. This is another good estimate of the average.

- 75%: The third quartile. 75% of the data has a value less than this number.

- max: The largest entry in each column.

4. Now, use the info() method to deliver a full list of columns, along with their types and the number of null values.

info() is especially valuable when you have hundreds of columns, and it takes a long time to horizontally scroll through each one:

```
df.info()
```

The output will be as follows:

```
<class 'pandas.core.frame.DataFrame'>
RangeIndex: 506 entries, 0 to 505
Data columns (total 14 columns):
 #   Column   Non-Null Count   Dtype
---  ------   --------------   -----
 0   CRIM     486 non-null     float64
 1   ZN       486 non-null     float64
 2   INDUS    486 non-null     float64
 3   CHAS     486 non-null     float64
 4   NOX      506 non-null     float64
 5   RM       506 non-null     float64
 6   AGE      486 non-null     float64
 7   DIS      506 non-null     float64
 8   RAD      506 non-null     int64
 9   TAX      506 non-null     int64
 10  PTRATIO  506 non-null     float64
 11  B        506 non-null     float64
 12  LSTAT    486 non-null     float64
 13  MEDV     506 non-null     float64
dtypes: float64(12), int64(2)
memory usage: 55.5 KB
```

Figure 10.32 – Output of df.info()

As you can see, df.info() reveals the count of non-null values in each column, along with the column type. Since some columns have less than 506 non-null values, you can infer that the other values are null.

In this dataset, there's a total of 506 rows and 14 columns. You can use the .shape attribute to obtain this information directly.

Now, confirm the number of rows and columns in the dataset:

```
df.shape
```

The output will be as follows:

```
(506, 14)
```

This confirms that you have 506 rows and 14 columns. Notice that `shape` does not have any parentheses after it. This is because it's technically an attribute and pre-computed.

In this exercise, you performed key operations on the entire dataset, such as finding the descriptive statistics, finding columns with null values, and finding the number of rows and columns.

In the next section, we will cover null values.

Null values

You need to do something about the null values. They will break machine learning algorithms (see *Chapter 11, Machine Learning*) that rely on numerical values as input. There are several popular choices when dealing with null values:

- Eliminate the rows. This is a respectable approach if null values are a very small percentage – that is, around 1% of the total dataset.

- Replace the null value with a significant value, such as the median or the mean. This is a great approach if the rows are valuable, and the column itself is reasonably balanced.

- Replace the null value with the most likely value, perhaps a 0 or 1. This is preferable to averages when the median or mean might be unrealistic based on other factors.

> **Note**
> **Mode** is the official term for the value that occurs the greatest number of times.

As you can see, which option you choose depends on the data. That's a general theme that rings true for data science: no one method fits all; your choice of action will ultimately depend on the data at hand.

Exercise 141 – viewing null values

In this exercise, you will view null values in the DataFrame. Follow these steps:

1. Open a new Jupyter Notebook where your Boston Housing data is stored.

2. Import pandas and choose a variable for storing the DataFrame to read in the HousingData. csv file:

```
import pandas as pd
df = pd.read_csv('HousingData.csv')
```

3. Now, find the values and columns in the dataset with null values, as shown in the following code snippet:

```
df.isnull().any()
```

The output will be as follows:

```
CRIM          True
ZN            True
INDUS         True
CHAS          True
NOX           False
RM            False
AGE           True
DIS           False
RAD           False
TAX           False
PTRATIO       False
B             False
LSTAT         True
MEDV          False
dtype: bool
```

Figure 10.33 – Output of the columns with null values

The .isnull() method will display an entire DataFrame of True/False values, depending on the Null value. Feel free to give it a try.

4. The .any() method returns the individual columns, as shown in *Figure 10.33*. Now, using the DataFrame, find the null columns.

You can use .loc to find the location of particular rows. Select the first five rows and all of the columns that have null values, as shown in the following code snippet:

```
df.loc[:5, df.isnull().any()]
```

The output will be as follows:

	CRIM	ZN	INDUS	CHAS	AGE	LSTAT
0	0.00632	18.0	2.31	0.0	65.2	4.98
1	0.02731	0.0	7.07	0.0	78.9	9.14
2	0.02729	0.0	7.07	0.0	61.1	4.03
3	0.03237	0.0	2.18	0.0	45.8	2.94
4	0.06905	0.0	2.18	0.0	54.2	NaN
5	0.02985	0.0	2.18	0.0	58.7	5.21

Figure 10.34 – DataFrame of columns with null values

5. Now, for the final step. Use the `.describe()` method on the null columns of the dataset:

```
df.loc[:, df.isnull().any()].describe()
```

This code can be broken down as follows:

- `df` is the DataFrame
- `.loc` allows you to specify rows and columns
- `:` selects all rows
- `df.isnull().any()` selects only columns with null values
- `.describe()` pulls up the statistics

The output will be as follows:

	CRIM	ZN	INDUS	CHAS	AGE	LSTAT
count	486.000000	486.000000	486.000000	486.000000	486.000000	486.000000
mean	3.611874	11.211934	11.083992	0.069959	68.518519	12.715432
std	8.720192	23.388876	6.835896	0.255340	27.999513	7.155871
min	0.006320	0.000000	0.460000	0.000000	2.900000	1.730000
25%	0.081900	0.000000	5.190000	0.000000	45.175000	7.125000
50%	0.253715	0.000000	9.690000	0.000000	76.800000	11.430000
75%	3.560263	12.500000	18.100000	0.000000	93.975000	16.955000
max	88.976200	100.000000	27.740000	1.000000	100.000000	37.970000

Figure 10.35 – Descriptive statistics of the columns with null values

Consider the first column, CRIM. The mean is way more than the median (50%). This indicates that the data is very right-skewed with some outliers since outliers pull the mean away from the median. Indeed, you can see that the maximum of 88.97 is much larger than the 3.56 value of the 75th percentile. This makes the mean a poor replacement candidate for this column.

It turns out that the median is a good candidate for replacing null values in all columns shown. Although the median is not better than the mean in some cases, there are a few cases where the mean is worse (CRIM, ZN, and CHAS).

The choice for replacing null values depends on what you ultimately want to do with the data. If the goal is straightforward data analysis, eliminating the rows with null values is worth considering. However, if the goal is to use machine learning to predict data, then perhaps more is to be gained by changing the null values into suitable replacements.

A more thorough examination could be warranted, depending on the data. For instance, when analyzing new medical drugs, it would be worth putting more time and energy into appropriately dealing with null values. You may want to perform more analysis to determine whether a value is 0 or 1, depending on other factors.

In this particular case, replacing all the null values with the median is warranted. For the sake of practice, however, let's replace the null values with various values in the following section.

Replacing null values

pandas includes a nice method, fillna, which can be used to replace null values. It works for individual columns and entire DataFrames. You will use three approaches: replacing the null values of a column with the mean, replacing the null values of a column with another value, and replacing all the null values in the entire dataset with the median.

Open the same Jupyter Notebook that you used in *Exercise 141 – viewing null values*. Ensure that all cells have been run since you opened the notebook.

Here are the steps to transform the null values:

1. Replace the null values in the AGE column with mean:

    ```
    df['AGE'] =df['AGE'].fillna(df.mean())
    ```

2. Replace the null values in the CHAS column with 0:

    ```
    df['CHAS'] = df['CHAS'].fillna(0)
    ```

3. Replace all remaining null values with median for the respective columns:

    ```
    df = df.fillna(df.median())
    ```

4.   Finally, check that all null values have been replaced:

```
df.info()
```

The output will be as follows:

```
<class 'pandas.core.frame.DataFrame'>
RangeIndex: 506 entries, 0 to 505
Data columns (total 14 columns):
 #   Column   Non-Null Count   Dtype
---  ------   --------------   -----
 0   CRIM     506 non-null     float64
 1   ZN       506 non-null     float64
 2   INDUS    506 non-null     float64
 3   CHAS     506 non-null     float64
 4   NOX      506 non-null     float64
 5   RM       506 non-null     float64
 6   AGE      506 non-null     float64
 7   DIS      506 non-null     float64
 8   RAD      506 non-null     int64
 9   TAX      506 non-null     int64
 10  PTRATIO  506 non-null     float64
 11  B        506 non-null     float64
 12  LSTAT    506 non-null     float64
 13  MEDV     506 non-null     float64
dtypes: float64(12), int64(2)
memory usage: 55.5 KB
```

Figure 10.36 – df.info() revealing no null values

Since all columns contain 506 non-null values, which is the total number of rows, you can infer that all null values have been eliminated. After eliminating all null values, the dataset is much cleaner. There may still be problematic outliers that may lead to poor predictions. These can sometimes be detected through visual analysis, which we will cover in the next section.

Creating statistical graphs

Most people interpret data visually. They prefer to view colorful, meaningful graphs to make sense of the data. As a data science practitioner, it's your job to create and interpret these graphs for others.

In *Chapter 4, Extending Python, Files, Errors, and Graphs*, you were introduced to matplotlib and many different kinds of graphs. In this section, you will expand upon your knowledge by learning about new techniques to enhance the outputs and information displayed in your histograms and scatterplots. Additionally, you will see how box plots can be used to visualize statistical distributions, and how heat maps can provide nice visual representations of correlations.

In this section, you will use Python – in particular, `matplotlib` and `seaborn` – to create these graphs. Although software packages such as Tableau are rather popular, they are essentially drag-and-drop. Since Python is an all-purpose programming language, the limitations are only what you know and are capable of doing. In other words, Python's graphing libraries give you the capacity to generate any output that you desire.

Histograms

As you have seen, creating a histogram is rather simple. You choose a column and place it inside of `plt.hist()`. The general idea behind a histogram is that it groups an x value into various bins. The height of the bin is determined by the number of values that fall into that particular range. By default, `matplotlib` selects 10 bins, but that number may be changed.

In the interest of generating professional graphs, we will use `seaborn` as a backdrop, and you will export the graphs as PNGs using the dots-per-inch of your choice. You must also provide clear labels for readability and choose an optimal size for the graph.

Exercise 142 – creating a histogram using the Boston Housing dataset

In this exercise, you will use MEDV, the median value of the Boston Housing dataset, as a future target column for machine learning. The following steps will enable you to complete this exercise:

1.   Open a new Jupyter Notebook where your Boston Housing data is stored.

2.   Import `pandas` as `pd` and choose a variable for storing the DataFrame while reading in the `HousingData.csv` file:

```
import pandas as pd
df = pd.read_csv('HousingData.csv')
```

3.   Import `matplotlib` and `seaborn`, then use `sns.set()` to create a nice gray background with white grid lines for your histogram:

```
import matplotlib.pyplot as plt
import seaborn as sns
sns.set()
```

4.   Store a title for your histogram as a variable for the display title, and for saving the output as a PNG:

```
title = 'Median Boston Housing Prices'
```

5. Adjust the figure size of your histogram using (horizontal, vertical) dimensions, as follows:

```
plt.figure(figsize=(14,8))
```

6. Now, create the histogram itself, using a green color since we are talking about money, and set the transparency, or the alpha, at the desired percentage to lessen the brightness and add a 3D effect:

```
plt.hist(df['MEDV'], color='green', alpha=0.6)
```

7. Now, add a title and labels, increasing the font size of your title as follows:

```
plt.title(title, fontsize=15)
plt.xlabel('1980 Median Value in Thousands')
plt.ylabel('Count')
```

8. Finally, export your histogram, making sure to set dpi, or dots per inch, to the desired value, and show the histogram itself:

```
plt.savefig(title, dpi=300)
plt.show()
```

Here is a screenshot of the Jupyter Notebook output, which is not the saved figure:

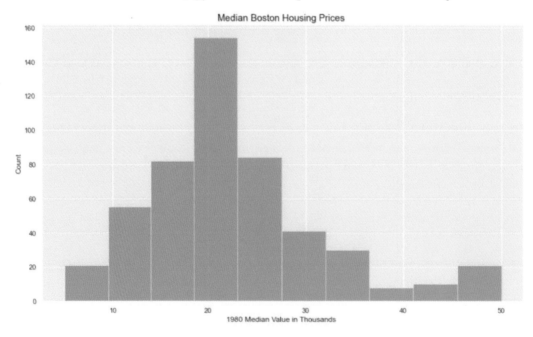

Figure 10.37 – Output of the Jupyter Notebook histogram

To access the saved figure, look in the folder where you created this notebook; it should be there. Just double-click to open it. The saved image will look far better than the Jupyter Notebook output on account of the `dpi` value. Although our input will not capture color and has been degraded since we inserted it into this editor, by printing it on the page, it should look crisper than the previous screenshot:

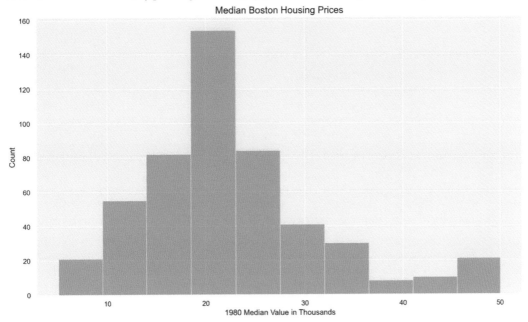

Figure 10.38 – Output of the exported PNG histogram with a 300 dpi value – it looks much stronger on screen!

Now, say you want to create another histogram. Should you keep copying the same code? Copying code repeatedly is never a good idea. It's better to write functions.

We'll create new histograms by implementing a histogram function in the following exercise.

Exercise 143 – creating histogram functions

Creating functions to display graphs is a little different from creating other functions for several reasons:

- Since you want to display the graph, it usually returns nothing
- It's not always clear what pieces of code should change
- There are customization options with the `matplotlib` graphs inside of functions

Instead of creating the most robust functions possible, we will include core concepts to make nice, repeatable histograms. You are encouraged to add customization options as desired.

Here are the steps to create professional-looking histograms using a histogram function:

1. Open the same Jupyter Notebook that you used in *Exercise 142 – creating a histogram using the Boston Housing dataset.*

2. Define your histogram function, as shown in the following code snippet:

```
def my_hist(column, title, xlab, ylab=' Count', color= '
green ', alpha=0.6, bins=10):
    plt.figure(figsize=(14,8))
    plt.hist(column, color=color, alpha=alpha)
    plt.title(title, fontsize=15)
    plt.xlabel(xlab)
    plt.ylabel(ylab)
    plt.savefig(title, dpi=300)
    plt.show()
```

It's not easy to create functions with `matplotlib`, so let's go over the parameters carefully. `figsize` allows you to establish the size of the figure. `column` is the essential parameter. – it's what you are going to be graphing. Many possible column customizations may be included as parameters (see the official documentation at `https://matplotlib.org/stable/api/_as_gen/matplotlib.pyplot.hist.html`). We have included `color` and `alpha` here. Next, you have `title`, followed by the labels for the x - and y - axes.

Finally, you save the figure and show the plot. Inside this function is the same code that you ran previously.

3. Call the histogram function while using the RM column as input:

```
 my_hist(housing_df['RM'], 'Average Number of Rooms
in Boston Households', 'Average Number of Rooms',
color='royalblue')
```

The output will be as follows:

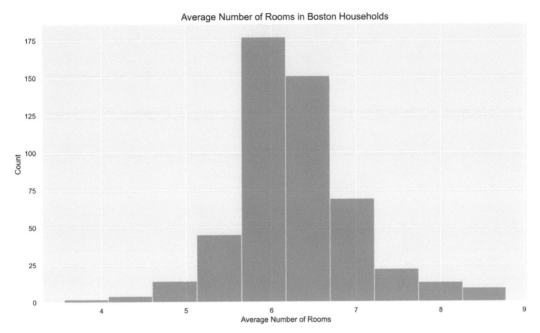

Figure 10.39 – Screenshot output of the histogram function

The output looks solid, but there's one glaring issue: it's the distribution of bins. It seems most rooms have an average of 6, but how many of those are closer to 7? Our graph could be improved if each histogram was clearly between two numbers on the plot. As df.describe() previously revealed, the range of rooms is between 3 and 9.

The strategy is to change both the number of bins and the range of the bins so that they fall exactly between the minimum and the maximum.

4. It's not uncommon to modify graphing functions to add customizations. Let's make these adjustments to nicely show the bins falling precisely between two numbers:

```
def my_hist(column, title, xlab, ylab='Count',
color='green', alpha=0.6, bins=10, range=None):
    plt.figure(figsize=(14,8))
    plt.hist(column, color=color, alpha=alpha, bins=bins,
range=range)
    plt.title(title, fontsize=15)
    plt.xlabel(xlab)
    plt.ylabel(ylab)
    plt.savefig(title, dpi=300)
    plt.show()
```

5. Now, call the improved histogram function:

```
my_hist(housing_df['RM'], 'Average Number of Rooms
in Boston Households', 'Average Number of Rooms',
color='skyblue', bins=6, range=(3,9))
```

The output will be as follows:

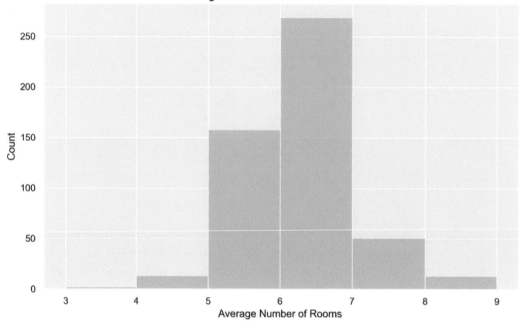

Figure 10.40 – Output of the improved histogram function clearly between the bins

As we can see, the highest average is between 6 and 7 rooms.

Now that you have understood how to create professional histograms using your own functions and customizations, let's shift from one-dimensional to two-dimensional data with scatter plots.

Scatter plots

Scatter plots are often used to compare the relationship between two variables of data. In this section, you will expand upon what you learned in *Chapter 4, Extending Python, Files, Errors, and Graphs*. You will create more advanced scatter plots in seaborn that include color and size variables to add more information.

Exercise 144 – creating a scatter plot for the Boston Housing dataset

In this exercise, you will create a `seaborn` scatter plot for our Boston Housing dataset that includes color and size variation.

The following steps will enable you to complete this exercise:

1. Open a new Jupyter Notebook where your Boston Housing data is stored.

2. Import `pandas` as `pd` and choose a variable for storing the DataFrame while reading in the `HousingData.csv` file:

```
import pandas as pd
housing_df = pd.read_csv('HousingData.csv')
```

3. Import `matplotlib` and `seaborn`, and set the gray seaborn background with the white grid:

```
import matplotlib.pyplot as plt
import seaborn as sns
sns.set()
```

4. Set the figure size and the title, as shown in the following code snippet:

```
plt.figure(figsize=(16,10))
my_title='Boston Housing Scatterplot'
plt.title(my_title, size=15)
```

Create a `seaborn` scatter plot with the `x` value set to the crime rate and the `y` value set to the median value of the house. Include color variation by setting the `hue` parameter equal to another column, and size variation by setting the `size` parameter equal to an additional column. Adjust the size of the dots as a tuple using the `sizes` parameter, and the color palette using the `palette` parameter. All may be executed as shown in the following code snippet:

```
sns.scatterplot(x=df['CRIM'], y=df['MEDV'],
                hue=df['RM'], size=df['AGE'],
                sizes=(20, 400),
                palette='Greens')
```

5. Save your figure and display the graph using the following code:

```
plt.savefig(my_title, dpi=225)
plt.show()
```

A screenshot of the output is as follows:

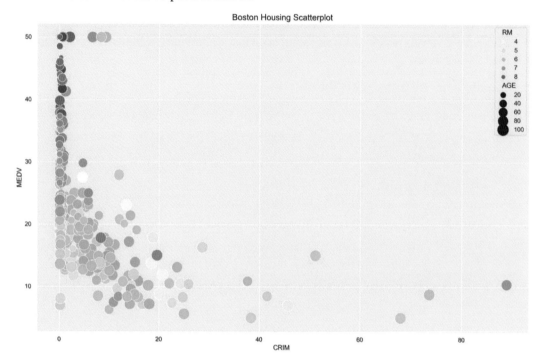

Figure 10.41 – Scatter plot output showing how crime, number
of rooms, and age affect the median house value

It's your job as a practicing data scientist to help interpret your graphs. There's a clear negative relationship, as expected, between crime and the median house value. As crime goes up, the median house value goes down. We can also see from the color variation that as the number of rooms goes up, according to the key on the right, the median house values go up. Finally, there does not seem to be much of a relationship between age, according to the key on the right, and the median house value.

`seaborn` comes with many nice default options, as shown in this graph. They automatically include a key, also called a legend, along with the labels of the columns. `seaborn` and `matplotlib` work well together, and can more or less be used interchangeably.

For more information on creating cool Seaborn graphs, click on any of the links in the Seaborn gallery: `https://seaborn.pydata.org/examples/index.html`.

The question of negative and positive association, as referenced earlier, can be more accurately determined by an important statistical concept called **correlation**, which we will examine next.

Correlation

Correlation is a statistical measure between -1 and +1 that indicates how closely two variables are related. A correlation of -1 or +1 means that the variables are dependent, and they fall in a perfectly straight line. A correlation of 0 indicates that an increase in one variable gives no information whatsoever about the other variable. Visually, this would involve points being all over the place. Correlations usually fall somewhere in the middle. For instance, a correlation of 0.75 represents a fairly strong linear relationship, whereas a correlation of 0.25 is a reasonably weak linear relationship. Positive correlations go up (meaning as x goes up, y goes up), and negative correlations go down.

Here is a great image from Wikimedia Commons that shows a range of scatter plots, along with their correlations:

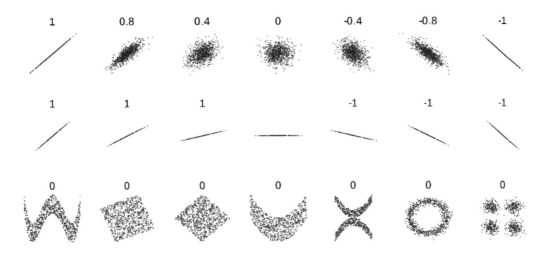

Figure 10.42 – Scatter plots and their respective correlations from Wikimedia Commons

In the following exercise, you will find the correlation values from the Boston Housing dataset and display them using a heatmap.

Exercise 145 – correlation values from the dataset

In this exercise, you will find the correlation values from the Boston Housing dataset and display them using a heat map. The following steps will enable you to complete this exercise:

1. Open a new Jupyter Notebook where your Boston Housing data is stored.

2. Import pandas as pd and choose a variable for storing the DataFrame while reading in the HousingData.csv file:

```
import pandas as pd
df = pd.read_csv('HousingData.csv')
```

3. Now, find the correlation value of the dataset, as shown in the following code snippet:

```
df.corr()
```

The output will be as follows:

	CRIM	ZN	INDUS	CHAS	NOX	RM	AGE	DIS	RAD	TAX	PTRATIO	B	LSTAT	MEDV
CRIM	1.000000	-0.191178	0.401863	-0.054355	0.417130	-0.219150	0.354342	-0.374166	0.624765	0.580595	0.281110	-0.381411	0.444943	-0.391363
ZN	-0.191178	1.000000	-0.531871	-0.037229	-0.513704	0.320800	-0.563801	0.656739	-0.310919	-0.312371	-0.414046	0.171303	-0.414193	0.373136
INDUS	0.401863	-0.531871	1.000000	0.059859	0.764866	-0.390234	0.638431	-0.711709	0.604533	0.731055	0.390954	-0.360532	0.590690	-0.481772
CHAS	-0.054355	-0.037229	0.059859	1.000000	0.075097	0.104885	0.078831	-0.093971	0.001468	-0.032304	-0.111304	0.051264	-0.047424	0.181391
NOX	0.417130	-0.513704	0.764866	0.075097	1.000000	-0.302188	0.731548	-0.769230	0.611441	0.668023	0.188933	-0.380051	0.582641	-0.427321
RM	-0.219150	0.320800	-0.390234	0.104885	-0.302188	1.000000	-0.247337	0.205246	-0.209847	-0.292048	-0.355501	0.128069	-0.614339	0.695360
AGE	0.354342	-0.563801	0.638431	0.078831	0.731548	-0.247337	1.000000	-0.744844	0.458349	0.509114	0.269226	-0.275303	0.602891	-0.394656
DIS	-0.374166	0.656739	-0.711709	-0.093971	-0.769230	0.205246	-0.744844	1.000000	-0.494588	-0.534432	-0.232471	0.291512	-0.493328	0.249929
RAD	0.624765	-0.310919	0.604533	0.001468	0.611441	-0.209847	0.458349	-0.494588	1.000000	0.910228	0.464741	-0.444413	0.479541	-0.381626
TAX	0.580595	-0.312371	0.731055	-0.032304	0.668023	-0.292048	0.509114	-0.534432	0.910228	1.000000	0.460853	-0.441808	0.536110	-0.468536
PTRATIO	0.281110	-0.414046	0.390954	-0.111304	0.188933	-0.355501	0.269226	-0.232471	0.464741	0.460853	1.000000	-0.177383	0.375966	-0.507787
B	-0.381411	0.171303	-0.360532	0.051264	-0.380051	0.128069	-0.275303	0.291512	-0.444413	-0.441808	-0.177383	1.000000	-0.369889	0.333461
LSTAT	0.444943	-0.414193	0.590690	-0.047424	0.582641	-0.614339	0.602891	-0.493328	0.479541	0.536110	0.375966	-0.369889	1.000000	-0.735822
MEDV	-0.391363	0.373136	-0.481772	0.181391	-0.427321	0.695360	-0.394656	0.249929	-0.381626	-0.468536	-0.507787	0.333461	-0.735822	1.000000

Figure 10.43 – Correlation values displayed as a DataFrame

This tells us the exact correlation values. For instance, to see what variables are the most correlated with Median Value Home, you can examine the values under the MEDV column. There, you will find that RM is the largest at 0.695360. But you also see a value of -0.735822 for LSTAT, which is the percentage of the lower status of the population. This is a very strong negative correlation.

4. Seaborn provides a nice way to view correlations inside of a heatmap. Begin by importing maplotlib and seaborn:

```
import matplotlib.pyplot as plt
import seaborn as snssns.set()
```

5. Now, display the heatmap, as shown in the following code snippet:

```
corr = df.corr()
plt.figure(figsize=(14,10))
sns.heatmap(corr, xticklabels=corr.columns.values,
```

```
ytosticklabels=corr.columns.values, cmap="Reds",
linewidths=1.25)
plt.show()
```

A screenshot of the output is as follows:

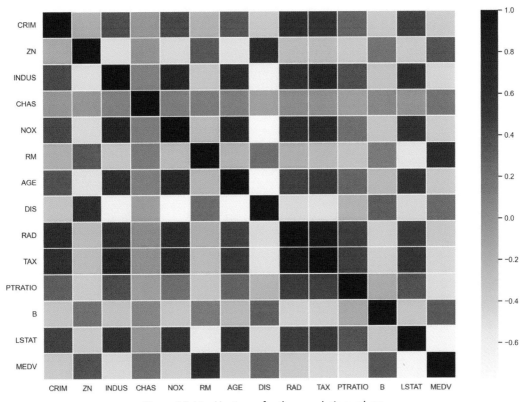

Figure 10.44 – Heatmap for the correlation values

The darker the squares, the higher the correlation, and the lighter the squares, the lower the correlation. Now, when examining the MEDV column, it's much easier to find the darkest square, RM, and the lightest square, LSTAT. You may have noticed that, technically, the MEDV square is the darkest. This has to be true because MEDV is perfectly correlated with itself. The same holds for each column along the diagonal.

In this exercise, you were able to work with correlation values from the dataset and get a visual aid for the data output.

In the next section, you will learn about regression.

Regression

Perhaps the most important addition to a scatter plot is the regression line. The idea of regression came from Sir Francis Galton, who measured the heights of the offspring of very tall and very short parents. The offspring were not taller or shorter than their parents on average, but rather closer to the mean height of all people. Sir Francis Galton used the term "regression to the mean," meaning that the heights of the offspring were closer to the mean of their very tall or very short parents. The name stuck.

In statistics, a regression line is a line that tries to fit the values of a scatter plot as closely as possible. Generally speaking, half of the points are above the line, and half of the points are below. The most popular regression line method is ordinary least squares, which minimizes the sum of the square of the distance from each point to the line.

There are a variety of methods to compute and display regression lines using Python.

Plotting a regression line

To create a regression line of our Boston Housing dataset, the following code steps need to be followed:

```
x = df['RM']
y = df['MEDV']
plt.figure(figsize=(14, 10))
sns.regplot(x,y)
plt.show()
```

The output will be as follows:

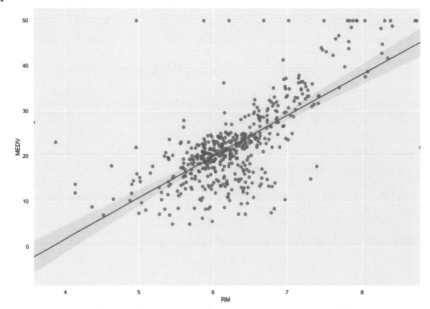

Figure 10.45 – Regression line predicting MEDV from RM with the 95% confidence interval shaded in

You may be wondering about the shaded part of the line. It represents a 95% confidence interval, meaning that Python is 95% confident that the actual regression line falls within that range. Since the shaded area is fairly small concerning the plot, this means that the regression line is reasonably accurate. Note that Seaborn provides a 95% confidence interval by default, and this number can be adjusted if desired.

The general idea behind regression lines is that they can be used to predict new y values from new x values. For instance, if there is an eight-room house, you can use regression to get an estimate of its value. You will use this general philosophy in a more sophisticated manner in *Chapter 11*, *Machine Learning*, using the machine learning version of linear regression.

Although this is not a course on statistics, if you want to go a little deeper, check out the next section, which explains how to obtain all of the key parameters of the ordinary least squares regression line. As a practicing data scientist, it's important to be able to obtain this information if needed.

StatsModel regression output

Import StatsModel and use its methods to print out a summary of the regression line:

```
import statsmodels.api as sm
X = sm.add_constant(x)
model = sm.OLS(y, X)
est = model.fit()
print(est.summary())
```

The strangest part of the code is adding the constant. This is the y-intercept. When the constant is not added, the y-intercept is 0. In our case, it makes sense that the y-intercept would be 0; if there are 0 rooms, the house should have no value. In general, however, it's a good idea to keep a y-intercept, and it's the default choice of the preceding Seaborn graph. It's a good idea to try both methods and compare the results of the data. A comparative analysis will improve your background in statistics. Finally, note that OLS stands for **ordinary least squares**, as described in the preceding section.

The expected output is as follows:

```
                            OLS Regression Results
==============================================================================
Dep. Variable:                   MEDV   R-squared:                       0.484
Model:                            OLS   Adj. R-squared:                  0.483
Method:                 Least Squares   F-statistic:                     471.8
Date:                Sat, 03 Sep 2022   Prob (F-statistic):           2.49e-74
Time:                        19:37:20   Log-Likelihood:                -1673.1
No. Observations:                 506   AIC:                             3350.
Df Residuals:                     504   BIC:                             3359.
Df Model:                           1
Covariance Type:            nonrobust
==============================================================================
                 coef    std err          t      P>|t|      [0.025      0.975]
------------------------------------------------------------------------------
const        -34.6706      2.650    -13.084      0.000     -39.877     -29.465
RM             9.1021      0.419     21.722      0.000       8.279       9.925
==============================================================================
Omnibus:                      102.585   Durbin-Watson:                   0.684
Prob(Omnibus):                  0.000   Jarque-Bera (JB):              612.449
Skew:                           0.726   Prob(JB):                     1.02e-133
Kurtosis:                       8.190   Cond. No.                         58.4
==============================================================================

Notes:
[1] Standard Errors assume that the covariance matrix of the errors is correctly specified.
```

Figure 10.46 – Summary of the regression line

There's a lot of important information in this table. The first is the value of R^2 at 0.484. This suggests that 48% of the data can be explained by the regression line. The second is the coefficient constant of -34.6706. This is the y-intercept. The third is the RM coefficient of 9.1021. This suggests that for every one-bedroom increase, the value of the house increased by 9,102 (keep in mind that this dataset is from 1980).

The standard error suggests how far off the actual values are from the line on average, and the numbers underneath the [0.025 0.975] column give the 95% **confidence interval** of the value, meaning statsmodel is 95% confident that the true increase in the value of the average house for every one-bedroom increase is between 8,279 and 9,925.

Box plots and violin plots

There's a great deal of data analysis in Python – far more than you can adequately cover in an introductory text. In this chapter, you covered histograms and scatter plots in considerable detail, including regression lines and heat maps. In *Chapter 4*, *Extending Python, Files, Errors, and Graphs*, you also covered line charts, bar charts, pie charts, density plots, contour plots, and 3D plots.

Two additional types of plots – box plots and violin plots – will be briefly highlighted before we move on to machine learning.

Exercise 146 – creating box plots

A box plot provides a nice visual of the mean, median, quartiles, and outliers of a given column of data.

In this exercise, you will create box plots using the Boston Housing dataset. The following steps will enable you to complete this exercise:

1. Open a new Jupyter Notebook where your Boston Housing data is stored.

2. Import `pandas` as `pd` and choose a variable for storing the DataFrame while reading in the `HousingData.csv` file:

```
import pandas as pd
housing_df = pd.read_csv('HousingData.csv')
import matplotlib.pyplot as plt
import seaborn as sns
sns.set()
```

3. Now, enter the following code to create a box plot:

```
plt.figure(figsize=(14, 10))
title='Box Plot of Boston Median House Values'
plt.title(title, size=15)
sns.boxplot(x = df['MEDV'])
plt.savefig(title, dpi=300)
plt.show()
```

Here is the output of the saved PNG file:

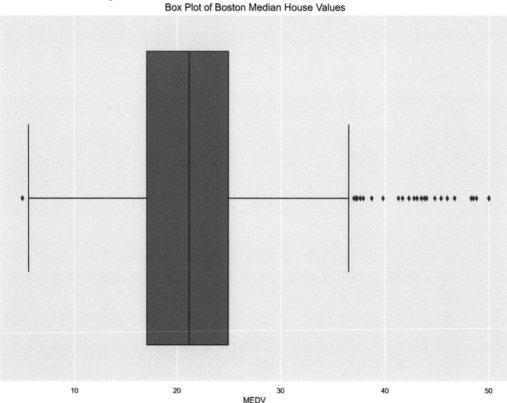

Figure 10.47 – Seaborn box plot output

Note that the small diamonds are considered outliers. The line in the middle is the median, while the bars at the end of the dark box are the 25th and 75th percentiles, or the first and third quartiles. The end bars represent the quartiles plus or minus 1.5 times the interquartile range. The value of 1.5 times the interquartile range is a standard limit in statistics that's used to define outliers, but it does not have universal acceptance since outliers must be judged, depending on the data at hand.

In this exercise, you created a box plot graph to visually represent a column of data.

Exercise 147 – creating violin plots

A violin plot is a different type of plot that conveys similar information as a box plot. In this exercise, you will create a violin plot by performing the following steps:

1.   Continue with the same Jupyter Notebook as in the previous exercise.

2. Enter the following code to create the violin plot:

```
plt.figure(figsize=(14, 10))
sns.violinplot(x = df['MEDV'])
plt.show()
```

The output will be as follows:

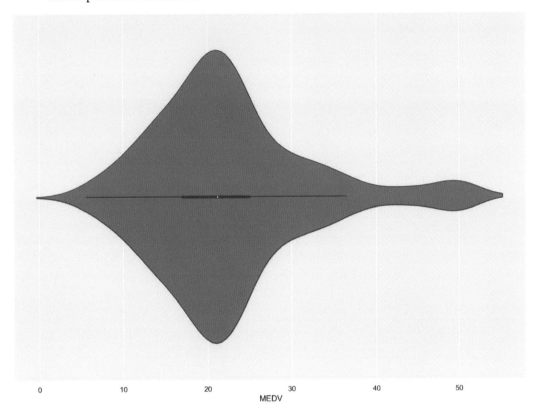

Figure 10.48 – Violin plot output

In the violin plot, the right and left edges define the minimum and maximum values, and the width of the plot indicates how many rows contain that particular value. The difference between the violin plot and the box plot is that the violin plot shows the overall distribution of the data as one continuous graph, whereas the box plot is partitioned.

That concludes our survey of visual graphs.

Now, you will complete an activity to see whether you can implement the concepts covered in this chapter.

Activity 24 – performing data analysis to find the outliers in pay versus the salary report in the UK statistics dataset

You are working as a data scientist, and you come across a government dataset that seems interesting concerning payments. But since the dataset values are cluttered, you need to use visual data analysis to study the data and determine whether any outliers need to be removed.

In this activity, you will be performing visual data analysis using histograms, scatter plots, regression lines, and box plots to arrive at your conclusion.

Follow these steps to complete this activity:

1. First, you need to copy the `UKStatistics.csv` dataset file into a specific folder.

2. Next, in a new Jupyter Notebook, import the necessary data visualization packages.

3. View the dataset file, then find the information about each column and the descriptive statistics.

4. Plot the histogram for `Actual Pay Floor (£)`.

5. Plot the scatter plot while using x as `Salary Cost of Reports (£)` and y as `Actual Pay Floor (£)`.

6. Now, get the box plot for the x and y values, as shown in *step 5*.

> **Note**
>
> `UKStatistics.csv` can be downloaded on GitHub at `https://github.com/PacktPublishing/The-Python-Workshop-Second-Edition/tree/main/Chapter10/`.
>
> More information on the `UKStatistics` dataset can be found at `https://packt.live/2BzBwqF`.

Here is the expected output with the outliers in one of the box plots:

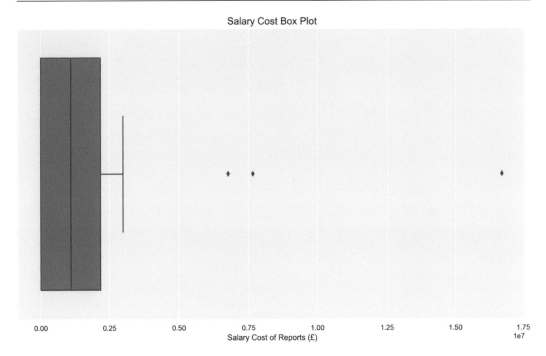

Figure 10.49 – The expected output for the box plot of the Salary Cost of Reports revealing outliers

> **Note**
> The solution for this activity can be found in the *Appendix* on GitHub.

Summary

We began our introduction to data analysis with NumPy, Python's incredibly fast library for handling massive matrix computations. Next, you learned about the fundamentals of pandas, Python's library for handling DataFrames. Taken together, you used NumPy and pandas to analyze the Boston Housing dataset by correcting null values and interpreting descriptive statistics, including the mean, standard deviation, median, quartiles, correlation, skewed data, and outliers. You also learned about advanced methods for creating clean, clearly labeled, publishable graphs, including histograms, scatter plots with variation in size and color, regression lines, box plots, and violin plots. You now have the fundamental skills to load, clean, analyze, and plot big data for technical and general audiences.

In *Chapter 11, Machine Learning*, you will make predictions from big data using some of the best machine learning algorithms in the world today.

11

Machine Learning

Overview

By the end of this chapter, you will be able to apply **machine learning** (**ML**) algorithms to solve different problems; compare, contrast, and apply different types of ML algorithms, including linear regression, logistic regression, decision trees, random forests, Naive Bayes, Adaptive Boosting (AdaBoost), and Extreme Gradient Boosting (XGBoost); analyze overfitting and implement regularization; work with `GridSearchCV` and `RandomizedSearchCV` to adjust hyperparameters; evaluate algorithms using a confusion matrix and cross-validation, and solve real-world problems using the ML algorithms outlined here.

Introduction

Computer algorithms enable machines to learn from data. The more data an algorithm receives, the more capable the algorithm is of detecting underlying patterns within the data. In *Chapter 10, Data Analytics with pandas and NumPy*, you learned how to view and analyze big data with `pandas` and `NumPy`. In this chapter, we will now extend these concepts to algorithms that learn from data.

Consider how a child learns to identify a cat. Generally speaking, a child learns by having someone point out "That's a cat", "No, that's a dog", and so on. After enough cats and non-cats have been pointed out, the child knows how to identify a cat.

ML implements the same general approach. A **convolutional neural network** (**CNN**) is an ML algorithm that distinguishes between images. Upon receiving images labeled cats and non-cats, the algorithm looks for underlying patterns within the pixels by adjusting the parameters of an equation until it finds an equation that minimizes the error.

After the algorithm has selected the best possible equation, given the data it has received, this equation is used to predict future data. When a new image arrives, the new image is placed within the algorithm to determine whether the image is a cat or not.

In this chapter on ML, you will learn how to construct linear regression, logistic regression, decision tree, random forest, Naive Bayes, AdaBoost, and XGBoost algorithms. These algorithms can be used to solve a wide range of problems, from predicting rainfall to detecting credit card fraud and identifying diseases.

Then, you will learn about Ridge and Lasso, two regularized ML algorithms that are variations of linear regression. You will learn about using regularization and cross-validation to obtain accurate results with data that the algorithm has never seen before.

After learning how to build an ML model in `scikit-learn` through an extended example with linear regression, you will take a similar approach to build models based on k-nearest neighbors, (KNN) decision trees, and random forests. You will learn how to extend these models with hyperparameter turning, a way of fine-tuning models to meet the specifications of the data at hand.

Next, you will move on to classification problems, where the ML model is used to determine whether an email is spam and whether a celestial object is a planet. All classification problems can be tackled with logistic regression, an ML algorithm that you will learn about here. In addition, you will solve classification problems with Naive Bayes, random forests, and other types of algorithms. Classification results can be interpreted with a confusion matrix and a classification report, both of which we will explore in depth.

Finally, you will learn how to implement boosting methods that transform weak learners into strong learners. In particular, you will learn how to implement AdaBoost, one of the most successful ML algorithms in history, and XGBoost, one of the best ML algorithms today.

To sum up, after completing this chapter, you will be able to apply multiple ML algorithms to solve classification and regression problems. You will be capable of using advanced tools such as a confusion matrix and a classification report to interpret results. You will also be able to refine your models using regularization and hyperparameter tuning. In short, you will have the tools to use ML to solve real-world problems, including predicting cost and classifying objects.

Here's a quick overview of the topics covered:

- Introduction to linear regression
- Testing data with cross-validation
- Regularization—Ridge and Lasso
- K-nearest neighbors, decision trees, and random forests
- Classification models
- Boosting algorithms

As for CNNs, you will learn how to build one when you conclude your ML and data science journey in Python at the end of the following chapter, *Chapter 12, Deep Learning with Python.*

Technical requirements

You can find the code files for this chapter on GitHub at https://github.com/PacktPublishing/ The-Python-Workshop-Second-Edition/tree/main/Chapter11.

Introduction to linear regression

ML is the ability of computers to learn from data. The power of ML comes from making future predictions based on the data received. Today, ML is used all over the world to predict the weather, stock prices, profits, errors, clicks, purchases, words to complete a sentence, recommend movies, recognize faces and many more things.

The unparalleled success of ML has led to a paradigm shift in the way businesses make decisions. In the past, businesses made decisions based on who had the most influence, but now, the new idea is to make decisions based on data. Decisions are constantly being made about the future, and ML is the best tool at our disposal to convert raw data into actionable decisions.

The first step in building an ML algorithm is deciding what you want to predict. When looking at a DataFrame, the idea is to choose one column as the **target** column. The target column, by definition, is what the algorithm will be trained to predict.

Recall the Boston Housing dataset introduced in *Chapter 10, Data Analytics with pandas and NumPy*. The median value of a home is a desirable target column since real-estate agents, buyers, and sellers often want to know how much a house is worth. People usually determine this information based on the size of the house, the location, the number of bedrooms, and many other factors.

Here is the Boston Housing DataFrame from *Chapter 10, Data Analytics with pandas and NumPy*. Each column includes features about houses in the neighborhood, such as crime, the average age of the house, and notably, in the last column, the median value:

	CRIM	ZN	INDUS	CHAS	NOX	RM	AGE	DIS	RAD	TAX	PTRATIO	B	LSTAT	MEDV
0	0.00632	18.0	2.31	0.0	0.538	6.575	65.2	4.0900	1	296	15.3	396.90	4.98	24.0
1	0.02731	0.0	7.07	0.0	0.469	6.421	78.9	4.9671	2	242	17.8	396.90	9.14	21.6
2	0.02729	0.0	7.07	0.0	0.469	7.185	61.1	4.9671	2	242	17.8	392.83	4.03	34.7
3	0.03237	0.0	2.18	0.0	0.458	6.998	45.8	6.0622	3	222	18.7	394.63	2.94	33.4
4	0.06905	0.0	2.18	0.0	0.458	7.147	54.2	6.0622	3	222	18.7	396.90	NaN	36.2

Figure 11.1 – Sample from the Boston Housing dataset

The meaning of the columns from *Chapter 10, Data Analytics with pandas and NumPy*, is displayed again for your reference:

```
CRIM     per capita crime rate by town
ZN       proportion of residential land zoned for lots over 25,000 sq. ft.
INDUS    proportion of non-retail business acres per town
CHAS     Charles River dummy variable (= 1 if tract bounds river; 0 otherwise)
NOX      nitric oxide concentration (parts per 10 million)
RM       average number of rooms per dwelling
AGE      proportion of owner-occupied units built prior to 1940
DIS      weighted distances to five Boston employment centers
RAD      index of accessibility to radial highways
TAX      full-value property-tax rate per $10,000
PTRATIO  pupil-teacher ratio by town
LSTAT    % lower status of the population
MEDV     median value of owner-occupied homes in $1,000s
```

Figure 11.2 – Dataset value representation

We want to come up with an equation that uses every other column to predict the last column, which will be our target column. What kind of equation should we use? Before we answer this question, let's have a look at a simplified solution.

Simplifying the problem

It's often helpful to simplify a problem. What if we take just one column, such as the number of bedrooms, and use it to predict the median house value?

It's clear that the more bedrooms a house has, the more valuable it will be. As the number of bedrooms goes up, so does the house value. A standard way to represent this positive association is with a straight line.

In *Chapter 10, Data Analytics with pandas and NumPy*, we modeled the relationship between the number of bedrooms and the median house value with the linear regression line, as shown here:

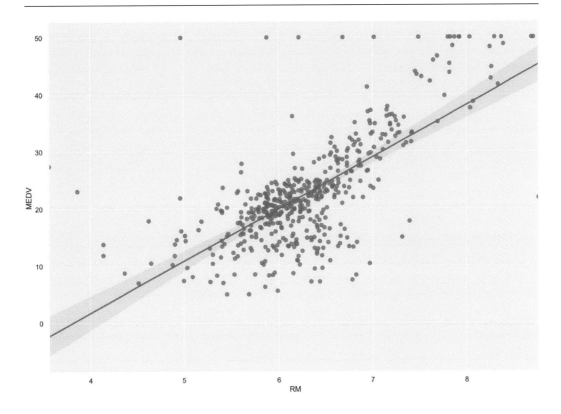

Figure 11.3 – Linear regression line for the median value and the number of bedrooms

It turns out that linear regression is a very popular ML algorithm. Linear regression is often worth trying when the target column takes on continuous values, as in this dataset. The value of a home is generally considered to be continuous. There is technically no limit to how high the cost of a home may be. It could take any value between two numbers, despite often rounding up.

By contrast, if we predict whether a house will sell after 1 month on the market, the possible answers are yes and no. In this case, the target column is not continuous but discrete.

From one to N-dimensions

Dimensionality is an important concept in ML. In math, it's common to work with two dimensions, x and y, in the coordinate plane. In physics, it's common to work with three dimensions, the x, y, and z axes. When it comes to spatial dimensions, three is the limit because we live in a three-dimensional universe. In mathematics, however, there is no restriction on the number of dimensions we can use theoretically. In superstring theory, 12 or 13 dimensions are often used. In ML, however, the number of dimensions is often the number of **predictor** columns.

There is no need to limit ourselves to one dimension with linear regression. Additional dimensions—in this case, additional columns—will give us more information about the median house value and make our model more valuable.

In one-dimensional linear regression, the slope-intercept equation is $y = mx + b$, where y is the target column, x is the input, m is the slope, and b is the y-intercept. This equation is now extended to an arbitrary number of dimensions using $Y = MX + B$, where Y, M, and X are vectors of arbitrary length. Instead of the slope, M is referred to as the weight.

> **Note**
>
> It's not essential to comprehend the linear algebra behind vector mathematics to run ML algorithms; however, it is essential to comprehend the underlying ideas. The underlying idea here is that linear regression can be extended to an arbitrary number of dimensions.

In the Boston Housing dataset, a linear regression model will select weights, which are numerical coefficients, for each of the columns. In order to predict the median house value for each row (our target column), the weights will be multiplied by the column entries and then summed, with the goal of getting as close as possible to the target value.

We will have a look at how this works in practice.

The linear regression algorithm

Before implementing the algorithm, let's take a brief look at the libraries that we will import and use in our programs:

- pandas: You learned how to use `pandas` in *Chapter 10, Data Analytics with pandas and NumPy*. When it comes to ML, in this chapter, all data will be handled through `pandas`. Loading data, reading data, viewing data, cleaning data, and manipulating data all require `pandas`, so `pandas` will always be our first import.

- NumPy: This was introduced in *Chapter 10, Data Analytics with pandas and NumPy*, as well and will often be used for mathematical computations on datasets. It's often a good idea to import `NumPy` when performing ML so that it's available when needed.

- LinearRegression: The `LinearRegression` library should be implemented every time linear regression is used. This library will allow you to build linear regression models and test them in very few steps. ML libraries do the heavy lifting for you. In this case, `LinearRegression` will place weights on each of the columns and adjust them until it finds an optimal solution to predict the target column, which in our case would be the median house value.

- `mean_squared_error`: In order to find optimal values, the algorithm needs a measure to test how well it's doing. Measuring how far the model's predicted value is from the target value is a standard place to start. In order to avoid negatives canceling out positives, we can use `mean_squared_error`. To compute the `mean_squared_error` value, the prediction of each row is subtracted from the target column or actual value, and the result is squared. Each result is summed, and the mean is computed. Finally, taking the square root keeps the units the same.

- `train_test_split`: Python provides `train_test_split` to split data into a **training** set and a **test** set. Splitting the data into a training set and test set is essential because it allows users to test the model right away. Testing the model on data the machine has never seen before is the most important part of building the model because it shows how well the model will perform in the real world.

Most of the data is included in the training set because more data leads to a more robust model. A smaller portion—around **20%**—is held back for the test set. An **80-20** split is the default, though you may adjust it as you see fit. The model is optimized on the training set, and after completion, it is scored against the test set.

These libraries are a part of `scikit-learn`, also known as `sklearn`. `scikit-learn` has a wealth of excellent online resources for beginners. See `https://scikit-learn.org/stable/` for more information.

Exercise 148 – using linear regression to predict the accuracy of the median values of our dataset

The goal of this exercise is to build an ML model using linear regression. Your model will predict the median value of Boston houses and, based on this, we will come to a conclusion about whether the value is optimal or not.

This exercise will be performed on a Jupyter Notebook with the following steps:

> **Note**
> To proceed with the exercises in the chapter, you will need the `scikit-learn` library installed that is mentioned in the *Preface* section. It should be available with any Anaconda distribution.

1. Open a new notebook file in the same folder as your `Data` folder.
2. Now, import all the necessary libraries, as shown in the following code snippet:

```
import pandas as pd
import numpy as np
from sklearn.linear_model import LinearRegression
```

```
from sklearn.metrics import mean_squared_error
from sklearn.model_selection import train_test_split
```

Now that we have imported the libraries, we will load the data.

3. Load the dataset and view the DataFrames to look at the first five rows:

```
# load data
housing_df = pd.read_csv('HousingData.csv')
housing_df.head()
```

Recall that, as mentioned in *Chapter 10, Data Analytics with pandas and NumPy,* housing_df = pd.read_cs('HousingData.csv') will read the CSV file in parentheses and store it in a DataFrame called housing_df. Then, housing_df.head() will display the first five rows of the housing_df DataFrame by default.

You should get the following output:

	CRIM	ZN	INDUS	CHAS	NOX	RM	AGE	DIS	RAD	TAX	PTRATIO	B	LSTAT	MEDV
0	0.00632	18.0	2.31	0.0	0.538	6.575	65.2	4.0900	1	296	15.3	396.90	4.98	24.0
1	0.02731	0.0	7.07	0.0	0.469	6.421	78.9	4.9671	2	242	17.8	396.90	9.14	21.6
2	0.02729	0.0	7.07	0.0	0.469	7.185	61.1	4.9671	2	242	17.8	392.83	4.03	34.7
3	0.03237	0.0	2.18	0.0	0.458	6.998	45.8	6.0622	3	222	18.7	394.63	2.94	33.4
4	0.06905	0.0	2.18	0.0	0.458	7.147	54.2	6.0622	3	222	18.7	396.90	NaN	36.2

Figure 11.4 – First five rows of the Boston Housing dataset

4. Next, enter the following code to clean the dataset of null values using .dropna():

```
# drop null values
housing_df = housing_df.dropna()
```

In *Chapter 10, Data Analytics with pandas and NumPy,* we cleared the null values by counting them and comparing them to measures of central tendency. In this chapter, however, we will use a swifter approach in order to expedite testing for ML. The housing_df.dropna() code will drop all null values from the housing_df DataFrame.

Now that the data is clean, it's time to prepare our X and y values.

5. Now, declare X and y variables, where you use X for the **predictor** columns and y for the **target** column:

```
# declare X and y
X = housing_df.iloc[:, :-1]
y = housing_df.iloc[:, -1]
```

The target column is MEDV, which is the median value of Boston house prices. The predictor columns include every other column. The standard notation is to use X for the predictor columns and y for the target column.

Since the last column is the target column, which is y, it should be eliminated from the predictor column—that is, X. We can achieve this split by indexing as already shown.

Before building the regression model, we are going to use `train_test_split()` to split X and y, the predictor and target columns, into training and test sets. The model will be built using the training set. Let's split the data in the following step.

6. Split X and y into training and test sets, as follows:

```
X_train, X_test, y_train, y_test = train_test_split(X, y,
test_size=0.2, random_state=0)
```

`test_size=0.2` reflects the percentage of rows held back for the test set. This is the default setting and does not need to be added explicitly. It is presented so that you know how to change it. The `random_state=0` parameter is also not required, but it will ensure that you have the same split as we do, later resulting in the same ML score.

7. We now build the actual linear regression model. Although many ML models are incredibly sophisticated, they can be built using very few lines of code.

Create an empty `LinearRegression()` model, as shown in the following code snippet:

```
reg = LinearRegression()
```

Finally, fit the model to the data using the `.fit()` method:

```
reg.fit(X_train, y_train)
```

The parameters are X_train and y_train, which is the training set that we have defined. `reg.fit(X_train, y_train)` is where ML actually happens. In this line, the `LinearRegression()` model adjusts itself to the training data. The model keeps changing weights, according to the ML algorithm, until the weights minimize the error.

The Jupyter Notebook shows the following output:

`LinearRegression()`

At this point, `reg` is an ML model with specified weights. There is one weight for each X column. These weights are multiplied by the entry in each row to get as close as possible to the target column, y, which is the median house value.

8. Now, find how accurate the model is. Here, we can test it on unseen data:

```
# Predict on the test data: y_pred
y_pred = reg.predict(X_test)
```

To make a prediction, we implement a method, `.predict()`. This method takes specified rows of data as the input and produces the corresponding predicted values as the output. The input is `X_test`, the `X` values that were held back for our test set. The output is the predicted `y` values.

9. We can now test the prediction by comparing the predicted `y` values (`y_pred`) to the actual `y` values (`y_test`), as shown in the following code snippet:

```
# Compute and print RMSE
rmse = np.sqrt(mean_squared_error(y_test, y_pred))
 print(f'RMSE: {rmse}')
```

The error—the difference between the two `np.array` instances—may be computed as `mean_squared_error`. We take the square root of the mean squared error to keep the same units as the target column.

The output is as follows:

RMSE: 5.371207757773587

Note that there are other errors to choose from. The square root of `mean_squared_error` is a standard choice with linear regression. `rmse`, short for root mean squared error, will give us the error of the model on the test set.

A root mean squared error of `5.37` means that, on average, the ML model predicts values approximately `5.37` units away from the target value, which is not bad in terms of accuracy given the range of column values of 45 and standard deviation of 9.1 (see `df['MEDV'].describe()`). Since the median value (from 1980) is in the thousands, the predictions are about 5.37 thousand off. Lower errors are always better, so we will see if can improve the error going forward.

In this very first exercise, we were able to load our dataset, clean it, and build a linear regression model to make predictions and check its accuracy.

Linear regression function

After building your first ML model, you may wonder what happens if you run it multiple times as a function. Will you get different results?

Let's do this, as shown in the following example, using the same Boston Housing dataset, this time without setting a random seed.

Let's put all the ML code, including the train-test split, in a function and run it again:

```
def regression_model(model):
  # Create training and test sets
  X_train, X_test, y_train, y_test = train_test_split(X, y,
```

```
test_size=0.2)
    # Create the regressor: reg_all
    reg_all = model
    # Fit the regressor to the training data
    reg_all.fit(X_train, y_train)
    # Predict on the test data: y_pred
    y_pred = reg_all.predict(X_test)
    # Compute and print RMSE
    rmse = np.sqrt(mean_squared_error(y_test, y_pred))
    print("RMSE: {}".format(rmse))
```

Now, run the function multiple times to see the results:

```
regression_model(LinearRegression())
```

Here are several sample outputs that we obtained:

```
RMSE: 4.085279539934423
RMSE:: 4.317496624587608
RMSE:: 4.7884343211684435
```

This is troublesome, right? The score is always different. Your scores are also likely to differ from ours.

The scores are different because we are splitting the data into a different training set and test set each time, and the model is based on different training sets. Furthermore, it's being scored against a different test set.

In order for ML scores to be meaningful, we want to minimize fluctuation, and ensure that our results are representative of reality. We will see how to do this in the next section.

Testing data with cross-validation

In cross-validation, also known as CV, the training data is split into five folds (any number will do, but **five is standard**). The ML algorithm is fit on one fold at a time and tested on the remaining data. The result is five different training and test sets that are all representative of the same data. The mean of the scores is usually taken as the accuracy of the model.

> **Note**
> For cross-validation, 5 folds is only one suggestion. Any natural number may be used, with 3 and 10 also being fairly common.

Cross-validation is a core tool for ML. Mean test scores on different folds are more reliable than one mean test score on the entire set, which we performed in the first exercise. When examining one test score, there is no way of knowing whether it is low or high. Five test scores give a better picture of the true accuracy of the model.

Cross-validation can be implemented in a variety of ways. A standard approach is to use `cross_val_score`, which returns an array of scores for each fold; `cross_val_score` breaks X and y into training and test sets for you.

Let's modify our regression ML function to include `cross_val_score` in the following exercise.

Exercise 149 – using the cross_val_score function to get accurate results on the dataset

The goal of this exercise is to use cross-validation to obtain more accurate ML results from the dataset compared to the previous exercise. The steps are as follows:

1. Continue using the same Jupyter Notebook from *Exercise 148 – using linear regression to predict the accuracy of the median values of our dataset.*

2. Now, import `cross_val_score`:

    ```
    from sklearn.model_selection import cross_val_score
    ```

3. Define the `regression_model_cv` function, which takes a fitted model as one parameter. The `k=5` hyperparameter gives the number of folds. Note that `cross_val_score` does not need a random seed because it splits the data the same way every time. Enter the code shown in the following snippet:

    ```
    def regression_model_cv(model, k=5):
        scores = cross_val_score(model, X, y, scoring='neg_
    mean_squared_ error', cv=k)
        rmse = np.sqrt(-scores)
        print('Reg rmse:', rmse)
        print('Reg mean:', rmse.mean())
    ```

    In `sklearn`, the scoring options are sometimes limited. Since `mean_squared_error` is not an option for `cross_val_score`, we choose `neg_mean_squared_error`. `cross_val_score` takes the highest value by default, and the highest negative mean squared error is 0.

4. Use the `regression_model_cv` function on the `LinearRegression()` model defined in the previous exercise:

    ```
    regression_model_cv(LinearRegression())
    ```

The output is as follows:

```
Reg rmse: [3.26123843 4.42712448 5.66151114 8.09493087
5.24453989]
Reg mean: 5.337868962878373
```

5.   Use the `regression_model_cv` function on the `LinearRegression()` model with 3 folds and then 6 folds, as shown in the following code snippet, for 3 folds:

```
regression_model_cv(LinearRegression(), k=3)
```

You may get something similar to the following output:

```
Reg rmse: [ 3.72504914 6.01655701 23.20863933]
Reg mean: 10.983415161090695
```

6.   Now, test the values for 6 folds:

```
regression_model_cv(LinearRegression(), k=6)
```

You may get something similar to the following output:

```
Reg rmse: [3.23879491 3.97041949 5.58329663 3.92861033
9.88399671 3.91442679]
Reg mean: 5.08659081080109
```

There is a significant discrepancy between the RMSE in the different folds. One reason is that we have a reasonably small dataset to begin with. Another reason is that some outliers may be causing problems in some of the folds. Going forward, we will keep five folds as our standard.

Regularization – Ridge and Lasso

Regularization is an important concept in ML; it's used to counteract overfitting. In the world of big data, it's easy to overfit data to the training set. When this happens, the model will often perform badly on the test set, as indicated by `mean_squared_error` or some other error.

You may wonder why a test set is kept aside at all. Wouldn't the most accurate ML model come from fitting the algorithm on all the data?

The answer, generally accepted by the ML community after research and experimentation, is no.

There are two main problems with fitting an ML model on all the data:

- There is no way to test the model on unseen data. ML models are powerful when they make good predictions on new data. Models are trained on known results, but they perform in the real world on data that has never been seen before. It's not vital to see how well a model fits known results (the training set), but it's absolutely crucial to see how well it performs on unseen data (the test set).

- The model may overfit the data. Models exist that may fit any set of data points perfectly. Consider the nine points in the following diagram. An eighth-degree polynomial exists that fits these points perfectly, but it's a poor predictor of the new data because it fails to pick up on general patterns:

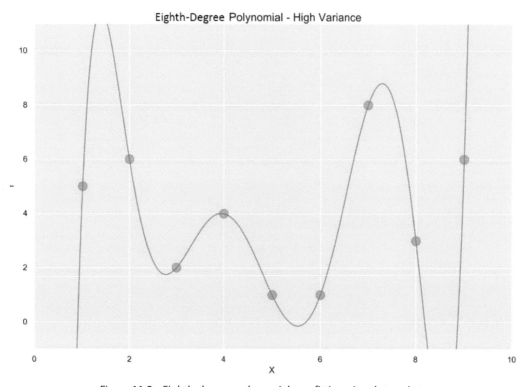

Figure 11.5 – Eighth-degree polynomial overfitting nine data points

There are many models and approaches to counteract overfitting. Let's go over a couple of linear models now:

- **Ridge** is a simple alternative to linear regression, designed to counteract overfitting. Ridge includes an L2 penalty term (L2 is based on Euclidean distance) that shrinks the linear coefficients based on their size. The coefficients are the weights—numbers that determine how influential each column is on the output. Larger weights carry greater penalties in Ridge.

- **Lasso** is another regularized alternative to linear regression. Lasso adds a penalty equal to the absolute value of the magnitude of coefficients. This L1 regularization (L1 is taxicab distance) can eliminate some column influence, but it's less widely used than Ridge on account of the L1 distance metric being less common than L2.

Let's look at an example to check how Ridge and Lasso perform on our Boston Housing dataset.

In this example, we perform regularization on the dataset using Ridge and Lasso to counteract overfitting. You can continue on the notebook from *Exercise 149 – using the cross_val_score function to get accurate results on the dataset*, to work on this example.

We begin by setting `Ridge()` as a parameter for `regression_model_cv`, as shown in the following code snippet:

```
from sklearn.linear_model import Ridge
regression_model_cv(Ridge())
```

The output is as follows:

```
Reg rmse: [3.52479283 4.72296032 5.54622438 8.00759231
5.26861171]
Reg mean: 5.414036309884279
```

Ridge has a comparable score to linear regression. This is not surprising because both algorithms use Euclidean distance, and the linear regression model is not overfitting the data by a significant amount.

Another basis of comparison is the worst score of the five. In Ridge, we obtained 8.00759 as the worst score. In linear regression, we obtained 23.20863933 as the worst score. This suggests that 23.20863933 is badly overfitting the training data. In Ridge, this overfitting is compensated.

Now, set `Lasso()` as the parameter for `regression_model_cv`:

```
from sklearn.linear_model import Lasso
regression_model_cv(Lasso())
```

You should get the following output:

```
Reg rmse: [4.712548 5.83933857 8.02996117 7.89925202
4.38674414]
Reg mean: 6.173568778640692
```

Whenever you're trying linear regression, it's often worth trying Lasso and Ridge as well since overfitting the data is common, and they only actually take a few lines of code to test. Lasso does not perform as well here because the L1 distance metric, taxicab distance, was not used in our model.

Regularization is an essential tool when implementing ML algorithms. Whenever you choose a particular model, be sure to research regularization methods to improve your results, as in the preceding example.

Now, let's get to know a developer's doubt. Although we have focused on overfitting the data, underfitting the data is also possible, right? Underfitting can occur if the model is a straight line, but a higher degree polynomial will fit the data better. By trying multiple models, you are more likely to find the optimal results.

So far, you have learned how to implement linear regression as an ML model. You have learned how to perform cross-validation to get more accurate results, and you have learned about using two additional models, Ridge and Lasso, to counteract overfitting.

Now that you understand how to build ML models using `scikit-learn`, let's take a look at some different kinds of models that will also work on regression but that will not underfit the data. In fact, some of these models are so good at picking up on nuances that they can overfit the data badly if you're not careful.

K-nearest neighbors, decision trees, and random forests

Are there other ML algorithms, besides `LinearRegression()`, that are suitable for the Boston Housing dataset? Absolutely. There are many regressors in the `scikit-learn` library that may be used. Regressors are a class of ML algorithms that are suitable for continuous target values. In addition to linear regression, Ridge, and Lasso, we can try k-nearest neighbors, decision trees, and random forests. These models perform well on a wide range of datasets. Let's try them out and analyze them individually.

K-nearest neighbors

The idea behind **k-nearest neighbors** (**KNN**) is straightforward. When choosing the output of a row with an unknown label, the prediction is the same as the output of its k-nearest neighbors, where k may be any whole number.

For instance, let's say that $k=3$. Given an unknown label, we take n columns for this row and place them in n-dimensional space. Then, we look for the three closest points. These points already have labels. We take the average of the three points for our new point; the value of the new point is determined by its three nearest neighbors.

KNN is commonly used for classification since classification is based on grouping values, but it can be applied to regression as well. When determining the value of a home—for instance, in our Boston Housing dataset—it makes sense to compare the values of homes in a similar location, with a similar number of bedrooms, a similar amount of square footage, and so on.

You can always choose the number of neighbors for the algorithm and adjust it accordingly. The number of neighbors denoted here is k, which is also called a **hyperparameter**. In ML, the model parameters are derived during training, whereas the hyperparameters are chosen in advance.

Fine-tuning hyperparameters is an essential task to master when building ML models. Learning the ins and outs of hyperparameter tuning takes time, practice, and experimentation. You will gain essential practice later in this chapter.

Exercise 150 – using k-nearest neighbors to find the median value of the dataset

The goal of this exercise is to use k-nearest neighbors to predict the optimal median value of homes in Boston. We will use the same function, `regression_model_cv`, with an input of `KNeighborsRegressor()`. Proceed as follows:

1. Continue with the same Jupyter Notebook from the previous exercise, *Exercise 149 – using the cross_val_score function to get accurate results on the dataset*.

2. Set and import `KNeighborsRegressor()` as the parameter on the `regression_model_cv` function:

    ```
    from sklearn.neighbors import KNeighborsRegressor
    regression_model_cv(KNeighborsRegressor())
    ```

    The output is as follows:

    ```
    Reg rmse: [ 8.24568226 8.81322798 10.58043836 8.85643441
    5.98100069]
    Reg mean: 8.495356738515685
    ```

    K-nearest neighbors did not perform as well as `LinearRegression()`, but it performed respectably. Recall that `rmse` stands for root mean squared error. So, the mean error is about `8.50` (or 85,000 since the units are tens of thousands of dollars).

    We can change the number of neighbors to see whether we can get better results. The default number of neighbors is 5. Let's change the number of neighbors to 4, 7, and 10.

3. Now, change the `n_neighbors` hyperparameter to 4, 7, and 10. For 4 neighbors, enter the following code:

    ```
    regression_model_cv(KNeighborsRegressor(n_neighbors=4))
    ```

    The output is as follows:

    ```
    Reg rmse: [ 8.44659788 8.99814547 10.97170231 8.86647969
    5.72114135]
    Reg mean: 8.600813339223432
    ```

    Change `n_neighbors` to 7:

    ```
    regression_model_cv(KNeighborsRegressor(n_neighbors=7))
    ```

    The output is as follows:

    ```
    Reg rmse: [ 7.99710601 8.68309183 10.66332898 8.90261573
    5.51032355]
    Reg mean: 8.351293217401393
    ```

Change n_neighbors to 10:

```
regression_model_cv(KNeighborsRegressor(n_neighbors=10))
```

The output is as follows:

```
Reg rmse:  [ 7.47549287  8.62914556  10.69543822  8.91330686
6.52982222]
Reg mean:  8.448641147609868
```

The best results so far come from 7 neighbors. But how do we know whether 7 neighbors give us the best results? How many different scenarios do we have to check?

scikit-learn provides a nice option to check a wide range of hyperparameters: GridSearchCV. The idea behind GridSearchCV is to use cross-validation to check all the possible values in a grid. The value in the grid that gives the best result is then accepted as a hyperparameter.

Exercise 151 – K-nearest neighbors with GridSearchCV to find the optimal number of neighbors

The goal of this exercise is to use GridSearchCV to find the optimal number of neighbors for k-nearest neighbors to predict the median housing value in Boston. In the previous exercise, if you recall, we used only three neighbor values. Here, we will increase the number using GridSearchCV. Proceed as follows:

1. Continue with the Jupyter Notebook from the previous exercise.

2. Import GridSearchCV, as shown in the following code snippet:

```
from sklearn.model_selection import GridSearchCV
```

3. Now, choose a grid. A grid is a range of numbers—in this case, neighbors—that will be checked. Set up a hyperparameter grid for between 1 and 20 neighbors:

```
neighbors = np.linspace(1, 20, 20)
```

We achieve this with np.linspace(1, 20, 20), where 1 is the first number, the first 20 is the last number, and the second 20 in the brackets is the number of intervals to count.

4. Convert floats to int (required by knn):

```
k = neighbors.astype(int)
```

5. Now, place the grid in a dictionary, as shown in the following code snippet:

```
param_grid = {'n_neighbors': k}
```

6. Build the model for each neighbor:

```
knn = KNeighborsRegressor()
```

7. Instantiate the `GridSearchCV` object, `knn_tuned`:

```
knn_tuned = GridSearchCV(knn, param_grid, cv=5,
scoring='neg_mean_squared_error')
```

8. Fit `knn_tuned` to the data using `.fit`:

```
knn_tuned.fit(X, y)
```

9. Finally, you print the best parameter results, as shown in the following code snippet:

```
k = knn_tuned.best_params_
print("Best n_neighbors: {}".format(k))
score = knn_tuned.best_score_
rsm = np.sqrt(-score)
print("Best score: {}".format(rsm))
```

The output is as follows:

```
Best n_neighbors: {'n_neighbors': 7}
Best score: 8.516767055977628
```

Figure 11.6 – Output showing the best score using n_neighbors after GridSearchCV

It appears that 7 neighbors gave the best results after all.

Now, moving on, let's see whether we can improve our results by using tree-based algorithms.

Decision trees and random forests

You may be familiar with the game *Twenty Questions*. It's a game in which someone is asked to think of something or someone that the other person will try to guess. The questioner asks binary *yes* or *no* questions, gradually narrowing down the search in order to determine exactly who or what the other person was thinking of.

Twenty Questions is a decision tree. Every time a question is asked, there are two possible branches that the tree may take depending upon the answer. For every new question, new branching occurs, until the branches end at a prediction, called a leaf.

Here is a mini-decision tree that predicts whether someone makes over 50K:

DECISION TREE – IMAGE

Census Dataset - max_depth=2

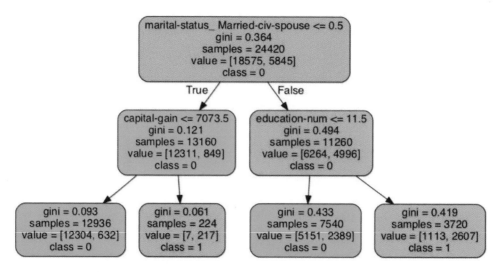

Figure 11.7 – Decision tree sample on the Titanic incident

This decision tree starts by determining whether the person is married. If the value is 0, presumably not married, the condition at the top of the decision tree is met, and you follow the `True` branch on the left in *Figure 11.7*. The next question is about the person's capital gain. If the person does not make less than 7073.5, the `False` branch on the right is followed and you end up at a leaf, where the given class is 1 with a value of 7 people who make less than 50K and 217 who make more than 50K.

Decision trees are very good ML algorithms, but they are prone to overfitting. A random forest is an ensemble of decision trees. Random forests consistently outperform decision trees because their predictions generalize to data much better. A random forest may consist of hundreds of decision trees.

A random forest is a great ML algorithm to try on almost any dataset. Random forests work well with both regression and classification, and they often perform well out of the box.

Let's try decision trees and random forests on our data.

Exercise 152 – building decision trees and random forests

The goal of this exercise is to use decision trees and random forests to predict median house values in Boston. Let's look at the steps for this exercise:

1. Continue with the same Jupyter Notebook from the previous exercise.

2. Use `DecisionTreeRegressor()` as the input for `regression_model_cv`. Include a random state set equal to 0 since decision trees have some randomness built in:

```
from sklearn import tree
regression_model_cv(tree.DecisionTreeRegressor(random_
state=0))
```

The output is as follows:

```
Reg rmse: [3.7647936   7.26184759 7.78346186 6.48142428
4.79234165]
Reg mean:  6.016773796161434
```

3. Use `RandomForestRegressor()` as the input for `regression_model_cv`:

```
from sklearn.ensemble import RandomForestRegressor
regression_model_cv(RandomForestRegressor(random_
state=0))
```

The output is as follows:

```
Reg rmse: [3.21859405 3.76199072 4.96431026 6.55950671
3.7700697 ]
Reg mean:  4.454894289804201
```

As you can see, the random forest regressor gives the best results yet. Let's see whether we can improve these results by examining random forest hyperparameters.

Random forest hyperparameters

Random forests have a lot of hyperparameters. Instead of going over them all, we will highlight the most important ones:

*   `n_jobs(default=None)`: The number of jobs has to do with internal processing. None means 1. It's ideal to set `n_jobs = -1` to permit the use of all processors. Although this does not improve the accuracy of the model, it may improve the speed.

*   `n_estimators(default=100)`: The number of trees in the forest. The more trees, the better. The more trees, the more RAM is required. It's worth increasing this number until the algorithm moves too slowly. Although 1,000,000 trees may give better results than 1,000, the gain might be small enough to be negligible. A good starting point is 100, and 500 if time permits.

- `max_depth(default=None)`: The maximum depth of the trees in the forest. The deeper the trees, the more information is captured about the data, but the more prone the trees are to overfitting. When set to the default `max_depth` value of `None`, there are no limitations, and each tree goes as deep as necessary. The max depth may be reduced to a smaller number of branches.

- `min_samples_split(default=2)`: This is the minimum number of samples required for a new branch or split to occur. This number can be increased to constrain the trees as they require more samples to make a decision.

- `min_samples_leaf(default=1)`: This is the same as `min_samples_split`, except it's the minimum number of samples at the leaves or the base of the tree. By increasing this number, the branch will stop splitting when it reaches this parameter.

- `max_features(default="auto")`: The number of features to consider when looking for the best split. The default for regression is to consider the total number of columns. For the classification of random forests, `sqrt` is recommended.

We could try `GridSearchCV` on a range of these hyperparameters to see whether we can find a better combination than the defaults, but checking every possible combination of hyperparameters could reach the order of thousands or millions and take way too long to build.

`sklearn` provides `RandomizedSearchCV` to check a wide range of hyperparameters. Instead of exhaustively going through a list, `RandomizedSearchCV` will check 10 random combinations and return the best results.

Exercise 153 – tuning a random forest using RandomizedSearchCV

The goal of this exercise is to tune a random forest to improve the median house value predictions for Boston. This will be done with the following steps:

1. Continue with the same Jupyter Notebook from *Exercise 152 – building decision trees and random forests*.

2. Use `RandomizedSearchCV` to look for a better combination of random forest hyperparameters than the defaults:

```
from sklearn.model_selection import RandomizedSearchCV
```

3. Set up the hyperparameter grid using `max_depth`, as shown in the following code snippet:

```
param_grid = {'max_depth': [None, 1, 2, 3, 4, 5, 6, 8,
10, 15, 20],
                'min_samples_split': [2, 3, 4, 5, 6],
```

```
                              'min_samples_leaf': [1, 2, 3, 4, 6, 8],
                              'max_features': [1.0, 0.9, 0.8, 0.7, 0.6,
         0.5, 0.4]}
```

4. Initialize the random forest regressor:

```
reg = RandomForestRegressor(n_jobs=-1, random_state=0)
```

5. Define the RandomizedSearchCV object as reg_tuned:

```
reg_tuned = RandomizedSearchCV(reg, param_grid, cv=5,
scoring='neg_mean_squared_error', random_state=0)
```

6. Fit reg_tuned to the data:

```
reg_tuned.fit(X, y)
```

7. Now, print the tuned parameters and score:

```
p = reg_tuned.best_params_
print("Best params: {}".format(p))
score = reg_tuned.best_score_
rsm = np.sqrt(-score)
print("Best score: {}".format(rsm))
```

The output is as follows:

```
Best params: {'min_samples_split': 5, 'min_samples_leaf':
2, 'max_features': 0.7, 'max_depth': 10}
Best score: 4.465574177819689
```

8. Keep in mind that with RandomizedSearchCV, there is no guarantee that the hyperparameters will produce the best results. Although the randomized search did well, it did not perform as well as the defaults. However, let's compare the results using 500 trees with the tuned model previously, and with the rest of the hyperparameters set to their defaults. Now, run a random forest regressor with n_jobs=-1 and n_estimators=500:

```
regression_model_cv(RandomForestRegressor(n_jobs=-1, n_
estimators=500))
```

The output is as follows:

```
Reg rmse: [3.17084646 3.7593559  4.8534035  6.49732743
3.94043004]
Reg mean: 4.4442726650747915
```

9. Now, run a random forest regressor using the tuned hyperparameters from the output in *step 6*:

```
regression_model_cv(RandomForestRegressor(n_jobs=-1, n_
estimators=500, random_state=0, min_samples_split=5, min_
samples_leaf=2, max_features=0.7, max_depth=10))
```

The output is as follows:

```
Reg rmse: [3.18498898 3.59234342 4.66618434 6.43013587
3.81099639]
Reg mean: 4.336929799775126
```

The is the best score yet. One reason is that many tuned parameters are designed to prevent overfitting, so it's often the case that scores will improve with more iterations because they give the algorithm more time to learn from the data.

> **Note**
>
> Increasing n_estimators generally may produce more accurate results, but the model takes longer to build.

Hyperparameters are a primary key to building excellent ML models. Anyone with basic ML training can build ML models using default hyperparameters. Using GridSearchCV and RandomizedSearchCV to fine-tune hyperparameters to create more efficient models distinguishes advanced practitioners from beginners.

Classification models

The Boston Housing dataset was great for regression because the target column took on continuous values without limit. There are many cases when the target column takes on one or two values, such as TRUE or FALSE, or possibly a grouping of three or more values, such as RED, BLUE, or GREEN. When the target column may be split into distinct categories, the group of ML models that you should try is referred to as **classification**.

To make things interesting, let's load a new dataset used to detect pulsar stars in outer space. Go to https://packt.live/33SD0IM and click on **Data Folder**. Then, click on **HTRU2.zip**, as shown:

Index of /ml/machine-learning-databases/00372

- Parent Directory
- HTRU2.zip

Apache/2.4.6 (CentOS) OpenSSL/1.0.2k-fips SVN/1.7.14 Phusion_Passenger/4.0.53 mod_perl/2.0.11 Perl/v5.16.3 Server at archive.ics.uci.edu Port 443

Figure 11.8 – Dataset directory on the UCI website

The dataset consists of 17,898 potential pulsar stars in space. But what are these pulsars? Pulsar stars rotate very quickly, so they have periodic light patterns. Radio frequency interference and noise, however, are attributes that make pulsars very hard to detect. This dataset contains 16,259 non-pulsars and 1,639 real pulsars.

> **Note**
>
> The dataset is from Dr. Robert Lyon, University of Manchester, School of Physics and Astronomy, Alan Turing Building, Manchester M13 9PL, United Kingdom, Robert.lyon'@'manchester.ac.uk, 2017.

The columns include information about an integrated pulse profile and a DM-SNR curve. All pulsars produce a unique pattern of emissions, commonly known as their "pulse profile". A pulse profile is similar to a fingerprint, but it is not consistent like a pulsar rotational period. An integrated pulse profile consists of a matrix of an array of continuous values describing the pulse intensity and phase of the pulsar. **DM** stands for **Dispersion Measure**, a constant that relates the frequency of light to the extra time required to reach the observer, and **SNR** stands for **Signal to Noise Ratio**, which relates how well an object has been measured compared to its background noise.

Here is the official list of columns in the dataset:

- Mean of the integrated profile
- Standard deviation of the integrated profile
- Excess kurtosis of the integrated profile
- Skewness of the integrated profile
- Mean of the DM-SNR curve
- Standard deviation of the DM-SNR curve
- Excess kurtosis of the DM-SNR curve
- Skewness of the DM-SNR curve
- Class

In this dataset, potential pulsars have already been classified as pulsars and non-pulsars by the astronomy community. The goal here is to see whether ML can detect patterns within the data to correctly classify new potential pulsars that emerge.

The methods that you learn for this topic will be directly applicable to a wide range of classification problems, including spam classifiers, user churn in markets, quality control, product identification, and others.

Exercise 154 – preparing the pulsar dataset and checking for null values

The goal of this exercise is to prepare the pulsar dataset for ML. The steps are as follows:

1. Open a new Jupyter Notebook in the same folder as your pulsar data file.

2. Import the libraries, load the data, and display the first five rows, as shown in the following code snippet:

```
import pandas as pd
import numpy as np
df = pd.read_csv('HTRU_2.csv')
df.head()
```

The output is as follows:

	140.5625	55.68378214	-0.234571412	-0.699648398	3.199832776	19.11042633	7.975531794	74.24222492	0
0	102.507812	58.882430	0.465318	-0.515088	1.677258	14.860146	10.576487	127.393580	0
1	103.015625	39.341649	0.323328	1.051164	3.121237	21.744669	7.735822	63.171909	0
2	136.750000	57.178449	-0.068415	-0.636238	3.642977	20.959280	6.896499	53.593661	0
3	88.726562	40.672225	0.600866	1.123492	1.178930	11.468720	14.269573	252.567306	0
4	93.570312	46.698114	0.531905	0.416721	1.636288	14.545074	10.621748	131.394004	0

Figure 11.9 – The first five rows of the pulsar dataset

Looks interesting, and problematic. Notice that the column headers appear to be in another row. It's impossible to analyze data without knowing what the columns are supposed to be, right?

Note that the last column is all 0s in the DataFrame. This suggests that this is the Class column, which is our target column. When detecting the presence of something—in this case, pulsar stars—it's common to use a 1 for positive identification, and a 0 for negative identification.

Since Class is last in the list, let's assume that the columns are given in the correct order presented in the Attribute Information list. The easiest way forward is to reload the data with no header and then change the column headers to match the attribute list.

3. Now, reload the data with no header, change the column headers to match the official list, and print the first five rows, as shown in the following code snippet:

```
df = pd.read_csv('HTRU_2.csv', header=None)
df.columns = [['Mean of integrated profile', 'Standard
deviation of integrated profile','Excess kurtosis
of integrated profile', 'Skewness of integrated
profile','Mean of DM-SNR curve', 'Standard deviation
of DM-SNR curve','Excess kurtosis of DM-SNR curve',
```

```
'Skewness of DM-SNR curve', 'Class' ]]
df.head()
```

The output is as follows:

	Mean of integrated profile	Standard deviation of integrated profile	Excess kurtosis of integrated profile	Skewness of integrated profile	Mean of DM-SNR curve	Standard deviation of DM-SNR curve	Excess kurtosis of DM-SNR curve	Skewness of DM-SNR curve	Class
0	140.562500	55.683782	-0.234571	-0.699648	3.199833	19.110426	7.975532	74.242225	0
1	102.507812	58.882430	0.465318	-0.515088	1.677258	14.860146	10.576487	127.393580	0
2	103.015625	39.341649	0.323328	1.051164	3.121237	21.744669	7.735822	63.171909	0
3	136.750000	57.178449	-0.068415	-0.636238	3.642977	20.959280	6.896499	53.593661	0
4	88.726562	40.672225	0.600866	1.123492	1.178930	11.468720	14.269573	252.567306	0

Figure 11.10 – Pulsar dataset with correct column headings

4. Now, let's find the information in the dataset using .info():

```
df.info()
```

You should get the following output:

```
<class 'pandas.core.frame.DataFrame'>
RangeIndex: 17898 entries, 0 to 17897
Data columns (total 9 columns):
 #   Column                                      Non-Null Count  Dtype
---  ------                                      --------------  -----
 0   (Mean of integrated profile,)               17898 non-null  float64
 1   (Standard deviation of integrated profile,) 17898 non-null  float64
 2   (Excess kurtosis of integrated profile,)    17898 non-null  float64
 3   (Skewness of integrated profile,)           17898 non-null  float64
 4   (Mean of DM-SNR curve,)                     17898 non-null  float64
 5   (Standard deviation of DM-SNR curve,)       17898 non-null  float64
 6   (Excess kurtosis of DM-SNR curve,)          17898 non-null  float64
 7   (Skewness of DM-SNR curve,)                 17898 non-null  float64
 8   (Class,)                                    17898 non-null  int64
dtypes: float64(8), int64(1)
memory usage: 1.2 MB
```

Figure 11.11 – Information based on the pulsar dataset

We can infer that there are no null values since all columns give a non-null count of 17898, which is the total number of rows. If there were null values, we would need to eliminate the rows or fill them in by taking the mean, the median, the mode, or another value from the columns, as explained in *Chapter 10, Data Analytics with pandas and NumPy*.

When it comes to preparing data for ML, it's essential to have clean, numerical data with no null values. Further data analysis is often warranted, depending on the goal at hand. If the goal is simply to try out some models and check them for accuracy, it's fine to go ahead. If the goal is to uncover deep insights about the data, further statistical analysis (as introduced in the previous chapter) is always warranted. Now that we have all this basic information, we can proceed ahead with the same notebook file.

Logistic regression

When it comes to datasets that classify points, logistic regression is one of the most popular and successful ML algorithms. Logistic regression utilizes the `sigmoid` function to determine whether points should approach one value or the other. As the following diagram indicates, it's a good idea to classify the target values as 0 and 1 when utilizing logistic regression:

SIGMOID EQUATION

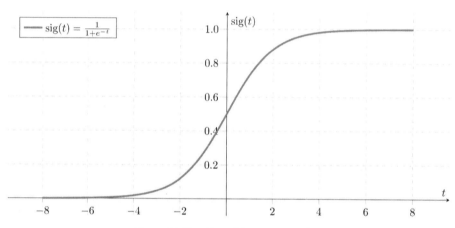

Figure 11.12 – Sigmoid curve on a plot

In the pulsar dataset, the values are already classified as 0s and 1s. If the dataset were labeled as Red and Blue, converting them in advance to 0 and 1 would be essential (you will practice converting categorical to numerical values in the activity at the end of this chapter).

The sigmoid curve in *Figure 11.12* approaches 1 from the left and 0 from the right, without ever reaching 0 or 1. In this respect, 0 and 1 function as horizontal asymptotes. Basically, every positive x value is given an output of 1, and every negative x value is given an output of 0. Furthermore, the higher up the graph, the higher the probability of a 1, and the lower down the graph, the higher the probability of 0.

Let's see how logistic regression works in action by using a similar function as before.

Note that by default, classifiers use percentage accuracy as the score output.

Exercise 155 – using logistic regression to predict data accuracy

The goal of this exercise is to use logistic regression to predict the classification of pulsar stars. The steps are set out here:

1. Import `cross_val_score` and `LogisticRegression`:

```
from sklearn.model_selection import cross_val_score
from sklearn.linear_model import LogisticRegression
```

2. Set up X and y matrices to store the predictors and response variables, respectively:

```
X = df.iloc[:, 0:8]
y = df.iloc[:, 8]
```

3. Write a classifier function that takes a model as its input:

```
def clf_model(model):
```

4. Create a `clf` classifier, as shown in the following code snippet:

```
clf = model
scores = cross_val_score(clf, X, y)
print('Scores:', scores)
print('Mean score:', scores.mean())
```

5. Run the `clf_model` function with `LogisticRegression()` as the input. Be sure to set the `max_iter` parameter equal to 1000 so that the algorithm has enough time to converge, otherwise you may get an error. Basically, `max_iter` allows you to increase the maximum number of iterations for the algorithm to learn the best weights to optimize results:

```
clf_model(LogisticRegression(max_iter=1000))
```

The output is as follows:

```
Scores: [0.97486034 0.97988827 0.98184358 0.97736798
0.9782062 ]
Mean score: 0.9784332723007113
```

These numbers represent accuracy. A mean score of 0.978433 means that the logistic regression model is classifying 97.8% of pulsars correctly.

Logistic regression is very different from linear regression. Logistic regression uses the Sigmoid function to classify all instances into one group or the other. Generally speaking, all cases that are above 0.5 are classified as a 1, and all cases that fall below 0.5 are classified as a 0, with decimals that are close to 1 more likely to be a 1, and decimals that are close to 0 more likely to be a 0. Linear regression, by contrast, finds a straight line that minimizes the error between the straight line and the individual points. Logistic regression classifies all points into two groups; all new points will fall into one of these groups. By contrast, linear regression finds a line of best fit; all new points may fall anywhere on the line and take on any value.

Other classifiers

We used KNN, decision trees, and random forests as regressors before. This time, we need to implement them as classifiers. For instance, there is `RandomForestRegressor`, and there is `RandomForestClassifier`. Both are random forests, but they are implemented differently to meet the output of the data. The general setup is the same, but the output is different. In the next section, we will have a look at Naive Bayes.

Naive Bayes

Naive Bayes is a model based on Bayes' theorem, a famous probability theorem based on a conditional probability that assumes independent events. Similarly, Naive Bayes assumes independent attributes or columns. The mathematical details of Naive Bayes are beyond the scope of this book, but we can still apply it to our dataset.

There is a small family of ML algorithms based on Naive Bayes. The one that we will use here is `GaussianNB`. Gaussian Naive Bayes assumes that the likelihood of features is Gaussian. Other options that you may consider trying is including `MultinomialNB`, used for multinomial distributed data (such as text), and `ComplementNB`, an adaptation of `MultinomialNB` that is used for imbalanced datasets.

Let's try Naive Bayes, in addition to the KNN, decision tree, and random forest classifiers mentioned previously.

Exercise 156 – using GaussianNB, KNeighborsClassifier, DecisionTreeClassifier, and RandomForestClassifier to predict the accuracy of our dataset

The goal of this exercise is to predict pulsars using a variety of classifiers, including `GaussianNB`, `KNeighborsClassifier`, `DecisionTreeClassifier`, and `RandomForestClassifier`. Let's go through the steps:

1. Begin this exercise on the same notebook file from the previous exercise.

2. Run the `clf_model` function with `GaussianNB()` as the input:

```
from sklearn.naive_bayes import GaussianNB
clf_model(GaussianNB())
```

The output is as follows:

```
Scores: [0.96061453 0.92374302 0.94273743 0.92847164
0.96451523]
Mean score: 0.9440163679814436
```

3. Now, run the `clf_model` function with `KNeighborsClassifier()` as the input:

```
from sklearn.neighbors import KNeighborsClassifier
clf_model(KNeighborsClassifier())
```

The output is as follows:

```
Scores: [0.96955307 0.96927374 0.97318436
0.9706622  0.97289746]
Mean score: 0.9711141653437728
```

4. Run the `clf_model` function with `DecisionTreeClassifier()` as the input:

```
from sklearn.tree import DecisionTreeClassifier
clf_model(DecisionTreeClassifier(random_state=0))
```

The output is as follows:

```
Scores: [0.96843575 0.96424581 0.96871508 0.96227997
0.96954457]
Mean score: 0.9666442360073738
```

> **Note**
> The output values may differ from the values mentioned in the book.

5. Run the `clf_model` function with `RandomForestClassifier()` as the input:

```
from sklearn.ensemble import RandomForestClassifier
clf_model(RandomForestClassifier(random_state=0))
```

The output is as follows:

```
Scores: [0.97709497 0.98324022 0.98072626 0.97485331
0.97848561]
Mean score: 0.978880074800083
```

All classifiers have achieved between 94% and 98% accuracy. It's unusual for this many classifiers to all perform this well. There must be clear patterns within the data, or something is going on behind the scenes.

You may also wonder how to know when to use these classifiers. The bottom line is that whenever you have a classification problem, meaning that the data has a target column with a finite number of options (such as three kinds of wine), many classifiers are worth trying. Naive Bayes is known to work well with text data, and random forests are known to work well generally. New ML algorithms are often being developed to handle special cases. Practice and research will help to uncover more nuanced cases over time.

Confusion matrix

When discussing classification, it's important to know whether the dataset is imbalanced, as we had some doubts about the results from *Exercise 156 – using GaussianNB, KNeighborsClassifier, DecisionTreeClassifier, and RandomForestClassifier to predict the accuracy of our dataset*. An imbalance occurs if the majority of data points have one label rather than another.

Exercise 157 – finding the pulsar percentage from the dataset

The goal of this exercise is to count the percentage of pulsars in our dataset. We will use the `Class` column. Although we have primarily been using `df['Class']` as a way to reference a particular column, `df.Class` will work as well (except in limited cases, such as setting values). Follow these steps:

1. Begin this exercise in the same notebook you used in the previous exercise.

2. Use the `count.()` method on `df.Class` to obtain the number of potential pulsars:

   ```
   df.Class.count()
   ```

   The output is as follows:

   ```
   Class     17898
   dtype: int64
   ```

3. Use the `.count()` method on `df[df.Class == 1]` to obtain the number of actual pulsars:

   ```
   df[df.Class == 1].Class.count()
   ```

   The output is as follows:

   ```
   Class     1639
   dtype: int64
   ```

4. Divide *step 2* by *step 1* to obtain the percentage of pulsars:

   ```
   df[df.Class == 1].Class.count()/df.Class.count()
   ```

The output is as follows:

```
Class     0.091574
dtype: float64
```

The results show that 0.09158 or 9% of the data is pulsars. The other 91% is not pulsars. This means that it's very easy to make an ML algorithm in this case with 91% accuracy by predicting that every sample (row) is not a pulsar.

Imagine that the situation is even more extreme and we are trying to detect exoplanets, and our dataset has only classified 1% of the data as exoplanets. This means that 99% are not exoplanets. This also means that it's super easy to develop an algorithm with 99% accuracy! Just claim that everything is not an exoplanet!

A confusion matrix was designed to reveal the truth behind imbalanced datasets, as illustrated here:

		True condition	
	Total population	Condition positive	Condition negative
Predicted condition	Predicted condition positive	True positive	False positive, Type I error
	Predicted condition negative	False negative, Type II error	True negative

Figure 11.13 – Overview of a confusion matrix

As you can see from *Figure 11.13*, the confusion matrix is designed to show you what happened to each of the outputs. Every output will fall into one of four boxes, labeled **True positive**, **False positive**, **False negative**, and **True negative**, as shown here:

True positive	Prediction positive and label positive
True negative	Prediction negative and label negative
False positive	Prediction positive but label negative
False negative	Prediction negative but label positive

Figure 11.14 – Prediction of the confusion matrix based on conditions

Consider the following example. This is a confusion matrix for the decision tree classifier we used earlier. You will see the code to obtain this shortly. First, we want to focus on the interpretation:

```
[[3985   91]
 [  65  334]]
```

Figure 11.15 – Confusion matrix

In `sklearn`, the default order is 0, 1. This means that the zeros or negative values are actually listed first. So, in effect, the confusion matrix is interpreted as follows:

```
           0      1
0  [[3985    91]
1  [   65   334]]
```

Figure 11.16 – Confusion matrix with the default orders

In this particular case, 3985 non-pulsars have been identified correctly, and 334 pulsars have been identified correctly. 91 in the upper-right corner indicates that the model classified 91 pulsars incorrectly, and 65 in the bottom-left corner indicates that 65 non-pulsars were misclassified as pulsars.

It can be challenging to interpret a confusion matrix, especially when positives and negatives do not always line up in the same columns. Fortunately, a classification report may be displayed along with it.

A classification report includes the total number of labels, along with various percentages to help make sense of the numbers and analyze the data.

Here is a classification report with the confusion matrix for the decision tree classifier:

```
Confusion Matrix:  [[3985    91]
                    [   65   334]]


Classification Report:
                 precision recall   f1-score    support

         0         0.98      0.98       0.98       4076
         1         0.79      0.84       0.81        399

avg / total        0.97      0.97       0.97       4475
```

Figure 11.17 – Classification report on the confusion matrix

In the classification report, the columns on the two ends are the easiest to interpret. On the far right, `support` is the number of labels in the dataset. It matches the indexed column on the far left, labeled 0 and 1. Support reveals that there are 4,076 non-pulsars (0s) and 399 pulsars (1s). This number is less than the total because we are only looking at the test set.

Precision is the true positives divided by all the positive predictions. In the case of 0s, this is 3985 / (3985 + 65), and in the case of 1s, this is 334 / (334 + 91).

Recall is the true positives divided by all the positive labels. For 0s, this is 3985 / (3985 + 91), and for 1s, this is 334 / (334 + 65).

The **f1-score** is the harmonic mean of the precision and recall scores. Note that the f1 scores are very different for the zeros than the ones.

The most important number in the classification report depends on what you are trying to accomplish. Consider the case of the pulsars. Is the goal to identify as many potential pulsars as possible? If so, a lower precision is okay, provided that the recall is higher. Or, perhaps an investigation would be expensive. In this case, a higher precision than recall would be desirable.

Exercise 158 – confusion matrix and classification report for the pulsar dataset

The goal of this exercise is to build a function that displays the confusion matrix along with the classification report. The following steps need to be executed for this:

1. Continue on the same notebook file from the previous exercise.

2. Now, import the `confusion_matrix` and the `classification_report` libraries:

```
from sklearn.metrics import classification_report
from sklearn.metrics import confusion_matrix
from sklearn.model_selection import train_test_split
```

To use the confusion matrix and classification report, we need a designated test set using `train_test_split`.

3. Split the data into a training set and a test set:

```
X_train, X_test, y_train, y_test = train_test_split(X, y,
test_size=0.25, random_state=0)
```

Now, build a function called `confusion` that takes a model as the input and prints the confusion matrix and classification report. The `clf` classifier should be the output:

```
def confusion(model):
```

4. Create a `model` classifier:

```
clf = model
```

5. Fit the classifier to the data:

```
clf.fit(X_train, y_train)
```

6. Predict the labels of the `y_pred` test set:

```
y_pred = clf.predict(X_test)
```

7. Compute and print the confusion matrix:

```
print(confusion_matrix(y_test, y_pred))
```

8. Compute and print the classification report:

```
print(classification_report(y_test, y_pred))
return clf
```

Now, let's try the function on our various classifiers.

9. Run the `confusion()` function with `LogisticRegression` as the input:

```
confusion(LogisticRegression(max_iter=1000))
```

The output is as follows:

```
[[4095   20]
 [  63  297]]
               precision    recall  f1-score   support

           0       0.98      1.00      0.99      4115
           1       0.94      0.82      0.88       360

    accuracy                           0.98      4475
   macro avg       0.96      0.91      0.93      4475
weighted avg       0.98      0.98      0.98      4475
```

Figure 11.18 – Output of the confusion matrix and classification report on LogisticRegression

As you can see, the precision of classifying actual pulsars (the 1 in the classification report) is 94%. Perhaps more significantly, the f1-score, which is the average of the precision and recall scores, is 98% overall, but only 88% for the pulsars (the 1s).

10. Now, run the `confusion()` function with `KNeighborsClassifier()` as the input:

```
confusion(KNeighborsClassifier())
```

The output is as follows:

```
[[4077   38]
 [  69  291]]
               precision    recall  f1-score   support

           0       0.98      0.99      0.99      4115
           1       0.88      0.81      0.84       360

    accuracy                           0.98      4475
   macro avg       0.93      0.90      0.92      4475
weighted avg       0.98      0.98      0.98      4475
```

Figure 11.19 – Output of the confusion matrix and classification report on KNeighborsClassifier

They're all high scores overall, but the 81% recall and 84% f1-score for the pulsars are a little lacking.

11. Run the `confusion()` function with `GaussianNB()` as the input:

```
confusion(GaussianNB())
```

The output is as follows:

```
[[3946  169]
 [  52  308]]
              precision     recall  f1-score   support

           0       0.99       0.96      0.97      4115
           1       0.65       0.86      0.74       360

    accuracy                            0.95      4475
   macro avg       0.82       0.91      0.85      4475
weighted avg       0.96       0.95      0.95      4475
```

Figure 11.20 – Output of the confusion matrix and classification report on GaussianNB

In this particular case, the 65% precision of correctly identifying pulsars is not up to par.

12. Run the `confusion()` function with `RandomForestClassifer()` as the input:

```
confusion(RandomForestClassifier())
```

The output is as follows:

```
[[4095   20]
 [  59  301]]
              precision     recall  f1-score   support

           0       0.99       1.00      0.99      4115
           1       0.94       0.84      0.88       360

    accuracy                            0.98      4475
   macro avg       0.96       0.92      0.94      4475
weighted avg       0.98       0.98      0.98      4475
```

Figure 11.21 – Output of the confusion matrix and classification report on RandomForestClassifier

We've now finished this exercise, and you can see that, in this case, the f1-score of 88% for the random forest classifier is the highest that we have seen along with logistic regression.

Boosting algorithms

Random forests are a type of bagging algorithm. Bagging combines bootstrapping, selecting individual samples with replacement and aggregation, and combining all models into one ensemble. In practice, a random forest builds individual trees by randomly selecting rows of data, called samples, before combining (aggregating) all trees into one ensemble. Bagging algorithms are as good as the trees that make them up.

A comparable ML algorithm is boosting. The idea behind boosting is to transform a weak learner into a strong learner by modifying the weights for the rows that the learner got wrong. A weak learner may have an error of 49%, hardly better than a coin flip. A strong learner, by contrast, may have an error rate of 1 or 2%. With enough iterations, weak learners can be transformed into very strong learners.

Unlike bagging algorithms, boosting algorithms can improve over time. After the initial model in a booster, called the base learner, all subsequent models train on the errors of the previous model with the goal of improving the overall results.

The early success of boosting models caught the attention of the ML community. In 2003, Yoav Freund and Robert Schapire won the 2003 Gödel Prize for developing **AdaBoost**, short for **Adaptive Boosting**. Other boosters soon followed, including **XGBoost**, short for Extreme **Gradient Boosting**, which won the Kaggle competition confirming the existence of the Higgs boson. Microsoft more recently developed **LightGBM**, short for **Light Gradient Boosting Machine**, which has also won many Kaggle competitions.

LightGBM is not part of the `sklearn` library, so we will not cover it here. AdaBoost, however, is included in the `sklearn` library, and a `sklearn` wrapper for XGBoost was developed in 2019. You will build AdaBoost and XGBoost models to close out this chapter.

AdaBoost

As with many boosting algorithms, AdaBoost has both a classifier and a regressor. AdaBoost adjusts weak learners toward instances that were previously misclassified. If one learner is 45% correct, the sign can be flipped to become 55% correct. By switching the signs of negatives to positives, the problematic instances are those that are exactly 50% correct because changing the sign will not change anything. The larger the percentage that is correct, the larger the weight given to sensitive outliers.

XGBoost

XGBoost consists of multiple classifiers and regressors, including the standard gradient-boosted trees implemented here. XGBoost includes many hardware and software advances from general gradient boosting, including parallelization, regularization, and cache awareness, among others. In XGBoost, multiple advancements are combined to give it a significant edge in terms of speed and accuracy. Partially due to its success in Kaggle competitions, XGBoost has one of strongest reputations among ML ensembles in the world today.

Let's see how AdaBoost and XGBoost perform on our datasets.

Exercise 159 – using AdaBoost and XGBoost to predict pulsars

The goal of this exercise is to predict pulsars using AdaBoost and XGBoost. This will be achieved with the following steps:

1. Begin this exercise in the same notebook you used in the previous exercise.

2. Now, import AdaBoostClassifier and use it as the input for clf_model():

```
from sklearn.ensemble import AdaBoostClassifier
clf_model(AdaBoostClassifier())
```

The output is as follows:

```
Scores: [0.97430168 0.97988827 0.98128492 0.97597094
0.97708857]
Mean score: 0.977706874833175
```

As you can see, the AdaBoost classifier gave one of the best results yet. Let's see how it performs on the confusion matrix.

3. Use AdaBoostClassifer() as the input for the confusion() function:

```
confusion(AdaBoostClassifier())
```

The output is as follows:

```
[[4094    21]
 [  63   297]]
              precision    recall  f1-score   support

           0       0.98      0.99      0.99      4115
           1       0.93      0.82      0.88       360

    accuracy                           0.98      4475
   macro avg       0.96      0.91      0.93      4475
weighted avg       0.98      0.98      0.98      4475
```

Figure 11.22 – Output of the confusion matrix and classification report on AdaBoostClassifier

Weighted averages of 98% for precision, recall, and the f1-score are outstanding. The f1-score of the positive pulsar classification (the 1s) is 93%, nearly performing as well as RandomForestClassifier.

XGBoost must be downloaded. You can download it to your computer inside your Jupyter Notebook, as follows:

```
import sys
!{sys.executable} -m pip install xgboost
```

4. Now, import the XGBClassifier from `xgboost` and place it inside of the `clf_model` function, as follows:

```
    from xgboost import XGBClassifier
clf_model(XGBClassifier())
```

The output is as follows:

```
Scores: [0.97765363 0.98156425 0.97932961 0.97680916
0.97876502]
Mean score: 0.9788243337532252
```

It's nearly identical to AdaBoost, but slightly higher.

5. Let's see how XGBoost works inside the confusion matrix and classification report:

```
confusion(XGBClassifier())
```

The output is as follows:

```
[[4083   32]
 [  56  304]]
              precision   recall  f1-score   support

           0       0.99     0.99      0.99      4115
           1       0.90     0.84      0.87       360

    accuracy                          0.98      4475
   macro avg       0.95     0.92      0.93      4475
weighted avg       0.98     0.98      0.98      4475
```

Figure 11.23 – Output of the confusion matrix and classification report on XGBClassifier

The prediction of the pulsars (the 1s) could use some work, but the prediction of the non-pulsars (the 0s) is outstanding, and the combined f1-score is an impressive 98%.

Now, let's see how XGBoost and AdaBoost perform as regressors.

Exercise 160 – using AdaBoost and XGBoost to predict median house values in Boston

The goal of this exercise is to predict median house value prices in Boston using AdaBoost and XGBoost. Let's go through the steps:

1. Head to the notebook file that you used for *exercises 148-153* and run all the cells in the notebook so that all the variables are stored.

2. Now, import `AdaBoostRegressor` and use `AdaBoostRegressor()` as the input for the `regression_model_cv` function:

```
from sklearn.ensemble import AdaBoostRegressor
regression_model_cv(AdaBoostRegressor())
```

The output is as follows:

```
Reg rmse: [3.79117796 3.50477724 5.90361934 6.24188092 4.20210617]
Reg mean: 4.72871232513736
```

Figure 11.24 – Mean score output using AdaBoostRegressor

It's no surprise that AdaBoost also gives one of the best results on the housing dataset. It has a great reputation for a reason.

3. Now, import `XGBRegressor` and use `XGBRegressor()` as the input for the `regression_model_cv` function:

```
from xgboost import XGBRegressor
regression_model_cv(XGBRegressor())
```

The output is as follows:

```
Reg rmse: [3.25617197 3.70205981 5.8595083  6.47060538 3.56108012]
Reg mean: 4.569885116033572
```

Figure 11.25 – Mean score output using XGBRegressor

It's also not a surprise that XGBoost outperforms AdaBoost. XGBoost consistently performs well on a wide range of tabular datasets (meaning datasets with rows and columns). Furthermore, it has many hyperparameters to fine-tune so that you can improve your scores even more.

> **Note**
>
> For more information on XGBoost, check out the official documentation at `https://xgboost.readthedocs.io/en/latest/`.

Activity 25 – using ML to predict customer return rate accuracy

In this activity, you will use ML to solve a real-world problem. A bank wants to predict whether customers will return. When customers fail to return, this is known as churn. They want to know which customers are most likely to leave. They give you their data, and they ask you to create an ML algorithm to help them target the customers most likely to leave.

The overview for this activity will be for you to first prepare the data in the dataset, then run a variety of ML algorithms that were covered in this chapter to check their accuracy. You will then use a confusion matrix and classification report to help find the best algorithm to recall potential cases of user churn. You will select one final ML algorithm along with its confusion matrix and classification report for your output.

Here are the steps to achieve this goal:

1. Download the dataset from `https://packt.live/35NRn2C`.

2. Open `CHURN.csv` in a Jupyter Notebook and observe the first five rows.

3. Check for `NaN` values and remove any that you find in the dataset.

4. In order to use ML on all the columns, the predictive column should be in terms of numbers, not `No` and `Yes`. You may replace `No` and `Yes` with `0` and `1`, as follows:

   ```
   df['Churn'] = df['Churn'].replace(to_replace=['No',
   'Yes'], value=[0, 1])
   ```

5. Set `X`, the predictor columns, equal to all columns except the first and the last. Set `y`, the target column, equal to the last column.

6. You want to transform all of the predictive columns into numeric columns. This can be achieved as follows:

   ```
   X = pd.get_dummies(X)
   ```

7. Write a function called `clf_model` that uses `cross_val_score` to implement a classifier. Recall that `cross_val_score` must be imported.

8. Run your function on five different ML algorithms. Choose the top three models.

9. Build a similar function using a confusion matrix and a classification report that uses `train_test_split`. Compare your top three models using this function.

10. Choose your best model, look at the hyperparameters, and optimize at least one hyperparameter.

    You should get an output similar to the following:

```
[[1186  129]
 [ 203  243]]
             precision    recall  f1-score   support

          0       0.85      0.90      0.88      1315
          1       0.65      0.54      0.59       446

   accuracy                          0.81      1761
  macro avg       0.75      0.72      0.74      1761
weighted avg      0.80      0.81      0.81      1761


AdaBoostClassifier()
```

Figure 11.26 – Expected confusion matrix output

> **Note**
> A solution for this activity can be found in *Appendix* on GitHub.

Summary

In this chapter, you have learned how to build a variety of ML models to solve regression and classification problems. You have implemented linear regression, Ridge, Lasso, logistic regression, decision trees, random forests, Naive Bayes, AdaBoost, and XGBoost. You have learned about the importance of using cross-validation to split up your training set and test set. You have learned about the dangers of overfitting and how to correct it with regularization. You have learned how to fine-tune hyperparameters using `GridSearchCV` and `RandomizedSearchCV`. You have learned how to interpret imbalanced datasets with a confusion matrix and a classification report. You have also learned how to distinguish between bagging and boosting, and precision and recall.

The value of learning these skills is that you can make meaningful and accurate predictions from big data using some of the best ML models in the world today.

In the next chapter, you will improve your ML skills by learning the foundations of **deep learning (DL)**. In particular, you will build **sequential neural networks (SNNs)** using `keras`, a state-of-the-art library that runs on top of Google's TensorFlow.

12

Deep Learning with Python

Overview

By the end of this chapter, you will confidently build and tune neural networks using the Sequential deep learning algorithm provided by Keras (TensorFlow). In particular, you will apply deep learning to make meaningful predictions from tabular numerical datasets, in addition to image-based datasets. You will compare the sequential deep learning algorithm to standard machine learning algorithms using regression and classification. You will tune Keras models by modifying Dense layers, Hidden layers, Dropout nodes, and Early Stopping to optimize your neural networks. Finally, you will learn how to classify images by building convolutional neural networks, which are some of the strongest machine learning algorithms in the world today.

Introduction

Deep learning is a specific branch of machine learning modeled after the human brain, commonly referred to as neural networks.

The human brain works by transferring external stimuli through a vast network of neurons. These neurons work together to produce a desired output. For instance, when you are driving a car and your eye detects a red light, the neurons in your brain work together to rapidly output a request to stop the car. This request is based on optimizing past data that your brain has received.

According to the National Library of Medicine (https://www.ncbi.nlm.nih.gov/pmc/articles/PMC2776484/), the most advanced human brains contain approximately 100 billion neurons. This is a very deep network. The general idea behind deep learning is to emulate the human brain by creating a deep algorithmic network that responds to incoming data.

Machine learning started with neural networks when Frank Rosenblatt's 1958 Perceptron demonstrated 100% efficiency in finding linear classifiers to distinguish between two classes of linearly separable data. Although time-consuming, and limited to success if the data was linearly separable, the original Perceptron revealed the potential of computers to establish meaningful neural networks (see https://news.cornell.edu/stories/2019/09/professors-perceptron-paved-way-ai-60-years-too-soon for more information).

In this chapter on deep learning, you will examine the infrastructure of neural networks by first comparing them to the standard machine learning networks that you built in *Chapter 11, Machine Learning*. After reviewing the math behind linear regression, you will better understand the mathematical advantages that deep learning provides.

You will build your first deep learning models using Keras, TensorFlow's high-level language developed by Google that is now more widespread than ever. You will build a Sequential algorithm with Hidden layers that are densely connected using the Boston Housing dataset from *Chapter 11, Machine Learning*.

After building your first deep learning model, you will experiment with different Hidden layers, Dropout, and Early Stopping in an attempt to optimize and regularize your model.

Next, you will build a comparable Sequential Keras model for classification, using different activation and learning loss functions for a larger dataset.

Then, you will use Keras to identify handwritten digits using the famous **Modified National Institute of Standards and Technology** (**MNIST**) dataset. For this final case study, you will learn how to use **convolutional neural networks** (**CNNs**) to classify numbers.

In summary, you will learn how to make meaningful predictions by implementing and modifying deep learning algorithms (synonymous with neural networks) in Keras for datasets that require regression, classification, and predictions based on images.

Here's a quick overview of the topics covered:

- Introduction to deep learning
- Your first deep learning model
- Regularization – Dropout
- Classification
- Convolutional neural networks

Technical requirements

You can find the code files for this chapter on GitHub at https://github.com/PacktPublishing/The-Python-Workshop-Second-Edition/tree/main/Chapter12, and within the following Colab notebook: https://colab.research.google.com/drive/14FUXbsuRvz3jO6bzAm1Mgas6faJ0G61-?usp=sharing.

The technical requirements are different for Colab notebooks and Jupyter Notebook. You will need to install Keras and TensorFlow for Jupyter Notebook, whereas they are included with Colab notebooks in advance.

Colab notebooks

In this chapter, I recommend using an online version of Jupyter Notebook, called Colab notebooks (short for **Google Colaboratory Notebooks**) for the following reasons:

- Colab notebooks allow you to use **graphical processing units** (**GPUs**), which will greatly speed up computations for high-demand processing. This is particularly beneficial for neural networks, which can be time-consuming when combining large datasets with deep networks. We will be using them in the last section on convolutional neural networks.

- Colab notebooks have become the standard online alternative to Jupyter Notebook for data science; as a practicing data scientist, it's beneficial to have practice with both.

- Colab notebooks do not require installing special libraries such as TensorFlow.

- Colab notebooks are very easy to share with others.

> **Note**
>
> Colab notebooks work optimally with private Gmail accounts. When logged into your Gmail account, Colab notebooks automatically save in your Google Drive in a `Colab Notebooks` folder.

For those of you using Colab notebooks, no prior installation is required.

Jupyter Notebook

If you prefer working in Jupyter Notebook, you need to install TensorFlow, which provides the backend for Keras.

If you are working with Anaconda, you may install TensorFlow with the following command in your terminal:

```
conda install -c conda-forge tensorflow
```

For more information on installing TensorFlow with Anaconda, visit `https://anaconda.org/conda-forge/tensorflow`.

If you are not working with Anaconda, you may install TensorFlow with the following commands:

```
pip install --upgrade pip
pip install tensorflow
```

You may confirm your installation of TensorFlow by running the following code, which will show the version of TensorFlow that you are running. Anything 2.8 or above should be sufficient:

```
import tensorflow as tf
tf.__version__
```

For those of you using Jupyter Notebook, after you have installed TensorFlow, you are ready to use Keras!

Introduction to deep learning

The neurons in a human brain are analogously referred to as nodes in deep learning algorithms. Individual nodes may be thought of as computational units. Although they may stand alone, they are more powerful when connected to one another.

As a visual, here is the Boston Housing DataFrame from *Chapter 11, Machine Learning*. Each column in the following DataFrame can be represented as a node, as can each entry:

	CRIM	ZN	INDUS	CHAS	NOX	RM	AGE	DIS	RAD	TAX	PTRATIO	B	LSTAT	MEDV
0	0.00632	18.0	2.31	0.0	0.538	6.575	65.2	4.0900	1	296	15.3	396.90	4.98	24.0
1	0.02731	0.0	7.07	0.0	0.469	6.421	78.9	4.9671	2	242	17.8	396.90	9.14	21.6
2	0.02729	0.0	7.07	0.0	0.469	7.185	61.1	4.9671	2	242	17.8	392.83	4.03	34.7
3	0.03237	0.0	2.18	0.0	0.458	6.998	45.8	6.0622	3	222	18.7	394.63	2.94	33.4
4	0.06905	0.0	2.18	0.0	0.458	7.147	54.2	6.0622	3	222	18.7	396.90	NaN	36.2

Figure 12.1 – Sample from the Boston Housing dataset

In linear regression, using the standard machine learning algorithm introduced in *Chapter 11, Machine Learning*, each column, or node, is multiplied by a constant, called a weight, and the individual weights are summed together to make a prediction, as in the following diagram:

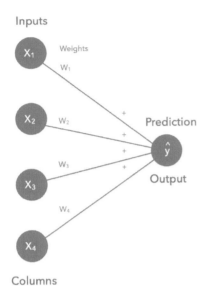

LINEAR REGRESSION

▸ This is one row of data.

▸ Picture depth for N rows.

▸ Multiply X by W and sum the results.

▸ Find Ws to minimize the error.

Figure 12.2 – Linear regression diagram from Berkeley Coding Academy, created by the author Corey Wade

The process is linear because it uses the simple technique of multiplication and addition; given any input X, after multiplication and addition, $Y = MX$ is a linear combination.

Complexifying the network for deep learning requires two shifts. The first is called an activation function. After multiplication and addition, the resulting nodes become activated through an activation function that allows for nonlinearity. The idea behind the activation function comes from the human brain. If you see a red light while in a car, only certain neurons become activated, such as one that tells your foot to step on the brake, and hopefully not one that tells you to reach for your cell phone. But in deep learning, the activation function runs deeper.

The output for logistic regression, as discussed in *Chapter 11, Machine Learning*, is the Sigmoid function, a nonlinear function used to classify data into two groups based on probability. Graphically, the Sigmoid function is clearly nonlinear, as the following figure reveals:

SIGMOID EQUATION

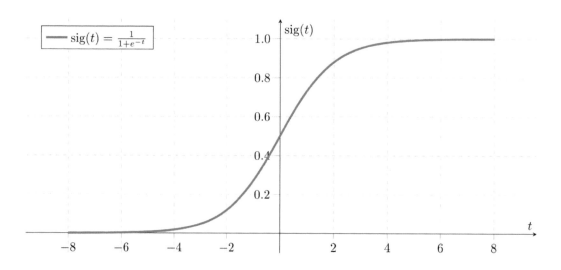

Figure 12.3 – Sigmoid curve on a plot from Berkeley Coding Academy, by the author Corey Wade

After the columns are multiplied by constants and summed together, the final result may be placed into the Sigmoid function, resulting in a nonlinear equation, as is the case with logistic regression. In deep learning, every additional node between the first and last layers becomes activated via an activation function. This general shift to nonlinearity in deep learning allows for much richer algorithms. With activation functions, all deep learning networks become non-linear. Other commonly used activation functions include the hyperbolic tangent (`tanh`), and the rectified linear unit (`relu`), which will be sampled in *Exercise 162 – using Sequential deep learning to predict the accuracy of the median house values of our dataset.*

In addition to activation functions, there is a second and perhaps more dramatic shift that differentiates deep learning from standard machine learning algorithms. Deep learning allows for as many nodes as desired. In other words, deep learning does not just aspire to the 100 billion neurons of the human brain; it exceeds it on demand.

To give you a flavor of the complexity of deep learning, consider the following diagram:

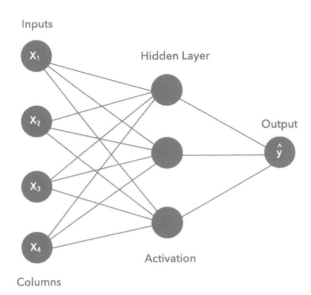

NEURAL NETWORK

This Neural Network has a hidden layer of 3 nodes. You can have as many hidden layers with as many nodes as you want. Each node after the first layer contains an activation function. This allows for nonlinearity and much greater complexity in models. The final node needs an activation function if the dataset requires classification; for regression it's uncommon.

Figure 12.4 – Simple neural network from Berkeley Coding Academy, by the author Corey Wade

The first column in this figure represents columns as nodes. In this densely connected network, each line represents a mathematical weight, and each node beyond the first column includes a nonlinear activation function. There are 15 total mathematical parameters in this relatively simple diagram.

As you can see in the next diagram, it's not uncommon for deep learning algorithms to contain tens of thousands, hundreds of thousands, or even more parameters depending on the project at hand:

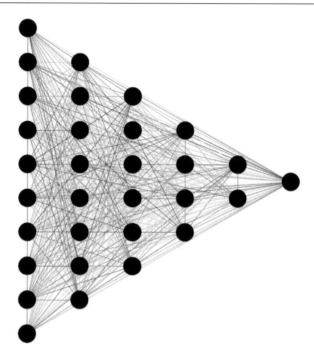

Figure 12.5 – Complex neural network, from https://openclipart.org/
detail/309343/neural-network-deep-learning-prismatic

Now that you have an idea of how deep learning compares to machine learning in terms of nonlinear activation functions and a much larger network size, it's time to build your first deep learning model.

Your first deep learning model

Let's use deep learning to predict the median house values in Boston to compare our results to the standard machine learning algorithms used in *Chapter 11, Machine Learning*.

First deep learning libraries

Before building your first deep learning model, let's take a brief look at the libraries that we will import and use:

- `pandas`: We need data to build a deep learning model, and `pandas`, Python's data analytics library, will remain our standard from *Chapter 10, Data Analytics with pandas and NumPy*, and *Chapter 11, Machine Learning*, to read and view data.

- `train_test_split`: We will use `train_test_split` as in *Chapter 11, Machine Learning*, to split the data into a **training** set and a **test** set.

- `TensorFlow`: `TensorFlow` has become the gold standard in deep learning. Created by Google in 2015, `TensorFlow` is a free, open source library developed by Google Brain. `TensorFlow` works on its own, but it is also the backend for `keras`.

- `keras`: A high-level version of `TensorFlow`, `keras` is an awesome, easy-to-use interface that allows you to focus on building powerful neural networks without worrying about tensors. `keras` is widely used all over the world to build elite deep learning models.

- `Sequential`: The `Sequential` model in `keras` provides a powerful framework to build neural networks that move from left to right in sequence. All deep learning models in this chapter will use `Sequential`.

- `Dense`: The nodes in `keras` that work together in sequence are referred to as layers. It's common for these layers to be densely connected, meaning that each node in one layer connects to every other node in the subsequent layer. These densely connected layers are initiated in `keras` as `Dense` layers.

- `EarlyStopping`: A valuable `keras` callback covered later in this chapter that stops neural networks when they peak.

- `Dropout`: A regularization technique in `keras` that drops out nodes by percentage within the network to prevent overfitting, also covered later in this chapter.

> **Note**
>
> For more information on the `keras` libraries, check out the official `keras` documentation at `https://keras.io/`.

Now that you have an idea of the libraries that we will use to create our first deep learning model, in the next exercise, we will import the libraries, load the data, and prepare the data for deep learning.

Exercise 161 – preparing the Boston Housing dataset for deep learning

The goal of this exercise is to prepare the Boston Housing dataset to get ready for Deep Learning.

This exercise will be performed in a Colab notebook (you may use Jupyter Notebook as well).

> **Note**
>
> If you are working in Jupyter Notebook, to proceed with the exercises in the chapter, you will need to download the `TensorFlow` library as outlined in the previous section.

Let's see the steps for this exercise:

1. For Colab users: log in to your private Google account, then open a new Colab notebook at `https://colab.research.google.com/` (for Jupyter users, open a new Jupyter notebook).

2. Import all the necessary libraries by entering the following code snippet in a coding cell:

```
import pandas as pd
from sklearn.model_selection import train_test_split
from tensorflow import keras
from keras.models import Sequential
from keras.layers import Dense, Dropout
from keras.callbacks import EarlyStopping
```

Press *Shift + Enter* in Colab to run the coding cell. After running the cell in Colab, your screen should appear as follows:

Figure 12.6 – Deep learning Colab notebook screenshot

Now that we have imported the libraries, we will load the data.

3. Load the dataset from the provided URL and view the DataFrame to look at the first five rows:

```
url ='https://raw.githubusercontent.com/PacktWorkshops/
ThePython-Workshop/master/Datasets/HousingData.csv'
df = pd.read_csv(url)
df.head()
```

After pressing *Shift + Enter* to run this code in Colab, you should get the following output, just as in *Chapter 11, Machine Learning*:

	CRIM	ZN	INDUS	CHAS	NOX	RM	AGE	DIS	RAD	TAX	PTRATIO	B	LSTAT	MEDV
0	0.00632	18.0	2.31	0.0	0.538	6.575	65.2	4.0900	1	296	15.3	396.90	4.98	24.0
1	0.02731	0.0	7.07	0.0	0.469	6.421	78.9	4.9671	2	242	17.8	396.90	9.14	21.6
2	0.02729	0.0	7.07	0.0	0.469	7.185	61.1	4.9671	2	242	17.8	392.83	4.03	34.7
3	0.03237	0.0	2.18	0.0	0.458	6.998	45.8	6.0622	3	222	18.7	394.63	2.94	33.4
4	0.06905	0.0	2.18	0.0	0.458	7.147	54.2	6.0622	3	222	18.7	396.90	NaN	36.2

Figure 12.7 – Output with the dataset displayed

> **Coding tip**
> You may load CSV files directly from URLs via GitHub if you click on **View Raw** after opening the CSV file.

4. Next, run the following code to clean the dataset of null values using `.dropna()`:

```
df = df.dropna()
```

Now that the data is clean, it's time to split the data.

5. Declare the X and y variables, where you use X for the **predictor** columns and y for the **target** column, then split the data into a training and test set as follows:

```
X = df.iloc[:,:-1]
y = df.iloc[:, -1]
X_train, X_test, y_train, y_test = train_test_split(X, y,
random_state=2)
```

The target column is MEDV, which is the median value of the Boston house prices. The predictor columns include every other column. The standard notation is to use X for the predictor columns and y for the target column. Using `random_state=2` is not required, but it guarantees that you will get the same split as ours.

At this point, the Boston Housing dataset is ready for deep learning.

In the next exercise, we will build our first deep learning model!

Exercise 162 – using sequential deep learning to predict the accuracy of the median house values of our dataset

In this exercise, we will apply the following steps to build a Sequential deep learning regressor using Keras:

1. Initialize a `Sequential()` model, as shown in the following code snippet:

    ```
    model = Sequential()
    ```

    This lets Python know that we are going to build a neural network that will connect nodes from left to right.

2. In `keras`, it's required to specify the number of columns as the input shape for the first Dense layer. You may set the number of columns as follows:

    ```
    num_cols = X.shape[1]
    ```

3. Now it's time to specify our first densely connected layer. We can choose the number of nodes in this new layer. Each new node will take as input the multiplication and sum from each of the previous nodes, which are columns, since they are coming from the first layer. Finally, the new nodes should be activated by an activation function. We will choose `relu`, which stands for **Rectified Linear Unit**; it simply returns 0 for negative values and the same input, or X value, for positive values, as shown in the following diagram:

$$\text{ReLU}(x) \triangleq \max(0, x)$$

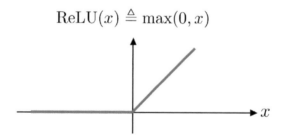

Figure 12.8 – ReLU function, from Wikimedia Commons: `https://upload.`
`wikimedia.org/wikipedia/commons/8/85/ReLU_and_`
`Nonnegative_Soft_Thresholding_Functions.svg`

Add a new Dense layer of 20 nodes, taking the number of columns (`num_cols`) as the input, and `relu` as the activation function, as in the following code snippet:

```
model.add(Dense(20, input_shape=(num_cols,),
activation='relu'))
```

We can continue adding new layers without the need to specify the input any longer.

4. Add a new densely connected layer of 10 nodes using the same activation function:

```
model.add(Dense(10, activation='relu'))
```

5. To arrive at an actual prediction, we must conclude with one final layer, densely connected, that only contains one node, without any activation so that all results are possible. We want all results because the desired output is the median house value, which means that we are dealing with regression. Here is the code for the last layer of our model:

```
model.add(Dense(1))
```

So far, we have not built an actual model. We have set up the parameters for the algorithm to build a model. To build the model, we need to feed it the data.

6. Add the following code to print out a summary of the model so far:

```
print(model.summary())
```

Here is the summary of the model provided by Keras:

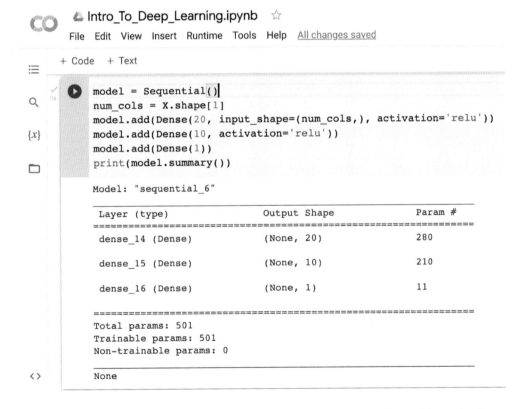

Figure 12.9 – Screenshot of initial code and model summary print-out from Colab notebook

The most interesting part of the model summary is the total number of parameters, which is 501. This means that the model will attempt to optimize 501 weights. The parameters are computed by multiplying the number of inputs by the number of nodes per layer + 1; the addition of one accounts for the resulting parameter after summing the nodes.

Note that the greater the number of dense layers and the length of the layers, the more parameters the model requires and the longer it will take to build. The next step is to compile the model. To do so, we need to specify an optimizer to find the desired weights, along with a loss function to determine how close the predictions are to reality.

7. Understanding optimizers requires calculus, which is beyond the scope of this book. We will stick with adam as our optimizer. Since the root mean squared error (RMSE) is not a default option, we will select the comparable mean squared error, abbreviated as mse, for the loss function. Both are combined in the following code snippet:

```
model.compile(optimizer='adam', loss='mse')
```

8. Finally, it's time to train the model using the .fit method, with X_train and y_train as parameters, along with a set number of epochs, which is the number of times that the model updates its weights in an attempt to minimize the loss using the preselected optimizer. The more epochs you specify, the longer the model will take to build. Let's start with a reasonably small number of 10 epochs, as shown in the following code snippet:

```
model.fit(X_train, y_train, epochs=10)
```

9. After the number of epochs completes, all that remains is to obtain a score on the test set. We can get the root mean squared error by taking the square root of the test set using the following code:

```
model.evaluate(X_test, y_test)**0.5
```

After you run all the previous code by pressing *Shift + Enter*, you should get an output comparable to the following:

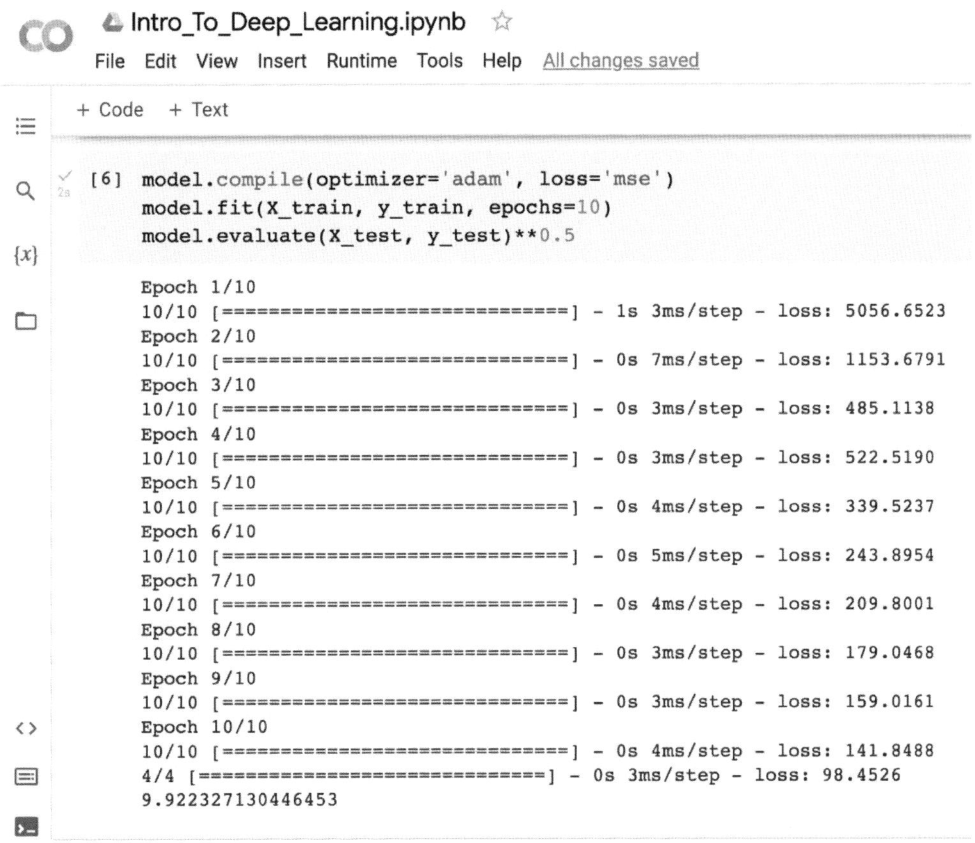

Figure 12.10 – Screenshot from Colab notebook – first deep learning score, RMSE of 9.92

If your score is much worse, don't panic. If it's better, great. Randomization is included in the weight initialization process, so the scores are going to be different.

A bigger point of emphasis is that 10 epochs are not enough time for the model to find convergence. A cool feature of Keras is that you can simply add more epochs; the following code snippet will add 50 epochs to the model:

```
model.fit(X_train, y_train, epochs=50)
model.evaluate(X_test, y_test)**0.5
```

After running this code, you should see an output similar to the following:

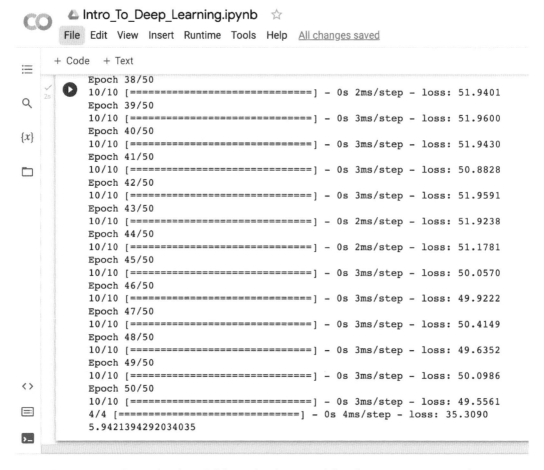

Figure 12.11 – Screenshot from Colab notebook – second deep learning score, RMSE of 5.94

A final RMSE of 5.9 is solid but does not surpass the best results obtained by linear regression in the previous chapter. Why?

First, deep learning is advantageous on very large datasets, along with unstructured data such as images or text. Second, deep learning models are very flexible in terms of the number and depth of densely connected layers, which we will explore in the next section to improve the model.

Tuning Keras models

We will look at several ways to improve scores by tuning Keras models. For additional ideas, check out the new Keras Tuner at `https://www.tensorflow.org/tutorials/keras/keras_tuner`.

Hidden layers

The densely connected layers between the input and the output are often referred to as **hidden layers** because they are not part of the input or output. The term *hidden layers* is suggestive of something going on beyond the human eye, although the programmer chooses the number and depth of these layers, and it's possible to retrieve model weights to figure out exactly what is going on.

So, what is an optimal strategy for choosing the number and depth of hidden layers?

The first answer in machine learning is always experimentation. Part of the fun of building neural networks is choosing your own hidden layers and numbers of nodes. Also, what works on one dataset may not work as well on another.

In our case, we want to improve the score of the model, so a natural first strategy is to increase the number of parameters by increasing the number of densely connected layers and nodes per layer.

To be more precise, increasing the number of parameters may be done as follows:

- Repeat the same densely connected layers multiple times
- Gradually increase or decrease the number of nodes in successive densely connected layers
- Use one large densely connected layer

Let's try these options in the next exercise.

Exercise 163 – modifying densely connected layers in a neural network to improve the score

The goal of this exercise is to lower the root mean squared error from the previous exercise by increasing the number of densely connected layers, and/or the number of nodes per layer. Let's start by increasing the number of nodes to 24, using only the first layer.

Here are the steps to change the densely connected layers and nodes:

1. Continue using the same Colab or Jupyter notebook from *Exercise 162 – using sequential deep learning to predict the accuracy of the median house values of our dataset*.

2. Create three densely connected layers of 24 nodes each with the `relu` activation function using 50 epochs in total with the following code:

```
model = Sequential()
model.add(Dense(24, input_shape=(num_cols,),
activation='relu'))
model.add(Dense(24, activation='relu'))
model.add(Dense(24, activation='relu'))
model.add(Dense(1))
print(model.summary())
model.compile(optimizer='adam', loss='mse')
model.fit(X_train, y_train, epochs=50)
model.evaluate(X_test, y_test)**0.5
```

After running this code, you should see the model summary before the model build as follows:

Model: "sequential_2"

Layer (type)	Output Shape	Param #
dense_6 (Dense)	(None, 24)	336
dense_7 (Dense)	(None, 24)	600
dense_8 (Dense)	(None, 24)	600
dense_9 (Dense)	(None, 1)	25

Total params: 1,561
Trainable params: 1,561
Non-trainable params: 0

Figure 12.12 – Screenshot from Colab notebook – model summary with 1561 parameters

As you can see from the model summary, the neural network contains a total of 1,561 parameters, which is approximately triple the previous 501.

Underneath the model summary, the results of the neural network after 50 epochs are as follows:

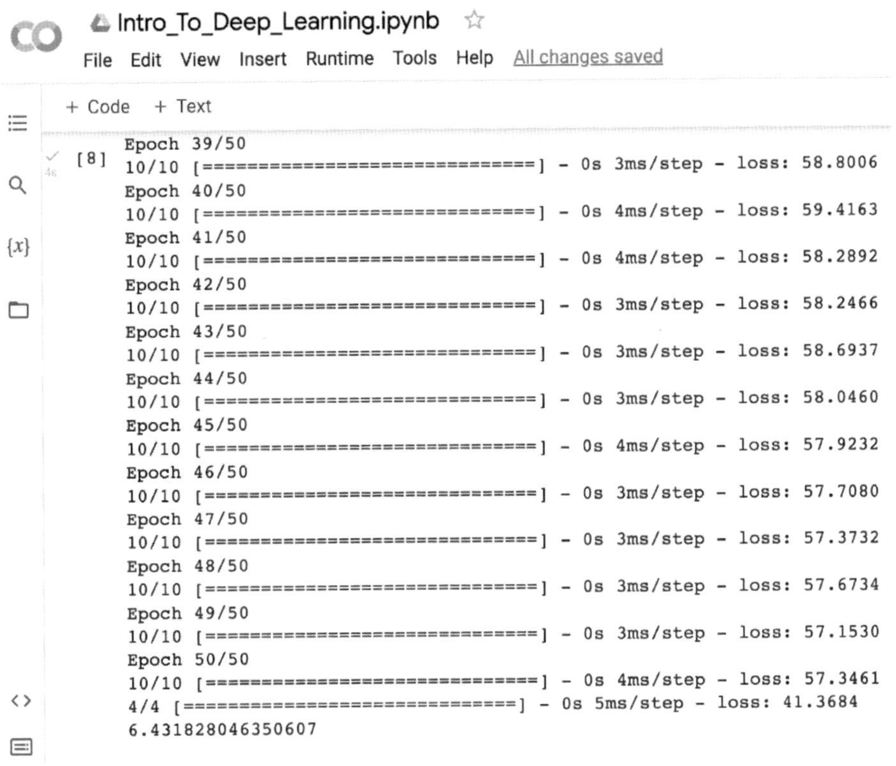

Figure 12.13 – Screenshot from Colab notebook – third deep learning score, RMSE of 6.43

Our score, however, has not improved, with an RMSE of 6.43. Notice that the loss on the right side, however, is steadily improving, so we could increase the number of epochs, a strategy that we will implement later.

3. Next, try creating two densely connected layers of 48 and 16 nodes each by running the following code snippet:

```
model = Sequential()
model.add(Dense(48, input_shape=(num_cols,),
activation='relu'))
model.add(Dense(16, activation='relu'))
model.add(Dense(1))
print(model.summary())
model.compile(optimizer='adam', loss='mse')
model.fit(X_train, y_train, epochs=50)
model.evaluate(X_test, y_test)**0.5
```

You should see the following model summary above the model build:

```
Model: "sequential_3"

Layer (type)                 Output Shape              Param #
=================================================================
dense_10 (Dense)             (None, 48)                672

dense_11 (Dense)             (None, 16)                784

dense_12 (Dense)             (None, 1)                 17

=================================================================
Total params: 1,473
Trainable params: 1,473
Non-trainable params: 0
```

Figure 12.14 – Screenshot from Colab notebook – model summary with 1,473 parameters

As you can see from this model summary, there are slightly fewer parameters; however, in this particular case, the following output at the end of the model build reveals that the RMSE has improved to a new low score of 5.086:

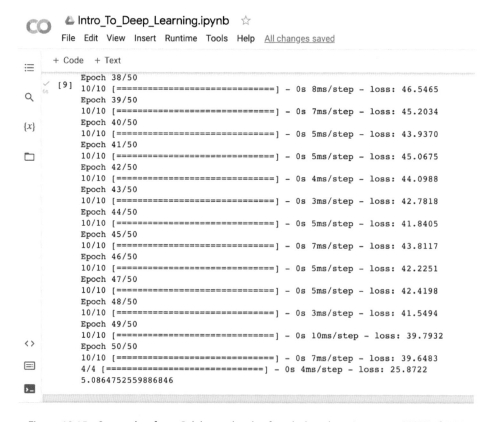

Figure 12.15 – Screenshot from Colab notebook – fourth deep learning score, RMSE of 5.09

4. Finally, create a Sequential model with one densely connected layer of 100 nodes by running the following code:

```
model = Sequential()
model.add(Dense(100, input_shape=(num_cols,),
activation='relu'))
model.add(Dense(1))
print(model.summary())
model.compile(optimizer='adam', loss='mse')
model.fit(X_train, y_train, epochs=50)
model.evaluate(X_test, y_test)**0.5
```

Here is the model summary, displaying a comparable number of parameters at 1,501:

```
Model: "sequential_4"
```

Layer (type)	Output Shape	Param #
dense_13 (Dense)	(None, 100)	1400
dense_14 (Dense)	(None, 1)	101

```
Total params: 1,501
Trainable params: 1,501
Non-trainable params: 0
```

Figure 12.16 – Screenshot from Colab notebook – model summary with 1,501 parameters

Running this code at different times can give very different answers. Try it! Here are the low and high results that occurred after running the previous code a few times.

Here is the low score from a single dense layer of 100 nodes:

```
CO    ▲ Intro_To_Deep_Learning.ipynb   ☆
      File  Edit  View  Insert  Runtime  Tools  Help

      + Code   + Text

   [26]  Epoch 38/50
         10/10 [==============================] - 0s 2ms/step - loss: 39.0250
         Epoch 39/50
         10/10 [==============================] - 0s 2ms/step - loss: 39.3789
         Epoch 40/50
         10/10 [==============================] - 0s 2ms/step - loss: 39.1006
         Epoch 41/50
         10/10 [==============================] - 0s 2ms/step - loss: 38.4823
         Epoch 42/50
         10/10 [==============================] - 0s 2ms/step - loss: 38.8776
         Epoch 43/50
         10/10 [==============================] - 0s 2ms/step - loss: 37.0495
         Epoch 44/50
         10/10 [==============================] - 0s 3ms/step - loss: 37.2557
         Epoch 45/50
         10/10 [==============================] - 0s 2ms/step - loss: 36.2107
         Epoch 46/50
         10/10 [==============================] - 0s 2ms/step - loss: 35.8049
         Epoch 47/50
         10/10 [==============================] - 0s 2ms/step - loss: 36.7325
         Epoch 48/50
         10/10 [==============================] - 0s 2ms/step - loss: 35.8743
         Epoch 49/50
         10/10 [==============================] - 0s 2ms/step - loss: 38.4962
         Epoch 50/50
         10/10 [==============================] - 0s 2ms/step - loss: 35.1725
         4/4 [==============================] - 0s 3ms/step - loss: 23.5795
         4.855870593161364
```

Figure 12.17 – Screenshot from Colab notebook – fifth deep learning score, RMSE of 4.86

Here is the high score from a single dense layer of 100 nodes:

```
CO       Intro_To_Deep_Learning.ipynb    ☆
         File  Edit  View  Insert  Runtime  Tools  Help   All changes saved

≔        + Code   + Text

✓   ▶    Epoch 38/50
3s       10/10 [==============================] - 0s 2ms/step - loss: 53.2083
Q        Epoch 39/50
         10/10 [==============================] - 0s 2ms/step - loss: 51.9169
{x}      Epoch 40/50
         10/10 [==============================] - 0s 3ms/step - loss: 52.1243
         Epoch 41/50
▢        10/10 [==============================] - 0s 2ms/step - loss: 51.6049
         Epoch 42/50
         10/10 [==============================] - 0s 2ms/step - loss: 51.3687
         Epoch 43/50
         10/10 [==============================] - 0s 2ms/step - loss: 51.0009
         Epoch 44/50
         10/10 [==============================] - 0s 2ms/step - loss: 50.7503
         Epoch 45/50
         10/10 [==============================] - 0s 2ms/step - loss: 50.5870
         Epoch 46/50
         10/10 [==============================] - 0s 3ms/step - loss: 50.4171
         Epoch 47/50
         10/10 [==============================] - 0s 2ms/step - loss: 49.9279
         Epoch 48/50
         10/10 [==============================] - 0s 2ms/step - loss: 49.4315
         Epoch 49/50
<>       10/10 [==============================] - 0s 2ms/step - loss: 49.8662
         Epoch 50/50
         10/10 [==============================] - 0s 2ms/step - loss: 49.2663
▤        4/4 [==============================] - 0s 3ms/step - loss: 38.8294
         6.231320352262395
▣
```

Figure 12.18 – Screenshot from Colab notebook – sixth deep learning score, RMSE of 6.23

You may wonder why the results are so different. The answer has to do with the initialization of random weights and the early learning that takes place. However, notice that in both cases, the learning loss is steadily decreasing indicating that we should use more epochs, which is what we will try next.

Number of epochs

The number of epochs, as mentioned before, is the number of times that the neural network adjusts the weights. In some respects, the more epochs the better. Overfitting the data, however, is definitely a concern, as mentioned in *Chapter 11*, *Machine Learning*, that will need addressing toward the end of this section.

Exercise 164 – modifying the number of epochs in the neural network to improve the score

The goal of this exercise is to lower the root mean squared error from the previous exercise by increasing the number of densely connected layers, and/or the number of nodes per layer:

1. Continue using the same Colab or Jupyter notebook from *Exercise 163 – modifying densely connected layers in a neural network to improve the score.*

2. Create a Sequential model with one hidden layer of 100 densely connected nodes with a `relu` activation function of 500 epochs, as shown in the following code:

```
model = Sequential()
model.add(Dense(100, input_shape=(num_cols,),
activation='relu'))
model.add(Dense(1))
print(model.summary())
model.compile(optimizer='adam', loss='mse')
model.fit(X_train, y_train, epochs=500)
model.evaluate(X_test, y_test)**0.5
```

The following figure shows the lowest score yet with 500 epochs using a single densely connected layer of 100 nodes:

Figure 12.19 – Screenshot from Colab notebook – seventh deep learning score, RMSE of 3.76

The 3.76 RMSE in the previous code is lower than any RMSE obtained in *Chapter 11, Machine Learning*. Just by estimating the number of nodes and densely connected layers, in conjunction with the number of epochs, we have achieved an optimal result.

We have tried a range of 10 epochs to 500. How can we find an optimal number of epochs?

One solution is to implement Early Stopping.

Early Stopping

Instead of guessing the number of epochs in advance, you can use the Early Stopping callback provided by Keras to find an optimal number of epochs. The Early Stopping callback works as follows:

1. You choose an arbitrarily high number of epochs that is not expected to be reached

2. The model starts working on optimizing weights as usual, one epoch at a time

3. The model stops building after the loss does not improve for N epochs in a row on a validation set, where N is a positive integer, called the patience, that you choose in advance

4. After completion, the model goes back to the top score after which no improvement was shown

The key number when using Early Stopping is the number of consecutive epochs N, the patience, that the model is guaranteed to build. In fact, the model will keep building, trying out new weights, until it fails to improve for N epochs in a row. A validation set is used to score the model on each round for early stopping instead of the training set so that the model is not at risk of grossly overfitting the training thereby undermining the Early Stopping advantage.

Choosing N should depend on how long it takes each epoch to run. During training, starting with a patience of 10 to 50 epochs for the early callback provides a nice balance between giving the model a chance to find new learning opportunities without waiting too long for the model to finish building.

Exercise 165 – optimizing the number of epochs with Early Stopping

The goal of this exercise is to optimize the number of epochs by using Early Stopping:

1. Continue using the same Colab or Jupyter notebook from *Exercise 164 – modifying the number of epochs in a neural network to improve the score*.

2. Import `EarlyStopping` from `keras.callbacks` and create a variable called `early_stopping_monitor` set equal to `EarlyStopping` with a parameter of patience set to 25:

```
from keras.callbacks import EarlyStopping
early_stopping_monitor = EarlyStopping(patience=25)
```

3. Create a Sequential model with one hidden layer of 100 densely connected nodes with a `relu` activation function. Compile the model using the standard `adam` optimizer and `mse` loss function as follows:

```
model = Sequential()
model.add(Dense(100, input_shape=(num_cols,),
activation='relu'))
model.add(Dense(1))
model.compile(optimizer='adam', loss='mse')
```

4. Fit the model on the training set with 50,000 epochs; include the `validation_split` parameter set equal to `0.2`, and `callbacks` set equal to a list that contains `early_stopping_monitor`. Evaluate the model on the test as well. Note that the validation split will split the training set, and the final evaluation is on a separate test set. Normally, this final evaluation would be withheld until the end of training, but we present an evaluation on the test set here to build on the consistency of previous results:

```
model.fit(X_train, y_train, epochs=50000, validation_
split=0.2, callbacks=[early_stopping_monitor])
model.evaluate(X_test, y_test)**0.5
```

The Early Stopping code and the beginning of training are shown in the following figure:

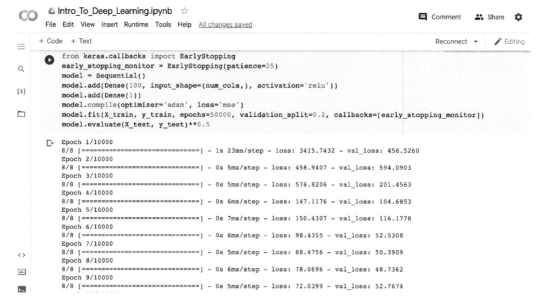

Figure 12.20 – Screenshot from Colab notebook – introducing Early Stopping

The following figure shows the end of the Early Stopping monitor with the final score:

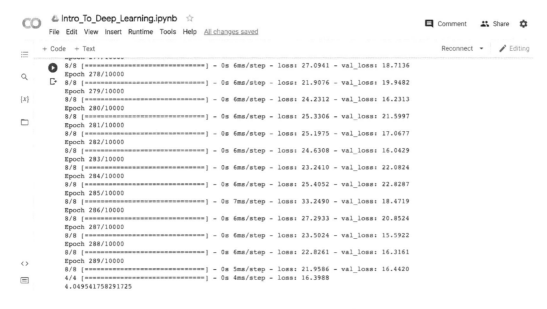

Figure 12.21 – Screenshot from Colab notebook – RMSE of 4.05 using Early Stopping

As you can see, our model finished after 289 epochs, so it failed to see an improvement in the validation score after the (*289-25=264*) 264th model.

Although the score is slightly worse than the model with 500 epochs, this is partially due to randomness. It's also possible to increase the patience. Finally, note that the Early Stopping callback stops building when the validation set fails to improve, so it's training on a smaller subset.

Additional regularization technique – Dropout

Regularization is built into the Early Stopping monitor because a validation test is used during each epoch to score against the training set. The idea is that even if the training set continues to improve, the model will stop building after the validation ceases to improve within the callback patience.

It's important to examine additional regularization techniques so that you can build even larger neural networks without overfitting the data.

Another very popular regularization technique widely used in neural networks is called the Dropout. Given multiple nodes in multiple layers result in thousands or millions of weights, neural networks can easily overfit the training set.

The idea behind Dropout is to randomly drop some nodes altogether. In densely connected networks, since all nodes in one layer are connected to all nodes in the next layer, any node may be eliminated except the last.

Dropout works in code by adding a Dropout with a certain percentage that is the probability of each node being eliminated between layers. Dropout percentages commonly range from 10 to 50%, although any number strictly between 0 and 100% is valid.

In our previous neural networks, for simplicity, we used one layer of 100 nodes. But now, by using Dropout with Early Stopping, it may be advantageous to increase the number of densely connected layers.

Exercise 166 – using Dropout in a neural network to improve the score

The goal of this exercise is to lower the root mean squared error from the previous exercise by using Dropout:

1. Open a new Colab or Jupyter Notebook. The code for our new notebook is here: https://colab.research.google.com/drive/1lhxPKvfVfWYh6ru0OTn4EapH0qo6NBLC?usp=sharing.

2. Import Dropout from keras.layers. Initialize a Sequential model, then add a densely connected layer with 128 nodes and a relu activation. After the first layer, add a Dropout of 0.1 as shown in the following code snippet:

```
from keras.layers import Dropout
model = Sequential()
model.add(Dense(128, input_shape=(num_cols,),
activation='relu'))
model.add(Dropout(0.1))
```

3. Add a Dense layer of 32 nodes with another relu activation followed by a Dropout of 0.1 and a Dense layer of one node. Compile the model as in the following code snippet:

```
model.add(Dense(32, activation='relu'))
model.add(Dropout(0.1))
model.add(Dense(1))
model.compile(optimizer='adam', loss='mse')
```

4. Set Early Stopping to a patience of 50, fit the model to the training set with an upper bound of 10,000 epochs, use a validation_split value of 0.2, and evaluate on the test set as follows:

```
early_stopping_monitor = EarlyStopping(patience=50)
model.fit(X_train, y_train, epochs=10000, validation_
split=0.2, callbacks=[early_stopping_monitor])
model.evaluate(X_test, y_test)**0.5
```

The following figure shows the code altogether along with the early results using Dropout:

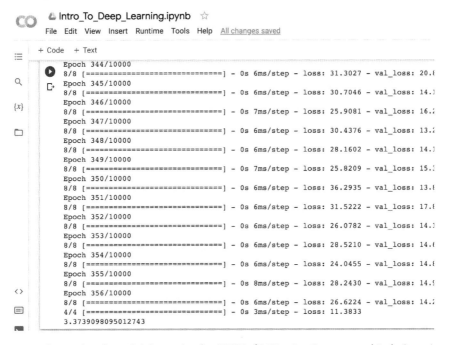

```
from keras.layers import Dropout
model = Sequential()
model.add(Dense(128, input_shape=(num_cols,), activation='relu'))
model.add(Dropout(0.1))
model.add(Dense(32, activation='relu'))
model.add(Dropout(0.1))
model.add(Dense(1))
model.compile(optimizer='adam', loss='mse')
early_stopping_monitor = EarlyStopping(patience=50)
model.fit(X_train, y_train, epochs=10000, validation_split=0.2, callbacks=[early_stopping_monitor])
model.evaluate(X_test, y_test)**0.5
```

```
Epoch 1/10000
8/8 [==============================] - 1s 26ms/step - loss: 536.5046 - val_loss: 44.3476
Epoch 2/10000
8/8 [==============================] - 0s 6ms/step - loss: 302.7124 - val_loss: 109.5779
Epoch 3/10000
8/8 [==============================] - 0s 6ms/step - loss: 228.4950 - val_loss: 43.9412
Epoch 4/10000
8/8 [==============================] - 0s 7ms/step - loss: 158.5551 - val_loss: 40.3001
Epoch 5/10000
8/8 [==============================] - 0s 6ms/step - loss: 149.4862 - val_loss: 49.3337
Epoch 6/10000
8/8 [==============================] - 0s 6ms/step - loss: 116.8722 - val_loss: 33.6004
Epoch 7/10000
```

Figure 12.22 – Screenshot from Colab notebook – Dropout

The next figure shows the end of the code with the Dropout added:

```
Epoch 344/10000
8/8 [==============================] - 0s 6ms/step - loss: 31.3027 - val_loss: 20.8
Epoch 345/10000
8/8 [==============================] - 0s 6ms/step - loss: 30.7046 - val_loss: 14.1
Epoch 346/10000
8/8 [==============================] - 0s 7ms/step - loss: 25.9081 - val_loss: 16.2
Epoch 347/10000
8/8 [==============================] - 0s 6ms/step - loss: 30.4376 - val_loss: 13.2
Epoch 348/10000
8/8 [==============================] - 0s 6ms/step - loss: 28.1602 - val_loss: 14.1
Epoch 349/10000
8/8 [==============================] - 0s 7ms/step - loss: 25.8209 - val_loss: 15.3
Epoch 350/10000
8/8 [==============================] - 0s 6ms/step - loss: 36.2935 - val_loss: 13.8
Epoch 351/10000
8/8 [==============================] - 0s 6ms/step - loss: 31.5222 - val_loss: 17.8
Epoch 352/10000
8/8 [==============================] - 0s 6ms/step - loss: 26.0782 - val_loss: 14.1
Epoch 353/10000
8/8 [==============================] - 0s 6ms/step - loss: 28.5210 - val_loss: 14.6
Epoch 354/10000
8/8 [==============================] - 0s 6ms/step - loss: 24.0455 - val_loss: 14.8
Epoch 355/10000
8/8 [==============================] - 0s 8ms/step - loss: 28.2430 - val_loss: 14.9
Epoch 356/10000
8/8 [==============================] - 0s 6ms/step - loss: 26.6224 - val_loss: 14.2
4/4 [==============================] - 0s 3ms/step - loss: 11.3833
3.3739098095012743
```

Figure 12.23 – Screenshot from Colab notebook – RMSE of 3.37 using Dropout and Early Stopping

The new RMSE of 3.37 is the lowest yet, and therefore the best. You are encouraged to experiment with the number of hidden layers and nodes, along with Dropout and Early Stopping, to aim for an even better score.

Building neural networks for classification

In the previous examples, the final output could have been any given number, so we were dealing with regression. But in many cases, the final output may be 0 or 1, "yes" or "no," or a range of distinct colors. In each of these cases, the type of machine learning algorithms that we are looking for fall under the general heading of classification.

In neural networks, one primary difference between regression and classification is the loss functions and scoring metrics. For classification, loss functions and scoring metrics are usually based on some kind of percentage of accuracy. It's standard to use `binary_crossentropy` as the loss function for classification and to include an `accuracy` metric, which is the percentage of cases the model predicts correctly.

Another important difference when building a classification model is the final node itself. In regression, we used a `Dense` layer with one node only and no activation function. All that is needed to shift the neural network to classification is a `sigmoid` activation function.

Why? Recall that the Sigmoid curve from *Chapter 11, Machine Learning,* transforms all possible X values to y values between 0 and 1. In machine learning, y values greater than 0.5 are mapped to 1, and y values less than 0.5 are mapped to 0. So, all that is needed to convert a regression model to a classification model in a neural network, in addition to selecting the appropriate loss function and metric, is to conclude with a `Dense` layer with one node only that includes a `sigmoid` activation function.

Exercise 167 – building a neural network for classification

We are now going to build a neural network for a dataset that requires classification.

The dataset that we are going to use is the famous *Census* dataset from the UCI Machine Learning Repository, which is commonly used to predict whether adults make more or less than 50K (USD) based on census data from a variety of locations in 1994 (Data source: `https://archive.ics. uci.edu/ml/datasets/census+income`).

We will use a clean version of this dataset with `pd.get_dummies()` already applied, as taken from Packt Publishing's *Hands-On Gradient Boosting with XGBoost and Scikit-Learn,* a machine learning book written by the author, which is a great follow-up book to this one if you are interested in gaining mastery over tree-based models.

Here are the steps to build a classifier as a neural network:

1. Continue with the same Colab notebook (or Jupyter notebook) from *Exercise 166 – using Dropout in a neural network to improve the score.*

2. Load and view the data with the following code, taking y, the target column, as the last column, and X as the remaining columns. Split the data into a training and test set and view the data as in the following code snippet:

```
url = 'https://media.githubusercontent.com/media/
PacktPublishing/Hands-On-Gradient-Boosting-with-XGBoost-
and-Scikit-learn/master/Chapter08/census_cleaned.csv'
df = pd.read_csv(url)
X = df.iloc[:, :-1]
y = df.iloc[:, -1]
X_train, X_test, y_train, y_test = train_test_split(X, y,
random_state=2)
df.head()
```

Here is the expected output:

	age	fnlwgt	education-num	capital-gain	capital-loss	hours-per-week	workclass_?	workclass_Federal-gov	workclass_Local-gov	workclass_Never-worked	...	native-country_Puerto-Rico
0	39	77516	13	2174	0	40	0	0	0	0	...	0
1	50	83311	13	0	0	13	0	0	0	0	...	0
2	38	215646	9	0	0	40	0	0	0	0	...	0
3	53	234721	7	0	0	40	0	0	0	0	...	0
4	28	338409	13	0	0	40	0	0	0	0	...	0

5 rows × 93 columns

Figure 12.24 – Census dataset, screenshot from Colab notebook

3. After setting the number of columns, initialize a Sequential model, then add a single dense layer with eight nodes and a relu activation function followed by an output layer with one node and the required sigmoid activation function. Include the model summary:

```
num_cols = X.shape[1]
model = Sequential()
model.add(Dense(8, input_shape=(num_cols,),
activation='relu'))
model.add(Dense(1, activation='sigmoid'))
print(model.summary())
```

Here is the expected output:

```
Model: "sequential"

Layer (type)                    Output Shape                   Param #
=====================================================================
dense (Dense)                   (None, 8)                      744

dense_1 (Dense)                 (None, 1)                      9

=====================================================================
Total params: 753
Trainable params: 753
Non-trainable params: 0
```

Figure 12.25 – Screenshot from Colab notebook shows 753 total parameters

4. Compile the model with the optimizer set to `adam`, the loss set to `binary_crossentropy`, and the metrics set to a list that only includes `accuracy`, as in the following code snippet:

```python
model.compile(optimizer='adam', loss='binary_
crossentropy', metrics=['accuracy'])
```

5. Set up an Early Stopping monitor with a patience of `10`. Next, fit the model to the training set, making sure to set a high number of epochs with a validation split, and add your Early Stopping monitor to the callbacks. Finally, evaluate the model on the test set and run your code as follows:

```python
early_stopping_monitor = EarlyStopping(patience=10)
model.fit(X_train, y_train, epochs=10000, validation_
split=0.2, callbacks=[early_stopping_monitor])
model.evaluate(X_test, y_test)
```

Your output should be comparable to the following:

```
Epoch 20/10000
611/611 [==============================] - 2s 3ms/step - loss: 12.8306 - accuracy: 0.7302 - val_loss: 2.5190 - val_accuracy: 0.8106
Epoch 21/10000
611/611 [==============================] - 2s 3ms/step - loss: 14.5757 - accuracy: 0.7367 - val_loss: 10.2165 - val_accuracy: 0.7969
Epoch 22/10000
611/611 [==============================] - 1s 2ms/step - loss: 13.4995 - accuracy: 0.7352 - val_loss: 5.3369 - val_accuracy: 0.8104
Epoch 23/10000
611/611 [==============================] - 2s 3ms/step - loss: 11.4023 - accuracy: 0.7411 - val_loss: 3.1207 - val_accuracy: 0.7244
Epoch 24/10000
611/611 [==============================] - 1s 2ms/step - loss: 14.6037 - accuracy: 0.7339 - val_loss: 21.1346 - val_accuracy: 0.3710
Epoch 25/10000
611/611 [==============================] - 1s 2ms/step - loss: 12.8796 - accuracy: 0.7313 - val_loss: 17.6294 - val_accuracy: 0.7916
Epoch 26/10000
611/611 [==============================] - 1s 2ms/step - loss: 9.2974 - accuracy: 0.7528 - val_loss: 2.5884 - val_accuracy: 0.8260
Epoch 27/10000
611/611 [==============================] - 1s 2ms/step - loss: 13.3042 - accuracy: 0.7384 - val_loss: 19.8166 - val_accuracy: 0.7985
Epoch 28/10000
611/611 [==============================] - 1s 2ms/step - loss: 11.3829 - accuracy: 0.7384 - val_loss: 4.6464 - val_accuracy: 0.8206
Epoch 29/10000
611/611 [==============================] - 1s 2ms/step - loss: 12.0870 - accuracy: 0.7468 - val_loss: 9.4172 - val_accuracy: 0.8133
Epoch 30/10000
611/611 [==============================] - 1s 2ms/step - loss: 10.2922 - accuracy: 0.7491 - val_loss: 3.9530 - val_accuracy: 0.8190
255/255 [==============================] - 0s 2ms/step - loss: 4.2645 - accuracy: 0.8048
[4.264492034912109, 0.8048151135444641]
```

Figure 12.26 – Screenshot from Colab notebook – accuracy is
on the right at 80.48 percent (loss is on the left)

Note that the output shows two numbers in a list. The number on the right, `0.8048`, is the accuracy, meaning the model is 80% accurate, and the number on the left is the loss.

That's all there is to it. As you can see, building a classifier is very similar to building a regressor provided that you take care of the loss function, the metric, and the final output layer.

Activity 26 – building your own neural network to predict whether a patient has heart disease

In this activity, you will build a neural network to solve a real-world problem. Doctors need more information to determine whether incoming patients have heart diseases after running some tests. They need a model that will correctly determine whether the patient has heart disease with 80% accuracy. They bring you on board to build a neural network that will take the patient data as input. Your goal is to predict whether new patients have heart disease. You will achieve this goal by training your neural network on the provided dataset, which includes a target column letting you know whether past patients have had heart disease or not.

Here are the steps to achieve this goal:

1. Download the dataset via the following URL: `https://media.githubusercontent.com/media/PacktPublishing/Hands-On-Gradient-Boosting-with-XGBoost-and-Scikit-learn/master/Chapter02/heart_disease.csv`.

2. Set `X`, the predictor columns, equal to all columns except the last. Set `y`, the target column, equal to the last column.

3. Split the data into a training and a test set.

4. Initialize a Sequential model.

5. Add your first Dense layer, making sure to include `input_shape=(num_cols,)`, along with the number of nodes and an activation function.

6. Include additional Dense layers and possible Dropout layers as needed.

7. Decide whether your final layer does not need an activation function, or whether it should have a `sigmoid` activation function.

8. Include an Early Stopping monitor to set the number of epochs.

9. Fit your data on the training set, making sure to include a `validation_split` value set to your desired percentage.

10. Adjust your neural network after your first scores come back until you achieve an accuracy of 80% or higher.

You should get an output similar to the following when you are finished. Recall that the accuracy is the second number in the list:

```
Epoch 72/1000
6/6 [==============================] - 0s 8ms/step - loss: 0.4675 - accuracy: 0.8232 - val_loss: 0.5302 - val_accuracy: 0.7174
Epoch 73/1000
6/6 [==============================] - 0s 9ms/step - loss: 0.3969 - accuracy: 0.8287 - val_loss: 0.3581 - val_accuracy: 0.8478
Epoch 74/1000
6/6 [==============================] - 0s 8ms/step - loss: 0.3702 - accuracy: 0.8343 - val_loss: 0.5377 - val_accuracy: 0.7174
Epoch 75/1000
6/6 [==============================] - 0s 8ms/step - loss: 0.3664 - accuracy: 0.8453 - val_loss: 0.4179 - val_accuracy: 0.8043
Epoch 76/1000
6/6 [==============================] - 0s 10ms/step - loss: 0.4303 - accuracy: 0.7845 - val_loss: 0.3773 - val_accuracy: 0.8478
Epoch 77/1000
6/6 [==============================] - 0s 8ms/step - loss: 0.4266 - accuracy: 0.8453 - val_loss: 0.6357 - val_accuracy: 0.6522
Epoch 78/1000
6/6 [==============================] - 0s 8ms/step - loss: 0.4155 - accuracy: 0.8232 - val_loss: 0.4632 - val_accuracy: 0.8261
Epoch 79/1000
6/6 [==============================] - 0s 9ms/step - loss: 0.4151 - accuracy: 0.8122 - val_loss: 0.4614 - val_accuracy: 0.7826
Epoch 80/1000
6/6 [==============================] - 0s 8ms/step - loss: 0.3488 - accuracy: 0.8453 - val_loss: 0.3515 - val_accuracy: 0.7826
3/3 [==============================] - 0s 4ms/step - loss: 0.4404 - accuracy: 0.8026
[0.44042325019836426, 0.8026315569877625]
```

Figure 12.27 – Sample final score from the neural network on the heart disease dataset

> **Note**
> A solution for this activity may be found here: `https://colab.research.google.com/drive/1O-F_0NwTlV3zMt6TrU4bUMeVhlsjLMY9#scrollTo=DUe9Oe2OGUDJ`.

Convolutional neural networks

Although deep learning performs well on tabular regression and classification datasets, deep learning has a bigger advantage when making predictions from unstructured data such as images or text.

When it comes to classifying images, deep learning shines by analyzing data not one-dimensionally, but two-dimensionally, using convolutional neural networks, or CNNs for short.

Convolutional neural networks are among the strongest machine learning algorithms in the world today for classifying images. In this section, you will learn the basic theory behind convolutions before building your own CNN.

MNIST

MNIST is the name of a famous dataset of handwritten digits from 1998 that has been widely used in computer vision. The dataset consists of 60K training images and 10K test images.

Google Colab includes a smaller sample of 20K training images, along with the 10K test images, that may be directly accessed in a Colab notebook and prepared for machine learning, as in the following exercise.

Exercise 168 – preparing MNIST data for machine learning

In this exercise, you will load the MNIST data, view the data, and prepare it for machine learning with the following steps:

1. Open up a new Colab notebook at `colab.research.google.com`, then enter and run the following code in a cell:

```
import pandas as pd
df=pd.read_csv('/content/sample_data/mnist_train_small.
csv', header=None)
df_test=pd.read_csv('/content/sample_data/mnist_test.
csv',header=None)
df.head()
```

The output is as follows:

	0	1	2	3	4	5	6	7	8	9	...	775	776	777	778	779	780	781	782	783	784
0	6	0	0	0	0	0	0	0	0	0	...	0	0	0	0	0	0	0	0	0	0
1	5	0	0	0	0	0	0	0	0	0	...	0	0	0	0	0	0	0	0	0	0
2	7	0	0	0	0	0	0	0	0	0	...	0	0	0	0	0	0	0	0	0	0
3	9	0	0	0	0	0	0	0	0	0	...	0	0	0	0	0	0	0	0	0	0
4	5	0	0	0	0	0	0	0	0	0	...	0	0	0	0	0	0	0	0	0	0

Figure 12.28 – MNIST one-dimensional data

> **Note**
>
> As the output indicates, the 0th column shows the digit that we are trying to predict, while the other 784 columns show the values of the pixels that make up the image. Most pixels have a value of 0 because there is nothing there.

2. Now, split the training and test data into X and y, choosing the 0th column as the y value, what you are trying to predict, and the remaining 784 columns as the X values:

```
X = df.iloc[:, 1:]
y = df.iloc[:, 0]
X_test = df_test.iloc[:, 1:]
y_test = df_test.iloc[:, 0]
```

3.   It's always worth viewing the actual images, the digits that you are trying to predict. Although this step is optional, it's definitely worth your while. Instead of viewing the data as a long string of individual pixels, it's going to be reshaped into 28x28 two-dimensional pixels and then displayed using the following annotated steps:

```python
import numpy as np
# Get random index between 0 and number of rows in X
random_index = np.random.randint(0, X.shape[0])
# Get the row with random index
random_row = X.iloc[random_index, :]
# Convert random row to numpy array for reshaping
np_random_row = np.array(random_row)
# reshape image from 1D 784 cols, to 2D 28 x 28
random_image = np_random_row.reshape(28, 28)
# Show image
import matplotlib.pyplot as plt
plt.imshow(random_image, cmap='Greys')
plt.axis('off')
plt.show()
print(y[random_index])
```

The output is random, so yours will likely be different than ours, but here is one possible sample:

3

Figure 12.29 – Sample MNIST pixelated image with a correct classification label

Don't worry that the image looks pixelated. It's supposed to! It's from 1998.

4. Next, we will one-hot encode the y values so that instead of being represented by the number 3, the 3 value will be encoded as follows: [0, 0, 0, 1, 0, 0, 0, 0, 0, 0]. This way, the 3 value stands alone, instead of being closer to 2 and 4 than other digits, which is not what we want for image classification:

```
from keras.utils.np_utils import to_categorical
y = to_categorical(y, num_classes=10)
y_test = to_categorical(y_test, num_classes=10)
```

5. Now let's standardize X and reshape it into the correct size of a NumPy array, which is four-dimensional: one dimension for the number of rows, two dimensions for the 28x28 2D representation, and the final dimension is 1, which can be adjusted to represent color. The code snippet is as follows:

```
# Standardize X
X = X/255
X_test = X_test/255
# convert X to numpy array
X = np.array(X)
X_test = np.array(X_test)
# reshape X to (rows, 28, 28, 1)
X = X.reshape(X.shape[0], 28, 28, 1)
X_test = X_test.reshape(X_test.shape[0], 28, 28, 1)
```

You are now ready to build a CNN!

CNN kernel

The main idea behind a CNN is the kernel. Since a CNN works on two-dimensional data, there must be a way of interacting with the data two-dimensionally. The general idea is to set up a kernel, which acts not on individual pixels but on squares of pixels, one square at a time.

Consider the following matrix:

$$\begin{bmatrix} 1 & 7 & 22 \\ 9 & 3 & 1 \\ 9 & 4 & 2 \end{bmatrix}$$

Figure 12.30 – Sample matrix

We can rotate through the matrix via a two-dimensional square as follows:

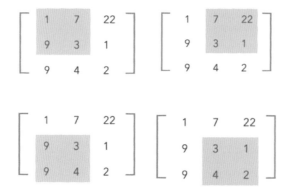

Figure 12.31 – The upper-left subset (top left), the upper-right subset (top right), the bottom-left subset (bottom left), and the bottom-right subset (bottom right) of the matrix

Each time we rotate through the matrix, we can perform a mathematical operation, also called a **convolution**, that will take each two-dimensional subset of the matrix as an input, and return a numerical output. One strategy is to choose a matrix of four numbers for the shaded square and perform the dot product with the given subset for each iteration.

Recall that the dot product of [0,1] and [1,2] is 0*1 + 1*2 = 2. The dot product multiplies each component together and sums the results.

The following three figures show how a randomly chosen matrix of [[1,2],[0,1]] may be used as a convolution to transform our original matrix into a new matrix:

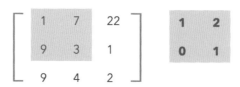

Figure 12.32 – Step A, preparing a convolution to take the dot product of the matrix on the right with the shaded matrix on the left

Figure 12.33 – Step B, the dot product of the two matrices, a convolution, gives the result of 18

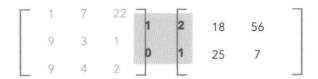

Figure 12.34 – Step C, the process of taking dot product may be repeated for each subset of the left matrix with [[1,2],[0,1]] to obtain the new matrix on the right

We started with an original matrix, then performed a convolution to transform the original matrix into a new matrix. With real data, a convolution will take the pixel values of an original image, and output variations of that image using different matrices, and different sizes of kernels. As a programmer, you choose the size of the kernel, and the neural network will choose the values of the matrix by first choosing random values, and then making adjustments to optimize predictions as before.

The theory of convolutions and computer vision is a deep and fascinating one. Although we are just scratching the surface, you now have enough background to understand the foundation behind building convolutional neural networks.

It's time to build your first CNN to optimize predictions with the MNIST dataset in the following exercise.

Exercise 169 – building a CNN to predict handwritten digits

Here are the steps to build your first CNN:

1. Import and initialize a `Sequential` model. Also import `Dense`, `Conv2D`, `Flatten`, and `MaxPool2D`:

```
from keras.models import Sequential
from keras.layers import Dense, Conv2D, Flatten,
MaxPool2D
model = Sequential()
```

2. Add a convolutional layer with 32 nodes that includes a kernel size of 3 and a `relu` activation. Be sure to specify `input_shape` as `(28, 28, 1)` where the 1 allows for the third dimension of color, which is not being used here. Also, note that `kernel_size` of 3 means a 3x3 matrix. It will rotate over the entire 28x28 matrix as shown in our previous example:

```
model.add(Conv2D(32, kernel_size=3, activation='relu',
input_shape=(28, 28, 1)))
```

3. Add a max pooling layer with a size of 2 (meaning 2x2). This will rotate over the entire matrix and take the largest value of every four entries. In other words, it highlights the brightest parts of the image:

```
model.add(MaxPool2D(2))
```

4. Add a second convolutional layer of 16 nodes with a kernel of 3, and another `relu` activation. Include another `MaxPool2D` layer:

```
model.add(Conv2D(16, kernel_size=3, activation='relu'))
model.add(MaxPool2D(2))
```

5. Before creating the output layer with 10 nodes (since 10 digits) using a `softmax` activation function, which is required for multi-classification, convert the entire image into one dimension by adding a `Flatten` layer:

```
model.add(Flatten())
model.add(Dense(10, activation='softmax'))
```

6. Finally, summarize and compile your model using the same techniques described earlier in this chapter for classification. Try 20 epochs, and be sure to evaluate on the test set. Before running your model, speed up your run time by switching to a GPU in Colab: **Runtime | Change runtime type | GPU**:

```
print(model.summary())
model.compile(optimizer='adam', loss='categorical_
crossentropy',
metrics=['accuracy'])
model.fit(X, y, epochs=20)
model.evaluate(X_test, y_test)
```

The output for the model summary is as follows:

```
Model: "sequential"
_____
 Layer (type)                Output Shape              Param #
=================================================================
 conv2d (Conv2D)             (None, 26, 26, 32)        320

 max_pooling2d (MaxPooling2D  (None, 13, 13, 32)       0
 )

 conv2d_1 (Conv2D)           (None, 11, 11, 16)        4624

 max_pooling2d_1 (MaxPooling  (None, 5, 5, 16)         0
 2D)

 flatten (Flatten)           (None, 400)               0

 dense (Dense)               (None, 10)                4010

=================================================================
Total params: 8,954
Trainable params: 8,954
Non-trainable params: 0
```

Figure 12.35 – The CNN contains 8,954 parameters that must be optimized

The output for the model is as follows:

```
Epoch 15/20
625/625 [==============================] - 13s 21ms/step - loss: 0.0157 - accuracy: 0.9948
Epoch 16/20
625/625 [==============================] - 13s 21ms/step - loss: 0.0124 - accuracy: 0.9958
Epoch 17/20
625/625 [==============================] - 13s 21ms/step - loss: 0.0131 - accuracy: 0.9958
Epoch 18/20
625/625 [==============================] - 13s 21ms/step - loss: 0.0105 - accuracy: 0.9964
Epoch 19/20
625/625 [==============================] - 13s 21ms/step - loss: 0.0085 - accuracy: 0.9975
Epoch 20/20
625/625 [==============================] - 13s 21ms/step - loss: 0.0103 - accuracy: 0.9961
313/313 [==============================] - 3s 8ms/step - loss: 0.0760 - accuracy: 0.9810
[0.07597225904464722, 0.9810000061988831]
```

Figure 12.36 – The CNN shows an accuracy of 98.1 percent

As you can see from the preceding figure, the model successfully predicts handwritten digits with 98% accuracy, an outstanding initial result. Have fun playing around with the parameters and see whether you can get 99% or better!

Here is a link to the Colab notebook that was used in this lesson:

```
https://colab.research.google.com/drive/1OQ0vMLsEj18THVLjCKqH8Ue7Z
mkA7-BE?usp=sharing.
```

Activity 27 – classifying MNIST Fashion images using CNNs

It's time to try CNNs on your own. Keras comes with an MNIST *Fashion* dataset that you can use to classify fashion images using the same general principles as you applied in *Exercise 169 – building a CNN to predict handwritten digits*.

The goal of this activity is to classify each fashion item that comes through a clothing sales website so that a range of sale prices may be suggested to the user depending on the type of item. Users just submit images of what they want to sell, and your job is to classify the images. You know that CNNs are the best in the world for classifying images, so you are going to use one to help your team.

Here are the steps to complete the activity.

1. Download the Keras MNIST *Fashion* dataset using the following code in a Colab notebook, making sure to set the runtime to GPU for optimal processing speed:

```
from keras.datasets import fashion_mnist
(X, y), (X_test, y_test) = fashion_mnist.load_data()
```

2. Import the necessary libraries to build your CNN. Along with `Sequential`, `Dense`, `Conv2D`, `MaxPool2D`, `Flatten`, and `Dense`, we recommend using `Dropout` to help prevent your model from overfitting and to improve scores.

3. Be sure to standardize and reshape X, and change y to `to_categorical` as in *Exercise 168 – preparing MNIST data for machine learning*. The MNIST *Fashion* dataset has the same number of categories, 10, and the data fits the same 28x28 shape as the MNIST dataset that you used to classify digits.

4. Initialize a Sequential model, then choose the size of your first convolutional layer, along with the size of your kernel.

5. Add max pooling layers, more convolutional layers, and Dropout layers as you see fit. Be judicious, recalling that more nodes result in more parameters and longer build times.

6. Evaluate your model on the test set.

7. Go back and make adjustments to improve your score.

Your output should be similar to the following:

```
Epoch 15/20
1875/1875 [==============================] - 6s 3ms/step - loss: 0.2109 - accuracy: 0.9232
Epoch 16/20
1875/1875 [==============================] - 7s 4ms/step - loss: 0.2068 - accuracy: 0.9244
Epoch 17/20
1875/1875 [==============================] - 6s 3ms/step - loss: 0.2037 - accuracy: 0.9257
Epoch 18/20
1875/1875 [==============================] - 6s 3ms/step - loss: 0.2019 - accuracy: 0.9255
Epoch 19/20
1875/1875 [==============================] - 6s 3ms/step - loss: 0.1955 - accuracy: 0.9269
Epoch 20/20
1875/1875 [==============================] - 6s 3ms/step - loss: 0.1952 - accuracy: 0.9282
313/313 [==============================] - 1s 3ms/step - loss: 0.2489 - accuracy: 0.9100
[0.24885225296020508, 0.9100000262260437]
```

Figure 12.37 – An output for Activity 27 with 91% accuracy

See whether you can beat our score of 91% accuracy!

Summary

In this chapter, you learned how to build neural networks using Keras, one of the best deep learning libraries in the world. You built Sequential dense models with a variety of hidden layers and nodes using the ReLU activation function and the Adam optimizer. You used Early Stopping to find an ideal number of epochs, and you used Dropout to help prevent overfitting. Furthermore, you trained both regressors and classifiers, making sure to use `binary_crossentropy` as the classification loss function and the `sigmoid` activation function. Additionally, you learned about the foundations behind convolutions and built convolutional neural networks to classify handwritten digits with over 98% accuracy.

Congratulations on completing your deep learning journey.

The next chapter is the final chapter of the second edition of the Python Workshop, *New Features in Python*, which includes updates from Python 3.7 to Python 3.11.

13

The Evolution of Python – Discovering New Python Features

Overview

By the end of his chapter, you will understand how Python continues to evolve and how to track that evolution to be up to date with the latest development. The chapter will introduce you to the **Python Enhancement Proposals (PEPs)** and show you the most significant enhancements of the language, from Python 3.7 to Python 3.11, allowing you to leverage the new features of the language.

Introduction

Across this book, we have seen how to use Python effectively, and the different tools and APIs that the language offers us. However, Python is not a language set in stone; it continues to evolve with every new release.

The Python development team cuts a release of the interpreter every year and provides a window of support, where bug fixes are backported, as well as a long-term support window for critical security fixes only.

In this chapter, we will see how to keep us up to date with the development of Python, how enhancements are made, and the changes that the latest versions of Python have published.

We will be covering the following topics:

- Python Enhancement Proposals
- New features released in Python from version 3.7 to version 3.11

Python Enhancement Proposals

The Python language evolves as its reference implementation changes (**CPython**). The process to introduce a change in the reference implementation and, therefore, the language is done by following the Python developer's guide (`https://devguide.python.org/`). An important part of the evolution of the language is the **Python Enhancement Proposal** (**PEP**), a step required for any *major* change in the language. The process starts with a core developer (a person with the commit bit in `python/cpython`) who sponsors or directly submits a draft PEP in the `python/peps` repository. Those proposals are usually first discussed in the Python ideas forum to gather a quick opinion by both developers and users alike on how useful they are or what issues they might face.

> **Tip**
> A great way to be involved in the evolution of the language is to subscribe to the forum and participate in those conversations.

After a core developer submits a PEP for review, the steering council, the governing body of the Python language, discusses it. The steering council takes input from the rest of the core developers, and if they find the change valid, it can be marked as *final* and accepted for the language. PEPs are used to propose changes to the language implementation or any process related to the development of Python. PEP 1 documents the process of submitting and reviewing PEPs.

> **Tip**
> Subscribe to the PEP discussions at `https://discuss.python.org/c/peps` to follow major changes in the language.

A PEP usually includes the following sections:

- A metadata header.

- An abstract with a short description and motivation of the PEP, and why it is needed.

- A rationale explaining the decisions taken when writing the PEP.

- A detailed PEP specification, how can it impact existing Python code, whether it has any security implications, and how you expect trainers to teach the new feature.

- A reference implementation, if available, rejected ideas when exploring the PEP, and a copyright note. You can find a template of a PEP in PEP 12 (`https://peps.python.org/pep-0012/`).

If you plan to work professionally using Python, I recommend you read some of the following PEPs:

- **PEP 8**: A style guide on Python code. This is a must-read if you are writing Python professionally. It allows Python developers across the globe to write and read Python with a common style, making it easier to read for everyone.

- **PEP 1**: A PEP that documents the purpose and instructions on how to submit a PEP. It explains what a PEP is, the workflow for submitting one, and detailed instructions on how to create a *good PEP*.

- **PEP 11**: The different levels of support that CPython offers on different platforms.

- **PEP 602**: The new Python annual release schedule.

In the next sections, we will be looking at new features available in each Python version, starting with Python 3.7.

Python 3.7

Python 3.7 was released in June 2018, received bug fixes until June 2020, and will receive security patches until June 2023.

Built-in breakpoint

The new built-in `breakpoint()` function allows you to quickly drop into a debugger by just writing it anywhere in your code. Rather than having to call the common idiom of `import pdb;pdb.set_trace()`, in this version of Python, you can just use the built-in `breakpoint()`, which not only works with the default Python debugger (`pdb`) but any other debugger that you might use.

Module dynamic attributes

Python is an object-oriented programming language. Everything is an object in Python, and with PEP 562, modules can behave more like classes! With the addition of the work done by PEP 562, you can now add a `__getattr__` function to your module that allows you to dynamically evaluate the querying of an attribute.

This is useful when you need to deprecate an attribute of your module, if you need to perform some catching, or if something that you initially declared as an attribute now needs to do some runtime evaluation.

Additionally, you can combine `__getattr__` with `lru_cache` to lazily evaluate the attributes of your module. This is useful when you have a module with constants that are expensive to compute. That allows you to move from the following:

```python
# constants_package.py
constant1 = expensieve_call()
constant2 = expensieve_call2()
```

To:

```python
# constants_package.py
_constant_resolution = {
    "constants1": expensive_call,
    "constants2": expensive_call2,
}
@functools.lru_cache(maxsize=None)
def __getattr__(name):
    try:
        return _constant_resolution[name]()
    except KeyError:
        raise AttributeError(f"module {__name__!r} has no
attribute {name!r}")
```

The second version of the code will allow you to get the same results without greedily evaluating those constants. In addition, by using `lru_cache`, no matter how many times users query the attribute, Python will execute each function only once.

Nanosecond support in a time module

As we saw in *Chapter 6*, *The Standard Library*, we can use the Python `time` APIs to get the current time in multiple ways via functions such as `time.time` and `time.monotonic`, but those APIs return the time in `float`, which is usually sufficient in most scenarios, but it might not be adequate if we need an accurate result that can be used with detailed precision. This resulted in PEP 564, which adds a new function to the `time` module that allows you to get the time with nanosecond precision as `integer`. The PEP added new functions that end with the `_ns` prefix, which can be used in situations where we care about getting the precise time. This new API allows the user to work with time using integers, therefore assuring that their computations will always preserve nanosecond precision.

The dict insertion order is preserved

Since Python 3.7, we can rely on Python dictionaries preserving their insertion order, allowing us to iterate them while having a deterministic result. You can see its effect by running the following code in an interpreter before 3.6 and one after 3.6, as even if this was already happening in 3.6, it was not until 3.7 that it was guaranteed by the standard:

```
x = {}
x["a"] = 1
x["b"] = 2
x[0] = 3
print(list(x))
```

In Python 2.7, the result will be `['a', 0, 'b']`, and you should not rely on the order of the keys, as there are no guarantees. However, if you are using Python 3.7+, you can be sure that the order of the keys is always going to be `['a', 'b', 0]`. That is fantastic, as it makes the dictionary (and sets) an ordered container (which is different from a sorted one). This is a property that few languages provide.

Dataclasses

PEP 567 brought dataclasses to Python 3.7. Before this version, users relied on the third-party `attrs` package, which had a continuously growing popularity. To know more about how to use dataclasses, refer to *Chapter 6, The Standard Library*, and *Exercise 86 – using the dataclass module*.

Importlib.resources

This new module in the standard library allows developers to load and read resources within modules. Using `importlib.resources` allows us to tell an interpreter to read a resource without having to provide paths, making it resilient to package managers that might relocate files. This module also allows us to model packages that might not have a disk representation.

Loading data that is part of a module could not be easier with this module now. There are two APIs that you will usually rely on: `importlib.resources.files(package)` to get all the files that a Python package provides and `importlib.resources.open_text/open_binary(package, resource)` to load a file.

Python 3.8

Python 3.8 was released in October 2019, received bug fixes until May 2021, and will receive security patches until October 2024.

Assignment expression

One of the most known additions to Python 3.8 is the assignment expression, also known as the **walrus** operator. It was quite a controversial addition to Python, which many people attribute to the stepping down of Guido van Rossum from the Python's final decision-making role in the CPython evolution.

This new syntax allows developers to write an assignment in the place of an expression. This allows for shorter code by combining what otherwise needs to be multiple lines of code. This is quite useful in control flow operations when combined with reading data or using regular expressions. See the following examples.

This is without PEP 572:

```
running = True
while running:
    data = get_more_data()
    if not data:
        running = check_if_running()
    business_logic(data)
```

This is with PEP 572:

```
while data := get_more_data():
    business_logic(data)
```

In the example, you can see how by using the : = operator, we save multiple lines of code, making the code quicker and arguably easier to read. You can treat the result of the assignment expression as an expression, allowing you to write the following code:

```
while len(data := get_more_data) >= 1
```

functools.cached_property

This new and terribly handy function allows you to optimize your code by allowing you to do in one line a common Python idiom that was used to cache a class attribute, which might be expensive to compute. Before Python 3.8, you would commonly find code like the following:

```
class MyClass:
    def __init__(self):
        self._myvar = None
    @property
    def myvar(self):
```

```
        if self._myvar is None:
            self._myvar = expensive_operation()
        return self._myvar
```

With the addition of `cached_property`, you can now simplify that to the following:

```
class MyClass:
    @functools.cached_property
    def myvar(self):
        return expensive_operation()
```

importlib.metadata

A new module was added in Python 3.8 that lets us read metadata about third-party packages that we have installed in our system. `importlib.metadata` can be used to replace usage of less efficient and third-party dependent code that relies on `pkg_resources`. See the following examples of how this new module is useful on a Python installation with `pytest` installed:

```
import importlib.metadata
importlib.metadata.version("pytest")
```

You get the following result:

`0.32.3`

Figure 13.1 – The pytest version

You can get any kind of metadata by getting it as a dictionary, by invoking the `metadata` function:

```
import importlib.metadata
importlib.metadata.metadata("pytest")["License"]
```

Here is the output:

`MIT license`

Figure 13.2 – The pytest license

typing.TypedDict, typing.Final, and typing.Literal

If you like to type your Python code, 3.8 brings three new classes to the typing module, which are quite useful to better qualify the types you use in your code.

Using `typing.Literal` allows you to type your code to specify what concrete values it can get beyond just documenting the type. This is specifically useful in situations where strings can be passed but there is only a known list of values. See the following example:

```
MODE = Literal['r', 'rb', 'w', 'wb']
def open_helper(file: str, mode: MODE) -> str:
```

Without `typing.Literal`, you will need to type mode as `str`, allowing other strings that are not valid types. In 3.8, you can also use `typing.Final`, which allows you to mark a variable as a constant, and the type checker will flag an error if you try to change the value of the variable.

Finally, we have `typing.TypedDict`, a great way to type your dictionaries when you know they need to have a specific set of keys. If you create a type with `Point2D = TypedDict('Point2D', x=int, y=int)`, the type checker will flag errors when you create dictionaries with a key that is neither x nor y.

f-string debug support via =

How many times have you written the name of a variable followed by its value? With Python 3.8, this just became a lot easier with debug support in f-strings using =. With this addition, you can now write code as follows to quickly debug your variables:

```
import datetime
name = "Python"
birthday = datetime.date(1991, 2, 20)
print(f'{name=} {birthday=}' )
```

This will produce the following output:

```
name='Python' birthday=datetime.date(1991, 2, 20)
```

Figure 13.3 – An f-string example

Positional-only parameters

If you are an API provider, you will definitely like this new addition to Python. With PEP570, you can now mark parameters as positional only, making the name of the function parameter `private`, and allowing you to change it in the future if so desired. Before Python 3.8, if you were creating an API with a signature such as `def convert_to_int(variable: float):`, users could call your function with the `convert_to_int(variable=3.14)` syntax. That could be an issue if you wanted to rename your variable in the future or wanted to move to `varargs`. With the addition of positional-only parameters to the language, you can now use new syntax to mark those arguments as positional only, preventing them from being passed using a `def convert_to_int(variable: float, /):` keyword. When / is specified, all arguments before it will be marked as positional only, similar to how * can be used to mark all arguments after it as keyword-only.

Python 3.9

Python 3.9 was released in October 2020, received bug fixes until May 2022, and will receive security patches until October 2025.

PEG parser

One of the most significant changes in Python 3.9 is the rewrite of the parser that sits at the core of an interpreter. After 30 years of using the LL1 parser, which was quite useful for Python, the core development team decided to move to a more modern and powerful parser, which enabled many enhancements to the language – from new syntax to better error messages. While this did not result in any big change directly for developers, it has helped the language to continue evolving. Take a read at `https://peps.python.org/pep-0617/` to understand the work that was done and how it is helping Python evolve.

Support for the IANA database

If you are working with time zones, you probably have used the IANA database (`https://www.iana.org/time-zones`) before. This database allows you to map strings to data that defines what offset to set for that time zone when given a date time. Before Python 3.9, two third-party packages, `dateutil` and `pytz`, provided this data to developers. With the implementation of PEP 615, developers can now fetch time zone information from their OS without the need to rely on a third-party package.

See the following example that converts a date time from the New York time zone to Los Angeles, all with the standard library:

```
import datetime
from zoneinfo import ZoneInfo
nyc_tz = ZoneInfo("America/New_York")
la_tz = ZoneInfo("America/Los_Angeles")
dt = datetime.datetime(2022, 5, 21, hour=12, tzinfo=nyc_tz)
print(dt.isoformat())
```

You will get the following result:

```
2022-05-21T12:00:00-04:00
```

Figure 13.4 – The datetime iso formatted

We can see how both the time and the offset change when we convert the datetime instance to a different time zone using astimezone:

```
print(dt.astimezone(la_tz).isoformat())
```

Now, the output will be the following:

```
2022-05-21T09:00:00-07:00
```

Figure 13.5 – The datetime iso formatted after the time zone change

Merge (|) and update (|=) syntax for dicts

Sets and dictionaries are getting closer and closer functionally. In this version of Python, dicts got support for the | union operator. This allows you to combine dictionaries with the following syntax:

```
d1 = dict(key1="d1", key3="d1")
d2 = dict(key2="d2", key3="d2")
print(d1 | d2)
```

This is the output:

```
{'key1': 'd1', 'key3': 'd2', 'key2': 'd2'}
```

Figure 13.6 – The dict merge output

Something to note is that if a key is present in both dictionaries, it will take the value from the last seen dictionary. Additionally, you can use the |= operator to merge an existing dictionary with another:

```
d1 = dict(key1="d1", key3="d1")
d1 |= dict(key2="d2", key3="d2")
print(d1)
```

The output observed is as follows:

```
{'key1': 'd1', 'key3': 'd2', 'key2': 'd2'}
```

Figure 13.7 – The dict merge operator output

str.removeprefix and str.removesuffix

With these two functions, we can remove the suffix or prefix of a string, something that many developers mistakenly used to do with `strip`. The `strip` function takes an optional list of characters to override the default and developers got confused, thinking that it was the exact string that would be removed. See the following example:

```
print("filepy.py".rstrip(".py"))
```

This gives the output as the following:

```
file
```

Figure 13.8 – The rstrip output

Users might have expected `filepy` as the result, but instead, just `file` is returned, as `strip` has been instructed to delete all p, y, and . characters from the end of the string. If you want to remove the suffix of a string, you can now use `str.removesuffix` instead:

```
print("filepy.py".removesuffix(".py"))
```

We will now get the expected output:

```
filepy
```

Figure 13.9 – The removesuffix output

Type hints with standard collections

Before Python 3.9, typing collections needed to import their types from the typing module. With the addition of PEP 585, developers can now use the standard library collections when type-hinting their code. This transforms the existing code from the following:

```
from typing import Dict, List
def myfunc(values: Dict["str", List[int]]) -> None:
```

To the following:

```
def myfunc(values: dict["str", list[int]]) -> None:
```

Python 3.10

Python 3.10 was released in October 2021, will receive bug fixes until May 2023, and will receive security patches until October 2026.

Pattern matching – PEP 634

By far, the most controversial addition to the Python 3.10 pattern matches was bringing `match` and `case` to the language. This addition consists of three different PEPS: PEP 634, PEP 635, and PEP 636. This new syntax allows you to mirror-switch structures that you might have seen in other languages:

```
match code:
    case 1:
        print("Working as expected")
    case -1 | -2 | -3:
        print("Internal Error")
    case _:
        print("Unknown code")
```

Note that to specify one of the multiple values, you need to use the | operator and not a comma. Using a comma will try to match a list. However, using dictionaries will be more correct for the previous example; the power of pattern matching comes from matching a variable, whose type or length in the case of containers is a lot more dynamic. Pattern matching allows you to evaluate specific properties of an object and copy those in variables when doing a match. See the following example:

```
match x:
    case {"warning": value}:
        print("warning passed with value:", value)
    case ["error", value]:
        print("Error array passed with value:", value)
```

Pattern matching is also useful when interacting with data in the form of containers and having to take different actions or create different objects based on their values. See the following example from the Python standard library:

```
match json_pet:
    case {"type": "cat", "name": name, "pattern": pattern}:
        return Cat(name, pattern)
    case {"type": "dog", "name": name, "breed": breed}:
        return Dog(name, breed)
    case _:
        raise ValueError("Not a suitable pet")
```

Note how pattern matching not only routes the code through one branch or another based on the attributes that we are matching but also captures others with specific variables. If you want to know more about pattern matching and understand how it works, we recommend you read `https://peps.python.org/pep-0636/`, which is a tutorial on how to use structural pattern matching.

Parenthesized context managers

Thanks to the introduction of the new PEG parser in Python 3.9, 3.10 was able to address a long-standing issue in Python grammar – allowing the use of parentheses in context managers.

If you have written multiple context managers in Python, you are probably aware of how hard it is to nicely format that code. This change allows you to move from having to write code such as the following:

```
with CtxManager1(
    ) as example1, CtxManager2(
    ) as example2, CtxManager3(
    ) as example3
):
```

To being able to write code such as the following:

```
with (
    CtxManager1() as example1,
    CtxManager2() as example2,
    CtxManager3() as example3,
):
```

Better error messages

Another advantage of the new parser is the new ability to write code to better handle errors in an interpreter. While Python errors are usually quite informative compared to other languages, when an error happens at parsing time, it is often quite cryptic.

Let's take the following code, which is missing a closing bracket in the first line:

```
d = {"key": "value", "key2": ["value"]
def func(): pass
```

Running it in a Python interpreter before Python 3.10 will give us the following error, which does not reference the first line at all and, therefore, is quite hard to debug:

```
$ python2.7 example.py
  File "example.py", line 2
    def func(): pass
       ^
SyntaxError: invalid syntax
```

Figure 13.10 – A previous error output

In Python 3.10, the error message will be the following:

```
$ python3.10 example.py
  File "/home/mcorcherojim/tmp/packt/example.py", line 1
    d = {"key": "value", "key2": ["value"]
        ^
SyntaxError: '{' was never closed
```

Figure 13.11 – The improved error output

This nicely points developers to the root cause of the issue.

Similar to missing brackets, there have been similar improvements to many other syntaxes, which saves developers time when developing by pointing them to the source of the issue.

Type union operator (|) – PEP 604

Python 3.10 brings some additional syntax sugar for typing. A common situation when type-hinting your code is that a parameter might have one of many types. This used to be handled by using the `typing.Union` type, but since Python 3.10, you can use the `|` operator to represent the same.

That allows you to move from writing code as the following:

```
def parse_number(text: str, pattern: typing.Union[str,
re.Pattern]) -> typing.Union[int, float]
```

To the following instead:

```
def parse_number(text: str, pattern: str | re.Pattern) ->int |
float
```

Statistics – covariance, correlation, and linear_regression

The Python 3.10 release adds functions to compute the covariance, the correlation, and the linear regression given two inputs:

```
>>> x = range(9)
>>> y = [*range(3)] * 3
>>> import statistics
>>> statistics.covariance(x, y)
0.75
>>> statistics.correlation(x, y)
0.31622776601683794
>>> statistics.linear_regression(x, y)
LinearRegression(slope=0.1, intercept=0.6)
```

Python 3.11

Python 3.11 was released in October 2022, will receive bug fixes until May 2024, and will receive security patches until October 2027.

Faster runtime

The new 3.11 is 22% faster than 3.10 when measured with the Python performance benchmark suite. The result depends a lot on your application and will usually range between 10% and 60%. A series of optimization into how code is parsed and run together with startup improvements have made this possible, as part of a project branded as **Faster CPython** that is focusing on making an interpreter faster.

Enhanced errors in tracebacks

Building on the success achieved with the improvement of error messages in Python 3.10, 3.11 has done substantial work to facilitate the debugging of errors in traceback through PEP 659. The interpreter will now point to the exact expression that caused the exception, allowing a developer to quickly figure out the root issue without using a debugger.

This is quite useful when navigating dictionaries, given the following code:

```
d = dict(key1=dict(key2=None, key3=None))
print(d["key1"]["key2"]["key3"])
```

Before Python 3.11, we will get the following error:

```
$ python3.9 example.py
Traceback (most recent call last):
  File "/home/mcorcherojim/tmp/packt/example.py", line 2, in <module>
    print(d["key"]["key2"]["key3"])
TypeError: 'NoneType' object is not subscriptable
```

Figure 13.12 – The previous dict error output

With Python 3.11, we get the following:

```
$ python3.11 example.py
Traceback (most recent call last):
  File "/home/mcorcherojim/tmp/packt/example.py", line 2, in <module>
    print(d["key"]["key2"]["key3"])
          ~~~~~~~~~~~~~~~~~^^^^^^^^
TypeError: 'NoneType' object is not subscriptable
```

Figure 13.13 – The enhanced dict error output

Note how the interpreter is now pointing us to the lookup that caused the error. Without this information, it would be hard to know where that NoneType was coming from. Here, the developer can easily realize that the exception was triggered when querying key3, meaning that the result of looking up key2 was None.

This is also quite useful when doing math operations. See the following code example:

```
x = 1
y = 2
str_num = "2"
print((x + y) * int(str_num) + y + str_num)
```

Before Python 3.11, we would get the following error:

```
$ python3.10 example.py
Traceback (most recent call last):
  File "/home/mcorcherojim/tmp/packt/example.py", line 4, in <module>
    print((x + y) * int(str_num) + y + str_num)
TypeError: unsupported operand type(s) for +: 'int' and 'str'
```

Figure 13.14 – The previous addition error output

In Python 3.11, we get the following instead:

```
$ python3.11 example.py
Traceback (most recent call last):
  File "/home/mcorcherojim/tmp/packt/example.py", line 4, in <module>
    print((x + y) * int(str_num) + y + str_num)
          ~~~~~~~~~~~~~~~~~~~~~~~~~~~^~~~~~~~~~
TypeError: unsupported operand type(s) for +: 'int' and 'str'
```

Figure 13.15 – The enhanced addition error output

The new tomllib package

Given the standardization and raising popularity of pyproject.toml, Python 3.11 has added a new module to facilitate reading TOML files. The tomllib package can be used to easily read your project configuration in files such as pyproject.toml. As an example, let's take the following .toml file:

```
[build-system]
requires = ["setuptools", "setuptools-scm"]
build-backend = "setuptools.build_meta"
[project]
name = "packt_package"
description = "An example package"
dependencies = [
        "flask",
        "python-dateutil",
]
[project.scripts]
example-script = "packt_package._main:main"
```

We can now read it in Python with the standard library with the following code:

```
import tomllib
import pprint
with open("pyproject.toml", "rb") as f:
    data = tomllib.load(f)
pprint.pprint(data)
```

This generates the following output:

```
$ python3.11 tomllib_example.py
{'build-system': {'build-backend': 'setuptools.build_meta',
                  'requires': ['setuptools', 'setuptools-scm']},
 'project': {'dependencies': ['flask', 'python-dateutil'],
             'description': 'An example package',
             'name': 'packt_package',
             'scripts': {'example-script': 'packt_package._main:main'}}}
```

Figure 13.16 – The tomllib output

This allows us to handle TOML similar to how we can handle JSON with `stdlib`. The main difference is that the `tomllib` module does not come with a method to generate TOML, for which developers have to rely on third-party packages, which have different ways of customization and formatting.

Required keys in dicts

If you have been type-hinting your code, this will allow you to go a more strict level in your Python dictionaries. In the past, we saw how we could use `TypeDict` to declare what keys a dictionary could take, but now with PEP655, there is a new way to mark whether keys are required or not. Using our previous example of a point, we can now add an optional map attribute as `TypedDict('Point2D', x=int, y=int, map=NotRequired[str])`. That will result in the type checker allowing `dict(x=1, y=2)` and `dict(x=1, y=2, map="new_york")` but not one that misses either the x or y keys, such as `dict(y=2, map="new_york")`.

The new LiteralString type

Another addition to type-hinting is the new `LiteralString` type. This is useful when we are passing strings that are going to be used in SQL statements or shell commands, as a type checker will require that only static strings be passed. That helps developers protect their code from SQL injection and other similar attacks that take advantage of strings interpolation. See the following example that defines an API for a database:

```
def get_all_tables(schema_name: str) -> list[str]:
    sql = "SELECT table_name FROM tables WHERE schema=" +
schema_name
    ...
```

The developer of this API intended that function to allow other developers to call it as a quick way to get all tables given a schema. The developer considered it safe code as long as the `schema_name` argument was under the control of the developer, but there was nothing to prevent that. A user of this API could write the following code:

```
schema = input()
print(get_all_tables(schema))
```

This allows the user to perform a SQL injection attack by passing to be input a string such as `X; DROP TABLES`. With PEP 675, the library developer can now mark `schema_name` as `LiteralString`, which will make the type checker raise an error if the string is not static and a part of the application code.

Exceptions notes – PEP 678

PEP 678 adds a new method, `add_note`, to all exceptions, allowing developers to enrich an exception without the need of having to raise a new one. Before this addition, it was quite common to find the following code, as developers wanted to enrich an exception with some additional information:

```
def func(x, y):
    return x / y
def secret_function(number):
    try:
        func(10_000 , number)
    except ArithmeticError as e:
        raise ArithmeticError(f"Failed secret function: {e}")
from e
```

With exception notes, we can now write the following:

```
def func(x, y):
    return x / y
def secret_function(number):
    try:
        func(10_000 , number)
    except ArithmeticError as e:
        e.add_note("A note to help with debugging")
        raise
```

This allows the exception to keep all its original information. Let's now run the following code:

```
secret_function(0)
```

We see the following traceback:

```
$ python3.11 exception_notes.py
Traceback (most recent call last):
  File "/home/mcorcherojim/tmp/packt/Chapter13/exception_notes.py", line 11, in <module>
    secret_function(0)
  File "/home/mcorcherojim/tmp/packt/Chapter13/exception_notes.py", line 6, in secret_function
    func(10_000, number)
  File "/home/mcorcherojim/tmp/packt/Chapter13/exception_notes.py", line 2, in func
    return x / y
           ~~^~~
ZeroDivisionError: division by zero
A note to help with debugging
```

Figure 13.17 – An exceptions notes example

With this, we conclude our review of the new Python features.

Summary

In this final chapter, you have taken your Python knowledge one step further by learning how to continue your journey of improving your Python skills. We have seen the process to enhance Python and the enhancements that the language has accommodated in the most recent releases. You are all set up to continue your Python learning and even ready to submit a proposal for enhancements if you have any good ideas on how to improve the language itself!

Index

W

X

Z

Other Books You May Enjoy

If you enjoyed this book, you may be interested in these other books by Packt:

Python for Geeks

Muhammad Asif

ISBN: 978-1-80107-011-9

- Understand how to design and manage complex Python projects
- Strategize test-driven development (TDD) in Python
- Explore multithreading and multiprogramming in Python
- Use Python for data processing with Apache Spark and Google Cloud Platform (GCP)
- Deploy serverless programs on public clouds such as GCP
- Use Python to build web applications and application programming interfaces
- Apply Python for network automation and serverless functions
- Get to grips with Python for data analysis and machine learning

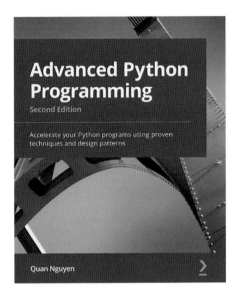

Advanced Python Programming - Second Edition

Quan Nguyen

ISBN: 978-1-80181-401-0

- Write efficient numerical code with NumPy, pandas, and Xarray
- Use Cython and Numba to achieve native performance
- Find bottlenecks in your Python code using profilers
- Optimize your machine learning models with JAX
- Implement multithreaded, multiprocessing, and asynchronous programs
- Solve common problems in concurrent programming, such as deadlocks
- Tackle architecture challenges with design patterns

Packt is searching for authors like you

If you're interested in becoming an author for Packt, please visit `authors.packtpub.com` and apply today. We have worked with thousands of developers and tech professionals, just like you, to help them share their insight with the global tech community. You can make a general application, apply for a specific hot topic that we are recruiting an author for, or submit your own idea.

Share Your Thoughts

Now you've finished *The Python Workshop, Second Edition*, we'd love to hear your thoughts! Scan the QR code below to go straight to the Amazon review page for this book and share your feedback or leave a review on the site that you purchased it from.

`https://packt.link/r/1-804-61061-5`

Your review is important to us and the tech community and will help us make sure we're delivering excellent quality content.

Download a free PDF copy of this book

Thanks for purchasing this book!

Do you like to read on the go but are unable to carry your print books everywhere?

Is your eBook purchase not compatible with the device of your choice?

Don't worry, now with every Packt book you get a DRM-free PDF version of that book at no cost.

Read anywhere, any place, on any device. Search, copy, and paste code from your favorite technical books directly into your application.

The perks don't stop there, you can get exclusive access to discounts, newsletters, and great free content in your inbox daily

Follow these simple steps to get the benefits:

1. Scan the QR code or visit the link below

https://packt.link/free-ebook/9781804610619

2. Submit your proof of purchase
3. That's it! We'll send your free PDF and other benefits to your email directly

Printed in Great Britain
by Amazon

38182698R00345